The
1800s

HEADLINES IN HISTORY

Books in the Headlines in History series:

The 1000s

The 1100s

The 1200s

The 1300s

The 1400s

The 1500s

The 1600s

The 1700s

The 1800s

The 1900s

The 1800s

HEADLINES IN HISTORY

James Miller, *Book Editor*

Bonnie Szumski, *Editorial Director*
Scott Barbour, *Managing Editor*

Greenhaven Press, Inc., San Diego, California

Every effort has been made to trace the owners of copyrighted material. The articles in this volume may have been edited for content, length, and/or reading level. The titles have been changed to enhance the editorial purpose.

Library of Congress Cataloging-in-Publication Data

The 1800s / James Miller, book editor.
    p. cm. — (Headlines in history)
    ISBN 0-7377-0543-4 (pbk. : alk. paper)—
    ISBN 0-7377-0544-2 (lib. bdg. : alk. paper)
      1. Nineteenth century. 2. World politics—19th century.
    3. Philosophy—History—19th century. 4. Revolutions—
    History—19th century. 5. Industrialization—History—
    19th century. 6. Civilization, Modern—19th century. I. Miller,
    James, 1943–   II. Headlines in history (San Diego, Calif.)

    CB415 .A16 2001
    909.81—dc21
                                                      00-048372

Cover photos: (top, left to right) painting by Edgar Degas,
Planet Art; American Civil War, Digital Stock;
(bottom, left to right) "Iron and Coal" by William Bell Scott,
National Trust, London/Art Resource, NY;
slaves preparing cotton for the gin,© William Clements Library,
University of Michigan/Bridgeman Art Library
Dover Publications, 112, 279
Library of Congress, 38, 105, 326
North Wind Picture Archives, 129, 160, 166, 262, 335
Prints Old and Rare, 155, 211

Copyright © 2001 by Greenhaven Press, Inc.
P.O. Box 289009 San Diego, CA 92198-9009

Printed in the USA

34.96

CONTENTS

Chapter 1: Heirs of the Revolutionary Era

1. Thomas Jefferson Assumes the American Presidency, 1801

At the very beginning of the nineteenth century, Thomas
Jefferson assumed the presidency after a bitterly contested
election—the first peaceful transfer of political power in
modern times—and called for national reconciliation and
limited government.

2. Inside Napoléon's Empire

Napoléon Bonaparte's accomplishments, not on the battle-
field, but as an administrator, lawgiver, and modernizer of
Europe, were far more enduring than his military conquests.

3. Latin America Wins an Ambiguous Independence

The revolutions that ended Spanish rule in most of Latin
America failed to build stable and prosperous new societies.

4. Reconciling Individualism and Community in the New American Republic

The great French commentator on the United States in
the 1830s analyzes how and why Americans felt impelled
to reconcile individualism and community spirit in their
new democratic society.

5. The Louisiana Purchase and the Lewis and Clark Expedition

The Louisiana Purchase made the Lewis and Clark Expedition an easier proposition for Jefferson and allowed for the
inevitable western expansion of the United States.

Chapter 2: Industrialization and Ideology

ing the Great Reform Era after 1855, with significant consequences on the Russian press, education, and politics.

Chapter 5: Europeans and the United States Dominate the Globe

China's fatal weaknesses, isolationism and its failure to industrialize.

and made it clear that the United States could and would become involved in world affairs.

Chapter 6: New Ideas

Chapter 7: A Century of Invention

Chronological time lines of history are mysteriously fascinating. To learn that within a single century Christopher Columbus sailed to the New World, the Aztec, Maya, and Inca cultures were flourishing, Joan of Arc was burned to death, and the invention of the printing press was radically changing access to written materials allows a reader a different type of view of history: a bird's-eye view of the entire globe and its events. Such a global picture allows for cross-cultural comparisons as well as a valuable overview of chronological history that studying one particular area simply cannot provide.

Taking an expansive look at world history in each century, therefore, can be surprisingly informative. In Headlines in History, Greenhaven Press attempts to imitate this time-line approach using primary and secondary sources that span each century. Each volume gives readers the opportunity to view history as though they were reading the headlines of a global newspaper: Editors of each volume have attempted to glean and include the most important and influential events of the century, as well as quirky trends and cultural oddities. Headlines in History, then, attempts to give readers a glimpse of both the mundane and the earth-shattering. Articles on the French Revolution, for example, are juxtaposed with the then-current fashion concerns of the French nobility. This creates a higher interest level by allowing students a glimpse of people's everyday lives throughout history.

By using both primary and secondary sources, students also have the opportunity to view the historical events both as eyewitnesses have experienced them and as historians have interpreted them. Thus, students can place such historical events in a larger context as well as receive background information on important world events.

Headlines in History allows readers the unique opportunity to learn more about events that may only be mentioned in their history textbooks, or may be ignored entirely. The series presents students with a variety of interesting topics that span cultural, historical, and political arenas. Such a broad span of material will allow students to wander wherever their curiosity will take them.

The Nineteenth Century: An Era of Accelerating Change

Except for the twentieth century, no hundred-year span of time in recorded history witnessed such startling or far-reaching changes as did the nineteenth. Consider these contrasts:

• In 1800, the exploitation of new sources of energy and the invention of new machinery for industrial production—the cluster of breakthroughs that historians call the Industrial Revolution—had already been under way for roughly forty or fifty years, but it was only beginning to spread from its cradle in England to the northeastern part of the United States; as yet it had made no significant impact on continental Europe, and was totally without influence anywhere else around the globe. By 1900, industrialization had moved far beyond the relatively simple steam-powered (and even simpler water-driven) machines of its early years, most of which were associated with the production of textiles; electrical power had been harnessed, a chemical industry had been created, and the list of countries boasting major industrial bases included not only Great Britain but also the United States, Germany, France, Belgium, Italy, Russia, and even distant Japan.

• In 1800, people, goods, and information moved no faster than human or animal muscles, wind, or water currents could carry them; it took a month or two (depending on the season and the weather) to cross the Atlantic Ocean. By 1900, steamships crossed the Atlantic in a little over a week and plied every major river in the world, steam-driven railroads crisscrossed almost every habitable part of the globe, the internal combustion engine and the automobile had recently been invented, telegraph and cable lines could carry messages almost instantaneously across oceans and over continents, experimentation in radio broadcasting was under way, and the first airplane flight lay only three years in the future.

• In 1800, the practice of medicine reflected a body of knowledge largely unchanged from medieval—if not ancient—times; bleeding (intended to remove harmful "humors" from a diseased body) was still a standard remedy, applied, for example, when in December 1799 George Washington contracted a fatal case of pneumonia; surgery, when resorted to at all, meant cutting into a fully conscious patient's body as rapidly as possible, with no thought to cleanliness and with nothing except an intoxicating drink to dull the pain. By 1900, the role of microorganisms in causing infection and illness was well understood, improvements in public health and sanitation were dramatically reducing the death toll of communicable diseases, anesthetics and sterile procedures were routinely used in operations, and X rays had recently been discovered.

• In 1800, even the most highly educated people had little reason not to believe that the heavens, the earth, and all living things (including human beings) had been created by God, perhaps only a few thousand years earlier. (Biblical scholars calculated the date as 4004 B.C.) By 1900, knowledge of geology had pushed back the earth's age hundreds of millions (if not several billion) years; overwhelmingly, educated Westerners understood that species—including the human species—were not unchanging through time, but rather had evolved from lower forms by means of natural selection; and the mechanism (genetics) for the transmission of evolving characteristics was at last beginning to be discovered.

• In 1800, the laws of physics as discovered in the late seventeenth century by Sir Isaac Newton seemed simple and universally valid. By 1900, baffling new phenomena such as radiation and the emission of light in "quanta" (which acted simultaneously as waves and as particles) were shaking scientists' faith in the validity of Newtonian physics, while a young patent-office examiner in Switzerland named Albert Einstein was only five years away from announcing his theory of special relativity, including the earth-shaking equation $E=mc^2$. This knowledge would enable twentieth-century physicists to unleash the natural force that holds together the atom—something that scientists in 1900 were also beginning to understand.

• In 1800, France had emerged from a decade of revolutionary upheaval as the strongest power on the European continent, against which were arrayed Great Britain and a coalition of absolute monarchies—all of them essentially the same kind of state that had thrived in the middle of the eighteenth century. By 1900, France was still a powerful nation-state, though its boundaries were much reduced from those of the revolutionary powerhouse of 1800; but across the European continent stood several other imposing nation-states where a century before there had been many traditional monarchies. Except for Russia and the Ottoman Empire, all the European states of 1900 were governed by constitutions (albeit an unwritten one in Great Britain), all of which recognized at least some role for popularly elected representatives and mass political parties. Great Britain, France, Italy, and some of western Europe's smaller states were vigorously democratic; in 1800, democratic government was still a tenuous experiment in the United States and was unknown anywhere else on earth.

• In 1800, the territory of the United States did not extend west of the Mississippi River, and settlement by its white and black population was only beginning to reach across the Allegheny Mountains. The influence of the United States in global affairs was practically negligible; its economy was largely agrarian and its population overwhelmingly rural; and about 20 percent of its settled population consisted of enslaved blacks. It shared the Western Hemisphere with a British colony in Canada and with Spanish and Portuguese colonies everywhere to its south. By 1900, the United States had grown into an industrial giant that spanned the continent, Canada also stretched to the Pacific and had achieved self-government, and almost two dozen Latin American republics had replaced the Spanish and Portuguese empires of 1800. Slavery had been abolished everywhere (although at the cost of a bloody American civil war); the United States, Argentina, Chile, and Brazil had attracted millions of European immigrants; and the United States, now with a colonial empire of its own, was taking its place among the global great powers.

• In 1800, the Western world and China were still roughly in equilibrium in terms of their relative power and population, and both were in the midst of population explosions. By 1900, however, China had become overwhelmed by rampant population growth, with which the nation's traditional economic and technological capabilities (once the most impressive on earth) utterly failed to keep pace. The Qing (or Manchu) dynasty, beset by endemic corruption and popular unrest, was staggering toward its collapse, and only the rivalries and mutual suspicions of the Western powers prevented them from partitioning the once-great empire among themselves and Japan.

• In 1800, Japan stood apart from the rest of the world in self-imposed isolation, aware of Western accomplishments in technology and science but viewing all but the most tenuous contact as a threat to the nation's feudal system. By 1900, Japan had adopted many features of Western life, but always with the aim of strengthening its own military and imperial power—an effort that proved so successful that within five years it would decisively defeat Russia in a major war.

• In 1800, sub-Saharan Africa was for Westerners "the Dark Continent," known only along the coasts where slavers still plied their trade in human beings, and with a tiny Dutch settlement at its southern tip. By 1900, almost all of black Africa had been partitioned among the European imperialist powers, and Great Britain was waging a difficult war to conquer the small Dutch-speaking* republics of South Africa.

A Revolution

So rapid and so dazzling were changes such as these that in the first years of the twentieth century the great American historian Henry Adams (1838–1916) mused in his autobiography that a boy born at the beginning of the nineteenth century stood closer in life-experience to a person who had been born in the year A.D. 1 than to someone born in A.D. 1900. And, added Adams with characteristically whimsical pessimism, the classical education that he, the grandson and great-grandson of two American presidents, had received had left him singularly ill-equipped to understand the world of 1900, with its mass politics, its powerful electrical dynamos, its wondrous science, and its enormously productive industry.

How are we to account for such stunning changes? A leading British historian, Eric Hobsbawm, used the term *Dual Revolution* to express the combined force of the transformations in life that radiated from Europe around the globe, whose sources were the Industrial and the French Revolutions—both of which began in the late eighteenth century but which were beginning to exert their sweeping influence about 1800. At first separate phenomena, the two revolutions became increasingly intertwined as the 1800s progressed, and their interrelationship was fully apparent by the time a wave of political and social upheavals convulsed Europe in 1848.

The onset of the Industrial Revolution is usually dated around 1760; its first great historical milestone came in 1769, when British inventor James Watt introduced his relatively efficient steam engine. The essence of the Industrial Revolution (or the Energy Revolution, an alternative name for the same processes that some historians to-day favor) was the discovery and exploitation of new ways to harness energy from natural sources, and the use of this energy to produce goods faster, with much less labor, and in much greater quantities. Great Britain had natural advantages that permitted it to take the lead: an abundance of easily mined coal; plentiful waterways (rivers, canals, and surrounding seas) over which coal could be hauled to places where it could be put to use as fuel; a relative absence of governmental economic regulation, which facilitated innovation in many spheres; resourceful tinkerers who had plenty of material incentives to invent new ways of doing things; a mobile

* More accurately, Afrikaans-speaking; Afrikaans is the Dutch-derived language spoken by the descendants of the original European colonizers of South Africa.

workforce that needed both to be employed and to be clothed; and sources of private capital that could be invested in new manufacturing ventures. Textiles were the first major industry to be revolutionized by the newly generated power (both steam and water) and the new machinery that could use it, and Great Britain not only produced wool on a large scale but also had access to plentiful imports of cotton—first from India and after 1800 from the American South.

After 1800 the effects of industrialization became fully apparent, first in Britain and then in other countries (the United States was one of the first) that were able to emulate British innovations. To be sure, early factories were ugly, and they spewed pollution and noxious wastes of every kind. Employers had plentiful incentives to demand long hours at low wages (particularly for women and children); traditional artisan crafts could not compete with industrial efficiency; and when the business cycle turned down (as it often did), workers had no protection against unemployment. Such human and environmental costs of industrialization cannot be minimized. Nevertheless, in the perspective of the nineteenth century's enormous overall productivity growth, the spread of industrialization was immensely beneficial to the people of the Western world, as comparison with areas (especially China) that experienced explosive population growth without corresponding enhancements of productivity readily shows. Ultimately the new middle class and working class that emerged from industrialization both benefited from access to more material goods and employment opportunities. Over time, and not without struggle, both classes secured rights of political participation that ensured that they would be not simply wage earners and taxpayers but also voters and citizens—status that enabled them to leverage a growing share of the material benefits that industrialization provided. And those benefits only increased over time. The application of steam power to waterborne and rail transportation was fully under way by the 1830s. By the 1840s and 1850s the need to deal with the disease, the crime, and the hopelessly inadequate sanitation of burgeoning industrial cities was beginning to engage the serious attention of Western governments. In the 1860s came the development of modern steelmaking and of petroleum as a new source of energy; in the 1870s and 1880s electricity was harnessed for power and new industries arose on the basis of breakthroughs in the science of chemistry.

The French Revolution

Paralleling the unfolding industrialization of the nineteenth-century Western world was the other half of the Dual Revolution—the reverberations of the French Revolution, which had begun in 1789. Narrowly conceived, the French Revolution ran its course in the ten-year period 1789–1799, during which the "old regime" of traditional social hierarchies collapsed, the monarchy was first reformed and then abolished, a radical phase marked by foreign invasion and domestic terror was endured, and finally order was restored under a series of regimes dominated by the new revolutionary elite that culminated in a coup d'état by a general named Napoléon Bonaparte in December 1799.

But during the years of Bonaparte's ascendancy—first as dictator of the French Republic and between 1804 and 1815 as Emperor Napoléon I—the lasting changes of the Revolution were consolidated and extended to much of the rest of Europe. These changes included the substitution of new elites recruited on the basis of wealth and ability for old elites of birth and privilege; the creation of a centralized, bureaucratic government whose main features still survive in France and most other democratic European states; and the establishment of the nation-state as the primary focus of citizens' loyalties. The French Revolution and all its works met fierce resistance by Europe's traditional monarchical governments—and often by ordinary people outside France, who with good reason resented French invaders, taxes, regulations, and military recruiters—but during the first half of the nineteenth century the French-style modernized state would prove its power as a model for much of the Continent.

A major reason why both the Industrial and the French Revolutions so influenced nineteenth-century Europe was the advent of revolutionary *ideologies*—a word coined in France in the early 1800s. An ideology is a set of ideas claiming to explain how society works and how it should be reformed, and all the ideologies that emerged in the Western world in the first decades of the nineteenth century constituted responses to the Industrial and French Revolutions—usually, in fact, to both. Four major ideologies were born in this era: liberalism, conservatism, nationalism, and socialism. Although the specific content of each ideology has changed considerably since the early 1800s, all of them still exert a powerful and enduring influence on modern life.

Liberalism, in its nineteenth-century form, called for limiting the power of government and maximizing individual freedom. It was above all the ideology of the new middle class that had been created economically by the Industrial Revolution and empowered politically by the French Revolution. Liberals tended to feel confident that change, overall, was a good thing—they believed, that is, in progress. They wanted as little interference from government in the workings of the capitalist market economy as possible, and usually agreed that the main functions of government should be to protect property and enforce contracts. They had confidence that some people, left to their own resources, could better their condition by diligence, frugality, and self-restraint. They chafed at the heavy hand of the church and clergy, rejected "superstition," professed themselves tolerant of different religious beliefs, and believed in the power of education. Although some were of aristocratic birth, they championed the principle of merit rather than birth in determining who should lead society and the state. They wanted constitutional government with a popularly elected legislature. They were not necessarily democrats who believed that every adult should vote, but they did expect that suffrage should be enlarged so that male "solid citizens" (that is, they themselves) would dominate national decision making.

Gradually, in the course of the nineteenth century, voting and other rights of political participation were in fact substantially extended to include most or all adult males: in the United States, for whites, as early as the 1830s; in Great Britain, through the enactment by Parliament of two Reform Bills in 1832 and 1867; in France, as a result of the Revolution of 1848; and in Germany, as part of the process of national unification between 1866 and 1871. (Male suffrage was as far as expansion of voting rights generally went in the nineteenth century. A movement for giving women the right to vote appeared in the United States and Great Britain between the 1840s and the 1860s, but even most male liberals refused to support it, and except in some locales including distant New Zealand women would not gain the vote until the early twentieth century.) Often, enlargement of suffrage to enfranchise peasants and workers undermined the "classical" liberalism of the nineteenth century, which had appealed to the educated and prosperous middle classes. By the end of the nineteenth century, liberalism either became the political faith of a small part of the electorate or else adopted a more activist, reformist stance that accepted a much larger role for government in solving society's problems—something, in short, much closer to what contemporary Americans understand as liberalism.

The Influence of Conservatism

Conservatism was also an ideology born in reaction to the French Revolution. In contrast to liberals, who felt inspired by the "progressive" gains of the French Revolution and wanted to build on them, conservatives disliked change, especially if it resulted from the application of such "abstract theories" as "progress" and "the rights of man." Conservatives believed that society and its institutions should change (if at all) slowly and as a result of natural, "organic" growth. They supported existing social hierarchies, tended to respect monarchy and the church, and revered customs and traditions inherited from the past. Unlike liberals, nineteenth-century conservatives generally viewed government positively, claiming that it protected ordinary people against the ruthless demands of the capitalist marketplace. (In this respect, contemporary conservatives and liber-

als have reversed the positions that their nineteenth-century coun-
terparts once held.) Conservatives were not necessarily reactionar-
ies—that is, people who wanted to bring back institutions that had
disappeared and who flatly rejected all change—but they did want
to slow the pace of change as much as possible. Nevertheless, some
conservative political leaders, including British prime minister Benjamin Disraeli and German chancellor Otto von Bismarck, were responsible for some of the most innovative social welfare legislation
enacted by nineteenth-century European governments.

Nationalism, one of the most powerful ideologies ever devised
and arguably the most significant on a worldwide scale today, is a
cluster of ideas quite different from simple patriotism. Nationalism
exalts the supposedly unique qualities of a whole people who are
united by language, history, and customs but who are not necessarily united under the same government; patriotism generally means
maintaining allegiance to the established government and expressing love for one's land. The roots of nationalism as a modern ideology can be traced to two sources. First is the emotional identification
of the French people with the Revolution and its famous principles
of "liberty, equality, fraternity," an identification that was supposed
to transcend divisions of wealth and class (but that deliberately excluded from "the people" those who refused to support the revolutionary regime). The second source is the efforts of German and
other Central European writers, teachers, historians, and journalists
of the early nineteenth century to rediscover the folk culture of their
native peoples and to evoke a community of "blood and soil" that
bound together all people of common speech and cultural heritage
regardless of the political boundaries that might separate them. Creating such a sense of community sometimes involved "purifying"
one of the dialects of a national language by formalizing it in dic-
tionaries and grammar textbooks, officially adopting its teaching in
schools, and creating a literature using it. Nationalism was thus generally a conscious creation of intellectuals (usually of middle-class
origin) who built on the natural but often inarticulate feelings of kin-
ship that ordinary people felt for others who spoke their language—
as well as their antipathy to foreigners (such as invading French
armies) who came among them.

The first half of the nineteenth century in Europe was a period of
intense nationalist development among many peoples, and because
political boundaries often did not coincide with the linguistic map,
the rise of nationalism presented a serious challenge to the political
stability of the Continent. This was especially evident in 1848, when
a series of social revolutions touched off by the tensions of industrialization became mixed with the aspirations of middle-class nationalists to unify their people. Germany and Italy, which were then

divided into many smaller states, and Hungary, which was part of the Austrian Empire, were the scenes of particularly intense nationalist movements. In the short run they failed, and the revolutions were put down by the established governments, largely because the middle classes of these countries became fearful of working-class unrest and thus sided with the authorities. But between the early 1850s and 1871, redrawing Europe's map along nationalist lines was on the political agenda of several major powers, and thus it became the focus of several swift but bloody wars. By 1871, Germany had been forged into a united state under the leadership of Prussia, Italy had become a united kingdom, and the Austrian Empire had been restructured as a "dual monarchy," Austria-Hungary, in which the Hungarians enjoyed wide autonomy (and were in a position to oppress other nationalities).

With the emergence of important new nation-states in mid-nineteenth-century Europe, nationalism won a victory more solid than anything achieved by liberalism during the same period, but that same victory also sowed the seeds of future instability. Nineteenth-century nationalism was highly competitive: Satisfying one nation's aspirations usually involved denying another's aspirations. Nationalists also tended to think of their particular nation as superior to all others, and so nationalism served to legitimize the tendency of mass society to foster resentments, fan hatreds, and search for easy answers to complicated problems. The bitter rivalries and the atmosphere of a constant struggle for power that poisoned international relations in the late nineteenth century and on the eve of World War I (1914–1918) owed much to overheated nationalism. In the name of nationalism, too, the great powers of Europe engaged in a frantic scramble to build overseas empires in the 1880s and 1890s—but in the long run it was the transfer of the European ideology of nationalism to colonial peoples that in the twentieth century would destroy these same empires.

The Influence of Socialism

Socialism, the fourth of the great nineteenth-century ideologies, was most directly a result of the Industrial Revolution. The earliest socialists were men such as the Duc de Saint-Simon (a French aristocrat), Charles Fourier (a middle-class French traveling salesman), and Robert Owen (a successful British industrialist), all of whom were shocked by the ugliness and social disruption caused by industrialization. They dreamed of finding ways to achieve the material wealth that the Industrial Revolution promised without paying the costs of injustice, inequality, and squalor. The answers that these and like-minded men (and a few women) found generally called for "ideal communities" where property would be owned in common, tasks and profits would be justly apportioned, and individualism would be subordinated to the common good. A few such ideal communities were founded in the 1830s and 1840s, both in Europe and in the United States. All of them—save for those created by deeply motivated religious movements, such as the Mormons—failed.

The German revolutionaries Karl Marx (1818–1883) and Friedrich Engels (1820–1895) scornfully dismissed these idealistic dreams as "utopian socialism." They claimed instead to have discovered what they called "scientific socialism," and in a pamphlet called *The Communist Manifesto*, published in Brussels by a tiny group of radicals on the eve of the Revolutions of 1848 (which Marx and Engels had nothing to do with precipitating), they announced their ideas to the world. All history, Marx and Engels declared, was the history of class struggle. In ancient times the antagonistic classes had been masters and slaves; between the Middle Ages and the eighteenth century they had been aristocrats and the middle class, or bourgeoisie. Now, claimed Marx and Engels, after the French Revolution had overthrown the aristocracies and given power to the bourgeoisie, a new class war pitted the capitalist middle class against an exploited and restive working class, or proletariat, who produced everything of value but received practically no reward. The laws of economics and history, supposedly as fixed as those of Newtonian physics, predicted that the ruthless competition among capitalists would inevitably lower wages to the bare minimum that workers needed for survival, while boom-and-bust fluctuations concentrated control of the economy in ever-fewer hands. Eventually the workers' misery would grow so great that they would rise in revolutionary fury and "expropriate the expropriators" by seizing the factories, railroads, and all other means of production. The result would be socialism—a form of social and political organization in which the means of production would be owned collectively and capitalism abolished. Yet socialism would be only a stage on the road toward humanity's ultimate transformation: the creation of a communist society in which all exploitation would cease and the governing principle would be "from each according to his ability, to each according to his needs." Historical change itself would cease, and the human race would finally achieve true happiness. All this, Marx and Engels insisted, would happen not because of the goodwill and idealism on which "utopian" socialists counted, but as a result of the "iron laws of history."

Few took Marx and Engels seriously in the mid–nineteenth century, and even when Marx produced, in 1867, the ponderous first volume of his book *Das Kapital*, the fruit of years of research in London, relatively few readers were convinced. But Marx was also a successful organizer. In 1864 he helped bring into existence the

International Workingmen's Association (the "First International"), a coalition of socialist parties in various European countries dedicated to advancing working-class interests and—Marx hoped—promoting the socialist revolution that his theory predicted would sooner or later come.

Not until the 1870s and and 1880s, however, did socialist parties begin to acquire mass followings, especially in Germany. And these parties generally dismayed Marx because they tended to stress improving the wages and working conditions of the proletariat while paying largely lip service to the sweeping revolutionary goals that Marx and Engels thought should be their objective. Marx was not a reformer; he saw no hope for saving "bourgeois society" or making capitalism tolerable for the working class. Yet, once the right to vote had been conceded to workers (as it increasingly was in Europe by this time, and had been for half a century in the United States), most of the working class was more interested in gaining marginal benefits within "the system" than in overthrowing it in a mighty uprising. Labor's struggle for social justice in the late nineteenth century was not always easy or entirely peaceful, but with the help of their unions (and in some countries, of their democratic socialist parties) by 1900 working people almost everywhere in the West enjoyed a much better standard of living and broader, more secure rights than had their predecessors in 1800 or 1850.

The chief exception to this generalization was Russia, where the autocratic czarist regime stubbornly denied all political rights to both the middle class and the working class that were emerging with the nation's belated industrialization. There, the revolutionary foundations of Marxism became a powerful force in the new Russian Social Democratic Party, and especially in the extremist Bolshevik faction that appeared by 1898. In 1917, when czarist Russia collapsed under the weight of having to wage World War I and a democratic middle-class republican regime failed to hold the country together, the Bolsheviks would take power in a coup. The Marxist regime established there would survive for most of the twentieth century and would serve as a model for many formerly colonial nations around the globe bent on modernizing quickly.

The Importance of Europe

This summary of the main currents of nineteenth-century history has so far been heavily Eurocentric, and with good reason. The Dual Revolution had its wellsprings in Europe and over the course of the nineteenth century reverberated around the globe. The balance among world civilizations, which had been slowly tilting in the West's direction during the 1700s, now shifted rapidly. With its technology, its political dynamism, its optimistic and aggressive world outlook, its pride, and its constant drive to control the resources and markets that its industrial economy demanded, the West made itself the master of the globe in the nineteenth century. This mastery manifested itself in several different ways.

First and most direct was the expansion of formal Western colonial empires. This expansion probably would not have been predicted at the beginning of the nineteenth century, when Western colonialism seemed to be in retreat. France had lost its large American holdings and its stake in India to the British in the great colonial wars that ended in 1763; Britain in turn lost its most valuable American colonies only twenty years later, when the United States successfully asserted its independence; and Spain was ejected from most of its vast American provinces by independence movements that prevailed by the early 1820s. The value of Europe's once-lucrative sugar-producing colonies in the West Indies was shrinking; France lost its largest sugar island when a slave rebellion at the beginning of the 1800s led to the creation of the Republic of Haiti; and in 1833 the British Parliament's abolition of slavery marked the end of the huge profits that absentee white plantation owners had squeezed from such Caribbean islands as Jamaica and Barbados. Even in India, British rule remained indirect, asserted through the corrupt and financially struggling East India Company. But these setbacks were temporary. As early as 1830, France began building a new colonial empire in North Africa, and in the 1860s it annexed southern Vietnam. The East India Company was meanwhile finding an enormously valuable if morally dubious source of profit in the export of opium from India to China, and in 1857–1858 it survived a bloody uprising—the Sepoy Mutiny—by its own native troops. After the mutiny's suppression, Parliament, fed up with the Company's manifest inefficiency, brought India under direct British rule. Then, between the 1860s and the early 1880s, Europeans "discovered" sub-Saharan Africa by conducting expeditions into the hitherto-unknown interior and bargaining for favorable treaty arrangements with the tribal groups they encountered. In 1885, the growing network of white outposts throughout Africa was converted into formal empires when a gathering of European diplomats in Berlin drew lines on the continent's map. Now almost all of Africa was partitioned among colonial powers, and by the early twentieth century only tiny Liberia (an American protectorate) and isolated Ethiopia (which in 1896 routed an invading Italian army) remained independent. Eventually, colonized Africans derived some benefits from the arrival of Western railroads, medicine, and ideas—including nationalism, which they would turn against their colonial masters—but they also paid a terrible price in forced labor and other forms of economic exploitation and in psychological devastation.

The second form of the nineteenth-century West's global expansion was the territorial spread of European communities across entire continents formerly inhabited solely by indigenous peoples. The most dramatic instance of this "manifest destiny" (to use a famous slogan of the 1840s) was the expansion of the United States all the way to the Pacific Ocean, which was accomplished in several stages: the Louisiana Purchase of 1803, in which the United States doubled its size by buying everything from the Mississippi River to the Rocky Mountains; a diplomatic deal with Great Britain, which brought it the Pacific Northwest in 1846; and a war with Mexico during which it annexed the Republic of Texas and a broad swath of Mexican land, including California and the Southwest, in 1846–1848. Subsequent purchases that included Alaska (from Russia, in 1867) rounded off the continental United States. By a combination of warfare, expulsion, and disease, the Native American population of the West was drastically reduced in both numbers and geographical distribution, thereby providing homes and farms for millions of white settlers (many of them immigrants from Europe) and profitable investments in railroads, mines, and livestock for East Coast and European capitalists. A similar, though less violent and more governmentally directed, process of expansion enabled Canada to reach the Pacific as well, and meanwhile the former British colony attained internal self-government in 1867. Two other English-speaking settlements were developed and expanded in the Southern Hemisphere: Australia, originally a British penal colony, which became internally self-governing in 1901; and New Zealand, which achieved self-government in 1907. In both countries, the arrival of European settlers and their livestock during the nineteenth century decimated the indigenous populations on a scale even surpassing the destruction of North America's native peoples. Russia also expanded by rounding out its Siberian borders at the expense of China, by annexing (to Britain's great alarm) large chunks of Central Asia that reached almost as far as the northern reaches of India, and by building railroads into these distant acquisitions that brought in Russian-speaking settlers—not always voluntarily, for many were exiled political prisoners.

The third means of Western global expansion was the building of "indirect" empires of commercial hegemony. Here, dominated lands remained formally independent, but economic control largely passed to the industrializing powers of Europe and North America. The earliest instance of such indirect domination was the economic penetration of Latin America by British firms after the region won its political independence from Spain. Railroads, mines, and other desirable economic enterprises came largely under British control in the course of the nineteenth century, although investors from the

United States also became quite active in the region by the 1880s. In the Old World, the Ottoman Empire (now Turkey and the Middle East) and Persia (now Iran) increasingly fell under the control of Western banks and corporations, but these lands were saved from partition largely because of bitter rivalries between Great Britain, Russia, and Germany, none of which wished to see the others annex territory.

For the same reason China, the greatest of all Asian empires, also escaped territorial dismemberment at the end of the nineteenth century, but still fell victim to Western encroachment. China's decline was one of the century's most important events, a process that reflected the flagging efficiency and morale of the Qing (or Manchu) dynasty, the overwhelming impact of Chinese population growth without corresponding increases in productivity, and the predatory impulses of aggressive Western powers that sensed an opportunity to take advantage of the once-haughty "Middle Kingdom's" distress. The first wedge that Westerners drove into China was the East India Company's drug trafficking, for when Chinese officials attempted to stop the import of opium, Great Britain responded by crushing Qing resistance. Britain's terms for ending this First Opium War (1840–1842) included opening a series of Chinese ports to Western merchants and exempting Westerners from Chinese jurisdiction, and soon the other Western powers were successfully claiming similar concessions. Then, between 1850 and 1864, China was torn by the most devastating civil war in nineteenth-century history, the Taiping Rebellion, a popular uprising that the Qing dynasty suppressed only by accepting Western aid on humiliating terms. Thereafter, Chinese history in the late nineteenth century was a story of the frustration of reformers who realized that the nation must learn from Western successes, of ever-increasing Western inroads on Chinese self-rule, and of the unchecked deterioration of popular respect for the Qing dynasty. In 1900, when an antiforeign insurrection known as the Boxer Rebellion was put down by the heavy-handed intervention of all the major Western powers (including the United States), China's fortunes seemed at their low point.

Of all the globe's non-Western societies in the nineteenth century, only one successfully withstood imperialist encroachments and met the Western challenge on its own terms. That society was Japan, where for hundreds of years the social and political order had borne striking similarities to that of medieval European feudalism. Almost totally closed to the outside world since about 1600, but aware of how the world was changing, Japan had continued to develop economically. In the early nineteenth century the conflict between social groups that saw the need to end Japan's isolation and those that wished to continue it in order to protect indigenous feudal relationships became acute. This conflict was exacerbated when in 1853 a U.S. naval contingent forced itself into Japanese waters and demanded that the country open itself to foreign commerce, in which American merchants saw particularly inviting opportunities for profit. This abrupt foreign challenge, coupled with the realization of what had happened when China attempted to resist Western incursions, set in motion a complicated political crisis in Japan. The crisis culminated in the overthrow of feudalism in 1868 and the establishment of a modernizing regime that was determined to make use of Western ways to ensure Japanese greatness. By 1900, Westernization had gone remarkably far; Japan was ready to treat the great powers of Europe and North America as equals and to demand a share of whatever imperial plunder was to be extracted from China; in 1905 it proved that it must be taken seriously by the West when it thoroughly whipped Russia's imposing army and navy in a war for dominance in Korea and southern Manchuria.

The nineteenth-century West's assertion of global leadership was both aided and symbolized by its impressive breakthroughs in science and technology. Ever since the sixteenth and seventeenth centuries—the era of the Scientific Revolution, when the discoveries of Copernicus, Galileo, and Newton had unveiled basic truths about the solar system and the physical laws governing visible phenomena—Western thinkers had been undermining worldviews shared by traditional cultures around the globe. In the eighteenth century the foundations of modern chemistry and biology had been laid by Western scientists, and in the cultural movement called the Enlightenment educated Western laypeople generally assimilated the new scientific outlook. Thus the way was prepared for the even more dramatic achievements of nineteenth-century science. One epoch-making discovery came in 1831 when British scientist Michael Faraday, building on Benjamin Franklin's eighteenth-century work in electricity, demonstrated that electromagnetism was a single natural force obeying regular physical laws. Simultaneously, in 1830–1833, British geologist Charles Lyell published the first edition of his *Principles of Geology*, asserting that analysis of rock strata showed the earth to be immensely older than hitherto suspected, and that changes in the physical environment generally occurred very slowly. Lyell's work gave currency to the word *evolution* and helped naturalist Charles Darwin formulate his theory that the process by which species (including the human species) evolved was what he called "natural selection," which popularizers soon dubbed "survival of the fittest." The publication of Darwin's books *The Origin of Species* in 1859 and *The Descent of Man* in 1871 was among the seminal events in modern history, setting off a boiling public controversy between critics and advocates of biblical literalism that even today shows no sign of abating. While Darwin's work was gaining immediate attention, equally important but virtually unknown experiments with peas were being carried out by an obscure Austrian monk named Gregor Mendel, which would establish the basic laws of genetics—the mechanism by which random mutations in living organisms are passed on to offspring, thus enabling Darwinian evolution by natural selection to occur. Also in the 1860s, the Russian chemist Dmitri Mendeleyev was working out the periodic chart of the elements, the basic blueprint for the physical world's structure, while several German chemists were formulating the discipline of organic chemistry and beginning to train university students in its theories and methods. In the 1880s came a series of fundamental discoveries in biology by such men as the Frenchman Louis Pasteur and the German Robert Koch, who identified the microorganisms responsible for such killer diseases as rabies, tuberculosis, anthrax, and cholera, as well as for fermentation, and also invented the process known ever since as the pasteurization of milk. In 1894, demonstrating that non-Westerners trained in modern science were equally capable of achieving major breakthroughs, Japan's Shibasaburo Kitasato codiscovered the bacillus that transmits bubonic plague, the dread disease that in earlier centuries had killed millions throughout the world.

In addition to these conceptual breakthroughs, nineteenth-century technology poured out an astonishing series of inventions, some of which built on the insights of theoretical science but many of which represented the responses of practical tinkerers to specific problems. Not long before the nineteenth century had come American inventor Eli Whitney's cotton gin (1793); in 1798 Whitney perfected the idea of manufacturing machinery with identical and interchangeable parts, with immense gains for industrial efficiency. Then, after 1800, came American Robert Fulton's steamboat (1805), Briton George Stephenson's adaptation of the steam engine to the railroad (1814); Michael Faraday's electric motor (developed between 1821 and 1831); the first railroad line (in England, 1824); the invention of photography by a series of Frenchmen in the 1830s; American Cyrus McCormick's grain reaper (1834); American Samuel Colt's revolver (1836); American Samuel F.B. Morse's first dispatch of a telegraph message (1844); Briton Henry Bessemer's blast furnace for the industrial manufacture of steel (1856); the laying of the first transatlantic cable (1866); Canadian Alexander Graham Bell's telephone (1876); Croatian-born American Nikola Tesla's discovery of the rotating magnetic field, which made possible the transmission of electric power (1877); American Thomas A. Edison's phonograph (1877) and incandescent electric light (1879); German Heinrich Hertz's discovery of radio waves and photoelectricity, which opened the way to the later development of radio and television (1885); German Gottlieb Daimler's internal combustion engine, key to the development of the automobile (1886–1887); and Italian Guglielmo Marconi's invention of wireless telegraphy (1895), by which in 1901 he was able to send a radio message across the Atlantic.

These and many other advances helped Western societies assert global dominance in the nineteenth century, helped raise Western living standards and added greatly to the comforts and conveniences of Western life, and helped convince all who became aware of them that the globe was experiencing an unprecedented surge of improvements—of progress, to use one of the century's key words. Yet change sometimes occurred in radically unexpected ways. For example, in 1887 the American physicists Edward Morely and Albert Michelson determined that light moves everywhere at the same speed, unimpeded by the supposed substance called ether, in the existence of which all physicists of the time believed. In 1895, German physicist Wilhelm Röntgen discovered an entirely new phenomenon, the X ray, and in 1898 French physicist Pierre Curie and his Polish-born wife Marie followed up Röntgen's work by observing radioactivity. These discoveries cast doubt on hitherto unquestioned assumptions of Newtonian physics and opened the way for two of the fundamental theories that would be advanced in the first years of the twentieth century: Max Planck's quantum theory (1900) and Albert Einstein's special theory of relativity (1905).

The restructuring of physics at the very end of the nineteenth century and the beginning of the twentieth was a major milestone in Western, indeed global, intellectual history. The lawlike regularities and predictability that Newtonian physics had proclaimed as central to the workings of the universe were now being revealed as nothing more than "special cases"—the simple regularities that we can observe with the naked eye. When we turn to the minute world of the atom (whose mysteries were now beginning to be explored) or to the vast world of solar systems and galaxies, we see not regularities but the unpredictable shimmering of particle emissions or the relativities of time and space. Darwin's theory of evolution by natural selection had seemed to remove all the special qualities that had made human beings unique among living creatures; now the physicists were making the universe a place where ordinary human standards of judgment were unreliable. The work of the Austrian psychologist Sigmund Freud, which purported to uncover the unconscious motivations that lie beneath our seemingly rational selves and that reveal themselves in obsessions and neuroses, burst upon the world about 1900, confirming for many thoughtful Westerners the pessimistic conclusion that rationality itself was a delusion. The mad rush of Europe's major powers toward ever more formidable armaments, even more bellicose political posturing, and ever more dangerous brinkmanship in international relations—for all of which there was plentiful evidence on display in 1900, and which would explode in World War I in the summer of 1914—can be interpreted as the public manifestation of the irrationality that Western culture was engendering as the nineteenth century gave way to the twentieth.

Was the nineteenth century truly the era of triumphant progress? Or was it, in the end, simply a time of dizzying change, increasingly disorienting to those who experienced it? The answer is best sought in how we evaluate the fruits of nineteenth-century civilization in their twentieth-century offspring.

Heirs of the Revolutionary Era

PREFACE

A common thread runs through revolutions that began in America in the 1770s and in France in 1789. That common thread is the insistence that "the people" are the source of all legitimate government and may change their form of government if it fails to serve its proper end—"life, liberty, and the pursuit of happiness," as the American Declaration of Independence put it, or "liberty, equality, fraternity," as a famous slogan of the French Revolution expressed the same basic goal.

But who were "the people," and who spoke for them? In both revolutions, it had been commonly assumed that only those who shared a determination to put the public good above private interest—those who lived and acted "virtuously," a word incessantly repeated by revolutionary activists—deserved to be counted among "the people." Divisions of wealth, of occupation, of status meant nothing, so it was assumed, among citizens united in their devotion to revolutionary regeneration. And those who selfishly rejected the common good—"Tories" and "monarchists" loyal to the British Crown in America, "aristocrats" and their dupes in the French Republic—had put themselves beyond the pale of "the people."

Such lofty abstractions may have served to whip up enthusiasm and self-sacrifice in the moments of crisis through which both revolutions passed, but they were impossible to sustain. "The people" consist of innumerable individuals, all driven by self-interest and none perfect. Aspirations to advance, resentment of those who are more fortunate, and fear of or contempt for those less well-off, or simply different, are all part of the human condition. Hopes that the American and French Revolutions had wrought fundamental changes in citizens' characters were dashed, and revolutionaries' expectations that republics could endure only as long as their citizens remained selflessly virtuous were called in question. The American states, that in 1776 declared their collective independence of Great Britain, were soon beset by partisan squabbling, profiteering, and bitter conflicts between debtors and creditors. In France, the turmoil went even deeper and the results were far more bloody. Not only aristocrats who lost their privileges, but also religious people who objected to ending the Catholic Church's traditional place in society and ordinary folk who resented the Revolution's tax collectors, military recruiters, and price controllers, all found themselves branded counterrevolutionary "enemies of the people." Nor did those who embraced the revolutionary cause remain united: By 1793–94, "terror" was the order of the day, as one faction of republicans after another beheaded their enemies on the guillotine. When order was finally restored, in the summer of 1794, the French Republic was in the hands of moderate revolutionaries who played down all talk of public "virtue" and winked at considerable graft and corruption.

Many historians see a similar pattern at work in America, especially after independence was assured by a peace treaty in 1783. By 1787, many moderate revolutionaries felt that the attempt to build small, "virtuous" republics in each state was failing. The Constitutional Convention that met in Philadelphia during the summer of 1787 was supposed to recommend only a few changes in the Articles of Confederation, the compact under which the states formed a loose but largely powerless union; instead, the Convention proposed a greatly strengthened federal union, and by skillful, not always scrupulous political maneuvering the advocates of the new Constitution engineered its adoption. In early 1789, just months before the Revolution broke out in France, George Washington was inaugurated president of the United States under the Constitution, and the First Congress opened its sessions. The new republic's fate indeed hung in the balance, and it could well have failed to survive the stormy years that followed. Partisan strife intensified as Washington's administration sought to win the support of rich urban creditors, much to the alarm of rural debtors. The Federalist Party, which supported Washington, had little patience with the democratic leanings of the opposition Republicans, led by Thomas Jefferson. To the Republicans, the new republic was quickly sinking back into the corrupt political practices of monarchical Great Britain, against which Americans had rebelled in the 1770s. When the French Revolution turned radical—executing the king, making war on monarchical Europe, and unleashing terror against domestic enemies—Americans were polarized. Federalists feared and hated what the French Revolution had become; Republicans admired and defended it. There was real danger that the United States would become embroiled in the war between revolutionary France and Britain, the probable result of which would have been civil war in America itself. The election of 1800 was fought against a background of government policies aimed at curbing critics of the Federalist administration and thwarting the Democratic Republican societies that supported Jefferson's candidacy. Because of constitutional peculiarities then in effect, the election ended in a deadlock, and in 1801 Jefferson was finally chosen as president by the House of Representatives only just before Inauguration Day. By that time, a successful and ambitious general, Napoléon Bonaparte, had already seized power in France and was consolidating a dictatorship that, he said, combined "order" with the social achievements of the Revolution.

Democracy had an uncertain future in the first years of the 1800s. Jefferson's election and the peaceful transfer of power to his democratically oriented party were momentous milestones, in pointed contrast to the ways in which power was transferred in the era of the French Revolution. Jefferson and his followers shared an unprecedented vision of America's democratic future: one in which the power of the state would be pared down to the absolute minimum, while the Union spread over the vast territory of the Louisiana Purchase, which Jefferson acquired from Napoléon and sent the famous Lewis and Clark Expedition to explore. The Jeffersonian hope for an "empire of liberty" in the New World contrasted sharply with the glamorous European empire that Napoléon was building with military conquests and administering with an impressive bureaucracy. Jefferson and Napoléon each saw himself as the fulfiller of the promise of the revolutionary era, yet how different were their creations.

How different, too, were the revolutionary states that emerged from the wreckage of the Spanish empire in America—a crisis set in motion when in 1808 Napoléon invaded Spain, overthrew its reactionary king, and thus confronted the Spanish colonies in the New World with the challenge of whether the government that claimed to rule them in Madrid was legitimate. The native-born upper class of Spanish America saw a golden opportunity to escape their domination by "peninsular" (Spanish-born) bureaucrats. It was these upper-class but politically powerless "Creoles" who led the Latin American revolutions of the early nineteenth century, and it was they who would hold virtually all power in the new Latin American nations that emerged; their grip on power remained virtually unchecked throughout the nineteenth and much of the twentieth century.

A generation later, in the mid-1830s, Europeans sensed the revival of the revolutionary democratic movement. The movement was still weak and highly controversial; many saw it not only as a challenge to the authoritarian governments that were in power across the Continent but also as a threat to property rights and law and order. By that time, most American states had broadened their suffrage requirements so that virtually all adult white men could vote (and in some cases specifically denied the vote to the relatively few free black men and white women who had been able to vote in Jefferson's time). Equally significantly, the United States now had a president—Andrew Jackson—who claimed a special mandate to lead because he alone, of all officeholders in the nation, had been elected by and thus spoke for the sovereign people. And a vigorous political party existed to mobilize popular support for Jackson and his policies, while an equally vigorous opposition party was arising that also sought a popular mandate to block Jackson's initiatives. By 1840, these opposing parties, the Democrats and the Whigs, would be waging exciting election campaigns, complete with torchlight parades, public barbecues, and impassioned political oratory, in which some three-fourths of eligible voters participated enthusiastically. This spectacle fascinated Europeans who visited the United States and avidly reported what they observed. Was democracy the wave of the future? How had Americans come to terms with it? Should Europeans be frightened at the prospect of mass democracy? One of the nineteenth century's most astute analysts, Alexis de Tocqueville, wrote a famous book to answer such questions.

Who were the people, and who should lead them? It was easy to claim that the people ruled, or should rule—but difficult to say how "the people" should be defined in a practical sense. *All* the people? All the adult *men*? All the men who had the education and the income to be able to devote themselves wisely to the public good? All those who spoke the same language and felt dedicated to the same nation? All those who worked, but not those who sat by idly and exploited the rest? All these choices, and others still, would be tested in the course of the nineteenth century, and the years beyond.

Thomas Jefferson Assumes the American Presidency, 1801

Thomas Jefferson

Although few people then alive would have understood its significance, one event from the years 1800–1801 stands out as truly significant for the coming century.

In 1800 the United States counted for very little in world affairs. Its population of a little more than 4 million (almost a quarter of them black slaves) was spread out mainly in Atlantic seaboard states, and settlers were crossing the Appalachian Mountains to settle the Mississippi River basin only in places. Its economy was mainly localized; for most states, trade with Great Britain was more important than with neighboring states. There was little sense of national cohesion, and the new federal Constitution that had gone into force at the beginning of 1789 still seemed a tenuous experiment. Partisan and regional rancor ran high; defenders and haters of revolutionary France were at each other's throats, civil liberties were under attack as a result of the Alien and Sedition Laws of 1798, and there was talk of breaking up the Union. The 1800 presidential election was a bitter contest between the Federalist and Democratic Republican Parties, which disagreed fundamentally over whether democracy was a good thing. Because of a flawed provision in the Constitution (which had not envisioned the existence

Excerpted from Thomas Jefferson's First Inaugural Address, 1801.

of competitive political parties), the two top contenders for the presidency were deadlocked in the electoral college as the year 1800 closed. Whether a president could even be inaugurated in March 1801, as scheduled, seemed questionable. The raw new American republic, isolated three thousand miles across the Atlantic on the outer fringe of the Western world, might well not survive. And if it failed, few in Europe would have mourned.

But survive it did. Thanks to the good sense of a few moderate Federalists, one vote shifted in Congress, which sufficed to permit Thomas Jefferson (1743–1826) to be formally elected president and to take the oath of office. Partisan rancor by no means disappeared, but because Jefferson and his victorious Republicans believed that government should be as weak and decentralized as possible, there were no serious reprisals against the losing Federalists—who indeed began to fade away as an organized party. Probably the United States owed its continued existence in those early years to the "antipower" beliefs of the dominant Republican Party. Whatever the reason, history's first peaceful transfer of political power between bitter political rivals had occurred as a result of the election of 1800, and the United States had a new lease on life. In the century to come, it would grow into a full-fledged democracy, an industrial giant, a continental nation stretching from the Atlantic to the Pacific and beyond. By 1900 it would stand poised to become the greatest power on the globe.

Jefferson's first inaugural address envisaged few of the dramatic changes that would transform the United States in the century to come. But as a testimonial to the hope of purposely keeping government as limited as possible, Jefferson gave voice to the ideals that would in fact permit the United States to make the transition to democracy and thus to what his great successor Abraham Lincoln would call "the last, best hope of earth."

During the contest of opinion through which we have passed the animation of discussions and of exertions has sometimes worn an aspect which might impose on strangers unused to think freely and to speak and to write what they think; but this being now decided by the voice of the nation, announced according to the rules of the Constitution, all will, of course, arrange themselves under the will of the law, and unite in common efforts for the common good. All, too, will bear in mind this sacred principle, that though the will of the majority is in all cases to prevail, that will to be rightful must be reasonable; that the minority possess their equal rights, which equal law must protect, and to violate would be oppression. Let us, then, fellow-citizens, unite with one heart and one mind. Let us restore to social intercourse that harmony and affection without which liberty and even life itself are but dreary things. And let us reflect that, having banished from our land that religious intolerance under which mankind so long bled and suffered, we have yet gained little if we countenance a political intolerance as despotic, as wicked, and capable of as bitter and bloody persecutions. During the throes and convulsions of the ancient world, during the agonizing spasms of infuriated man, seeking through blood and slaughter his long-lost liberty, it was not wonderful that the agitation of the billows should reach even this distant and peaceful shore; that this should be more felt and feared by some and less by others, and should divide opinions as to measures of safety. But every difference of opinion is not a difference of principle. We have called by different names brethren of the same principle. We are all Republicans, we are all Federalists.

If there be any among us who would wish to dissolve this Union or to change its republican form, let them stand undisturbed as monuments of the safety with which error of opinion may be tolerated where reason is left free to combat it. I know, indeed, that some honest men fear that a republican government can not be strong, that this Government is not strong enough; but would the honest patriot, in the full tide of successful experiment, abandon a government which has so far kept us free and firm on the theoretic and visionary fear that this Government, the world's

Thomas Jefferson

best hope, may by possibility want energy to preserve itself? I trust not. I believe this, on the contrary, the strongest Government on earth. I believe it the only one where every man, at the call of the law, would fly to the standard of the law, and would meet invasions of the public order as his own personal concern. Sometimes it is said that man can not be trusted with the government of himself. Can he, then, be trusted with the government of others? Or have we found angels in the forms of kings to govern him? Let history answer this question.

Let us, then, with courage and confidence pursue our own Federal and Republican principles, our attachment to union and representative government. Kindly separated by nature and a wide ocean from the exterminating havoc of one quarter of the globe; too high-minded to endure the degradations of the others; possessing a chosen country, with room enough for our descendants to the thousandth and thousandth generation; entertaining a due sense of our equal right to the use of our own faculties, to the acquisitions of our own industry, to honor and confidence from our fellow-citizens, resulting not from birth, but from our actions and their sense of them; enlightened by a benign religion, professed, indeed, and practiced in various forms, yet all of them inculcating honesty, truth, temperance, gratitude, and the love of man; acknowledging and adoring an overruling Providence, which by all its dispensations proves that it delights in the happiness of man here and his greater happiness hereafter—with all these blessings, what more is necessary to make us a happy and a prosperous people? Still one thing more, fellow-citizens—a wise and frugal Government, which shall restrain men from injuring one another, shall leave them otherwise free to regulate their own pursuits of industry and improvement, and shall not take from the mouth of labor the bread it has earned. This is the sum of good government, and this is necessary to close the circle of our felicities.

About to enter, fellow-citizens, on the exercise of duties which comprehend everything dear and valuable to you, it is proper you should understand what I deem the essential principles of our Government, and consequently those which ought to shape its Administration. I will compress them within the narrowest compass they will bear, stating the general principle, but not all its limitations. Equal and exact justice to all men, of whatever state or persuasion, religious or political; peace, commerce, and honest friendship with all nations, entangling alliances with none; the support of the State governments in all their rights, as the most competent administrations for our domestic concerns and the surest bulwarks against anti-republican tendencies; the preservation of the General Government in its whole constitutional vigor, as the sheet anchor of our peace at home and safety abroad; a jealous care of the right of election by the people—a mild and safe corrective of abuses which are lopped by the sword of revolution where peaceable remedies are unprovided; absolute acquiescence in the decisions of the majority, the vital principle of republics, from which is no appeal but to force, the vital principle and immediate parent of despotism; a well-disciplined militia, our best reliance in peace and for the first moments of war, till regulars may relieve them; the supremacy of the civil over the military authority; economy in the public expense, that labor may be lightly burthened; the honest payment of our debts and sacred preservation of the public faith; encouragement of agriculture, and of commerce as its handmaid; the diffusion of information and arraignment of all abuses at the bar of the public reason; freedom of religion; freedom of the press, and freedom of person under the protection of the habeas corpus, and trial by juries impartially selected. These principles form the bright constellation which has gone before us and guided our steps through an age of revolution and reformation. The wisdom of our sages and blood of our heroes have been devoted to their attainment. They should be the creed of our political faith, the text of civic instruction, the touchstone by which to try the services of those we trust; and should we wander from them in moments of error or of alarm, let us hasten to retrace our steps and to regain the road which alone leads to peace, liberty, and safety.

Inside Napoléon's Empire

Michael Broers

Napoléon Bonaparte's France stood, in many ways, at the opposite extreme from Thomas Jefferson's United States. Bonaparte (1769–1821) was the French Revolution's most successful general, a man who had led his armies to victory on many battlefields and who in 1799 seized power from the ineffectual politicians who were trying to run the country. He was named "first consul" of the Republic, and in 1804 he crowned himself Emperor Napoléon I. But whatever his title, he was the dictator. If in Jefferson's America the ideal was decentralization and "antipower," in Napoleonic France the goal was an efficiently run, centralized, bureaucratic state, capable of extending its power across all of Europe. Jeffersonian America might not have been fully democratic (and certainly was disfigured by the institution of slavery), but its leaders wanted to encourage the growth of democracy. Napoleonic France and its satellites were anything but democratic in practice.

But both Napoléon and Jefferson were sons of the revolutions—French and American, respectively—that had made them great figures in history. Jefferson saw himself as a champion of religious freedom, limited government, education, science, and enlightenment. Napoléon wanted to preserve and extend what he considered the positive benefits of the French Revolution: its centralized, rational state, its subordination of religious "superstition," its aim of providing every individual with the opportunity to rise as far as his (not "her"; he was no feminist) talents would permit—and like Jefferson, of promoting education, science, and enlightenment.

In the article that follows, British historian Michael Broers concentrates not on Napoléon's fabled career as a military conqueror but rather on his

Reprinted from "The Empire Behind the Lines," by Michael Broers, *History Today,* January 1998. Reprinted with permission from *History Today.*

activities as an administrator and a law giver to the many peoples of Europe over whom his French armies had been victorious. His work of consolidating and spreading the legacy of the French Revolution would in fact be much more enduring and historically important than the ephemeral empire that he ruled from Spain to Poland.

Napoléon is best remembered as a great military commander, and it is usually the story of how he built—and then lost—his great empire that first evokes an interest in his life and times. Napoléon's other distinguishing feature in the eyes of the world is that he was French—indeed, that he was the greatest Frenchman of modern times, if not of all time. Our own times are obsessed with the 'charisma' of public figures, and few people have possessed as much of it as Napoléon. He fascinated his contemporaries at least as much as later generations. Even a fierce enemy like the French Royalist and intellectual, Chateaubriand, made no attempt to conceal his fascination for him:

> Bonaparte was a poet in action, a total genius in war, an able, indefatiguable, alert mover when it came to administration, a careful and reasoned law-maker. That is why he gripped people's imaginations so much . . .

The Duke of Wellington said of him, bluntly, that 'His presence on the field made a difference of 40,000 men'. The German poet, Goethe—probably the most popular European writer of his times—simply called Napoléon 'the spirit of the age', while still deploring him. If this was how his enemies spoke of him, the words of his many admirers need only be imagined.

However, there was far more to the career of Napoléon, and to the nature of his empire, than this, although the aura of his personality makes it hard for the historian to get beyond the myth and, by extension, beyond the legendary—and glamorous—military exploits. Indeed, to dwell on these aspects of his career is to do Napoléon something of an injustice, for the battles, romantic tangles and heroic posturing are not his most lasting achievements. Napoléon was the ruler of a truly European empire and he devoted enormous energy to governing it, at least as much as he did to conquering it in the first place. The story of the 'home front'—of what went on behind the frontlines of conflict and conquest—came to embrace the history of all the peoples of Western and Central Europe in one way or another. The experience of Napoleonic rule— his rise and fall—proved formative for the collective future of modern Europe.

There are two angles from which the internal history of the Napoleonic empire must be viewed: from that of the ruler, and from that of the ruled. The first comprises the policies Napoléon developed to rule his subjects; the second involves their response to those policies. Only by putting the two together, can any real understanding be gained of the history of the fate of Europe under Napoléon. Even before his grip was secured on any given part of the continent, the experience of war and conquest had, in itself, created circumstances of crucial, often determining, importance for the character of imperial rule that was to follow. The mess created by the military advance of Napoleonic imperialism was the first thing Bonaparte had to deal with, wherever his armies went, just as it was the overwhelming preoccupation of all those he brought under his sway, for in every case, he owed his empire to military conquest, and to that alone.

War was the most widespread, common experience of the peoples of Western and Central Europe at this time. Every area which came into the Napoleonic empire had first to pass through the horrors of war and military occupation. Reduced to its human essentials, this meant that almost all the subject peoples of the empire endured rape and pillage on a grand scale, as a prelude to imperial rule and, when this hard truth is remembered, it is something of a miracle that any semblence of peaceful co-operation ever emerged between the conquered and the invaders. This was even true within France itself, in areas which had seen early counter-revolutionary resistance to the new order, the major example being the Vendée. But large parts of southern France—the Midi—were also theatres of armed resistance to the Revolution, particularly in the Rhone valley, along the border with Spain, in the Pyrenees and in Provence, the foothills of the Alps.

When they began their war with the rest of Europe in 1792, the French revolutionary armies had assumed they would be greeted with open arms by the common people of Europe. In fact, the prospect of invasion and occupation stirred much older, atavistic fears among the inhabitants of the Low Countries, the Rhineland, northern Spain, north-western Italy, and the British Isles, all of whom had strong folk memories of earlier wars with France and their attendant atrocities. It was irrelevant what ideological banner the French came under—whether it be that of the aggressive, expansionist Bourbon monarchy of old, or as the 'friends of humanity and the rights of man'—they were still the French, the ancestral, powerful and pitiless enemy.

An Irish traveller in the German Rhineland during the fighting of the 1790s recorded how ordinary people made a direct connection between the fate suffered by their ancestors in the wars against Louis XIV, and their own confrontation with the armies of the French Revolution:

> The particulars of that dismal scene have been transmitted from father to son, and are still spoken of with horror by the peasantry of this country, among whom the French nation is held in detestation to this day.

These latent, almost subconscious fears were fanned, and their forms crystallised, by the propaganda war waged against the Revolution by the Catholic Church, still the greatest single influence on the common people of Western Europe, and their most important source of information about the outside world.

When the French revolutionaries turned the Catholic Church against them—first in 1790, with the Civil Constitution of the Clergy, then with repeated outbursts of religious persecution, which lasted throughout the 1790s—they handed the governments of the surrounding states a powerful propaganda tool, which they employed to considerable effect. When the clergy touched on the deeper, semi-articulated fear of the French harboured by ordinary people, the ground was well presented for ferocious resistance to their advance.

In the end, the Church need not have bothered to stir these embers on behalf of the old order. The violent, rapacious conduct of the French armies was enough to rouse hatred, resentment and resistance on its own. The new 'citizen soldier' of the revolutionary armies saw himself as a citizen of one nation only, France, and when he left its frontiers, he did not carry with him the wider, internationalist aspirations of some revolutionary leaders, such as the Girondins. In his conduct towards non-French peoples, it is clear that the soldier of the Republic had not absorbed the universalism of the original battle-cry of the 'war party' in 1792—'War on the castle, peace to the cottage'—but he had become imbued with a ferocious sense of French nationalism, which meant a marked sense of superiority towards all those he encountered.

As the war tipped in their favour, French troops found themselves further from home and from their supply bases. Badly paid and supplied—indeed, often left to 'live off the land' as a deliberate policy—the revolutionary armies descended on the rest of Europe like a savage, barbarian horde. The analogy is not an exaggeration, for as time passed, away from their native villages and families, the troops began to form loyalties that had less to do with France, itself, and more to do with their own units. They were 'revolutionised' less by the efforts of government propaganda, than by this sense of root-lessness, reinforced by a reciprocal hatred for foreign populations which resisted them, often by cruel means, and by other aspects of government policy.

Just as the French soldier often did not divorce the political cause he defended from the quest for booty and supplies, so the civilian populations he invaded did not distinguish between the behaviour of the French troops and the revolution they carried with them. This hate-filled interaction began in earnest in the Vendée, and during the suppression of the Federalist revolts of 1793–94 when the large southern cities rose against Paris. It was nurtured within France itself, but as the armies pushed forward, it became a phenomenon of European dimensions.

In the context of the Napoleonic empire, perhaps the most important point to bear in mind—and it is often forgotten—is that this process was, truly, 'ongoing'. It did not end with the change of regime in 1799, nor did it soften in any way, as time progressed. Napoléon made many compromises with the enemies of the Revolution, as shall be seen, but he never allowed this to touch the armies. He made sure they remained bastions of republicanism; in so far as they had clear political views, the troops were just as imbued with anti-clericalism and hatred of the old order, as in the 1790s. Perhaps the clearest evidence of this is that Napoléon never allowed his troops to have chaplains with them, in accordance with revolutionary tradition. The armies became more, not less, cut off from the peasant society they had left behind, after 1799, and they remained just as contemptuous of the new populations they encountered, with every military success.

What changed after 1799 was not the conduct and attitude of the armies or the peoples who had to endure their presence, but rather that the battlelines moved away from the original fronts, around the eastern and southern borders of France. The war and its attendant horrors shifted from the Low Countries, western and central Germany and northern and central Italy, and with this the French—at last—saw the chance to create a new stability, on their own terms, a

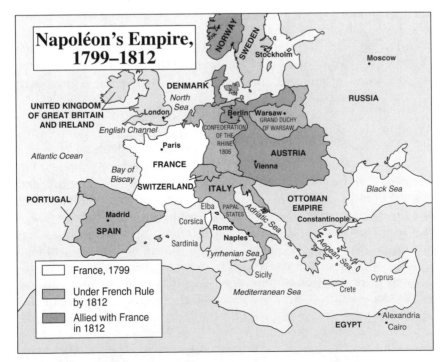

chance to clean up their own mess. The 'war syndrome' moved on: to Spain and Portugal in 1808—where the French, themselves, continued to compare circumstances to the Vendée—and to the North Sea and Adriatic coasts and southern Italy, where a 'monstrous little war' raged until 1814 between the French and the bandits of Calabria. These last named regions became the outer fringe of the 'Grand Empire', never really absorbed by Napoléon, and always the scenes of bitter guerrilla wars.

By contrast, those areas first conquered and furthest from the fighting, became an 'inner' empire, where French rule was stable and secure for most of the period 1801–12. It is essential to grasp this distinction within Napoléon's territories, for it is far more important than the largely artificial differences between satellite kingdoms, allied states and the non-French departments, ruled directly from Paris. Whereas the latter were the makeshift creations of improvised diplomacy, the concept of 'inner' and 'outer' empires rests on genuine, practical levels of stability and control.

In the lands of the 'inner empire', it became possible to create a stable, civilian administrative system of local government, based on the prefects, and to allow the laws of the Napoleonic Civil Code to operate in full, with all the guarantees for the protection of persons and property they allowed. These areas settled into relative peace and security early in the period, and this was where the Napoleonic reforms in justice and administration really took root. This happened directly in those vast parts of Western Europe annexed to France, including much of western Germany and north-western Italy, as well as all of modern Belgium—and by imitation in the satellite kingdoms of Italy—centred on Milan, and in Holland, or in those states closely allied with France, such as Bavaria, Baden and Wurtemberg in southern Germany.

The broad outlines of the centralised administrative system devised in France during the Revolution, and the general concepts of the Napoleonic Code had become 'the norms' in these parts of Europe by the fall of Napoléon in 1814. The Code brought an end to the power of the guilds to regulate many aspects of working life, and almost complete freedom of profession; it brought equality before the law for all citizens, where it was applied in full—which it was not in Bavaria, where Jews were still denied full civil rights—and the equal division of property among all citizens. Many of these changes were far from welcomed by ordinary people, as they represented the destruction of numerous deeply-rooted customs and traditions, and often spelled the loss of important privileges, not just for the nobility, but for whole cities and provinces. No one was exempt from the ferocious conscription laws Napoléon imposed on his own state and all his allies, to raise his massive armies. However, the long period of stability between 1801 and 1812 made millions of Western Europeans accustomed to both the good and the bad aspects of Napoleonic methods of government.

Napoléon sought to apply the same sets of policies to all the territories he came to control, regardless of when he seized them or whether he ruled them directly, as French departments, by proxy in his satellite kingdoms, or by indirect pressure, as in the independent, allied states of the Confederation of the Rhine. How successful he was depended essentially on how well a given part of his empire got over the initial shock of its conquest by his armies. Put another way, it depended on how much time his officials had to repair the ravages of war and win the trust of those they administered. Broadly, they made some progress in the lands of the 'inner empire', but they failed beyond them, in the areas Napoléon seized after about 1806.

In Spain, central and southern Italy, the northern coast of Germany, the Adriatic coast of modern Croatia, and in the 'Grand Duchy of Warsaw'—the core of modern Poland—Napoleonic rule was disruptive and traumatic. Usually, it brought with it only the horrors of war, conscription and heavy taxation, with none of the benefits felt further west. To this day, in Slovenia, peasants call taxes *fronki*—'French'—a sign of how Napoleonic rule is remembered in the more far flung parts of the 'Grand Empire'. In total contrast, when Prussia acquired most of the Rhineland at the Congress of Vienna in 1814, its rulers wisely decided to allow the region to retain almost all of the Napoleonic Code, because for the propertied and educated classes, at least, it had come to be regarded as a guarantee of civil liberties.

Attitudes to policing followed a similar pattern to the reception of the laws it enforced. Within the lands of the 'inner empire', the Gendarmerie—a paramilitary police force devoted to policing the countryside—proved popular and durable, at least among the better-off and isolated peasant communities. The Gendarmes were hated as the enforcers of conscription, but they also assured basic order where once banditry had been rife. Consequently, they were imitated or retained in many countries after the end of Napoleonic rule. The Netherlands and many Italian states retained Gendarmeries after 1814, while the Prussians adopted many of their methods.

The contrast with Spain, however, is striking. Here, French rule provoked the massive people's war against Napoléon, called the *guerrilla*. This true 'war of liberation' may have been a glorious chapter in Spanish history, but it had the devastating side-effect of turning a once peaceful country into a sea of banditry, as the guerrilla bands, the *partidas,* often refused to return to normal life and turned to crime, with no effective police force to cope with them. All over Europe, millions of soldiers were 'demobilised' in the years after 1814, usually returning to civilian life at a time of economic recession and poor harvests; yet in most of the lands of the 'inner empire', a semblence of civil order was maintained in the face of these difficult circumstances. In Spain, however, the collapse of all effective administration led to disorder on a huge scale that was not mastered for decades to come.

None of this meant that Napoleonic officials did not try to enforce the imperial system of government in these 'frontier' regions. In the Spanish Pyrenees, one young French prefect, Viefville, sent to govern an area infested with rebels was not even able to enter the main town of his department for the first eight months of his appointment in 1812. Once there, he had a serious nervous breakdown. Yet Viefville recovered, stayed at his post to the end, and did what he could to better the area, building a hospital and introducing proper sanitation methods to the town. Ultimately, however, he failed to make any real impact on the region; the war was always too close and the local rebels too strong for him.

Clearly, it depended very much on where you were, as to whether you saw any of the benefits of Napoleonic rule. Even within the 'inner empire' there were always tensions between its positive and negative aspects which made the impact of the Napoleonic state very much a mixed blessing, even in its heartlands. Conscription cast a shadow over most parts of Europe Napoléon controlled. Indeed, the French regarded their ability to raise men from a particular area as the benchmark of whether they really had a grip on it or not. Outside France itself, northern Italy, Belgium and the German states, became reliable sources of recruits, whereas the French never dared introduce it in the Kingdom of Naples—the southern half of the Italian peninsula—or in those parts of Spain they controlled. Even within France, itself, Napoléon exempted the volatile western region centred on the Vendée for as long as he could and, after 1812, kept its quotas low; along the border with Spain, it broke down altogether by the end of his rule.

Everywhere, conscription was hated, even in the heart of France itself. The novelist, Alfred de Musset was a schoolboy during the Napoleonic wars, and has left us this vivid impression in his memoirs:

> During the wars of the Empire . . . worried mothers brought a . . . nervous generation into the world, conceived between two battles, brought up in colleges to the role of drums, thousands of children looked around at each other with sombre eyes. . . . Every year France made a present to this man (Napoléon) of 300,000 youths. . . . Never were there so many sleepless nights as in the time of this man; never were there to be seen, leaning over the ramparts of town walls, such a nation of sorrowing mothers; never did such silence envelop those who spoke of death.

Napoléon had many battles to fight on his 'home front' and, on one level, he won several of them, at least within the 'inner empire'.

Life was regulated by a clear, rational and usually fair legal code. In what has become the core of the modern European Union, all these characteristics of the Napoleonic empire can still be seen at work, because they did just that—work. However, it took the end of the wars, and the suffering they brought, even well behind the lines, for these benefits to become obvious to most of the ordinary people of Europe. Nevertheless, by the 1820s and 1830s, it was clear to most educated Europeans that the best way to run a state efficiently was still very close to the models Napoleon had introduced them to.

One of the enduring questions about Napoléon among historians has always been to what extent he should be considered the heir to the French Revolution, or whether he destroyed its legacy in order to erect an authoritarian system of his own in its place. There is no real doubt that he stiffled the experiment in elected, representative government begun in 1789, but it is a very grave error to see this as the only—or even the most important—aspect of the French Revolution. By 1799, France had evolved a centralised, professional, modern system of administration and unleashed a pitiless war on the rest of Europe, and on many sectors of its own people. Napoléon intensified both, and made the civil war engendered by the French Revolution a truly European phenomenon. He brought war and good government at one and the same time to the peoples of Europe. His impact on European politics was as full of paradoxes as his own personality. The 'Napoleonic experience' was both a trauma and a ray of light on the future for all who lived through it.

Latin America Wins an Ambiguous Independence

John Lynch

The revolt of British North Americans in the 1770s was the first wave of anticolonial rebellion in the modern world; the second began in 1808 with the attempt of most of Spanish-speaking America to gain independence from Spain.

John Lynch, a British expert on Latin American history, makes clear in the following selection that significant differences separated the revolutionary experiences of British and Spanish (Latin) Americans. Before the 1760s, the old British Empire had been a ramshackle, decentralized collection of colonies, only loosely governed by the mother country as local elites of merchants, lawyers, and planters jealously guarded their political autonomy. Spanish America, however, had been vigorously and surprisingly efficiently governed by Spanish royal officials, who excluded the local American-born upper class from any significant political role. Moreover, in Spanish America there was an elaborate hierarchy of mixed-race peoples whose legal rights depended on their ethnic heritage, whereas in British America there were only three sharply separated categories: whites, blacks (who were overwhelmingly slaves), and Indians.

The revolt of the North American colonial population against British rule escalated rapidly after the mid-1760s because, for the first time,

Parliament attempted to extend direct control over the colonies, taxing them and depriving the local elites of their accustomed influence (for example, to flout trade restrictions). The result, broadly speaking, was a tendency for the white North American population to rally together against the perceived British threat to local liberty. In Spanish America, on the other hand, it was the *collapse* of royal authority when Napoléon invaded Spain and dethroned the king in 1808 that gave American-born (Creole) elites an unprecedented opportunity to assert themselves against the Spanish officialdom, or *peninsulares* ("people from the [Spanish] peninsula").The result was a series of local rebellions led by the Creole upper class in what is now Argentina, Peru, Colombia, Venezuela, and Mexico—regions too distant from one another to share any interest except throwing off "peninsular" domination. Once these revolts started, there was too little common interest among the subordinate categories of nonelite peoples for the Creole elites to do anything except dominate those lower on the social hierarchy—unlike the North American elites, who instinctively sought to rally nonelite whites behind their leadership.

Lynch emphasizes that Spanish American Creole leaders like Simón Bolívar in Gran Colombia (modern Colombia and Venezuela), José de San Martín in Peru, and the elites of Mexico and La Plata (modern Argentina) could only lead local rebellions. In turn, these ultimately successful rebellions spawned other revolts, in Central America, Ecuador, Bolivia, Chile, Paraguay, and Uruguay, but there was never a serious chance that these revolts would swell into a movement to unite Spanish America.Moreover, because of the deep social divisions and authoritarian political traditions of the old Spanish American empire, the result of successful revolt was always the same: the creation of oligarchic local dictatorships under military strongmen, called *caudillos,* rather than any serious attempt to limit governmental power or to maximize republican liberty—perhaps the chief ideological legacy of the North American revolution.

By the mid-1820s, almost all of Spanish America had broken free of peninsular rule; only in such Caribbean colonies as Cuba and Puerto Rico did Spanish authority remain effective. (Portuguese-ruled Brazil gained its independence by the simple process of the Portuguese royal family fleeing there after Napoléon invaded the mother country; in some ways, it was Portugal, liberated from Napoleonic occupation by the British army, that seceded from Brazil rather than vice versa.) Post-Napoleonic Spain alone was too weak to reestablish its old domination in Latin America, although it fought hard to do so. The reactionary governments of continental Europe were eager to help Spain reconquer its empire, but in 1823 Great Britain, which dominated the Atlantic Ocean and saw a golden opportunity to gain access to Spanish America's once-closed markets, proposed that the United States join in issuing a declaration of intervention. Knowing that the Royal Navy alone could keep European armies out of Latin America, the canny U.S. secretary of state John Quincy Adams refused to act as Britain's subordinate, but instead had President James Monroe announce unilaterally the U.S. policy insisting that the Americas no longer be subject to Old World colonization. This was the famous Monroe Doctrine, a statement initially important mainly as a declaration of American nationalism. As a practical matter, Latin America in the nineteenth century came largely under British protection and economic domination. Only in the late nineteenth and twentieth centuries would Yanqui influence become dominant—and widely resented—in the Latin American republics.

The Bourbon state in Spanish America [the Spanish empire] was not succeeded immediately by new nation states. There was an intermediate stage in which liberating armies or caudillo [warlord] bands first challenged the political and military power of Spain and then destroyed it. In some cases this was a lengthy process and involved the creation of rudimentary wartime states, capable of raising taxes and recruiting troops. But these states were not necessarily nations. Even after independence had been won the establishment of new states preceded the formation of nations. For the growth of national consciousness was slow and partial. . . . Yet there were new factors favouring a more positive concept of nation. The revolutionary war was itself a noble cause, for which the insurgent armies fought glorious battles, and the people made great if grudging sacrifices. . . .

The symbols and the language of nationalism acquired a new urgency. . . . [For example], the porteño [Buenos Aires, Argentina] leaders exulted in the revolution of 1810 and quickly crowned it with national symbols. . . . They sang of the heroes of independence, victories over the Spanish tyrants, the greatness of Argentina. When independence was complete these effusions were collected and published by authority in a volume entitled *La lira argentina* (1824), a hopeful gesture at a time when the nation was threatened at best by extreme federalism, at worst by utter anarchy.

Mexican nationalism, anticipated in the intellectual euphoria of the late colonial period, advanced a stage further during the revolutionary wars. . . . In the early days of the revolution Mexican nationalists . . . used the term 'American' to describe their country, and they referred to themselves as 'Americanos'. . . . To appropriate the wider name—as the United States did more decisively—was not to deny but to affirm their nationality. . . .

To what extent did Americans achieve economic independence? Economic nationalism, hostility to foreign penetration, resentment of external control, these later ingredients of Latin American nationalism were almost completely absent from contemporary attitudes. While the new nations rejected the Spanish monopoly, they welcomed foreigners who subscribed to free competition and who brought much needed capital, manufactured goods and entrepreneurial skills. Latin Americans were positively deferential to Britain. 'Politically,' wrote Bolívar, 'alliance with Great Britain would be a greater victory than Ayacucho[a battle with the Spanish], and if we procure it you may be certain that our future happiness is assured. The advantages which will result for Colombia, if we ally ourselves with that mistress of the universe, are incalculable.' These views contained a large measure of self-interest and betrayed the anxiety of young and weak states to acquire a protector—a liberal protector— against the Holy Alliance. In general, Latin American leaders overestimated the extent to which their countries needed protection: the fact was that the powers of Europe had neither the will nor the means to intervene militarily in the Americas. The Monroe Doctrine, first proclaimed in 1823, had only slight relevance at the time. It meant little to Latin Americans and indeed was not primarily directed to them: it was a unilateral statement of United States policy, warning off European incursions in the Americas, either for new colonization or for recolonizing the new states. The United States subsequently made no move to implement the doctrine unless its own interests were directly at stake. Britain too sought to pose as a protector of the new states, with no more justification but with more success. Latin Americans continued to look to British sea power and British commercial power as the best pledges of their security. And they were prepared to invite a greater British stake in their countries than would be tolerable to later generations. 'Here [Peru], I have sold the mines for two and a half million pesos, and I expect to obtain far more from other sources. I have suggested to the Peruvian government that it sell in England all its mines, lands, properties, and other government assets to cover the national debt, which is at least twenty million pesos.' This is not the language of modern nationalism. But what did it mean? Had the new states a realistic choice between autarchy and dependence, between development and underdevelopment?

Independence ended the Spanish monopoly . . . and gave Spanish America direct access to the world economy. British merchants and industrialists, or their agents, promptly moved into the new markets, looking for quick sales at low prices and selling to the popular sectors as well as to the elite. Britain was not only the leading exporter to Latin America—followed at some distance by the United States, France and Germany—but also the principal market for Latin American exports. There was at first an imbalance of trade, as Spanish American agricultural and mining exports stagnated and local capital was expended on imports rather than accumulated for investment. The principal owners of capital—Church and merchants—had little inducement to invest in industry in the absence of a strong and protected market. It was easier to allow British manufactures to flood the market and force out national products. Moreover, the superior supplies, credit and shipping resources of the British made it difficult for local merchants to compete and drove many of them out of business. Yet there were compensations. These were years of further industrial growth in Britain when the price of exports fell; and they fell more substantially than did the price of primary products. . . . Meanwhile British merchants had very little political leverage in Latin America and no influence over the tariff policy of the new states; unlike Spain, the new commercial metropolis could not be accused of fiscal extortion.

Yet the Latin American economies did not respond immediately to emancipation. The wars of independence were destructive of life and property; terror and insecurity, moreover, caused flight of labour and capital, which made it difficult to organise recovery and even more difficult to diversify the economy. Lack of internal accumulation and absence, as yet, of foreign investment further impeded economic growth. Mining in particular suffered from wartime dislocation and subsequent lack of capital. Other sectors needed less capital. Cattle ranching in Argentina and Venezuela could yield profits without great investment, assisted as it was by liberalisation of trade and access to stable markets. Tropical agriculture was less buoyant, but also found ways of surviving and expanding. The different economic sectors competed for influence but the metropolis no longer arbitrated.

Policy was made by the new leaders and national economic groups. These sought to . . . reduce other regions or provinces to a kind of colonial dependence upon themselves. Capitals or ports such as Buenos Aires thus tried to monopolize the fruits of independence, interposing themselves as a controlling interest in national and overseas trade. The subregions had to insist on economic autonomy in order to protect themselves; Uruguay and Paraguay opted for complete independence; the interior provinces of Argentina chose the way of federalism. In Mexico the artisan textile industry was less successful in protecting itself against the merchants of the capital who preferred to import British manufactures; Colombian industry suffered a similar fate. The national economies, therefore, were divided originally by internal rivalry, by conflict between the centre and the regions, between free trade and protection, between agriculturalists seeking export outlets and those who favoured industry or mining, between supporters of cheap imports and defenders of national products. On the whole the promoters of primary exports and cheap imports won the argument, and the British were waiting to take advantage.

But in the final analysis the prospects of national economic development were defeated by the social structure of the new states. The polarization of Latin American society into two sectors, a privileged minority monopolizing land and office, and a mass of peasants and workers, survived independence and continued with greater momentum. Perhaps economic growth would have raised the living standards of the people and nurtured a native middle class; in some countries, such as Mexico, upward mobility was already producing a middle group. But social rigidity and false social values were a cause as well as a result of economic retardation. Many landowners regarded their property as a social rather than economic investment, and their greatest economic activity was conspicuous consumption. Even if the consumption level of the upper income groups could have been reduced, there was no guarantee that the savings would have been invested in industry. As for the peasants, they were victims of grotesque inequality—and a helpless obstacle to development. Without agrarian reform there was no prospect of raising the living standards of the mass of the people, and without this there was no possibility of industrial development. The agrarian sector was only one stage removed from a slave economy. Peasants living at subsistence level could not be consumers of manufactures; and urban workers had to spend too much on food to have anything left for consumer goods. In these circumstances there was no mass market for national industries: Latin America either took foreign imports or went without consumer goods. Meanwhile the new nations relapsed into classical export economies, producing raw materials for the world market, exploiting the area's primitive assets—land and labour.

The basic economic institution, therefore, was the hacienda [the great landed estate], a relatively inefficient organization, producing for national consumption or for export to the world market, absorbing too much land and too little capital, and carried ultimately on the back of cheap labour, seasonal or servile. But the hacienda had more than an economic function. It was a social and political organization, a means of control, a base of the ruling oligarchy. Independence strengthened the hacienda. As the colonial state and its institutions withered, the hacienda grew more powerful; amidst the insecurity of revolution and civil war it stood firm, a bastion for its owner, a refuge for its many inhabitants. It also grew at the expense of the Church, continuing a process begun in 1767 when the vast and highly commercial estates of the Jesuits were auctioned at ridiculously low prices to neighbouring hacendados [hacienda owners] and incoming land-owners. The precedent was not lost on the new regimes. Lands of the Inquisition and of religious orders were often confiscated and sold to buyers on easy terms. And hacendados, backed by friendly governments, sometimes managed to free themselves from ecclesiastical mortgages on their property. If the war of independence was a struggle for power, it was also a dispute over resources and the creoles fought for land as well as for liberty. A new elite of landowners, rewarded from royalist property or from public land, joined the colonial proprietors and in some cases replaced them. The formation of estates went hand in hand with state building. The landowners were the new ruling class, taking over from the old colonial urban sectors of mining, trade and bureaucracy. The political ambitions of the new elite were placated by office and representation; and to satisfy their economic needs they were ready in effect to do a deal with foreigners, obtaining from the more developed nations of the northern hemisphere the credit, markets and luxury imports which Latin America itself could not provide.

The new nationalism was almost entirely devoid of social content. It is true that independence was inspired by liberal and even egalitarian ideas which rejected the rigid stratification of the colonial period. . . . But in practice the mass of the people had little loyalty to the nations in which they found themselves; they had to be forcibly conscripted during the war and closely controlled thereafter. The absence of social cohesion caused idealists like Bolívar to despair of creating viable nations. Negro slaves and the tied peons [peasants bound to the land by debt] who succeeded them, receiving few of the fruits of independence, had few reasons to feel a sense of national identity. The slave trade did not long survive independence, but slavery itself was another matter. The chronology of abolition was determined by the importance of slaves in a given economy and by the numbers available. Where there were few slaves, as in Chile, Central America and Mexico, abolition was decreed soon after independence, in the 1820s. Elsewhere, as in Argentina, Venezuela, Colombia and Peru, it survived until the 1850s, effectively barring slaves and ex-slaves from the process of nation building. The Indian population, too, remained unaware of nationality. The Indians were not integrated into the new nations. As they emerged from the colony they were an isolated and to some extent protected people, whose closest relations were with the hacienda or the Indian communities, not with the state.

The colonial caste structure [the hierarchy of mixed-race people], of which Indians were a part, did not survive the wars of independence. For caste society generated tensions between its components which threatened to destroy the traditional order in a holocaust of socio-racial violence. The creoles were haunted by the spectre of caste war. And to some degree the chronology of their conversion to independence depended upon two factors—the strength of popular agitation, and the capacity of the colonial government to control it. In Mexico and Peru, where viceregal [Spanish viceroys'] authority had the nerve and the means to govern effectively, the creoles did not hasten to desert the shelter of imperial government. But where the colonial regime was thought to be weak and social explosion imminent—in northern South America—then the obsession of the creoles with law and order and their anxiety to preserve the social structure persuaded them to make a bid for power from the very beginning. In any case, popular rebellion added a new dimension to the revolution which caused the creoles moments of near panic. There was, therefore, a causal connection between the radicalism of the masses and the conservatism of independence. Spanish America retained its colonial heritage not because the masses were indifferent to the creole revolution but because they were a threat to it. During the wars of independence popular revolt, while not successful, was menacing enough to compel the creoles to tighten their grip on the revolution: they had to contain the resentment of the Indians and the ambitions of the pardos and mestizos [people of mixed race]. And after the wars they sought to ease the less tolerable tensions in society by abolishing the caste system and preparing the way for a class society, simultaneously ending discrimination against those of mixed race and maintaining their own social and economic predominance.

The Indians, however, remained a people apart, ignored by conservatives and harassed by liberals. The latter regarded the Indians as an impediment to national development, and believed that their autonomy and corporate identity must be destroyed by forcing them into the nation through political dependence and economic participation. . . . Legislation in Peru, New Granada and Mexico sought to destroy communal and corporate entities in order to mobilize Indian lands and funds and to force the Indians out of their special status into a market economy and a national society. This involved the division of Indian communal lands among individual owners, theoretically among the Indians themselves, in practice among their more powerful white neighbours. Legislation in itself, of course, could not abolish Indian communities, which had their own mechanisms of survival. And community land was often protected in effect by the stagnation of commercial agriculture and the absence of competition for land in the decades immediately after independence. But once demographic and market pressures increased, and Spanish America became more closely integrated into the international economy, then it would be found that the Indian communities had been stripped of their defences and were open to the encroachment of the hacienda. Meanwhile, liberal policy did not integrate the Indians into the nation; it isolated them still further in hopeless poverty, their only outlet in blind and unavailing rebellion. The fruits of revolution were not all sweet and not all shared. . . .

The political systems of the new states represented the creole determination to control the Indians and Negroes, the rural labour force, and to curb the castes [mixed-blood people], the most ambitious of the lower classes. They also reacted inevitably to economic divisions and regional interests. What institutions were most appropriate to these tasks? Conservatives and liberals, products of the same elite, had different, though not consistently different, answers. A Colombian conservative remarked on the irritating self-righteousness of liberals: 'They alone tell the truth, they alone are men of honour, they alone are patriots. Those of us who do not belong to their party are dishonest, traitors, absolutists.' But he conceded that at least the liberals had a coherent doctrine, whereas the conservatives stood only for personal groupings. The distinction was not entirely valid. It is true that liberals had a policy: they stood for constitutional government, the basic human freedoms, economic *laissez-faire* [government nonintervention in the economy], opposition to military and ecclesiastical privilege. Constitutions in Mexico, Colombia, Venezuela and Chile . . . embodied typical liberal values, though even among liberals there was a tendency in Spanish America to grant the president extraordinary powers and to restrict the franchise to propertied literates. Conservatives favoured a more paternalist form of government, a virtual king with the name of president. . . .To some extent liberalism and conservatism represented different interests, urban versus rural groupings, entrepreneurial versus aristocratic values, province versus capital. But these interest alignments often dissolved, leaving a residue of ideas and convictions as the major factor of division. And there remained always an element of opportunism. In theory liberals favoured federalism, supposedly a decentralized and democratic form of government, while conservatives demanded a strong executive and central control. But when the opportunity occurred liberals would impose liberalism by central institutions in a unitary regime. . . . And to preserve their control in particular provinces, or if they happened to be the 'outs', conservatives might well be federalists. Federalism, therefore, was not necessarily a 'progressive' force. It also tended to be an expensive form of government. The proliferation of state governments and legislatures was a means by which regional ruling classes took a firm grip of offices and patronage in their region and created jobs and sinecures for themselves. The rank growth of bureaucracies, federal and provincial, were intolerable parasites on the new states; as Bolívar complained, 'there is not a town, no matter how insignificant, that does not have a court of justice and a thousand other tribunals to devour the insubstantial revenue of the state'. Moreover, the new states had expenses unknown to colonial government. Congressmen, judges, ministers, diplomats had to be paid salaries, new schools, hospitals and rudimentary social services had to be financed, all out of a revenue which the bureaucracy, sons or clients of the ruling class, regarded as fair game for plunder. One of the largest items of expenditure was the military budget. And one of the largest potential sources of revenue was the Church.

Independence weakened some of the basic structures of the Church.

Many bishops deserted their dioceses and returned to Spain. Others were expelled. Others died and were not replaced. . . . [Many] parishes were left unattended. The economic assets of the Church were also shrinking. . . . The new rulers, conservatives and liberals alike, coveted church property and income, not to redistribute them in society but as a rightful revenue of the state; and most property owners were anxious to unburden themselves of ecclesiastical loans or liens. Yet the Church survived, and if it was temporarily weak, the state was weaker. In the aftermath of independence the Church was more stable, more popular, and apparently more wealthy than the state. Many politicians, particularly liberals, saw the Church as a rival focus of allegiance, an obstacle to state building, and they reacted by seeking to control and to tax the Church . . . and to reduce its power. Some of these objectives were also extended to that other focus of interest and allegiance, the military.

The size and expense of armies were out of all proportion to their function, particularly after the last Spanish bases had been removed; for it needed little insight to appreciate that European invaders would have little chance of survival in independent Latin America. So the new states were left with virtual armies of occupation, whose function was principally the welfare of their own members.To disband them was difficult because it was expensive. In the immediate aftermath of the war the Colombian army stood at twenty-five to thirty thousand, and its budget represented three-quarters of the total expenditure of Santander's government. Republican armies were relatively democratic institutions: while the creole aristocracy monopolized the higher commands, men of humble origin . . . could work their way up to middle officer rank. But wages were inadequate and often in arrears; the inevitable results were desertion, mutiny, pillage and general delinquency. Far from providing law and order, the army was often a prime cause of violence and anarchy. . . . The great liberating armies and their successors, therefore, were regarded by civilians with mixed feelings. Liberals were positively hostile to standing armies, preferring state militias; and they tried various devices to take the menace out of the military. . . . Unlike the other great power groups, the hacendados and the Church, the military did not have an independent source of income. They were therefore tempted to dominate the state and control the allocation of resources. Latin America became the primeval home of the golpe [coup] and the caudillo [dictator]. . . .

The caudillo was a regional chieftain, deriving his power from control of local resources, especially of haciendas, which gave him access to men and supplies. Classical caudillism took the form of armed patron-client bands, held together by personal ties of dominance and submission, and by a common desire to obtain wealth by force of arms. The caudillo's domain might grow from local to national dimensions. Here, too, supreme power was personal, not institutional; competition for offices and resources was violent and the achievements were rarely permanent. Caudillism was not born in colonial society. The Spanish empire was governed by an anonymous bureaucracy and maintained itself with a minimum of military sanction. The caudillo was a product of the wars of independence, when the colonial state was disrupted, institutions were destroyed, and social groups competed to fill the vacuum. Local proprietors or chieftains recruited followers who often progressed from vagrant, to bandit, to guerrilla fighter. While such bands might enlist under one political cause or another, the underlying factors were rural conditions and personal leadership. The countryside was often impoverished by destruction, and people were ruined by war taxes and plunder. As the economy reached breaking point, so men were forced into bands for subsistence under a chieftain who could lead them to booty and in the early years of the war banditry was stronger than ideology. Even when the political motivation became stronger the revolutionary armies were not professional armies, nor were the caudillos necessarily professional soldiers; the armies came together as an informal system of obedience from various interests whom the caudillos represented and could assemble. The caudillo, then, was a war leader. He was born of a perennial and universal human instinct in time of war to confer absolute power on a strong man, a single executive, who can recruit troops and commandeer resources. The process was then perpetuated by postwar conflicts, between unitarians and federalists in Argentina, between neighbouring states such as Colombia and Peru, and in the north between Mexico and the United States. . . .

Caudillism reflected the weakness of republican institutions, which did not reassure or convince, and which could not immediately fill the gap left by the collapse of colonial government. Yet the rise and fall of caudillos, the frequent turnover of presidents, the repeated golpes, the suspension of constitutions, the constant political clamour, masked a basic stability and durability in post-independence society which made Latin America one of the least revolutionary places in the world. For these were superficial changes, struggles for power within the ruling class, factional not revolutionary conflicts, and they did not affect the mass of the people. Independence was a powerful yet finite force, which tore through Spanish America like a great storm, sweeping away the lines of attachment to Spain and the fabric of colonial government, but leaving intact the deeply rooted bases of colonial society. The Mexican peasants saw it as the same rider on a new mule, a political revolution in which one ruling class displaced another. Political independence was only the beginning. Latin America still awaited those further changes in social structure and economic organization without which its independence remained incomplete and its needs unfulfilled.

Reconciling Individualism and Community in the New American Republic

Alexis de Tocqueville

In 1831–1832 a young French aristocrat, Alexis de Tocqueville, toured the United States at the request of the French government, officially to investigate and report on the American prison system. Instead of merely confining criminals in dank jails, or executing them, several American states were creating prisons designed to rehabilitate offenders. Those convicted of crimes were now expected to do useful work that would repay their debt to society, to meditate on why they had done wrong, and eventually to realize that they must reform themselves. Some of the new prisons featured harsh work details in which the prisoners marched in lockstep, performed repetitive tasks, and were forbidden to speak; others were designed to hold prisoners in solitary confinement where they could meditate on their offenses and make their peace with God. Today, both approaches seem cruel and psychologically abusive, but in the early nineteenth century they fit perfectly with the ideas of the social and religious movement known as the Second Great Awakening, which maintained that sinners, even hardened criminals, were capable of repentance and had a duty to seek God's saving grace.

Tocqueville dutifully observed American prisons, talked to reformers, and filed his report to the French government. But, being a man of high intelligence and keen observational skill, he went far beyond his official assignment. While traveling through the United States he made notes that a few years later furnished the basis for one of the great books of the nineteenth century, his *Democracy in America*. Unlike most members of Europe's upper class, Tocqueville did not automatically reject democracy; he was fascinated by it and was convinced that it was the wave of the future, even in France. But he was no uncritical admirer of democracy, either. What he saw in America was that the destruction of traditional privileges—and in the old European social order *everyone's* position was defined by certain legal rights, duties, and privileges—would produce a society of unattached, restless, dissatisfied, and anxious *individuals*. No one would know exactly where he or she stood, but all would know that society expected them to rise by their own efforts. The possibility definitely existed that these individuals, buffeted by changes beyond their control, would rush blindly after demagogues and would-be dictators. More likely, Tocqueville thought, individuals would band together spontaneously to create associations—churches, civic groups, reform movements, charitable institutions, booster groups, clubs and fraternal organizations, political parties. They would be gnawed by status insecurity, to be sure; they would be driven by an itch to prosper, even at their neighbors' expense. But offsetting these divisive, frustrating tendencies would be people's inclination to be joiners. It was in this inclination that Tocqueville saw the hope and promise of democratic society, even as he warned against the dangers of conformity and mediocrity that it would also breed. His thoughts on these matters continue to make *Democracy in America* one of the few truly enduring books of social and political commentary written in the nineteenth century, and well worth reading even at the beginning of the twenty-first century.

M en cannot enjoy political liberty without some sacrifice, and they have never won it without great effort. But equality offers its pleasures free; each little incident in life occasions them, and to taste them one needs but to live.

Democratic peoples always like equality, but there are times when their passion for it turns to delirium. This happens when the old social hierarchy, long menaced, finally collapses after a severe internal struggle and the barriers of rank are at length thrown down. At such times men pounce on equality as their booty and cling to it as a precious treasure they fear to have snatched away. The passion for equality seeps into every corner of the human heart, expands, and fills the whole. It is no use telling them that by this blind surrender to an exclusive passion they are compromising their dearest interests; they are deaf. It is no use pointing out that freedom is slipping from their grasp while they look the other way; they are blind, or rather they can see but one thing to covet in the whole world.

The foregoing applies to all democratic nations, what follows only to the French.

Among most modern nations, especially those of Europe, the taste for freedom and the conception of it only began to take shape and grow at the time when social conditions were tending toward equality, and it was a consequence of that very equality. It was the absolute monarchs who worked hardest to level down ranks among their subjects. For the peoples equality had come before liberty, so equality was an established fact when freedom was still a novelty; the one had already shaped customs, opinions, and laws to its use when the other was first stepping lonely forward into broad daylight. Thus the latter was still only a matter of opinion and preference, whereas the former had already insinuated itself into popular habits, shaped mores, and given a particular twist to the slightest actions of life. Why, then, should we be surprised that our contemporaries prefer the one to the other?

I think democratic peoples have a natural taste for liberty; left to themselves, they will seek it, cherish it, and be sad if it is taken from them. But their passion for equality is ardent, insatiable, eternal, and invincible. They want equality in freedom, and if they cannot have that, they still want equality in slavery. They will put up with poverty, servitude, and barbarism, but they will not endure aristocracy.

This is true at all times, but especially in our own. All men and all powers who try to stand up against this irresistible passion will be overthrown and destroyed by it. In our day freedom cannot be established without it, and despotism itself cannot reign without its support. . . .

"Individualism" is a word recently coined to express a new idea. Our fathers only knew about egoism.

Egoism is a passionate and exaggerated love of self which leads a man to think of all things in terms of himself and to prefer himself to all.

Individualism is a calm and considered feeling which disposes each citizen to isolate himself from the mass of his fellows and withdraw into the circle of family and friends; with this little society formed to his taste, he gladly leaves the greater society to look after itself.

Egoism springs from a blind instinct; individualism is based on misguided judgment rather than depraved feeling. It is due more to inadequate understanding than to perversity of heart.

Egoism sterilizes the seeds of every virtue; individualism at first only dams the spring of public virtues, but in the long run it attacks and destroys all the others too and finally merges in egoism.

Egoism is a vice as old as the world. It is not peculiar to one form of society more than another.

Individualism is of democratic origin and threatens to grow as conditions get more equal. . . .

Each citizen of an aristocratic society has his fixed station, one above another, so that there is always someone above him whose protection he needs and someone below him whose help he may require.

So people living in an aristocratic age are almost always closely involved with something outside themselves, and they are often inclined to forget about themselves. It is true that in these ages the general conception of *human fellowship* is dim and that men hardly ever think of devoting themselves to the cause of humanity, but men do often make sacrifices for the sake of certain other men.

In democratic ages, on the contrary, the duties of each to all are much clearer but devoted service to any individual much rarer. The bonds of human affection are wider but more relaxed.

Among democratic peoples new families continually rise from nothing while others fall, and nobody's position is quite stable. The woof of time is ever being broken and the track of past generations lost. Those who have gone before are easily forgotten, and no one gives a thought to those who will follow. All a man's interests are limited to those near himself.

As each class catches up with the next and gets mixed with it, its members do not care about one another and treat one another as strangers. Aristocracy links everybody, from peasant to king, in one long chain. Democracy breaks the chain and frees each link.

As social equality spreads there are more and more people who, though neither rich nor powerful enough to have much hold over others, have gained or kept enough wealth and enough understanding to look after their own needs. Such folk owe no man anything and hardly expect anything from anybody. They form the habit of thinking of themselves in isolation and imagine that their whole destiny is in their own hands.

Thus, not only does democracy make men forget their ancestors, but also clouds their view of their descendants and isolates them from their contemporaries. Each man is forever thrown back on himself alone, and there is danger that he may be shut up in the solitude of his own heart. . . .

The general business of a country keeps only the leading citizens occupied. It is only occasionally that they come together in the same places, and since they often lose sight of one another, no lasting bonds form between them. But when the people who live there have to look after the particular affairs of a district, the same people are always meeting, and they are forced, in a manner, to know and adapt themselves to one another.

It is difficult to force a man out of himself and get him to take an interest in the affairs of the whole state, for he has little understanding of the way in which the fate of the state can influence his own lot. But if it is a question of taking a road past his property, he sees at once that this small public matter has a bearing on his greatest private interests, and there is no need to point out to him the close connection between his private profit and the general interest.

Thus, far more may be done by entrusting citizens with the management of minor affairs than by handing over control of great matters, toward interesting them in the public welfare and convincing them that they constantly stand in need of one another in order to provide for it. . . .

Local liberties, then, which induce a great number of citizens to value the affection of their kindred and neighbors, bring men constantly into contact, despite the instincts which separate them, and force them to help one another.

In the United States the most opulent citizens are at pains not to get isolated from the people. On the contrary, they keep in constant contact, gladly listen and themselves talk any and every day. They know that the rich in democracies always need the poor and that good manners will draw them to them more than benefits conferred. For benefits by their very greatness spotlight the difference in conditions and arouse a secret annoyance in those who profit from them But the charm of simple good manners is almost irresistible. Their affability carries men away, and even their vulgarity is not always unpleasant. . . .

It would seem as if in the United States every man's power of invention was on the stretch to find new ways of increasing the wealth and satisfying the needs of the public. The best brains in every neighborhood are constantly employed in searching for new secrets to increase the general prosperity, and any that they find are at once at the service of the crowd.

If one takes a close look at the weaknesses and vices of many of those who bear sway in America, one is surprised at the growing prosperity of the people, but it is a mistake to be surprised. It is certainly not the elected magistrate who makes the American democracy prosper, but the fact that the magistrates are elected.

It would not be fair to assume that American patriotism and the universal zeal for the common good have no solid basis. Though private interest, in the United States as elsewhere, is the driving force behind most of men's actions, it does not regulate them all.

I have often seen Americans make really great sacrifices for the common good, and I have noticed a hundred cases in which, when help was needed, they hardly ever failed to give each other trusty support.

The free institutions of the United States and the political rights enjoyed there provide a thousand continual reminders to every citizen that he lives in society. At every moment they bring his mind back to this idea, that it is the duty as well as the interest of men to be useful to their fellows. Having no particular reason to hate others, since he is neither their slave nor their master, the American's heart easily inclines toward benevolence. At first it is of necessity that men attend to the public interest, afterward by choice. What had been calculation becomes instinct. By dint of working for the good of his fellow citizens, he in the end acquires a habit and taste for serving them.

There are many men in France who regard equality of conditions as the first of evils and political liberty as the second. When forced to submit to the former, they strive at least to escape the latter. But for my part, I maintain that there is only one effective remedy against the evils which equality may cause, and that is political liberty. . . .

In the United States, political associations are only one small part of the immense number of different types of associations found there.

American of all ages, all stations in life, and all types of disposition are forever forming associations. There are not only commercial and industrial associations in which all take part, but others of a thousand different types—religious, moral, serious, futile, very general and very limited, immensely large and very minute. Americans combine to give fêtes, found seminaries, build churches, distribute books, and send missionaries to the antipodes. Hospitals, prisons, and schools take shape in that way. Finally, if they want to proclaim a truth or propagate some feeling by the encouragement of a great example, they form an association. In every case, at the head of any new undertaking, where in France you would find the government or in England some territorial magnate, in the United States you are sure to find an association.

I have come across several types of association in America of which, I confess, I had not previously the slightest conception, and I have often admired the extreme skill they show in proposing a common object for the exertions of very many and in inducing them voluntarily to pursue it.

Since that time I have traveled in England, a country from which the Americans took some of their laws and many of their customs, but it seemed to me that the principle of association was not used nearly so constantly or so adroitly there.

A single Englishman will often carry through some great undertaking, whereas Americans form associations for no matter how small a matter. Clearly the former regard association as a powerful means of action, but the latter seem to think of it as the only one.

Thus the most democratic country in the world now is that in which men have in our time carried to the highest perfection the art of pursuing in common the objects of common desires and have applied this new technique to the greatest number of purposes. Is that just an accident, or is there really some necessary connection between associations and equality?

In aristocratic societies, while there is a multitude of individuals who can do nothing on their own, there is also a small number of very rich and powerful men, each of whom can carry out great undertakings on his own. . . .

But among democratic peoples all the citizens are independent and weak. They can do hardly anything for themselves, and none of them is in a position to force his fellows to help him. They would all therefore find themselves helpless if they did not learn to help each other voluntarily. . . .

When several aristocrats want to form an association, they can easily do so. As each of them carries great weight in society, a very small number of associates may be enough. So, being few, it is easy to get to know and understand one another and agree on rules.

But that is not so easy in democratic nations, where, if the association is to have any power, the associates must be very numerous.

I know that many of my contemporaries are not the least embarrassed by this difficulty. They claim that as the citizens become weaker and more helpless, the government must become proportionately more and more skillful and active, so that society should do what is no longer possible for individuals. They think that answers the whole problem, but I think they are mistaken.

A government could take the place of some of the largest associations in America, and some particular states of the Union have already attempted that. But what political power could ever carry on the vast multitude of lesser undertakings which associations daily enable American citizens to control?

It is easy to see the time coming in which men will be less and less able to produce, by each alone, the commonest bare necessities of life. The tasks of government must therefore perpetually increase, and its efforts to cope with them must spread its net ever wider. The more government takes the place of associations, the more will individuals lose the idea of forming associations and need the government to come to their help. That is a vicious circle of cause and effect. Must the public administration cope with every industrial undertaking beyond the competence of one individual citizen? And if ultimately, as a result of the minute subdivision of landed property, the land itself is so infinitely parceled out that it can only be cultivated by associations of laborers, must the head of the government leave the helm of state to guide the plow?

The morals and intelligence of a democratic people would be in as much danger as its commerce and industry if ever a government wholly usurped the place of private associations.

Feelings and ideas are renewed, the heart enlarged, and the understanding developed only by the reciprocal action of men one upon another. . . .

The first time that I heard in America that one hundred thousand men had publicly promised never to drink alcoholic liquor, I thought it more of a joke than a serious matter and for the moment did not see why these very abstemious citizens could not content themselves with drinking water by their own firesides.

In the end I came to understand that these hundred thousand Americans, frightened by the progress of drunkenness around them, wanted to support sobriety by their patronage. They were acting in just the same way as some great territorial magnate who dresses very plainly to encourage a contempt of luxury among simple citizens. One may fancy that if they had lived in France each of these hundred thousand would have made individual representations to the government asking it to supervise all the public houses throughout the realm.

Nothing in my view, more deserves attention than the intellectual and moral associations in America. American political and industrial associations easily catch our eyes, but the others tend not to be noticed. And even if we do notice them we tend to misunderstand them, hardly ever having seen anything similar before. However, we should recognize that the latter are as necessary as the former to the American people; perhaps more so.

In democratic countries knowledge of how to combine is the mother of all other forms of knowledge; on its progress depends that of all the others.

Among laws controlling human societies there is one more precise and clearer, it seems to me, than all the others. If men are to remain civilized or to become civilized, the art of association must develop and improve among them at the same speed as equality of conditions spreads.

The Louisiana Purchase and the Lewis and Clark Expedition

Eleanor J. Hall

Although Thomas Jefferson planned to send a "Corps of Discovery" to explore the Louisiana Territory even before he was able to purchase it from France, the fact that France sold it to him made arranging the Lewis and Clark expedition much easier. In the following selection, author Eleanor J. Hall describes Jefferson's hopes for the expedition, his choice of Meriwether Lewis and William Clark to lead it, and its lasting impact on the young United States. Hall is a retired anthropology and history teacher.

Historians differ over what was in Thomas Jefferson's mind in February 1801 when he wrote a letter asking Captain Meriwether Lewis to become his private secretary. Jefferson had just been elected president of the United States and needed an assistant. Lewis was serving as paymaster of the First Infantry Regiment at Pittsburgh.

Historian Bernard DeVoto believes that Jefferson picked Lewis to be his secretary because he had already decided to send him on an expedition west of the Mississippi River. DeVoto says Lewis was uniquely qualified for a project which Jefferson had cherished for many years, the exploration of the Missouri River and the lands west of its source. Obviously, Jefferson entered office determined to carry out the project as soon as possible and took Lewis into his personal and official household for that purpose.

Indeed, DeVoto's statement seems to be supported by Jefferson's letter, which reads in part, "Your knolege [Jefferson's spelling] of the Western Country, of the army and all of its interests and relations have rendered it desireable for public as well as private purposes that you should be engaged in that office."

Another historian, David Lavender, disagrees with DeVoto's conclusion, however. In contending that Jefferson had no plans for an expedition when he hired Lewis, Lavender says:

Why did he hire Meriwether Lewis? The reasons were immediate, pragmatic, and political.

Dressed in a dark uniform crisscrossed with white belts, and wearing a cocked hat with an eagle medallion in its front, the captain would lend dignity to the confidential messages he carried. He could serve as a decorative and charming host at presidential dinners—a real need for Jefferson was a widower and his daughters could not often leave their households to help. More important, Lewis was a stalwart Republican.

Which theory is the correct one we shall never know. What we do know is that two years after becoming Jefferson's secretary, Meriwether Lewis was off on the greatest adventure of his life, an adventure that would place his name among those of the most honored explorers in American history.

Why Jefferson Organized the Expedition

Jefferson had many reasons for wanting to send an expedition to the Pacific Ocean. One of these was a deep curiosity about what lay in the unexplored lands west of the Mississippi River. Before becoming president, Jefferson had supported two separate, and unsuccessful, attempts to explore the western country. He even had approached Revolutionary War hero George Rogers Clark (an older brother of William Clark) about undertaking such a trip, but Clark was unable to go at that time.

After his inauguration in March 1801, Jefferson was ready to try again. This time he had the resources and the authority to organize an expedition. There was so much he wanted to know. He was anxious to learn about the botany (plants), zoology (animals), and geography of the West. He was curious about the customs and languages of the Indians.

Of course, it was not only curiosity that prompted the expedition. Serious political issues also influenced Jefferson's decision. One of these had to do with control of the Louisiana Territory.

In 1800, the Mississippi River was the western boundary of the United States. Spain claimed the Louisiana Territory, which lay west of the river. However, many Americans, including Jefferson, expected that this vast region would eventually become part of the United States. The Spanish empire in the New World had grown so large that Spain could no longer control or defend all of it.

It was in the best interests of the United States, therefore, to learn as much as possible about the Louisiana Territory. Did the Missouri River run all the way to the sea? How high were the mountains? What minerals and other resources did the territory have? Was farm land available? What kinds of animals inhabited the territory? Were the Indians friendly or hostile?

The desire to establish contact with the Indians west of the Mississippi was another important reason for sending the expedition. Powerful tribes were known to exist along the Missouri River, which was an area rich in furs. British fur traders from Canada were trying to expand their business into the Louisiana Territory. To keep the British out, and perhaps to cash in on the profitable fur trade as well, the United States needed to gain the friendship and loyalty of the Indian tribes as soon as possible. In his letter of instructions to Meriwether Lewis in 1803, Jefferson said:

> Treat them [the Indians] in the most friendly & conciliatory manner which their own conduct will admit; Allay [lessen] all jealousies as to the object of your journey, satisfy them of its innocence, make them acquainted with the position, extent, character, peaceable and commercial dispositions of the U.S. of our wish to be neighborly, friendly & useful to them, & of our dispositions to a commercial intercourse with them . . . [and] if a few of their influential chiefs, within practicable distance, wish to visit us, arrange such a visit with them . . . [and] if any of them should wish to have their young people brought up with us, & taught such arts as may be useful to them, we will receive, instruct, & take care of them.

Indians living east of the Mississippi River were also of concern to Jefferson, but in a different way. By 1800 tribes along the Atlantic seacoast had lost most of their lands to white settlers, and now large numbers of pioneers were crossing the Appalachian Mountains into Indian territory on the frontier. As a result, violence and bloodshed between the two groups were increasing.

Jefferson believed both Indians and settlers could find room in the new nation. In 1803 he wrote to a frontier army officer saying, "In truth, the ultimate point of rest & happiness for them [the Indians] is to let our settlements and theirs meet and blend together, to intermix, and become one people."

Like most Americans of his day, however, Jefferson expected the

Indians to do all the changing. He wanted them to settle down on farms so they would not need so much land. If that didn't work, perhaps Indians who insisted on keeping their hunting lifestyle could move into the Louisiana Territory. In a letter to William H. Harrison, governor of the Indiana Territory, Jefferson wrote, "our settlements will gradually circumscribe and approach the Indians, and they will in time either incorporate with us as citizens of the United States, or remove beyond the Mississippi."

Congress Approves the Expedition

With so much to be gained by exploring the lands west of the Mississippi, Jefferson decided to ask Congress to authorize an expedition into the Louisiana Territory regardless of who claimed it. On January 18, 1803, he sent a secret message to Congress asking for funding for a scientific expedition to be led by his secretary, Meriwether Lewis. He would seek Spain's permission later. Congress approved, and Lewis began to make preparations.

It was then that an unexpected event took place that changed the nature of the expedition and made it more important than ever. That event was the purchase by the United States of the Louisiana Territory from France, to whom Spain had secretly transferred these lands.

The Louisiana Purchase

Napoléon Bonaparte had recently come to power in France. Years before, France had lost all its holdings in North America and now Napoléon, a strong military leader, wanted them back. He had begun his campaign peacefully enough, by persuading Spain to return the Louisiana Territory, which France had given to Spain in 1762 to keep Great Britain from getting it at the end of the French and Indian Wars.

The news of the soon-to-be-completed transfer greatly worried Jefferson. France was a much more powerful and aggressive nation than Spain and could pose a threat to the newly formed United States. Napoléon had already established a foothold in North America. By a treaty with Spain in 1795, he gained possession of the Caribbean island of Hispaniola (today the countries of Haiti and the Dominican Republic). Many years before, France had established a sugar producing colony on the west end of Hispaniola operated by slave labor. In 1791, under the leadership of Toussaint L'Ouverture, the slaves rebelled and expelled the French. In 1802, Napoléon dispatched twenty thousand troops across the ocean to retake the rebellious colony and to establish Hispaniola as his base of operations in the New World. When that had been accomplished, he intended to occupy the Louisiana Territory, which included the port of New Orleans.

In a separate incident in 1802, the Spanish commander in New

Orleans closed the port to American shipping. This was a serious blow to farmers on the frontier, who brought their products down the river to New Orleans for reshipment to other markets.

Because it was known that Spain was in the process of transferring the Louisiana Territory to France, many settlers thought Napoléon had closed the port. Actually, Napoléon had nothing to do with the closing, and the port was reopened several months later. Nevertheless, the incident made it very clear that the United States needed to own New Orleans. It was not in U.S. interests for any European country to be able to close the port for any reason.

To avoid the possibility of another port closing when France took over the Louisiana Territory, many Americans wanted to go to war with Napoléon immediately. Jefferson, however, was determined to solve the matter through diplomacy if he could. He instructed Robert Livingston, the American ambassador in Paris, to try to buy the port of New Orleans. As directed, Livingston began negotiations with Charles Maurice de Talleyrand, Napoléon's minister of foreign affairs. Talleyrand did not like America, and for weeks, Livingston's efforts to make a deal were unsuccessful.

Early in the morning of April 11, 1803, Napoléon called his finance minister, François Barbé-Marbois, to his living quarters. Napoléon was distressed. His scheme of returning France to power in the New World was not going well. Thousands of the soldiers he had sent to the Caribbean had been killed in combat or had died from yellow fever. Moreover, he needed money to wage his wars in Europe.

To Marbois, Napoléon said, "I renounce Louisiana. It is not only New Orleans that I cede; it is the whole colony, without reserve. . . . I know the price of what I abandon. . . . I renounce it with greatest regret; to attempt obstinately to retain it would be folly. I direct you to negotiate the affair. Have an interview this very day with Mr. Livingston."

A few hours later, Talleyrand met with Ambassador Livingston, whom he completely surprised by asking what the United States would be willing to pay for the entire Louisiana Territory. Livingston said he needed time to consult with James Monroe, then ambassador to Spain, who had just arrived in Paris.

When Livingston told Monroe about the offer, the future president was greatly surprised, too. Jefferson had instructed his ambassadors to buy only New Orleans (from France) and perhaps Western Florida (from Spain). Yet the diplomats were unable to ask Jefferson what to do because it took six weeks for mail to travel from Paris to Washington. Using their own judgment, the two ambassadors decided to accept the offer. After many days of bargaining over terms and price, Monroe and Livingston signed a treaty on May 2, 1803 (but dated April 30), in which the United States agreed to pay 15 million dollars for the entire Louisiana Territory.

President Jefferson received unofficial news of the Louisiana Purchase on July 3, 1803, just in time for the Fourth of July celebration the next day. The treaty itself arrived on July 14. Jefferson immediately wrote of the acquisition to Captain Lewis, who was on his way to Pittsburgh to have a keelboat made for the coming expedition. When Lewis received the letter on July 22, he, too, was very pleased. Now he would be exploring in his own country.

Effects of the Louisiana Purchase on the Expedition

Although the Louisiana Purchase was not the original reason for the Lewis and Clark expedition (as is often supposed), the transfer of land ownership made official arrangements for the project less difficult. Jefferson no longer had to seek permission from Spain or France to explore the territory. He no longer had to pretend that it was purely a scientific expedition, but could openly include political and commercial goals as well. Owning the territory made it more important than ever to learn what the western country was like and what resources it held.

Originally, to keep from arousing Spain's suspicions, the exploring party was to be limited to twelve to fifteen men. Now it could be a larger, better equipped operation. As the size of the project grew, Jefferson thought it would be wise to have a second officer along in case something happened to Captain Lewis on the long journey. For that

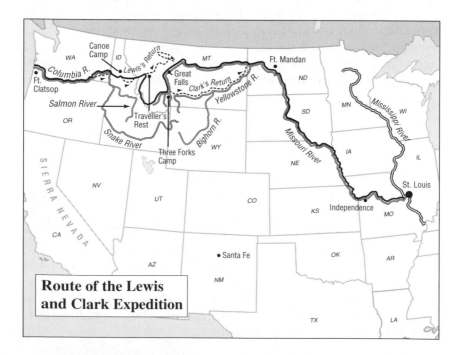

Route of the Lewis and Clark Expedition

position, Lewis chose his friend William Clark, whom he had known since 1795, when Lewis was sent to Fort Greenville, Ohio, to join a rifle company commanded by Lieutenant Clark.

As it turned out, the choice of Clark was a good one. Although he and Lewis had very different personalities, they got along very well. Both were young—Lewis was twenty-nine years old and Clark was thirty-three when the expedition began. Both were well suited for the journey, having spent much of their early lives outdoors in the fields and forests. As trained army officers, both were experienced at commanding men, and Clark was a veteran of the frontier Indian wars.

The Stage Is Set

The stage was now set for one of the most famous explorations in American history. Not only would the curiosity of Jefferson (and other scholars) be satisfied, but the political and commercial interests of the United States would be promoted. Questions about the worth of the newly acquired territory would be answered. (Some Americans thought the government had squandered money on a worthless tract of wilderness.) Last, but very important, the expedition would serve notice to the great powers of Europe that the United States of America was becoming a strong nation, capable of looking after its own interests. . . .

Looking Backward

The significance of a historic event cannot be fairly evaluated until many years after its occurrence. Historian Henry Adams, writing in 1889, attached little importance to the Lewis and Clark expedition. "Creditable as these expeditions were to American energy and enterprise," he wrote, "they added little to the stock of science or wealth. . . . The crossing of the continent was a great feat but was nothing more." A century later, many historians disagree, feeling that the expedition influenced future events in American history in several ways.

Although it would be several decades before wagon trains started pushing overland, the Lewis and Clark expedition took some of the fear and mystery out of the uncharted West. The journey undertaken by the Corps had been long and hard, but it had succeeded. The party had even included a woman and a baby! For the most part, the encounters with Indian tribes had been friendly, a matter of great concern to white people on the frontier. Moreover, the natural wonders described by Corps members stirred the blood of many restless men and women who longed to see those marvels for themselves.

In addition, the expedition ushered in the American fur trade that took place during the next few decades by bringing back good news about the abundance of beaver, and about waterways on which to transport the fur, and the fur trade had a side effect that was probably more important than the trade itself. While trapping beaver, many hardy "mountain men" roamed all over the West. In doing so, they greatly expanded the geographical data acquired by Lewis and Clark. Trappers often brought new information to William Clark, who continued to work on mapping the region west of the Mississippi long after the expedition.

Claim to the Oregon Country

In the early nineteenth century, both Great Britain and the United States competed for possession of the Oregon Territory, particularly the Columbia River region. The British felt it was rightfully theirs because they had been there a long time and had established many fur trading posts. The United States had a foothold in the area, however, because Robert Gray, who sailed to the mouth of the Columbia River in 1792, was an American.

This claim was greatly strengthened when Lewis and Clark traveled through the Oregon Territory and down the Columbia River to the Pacific. It was further strengthened when John Jacob Astor established a fur trading post on the Oregon coast in 1811, only five years after the expedition. "It was the journey of Lewis and Clark that gave the American people a conviction that Oregon was theirs," Bernard DeVoto says, "and this conviction was more important than the claim. And . . . the establishment of Fort Astoria by Astor's party won the British-American race to the Pacific."

The Future of the Indians

The Corps of Discovery owed a heavy debt to many of the Indian tribes they encountered along the way. Without the periodic assistance of Indians they might not have survived. Food, shelter, information, horses, guides, and many unnamed kindnesses were provided by Indians at one time or another. In turn Lewis and Clark treated the Indians with respect and tried to learn as much as possible about their cultures, as Jefferson had requested. With a few exceptions, relationships with Indian groups were friendly and positive.

Nevertheless, when Lewis and Clark "opened" the West, they sowed the seeds of destruction for the Indian nations residing there. Lewis and Clark's mission was not undertaken primarily for the benefit of the continent's earliest inhabitants. Its immediate purposes were to open the Missouri River for American traders and to discourage the Indians from trading with the British. Its long-range purpose was to evaluate the prospects for future white settlement.

When the expedition neared St. Louis, the group stopped at Fort Bellfontaine to let Chief Sheheke and his family obtain new clothing. James P. Ronda writes:

As the Indian [Chief Sheheke] searched through the stacks of calico shirts, fancy handkerchiefs, and colored beads, he symbolized the first fruits of the Lewis and Clark expedition. The explorers brought Indian America face to face with the Industrial Revolution and a rising American empire. . . . The Mandan chief, dressed in the best the young Republic could afford, did not know how much those explorers had forever changed his world.

In 1806 the new American nation, often scorned by Europeans, needed a dose of national pride. Lewis and Clark and the Corps of Discovery provided it. On December 2, 1806, President Jefferson sent the following message to Congress:

The expedition of Messrs. Lewis and Clarke, for exploring the river Missouri, and the best communication from that to the Pacific Ocean, has had all the success which could have been expected. They have traced the Missouri nearly to its source, descended the Columbia to the Pacific Ocean, ascertained with accuracy the geography of that interesting communication across our continent, learned the character of the country, of its commerce, and inhabitants; and it is but justice to say that Messrs. Lewis and Clarke, and their brave companions, have by this arduous service deserved well of their country.

If Lewis and Clark had not crossed the continent, someone else would have. It was not the journey alone that made the expedition an enduring part of American history, but the people themselves and the relationships that developed among them.

It would be hard to imagine a more colorful group—two young captains with very different personalities, a mixed crew from diverse cultural backgrounds, a Negro slave, a French/Indian interpreter, a young Indian girl carrying a baby on her back, and a big black dog!

As interesting as the individuals were, it was the harmonious relationships among them that often made the difference between success and failure. In good times, they danced and sang together. In bad times they drew close to one another and endured what had to be endured. The friendship between the captains, the loyalty and dedication of the men, the encouragement of Sacagawea, the fiddle playing of Cruzatte, the excited barking of a dog, the surprising sound of a child's voice—all these things worked together to make the Lewis and Clark expedition a one-of-a-kind event in American history.

Industrialization and Ideology

The ideologies of nineteenth-century liberalism and socialism had a particularly close connection with industrialization. Liberals overwhelmingly greeted the arrival of the Industrial Revolution as one more sign of the triumphant sweep of progress. For well-to-do people of liberal persuasion, this immense expansion of the energy available for human use promised to release society's productive forces. Government, they believed, must simply allow such forces to surge forward freely, allowing human ingenuity to seek its own reward. True, many individuals found themselves disadvantaged by the turbulent changes that industrialization sent coursing through nineteenth-century society. Artisan families who pursued the traditional crafts that the factory system destroyed lost their livelihoods; factory workers might find plentiful employment in good times, but even then their wages were by today's standards pitifully low and their living conditions almost always appalling. Liberals might deplore such consequences, but generally they assumed that the only remedy was for the working class to adopt the middle-class values of hard work, thrift, cleanliness, moral restraint, and a drive for self-improvement. In nineteenth-century politics, it was usually the conservatives who, rather paternalistically, saw in the stresses of industrialization a need for government to exercise its authority to control social disorder, regulate economic institutions, and maintain traditional hierarchies.

Socialism, on the other hand, was a European ideology that passionately defended the interests of the working classes, whether they were struggling artisans or poorly paid and housed factory employees. Like liberals, socialists also believed in "progress," and increasingly they saw industrialization as a great boon that could create bounty for humanity. But in bitter contrast to liberals, they viewed the capitalist employers of the working class as exploiters who unjustly appropriated for themselves far too much of the new economy's profits. Most early socialists came from the middle or upper classes, but after the 1840s men and women of working-class origin were also drawn to the movement. Eventually, as political democracy broadened in Europe beginning in the 1860s, socialism became a mass political movement, often mellowing its revolutionary rhetoric as it gained a share of actual power through the ballot box. In Russia, however, where the czarist autocracy never relinquished significant political power, the socialist movement remained genuinely revolutionary, and in 1917, during World War I, the Bolshevik faction within Russian socialism would seize power and create the Soviet Union, which would exert a powerful influence on the twentieth-century non-Western world. The main current of the socialist movement in Western Europe, however, would remain democratic and committed to the building of a "welfare state" dedicated to social justice—a goal that middle-class liberalism also increasingly adopted in the twentieth century.

This chapter reflects the range of the issues with which scholars deal in tracing the history of the great nineteenth-century ideologies. In the first reading, two leading contemporary economic historians assess the question of whether the Industrial Revolution did more harm than good for the West's working people. Their answer is an unequivocal defense of the benefits that industrialization wrought; the question remains, however: Was it just that the first generations of workers experiencing industrialization had to pay so costly a price for later generations' benefit? The second and third readings form an interesting contrast on the emergence of middle-class political participation in Great Britain in the 1830s. One focuses on the public agitation that demanded reform of the way in which the House of Commons was elected—an agitation that united the prosperous middle class (many of whose members up to then had no representation in Parliament) and the humbler artisans (who were even less likely to enjoy the right of political participation). The Great Reform Bill that was in fact enacted on the pressure of this agitation, in 1832, opened the way for political participation by considerably more of the middle class, but it deliberately excluded the workers who had supported the reform agitation. The second of this pair of readings, therefore, focuses on the effect of excluding artisans and others who worked at manual trades, thereby confirming to these people that they constituted a distinct social and economic group—"the working class." British politics from that point developed an antagonistic class basis, of which significant traces remain even today.

The chapter's last two readings highlight the contrasts of the class struggle as it seemed to mid-nineteenth-century people. In the first, an excerpt from *The Communist Manifesto,* Karl Marx and Friedrich Engels throw down a defiant challenge to "the bourgeoisie," complimenting them on the progress they have ushered in but predicting their coming downfall in the face of a proletarian revolution. In the second, Great Britain's middle class celebrates the triumph of industrialism and the prospect of social peace within England's borders with the Great Exhibition in London in 1851.

Early Factories Improved Workers' Lives

Nathan Rosenberg and L.E. Birdzell Jr.

The low pay, squalor, pollution, and disease endured by workers who crowded into manufacturing centers like Manchester, Birmingham, or Leeds in early-nineteenth-century Britain, and later into new industrial cities throughout the Western world, have been well documented in official reports, newspaper polemics, contemporaries' impressions, works of literature and art, and early photographs. Conditions in these manufacturing centers rivaled the worst that can be encountered in the slums of developing countries today.

Why did workers continue to pour into these cities? Much of the answer lies in the conditions from which ordinary people were escaping—the overpopulation, underemployment, and poverty of the countryside or the poverty and constricted opportunities offered by artisan labor in urban locales. The horrors of the Industrial Revolution, on which many writers have dwelt for two centuries or more, must be balanced against the horrors of traditional poverty that had been growing at least since the fifteenth and sixteenth centuries, when European manufacturing by traditional processes had been moved out of towns and away from tight guild regulations and into rural areas where peasant families could be set to miserably underpaid piecework.

Historians' disagreements over the costs of the Industrial Revolution often resemble arguments over whether a glass should be considered half-empty or half-full. Today, however, there are signs of an emerging con-

Excerpted from *How the West Grew Rich: The Economic Transformation of the Industrial World*, by Nathan Rosenberg and L.E. Birdzell Jr. Copyright © 1986 by BasicBooks, Inc. Reprinted with permission from BasicBooks, a member of Perseus Books, LLC.

sensus that, if we consider the long-range opportunities that participating in a market economy presented, the working class benefited more than it suffered. Certainly this is the viewpoint of contemporary economic historians Nathan Rosenberg and L.E. Birdzell Jr., whose 1986 book *How the West Grew Rich: The Economic Transformation of the Industrial World* vigorously defends the Industrial Revolution as opening a new era of productivity and abundance that is still unfolding.

The romantic view that workers in pre-industrial Europe lived well may safely be dismissed as pure fantasy. . . . [I]f early factory work was oppressive, the alternatives open to those who voted with their feet for factory work were worse. The early factories were able to attract workers with low wages because the wages were still well above the poverty level . . . and better than anything available elsewhere to an impoverished agricultural population. Victorian England was revolted by the fact that children labored in the factories for a few shillings a week, but when Parliament prohibited child labor, their places were quickly taken by landless Irish immigrants equally eager to work for a few shillings a week. The low wages, long hours, and oppressive discipline of the early factories are shocking in that the willingness of the inarticulate poor to work on such terms bespeaks, more forcefully than the most eloquent words, the even more abysmal character of the alternatives they had endured in the past. But this was not the way the romantics of the nineteenth century read the message of the factories. . . .

To evaluate the impact of the factory on [those who] . . . in current terms [were] the least-advantaged members of eighteenth-century society, it is necessary to consider the part played by the antecedent apprentice system in the antecedent artisan industry. There, it was customary to train workers through a long apprenticeship. Access to an apprenticeship was frequently restricted at the outset by the necessity of paying the master a substantial sum in advance, both for the support of the apprentice and for the master's instruction. Access was also restricted by guild rules limiting the number of apprentices a master might teach at one time.

An even more fundamental restriction was the practice of prolonging the apprenticeship. The usual term of the medieval apprenticeship was seven years. One purpose was to teach the apprentice all aspects of the craft. In some crafts, this meant acquiring skill in every step of producing the final product. In crafts where there was no specific product to be produced repetitively, it meant acquiring a range of skills defined in some other way, perhaps by the material being shaped (gold, silver, wood, leather, for examples). A second purpose of the prolonged apprenticeship was to give the master the benefit of the apprentice's labor for a period of time. This unpaid labor was rationalized as part of the master's compensation for instructing the apprentice.

The apprentice system restricted access to employment and it also restricted the production of goods. Its effect on the prices exacted of those outside the system—often buyers poorer than the guildmasters—was monopolistic, resulting from the restriction of access to the guild trades and the consequent restriction of the supply of goods. Secondarily, it reflected the wastefulness of unnecessarily prolonged training. Its persistence can be attributed to the fact that the guilds exercised combined political and economic functions, and so had the power to enforce uneconomic arrangements highly beneficial to themselves and highly injurious to the other members of society, including the very poor. Happily, the guilds were typically municipal political agencies, so that their writ did not run to the countryside. When factories were introduced, the legal power of the guilds was evaded by locating them in areas outside the guilds' jurisdiction. The medieval flight to the cities to escape the oppression of the manors ended as a return to the countryside to escape the oppression of the guilds.

There were, in the eighteenth century, a numerous subproletariat who had no funds to buy tools, no skills in their use, no possibility of supporting themselves through the years of an apprenticeship, none of the personal influence needed to obtain an apprenticeship, and no money to buy one. It was from this subproletariat that the early factories often drew their labor, even to the point of emptying an occasional poorhouse en masse.

Neither the entrepreneurs who built the factories nor anyone else supposed that they were engaged in a work of charity or an exercise of social conscience. But whatever the moral quality of their intentions, their actions advanced the interests of a down-trodden subproletariat—a subproletariat in part, perhaps, characteristic of pre-industrial societies and, in part, drawn from an agricultural work force hard pressed by the enclosure movement and a high rate of growth in agricultural productivity.

The reaction of the English middle class to all this remains a fascinating case study in social pathology. Having for centuries seen no better use for the poor than supplying an opportunity for their betters to exercise, with due moderation and modesty, the virtues of charity and compassion, much of middle-class England perceived the factory system not as a significant social advance, but as ruthless exploitation of the poor. Just below the middle class were the artisans, whose guild rules had long blocked all but privileged access to much of the everyday world of work. They did not think of themselves as monopolists at long last caught up with, but as victims of a new and highly unfair form of competition. Literary England, by and large, shared the opinion of both the middle class and the artisans. The reality could hardly have been more absurdly caricatured. . . .

If the way the early factory workers voted with their feet is evidence that the textile factory system improved *their* condition, it cannot be assumed that the factory system improved the condition of the cottage workers whom it displaced. The decline in their earnings, followed by new employment in circumstances not of their own making, could have been beneficial only for a lucky few. It may well be that the factory system improved the *average* condition of workers from the beginning, but the issue is complex, because, as [economic historian] T.S. Ashton has pointed out, the initial years of rapid growth of the factory system were also years of the Napoleonic Wars, which had a material impact on the cost of living and on the distribution of income. Ashton's general conclusion is that the distribution of income changed adversely for workers during the Napoleonic Wars and that their real income fell. By about 1820, the effects of the Napoleonic Wars on the British economy had worn off, and the conditions of the workers' lives began to improve steadily. The improvement was not uniform for all workers, and there were some, notably those skilled in crafts made obsolete by the factories, who suffered loss rather than benefit. . . .

While it is widely assumed that factory workers in the early textile mills earned less than handloom weavers had earned under the putting-out system, the reality was complicated by large differences in earnings among cottage weavers—a phenomenon still associated with piece rate systems—and a tendency to compare the earnings of skilled weavers with those of unskilled factory workers. Moreover, the statistics need to be interpreted carefully. . . . Scottish adult men worked as handloom weavers for about 10 or 12 shillings a week in the 1790s. By comparison, adult males working at power looms in Manchester in 1842 (still a time of transition) were earning about 20 shillings a week. Adult women were earning 8 to 12 shillings, and girls of twelve to sixteen years of age earned 5 to 7 shillings. . . . [P]iece rates for handlooming fell steadily all through the early nineteenth century, especially after the depression of 1826, causing severe hardship among handloom weavers. But the question whether handloom weavers earned more or less, before the advent of power looms, than the workers who ran the early power looms, can be answered either way, depending on how much one allows for differences in skills. . . .

The passage of time and changes in values, attitudes, assumptions, and expectations make it difficult to evaluate what was happening in the transition from the pre-industrial to the industrial era.

Consider, for example, the fact that hours of work in the factories were longer than those of most workers before the advent of factories. The longer hours may imply either a retrogression in the worker's welfare or a gain in opportunities for employment.

There is, however, a third possibility that may lie closer to the truth. It is based in part on observations of present-day conditions in Third World countries. The hours of work in pre-industrial economies are likely to be short simply because an undernourished population lacks the energy to work any longer. Shorter hours are not necessarily a choice of leisure over work; they may be compelled by the need to limit one's activity to what an inadequate diet can support. Considering the marginal standards of subsistence in Western Europe in the eighteenth century, and for long before, it is not clear that the hours of labor were short because the workers preferred leisure over wages; they may have been short, as in Third World countries, because of malnutrition. The improvement in English agriculture before the Industrial Revolution, and the resulting improvement in the English national diet, may have been a contributing cause of the Industrial Revolution and a possible explanation of why it occurred first in England. The thought that increased hours of labor can be an indication of improved worker welfare seems nearly incomprehensible today, but then neither are we accustomed to assume in our thinking that workers as a class may not be fed enough to work very long, or very hard.

The conditions faced by Western European working classes were harsh before the Industrial Revolution; they were harsh during the Industrial Revolution; and they were harsh for a long time afterward. But the balance of evidence is that the Industrial Revolution did not initially benefit all workers. It did not, even at its beginning, make matters any *worse,* on average, and once the effects of the Napoleonic Wars were shaken off, it led to major advances in the welfare of the working class. This point has a bearing on late-twentieth-century economic problems, in that the Industrial Revolution is not, as many have thought, a precedent for imposing sacrifices on the living generation (especially its working members) in the hope that things will be better for later generations. So far as this primary historic example of rapid economic progress teaches us anything about the need for social sacrifice, its lesson is that economies progress rapidly when the fruits of progress are widely and contemporaneously enjoyed.

The Struggle for Political Reform in Great Britain

Michael Brock

The 1830s was a key decade in the United States during which democratic institutions, practices, and attitudes took root during the presidential administrations of Andrew Jackson and his successor, Martin Van Buren. The same decade saw a much more limited, but also highly significant, breakthrough in the political culture of Britain, epitomized by Parliament's enactment of the Great Reform Act of 1832. The Reform Act did not make Britain a democracy, but it was decisive in giving direction and purpose to the ideology of liberalism, whose adherents were largely middle-class beneficiaries of industrialization. It also marked the definitive split between the middle class and the working class, who (unlike white male factory and artisan workers in the United States) did not gain the right to vote.

In this selection, British historian Michael Brock analyzes the arguments made for and against extending suffrage to prosperous middle-class voters during parliamentary debates over the Reform Bill, and also describes the angry public protest that arose when it seemed that the aristocratic House of Lords would block the bill's enactment. It is important to realize that the debates over whether to accept the Reform Bill occurred within a Parliament still chosen according to the jumble of rules dating from the eighteenth century and even earlier. Many seats in the House of Commons were literally controlled by a handful of aristocratic landlords who owned "rotten boroughs"—a bit of property legally entitled to representation in Parliament but where few (in some cases *no*) voters actually lived. Many other seats were filled by small groups of privileged voters who literally sold the seat to the highest bidder. In some places active campaigning went on, but this electioneering often consisted of spending large sums on free drinks for local voters, who then (if they were still sober) had to announce their votes publicly. On the other hand, large new industrial cities like Birmingham and Leeds, which had been tiny villages in the eighteenth century, had no representation at all. Corruption was rampant and extremely expensive. One of the arguments motivating upper-class advocates of the Reform Bill was that such lavish politicking was bankrupting them.

No great ideological issues separated the Whig and Tory politicians who debated the Reform Bill. The Whigs were the great landowners and their gentry allies who had been politically dominant during much of the eighteenth century, but who had lost control of the House of Commons to the Tory landowners during the era of the American and French Revolutions. Originally, Whigs had been more devoted to parliamentary supremacy, and Tories to upholding the authority of the Crown and the Anglican Church, but these positions had eroded in the course of the eighteenth century. Sir Robert Peel, a leading Tory, was actually the son of a rich manufacturer. The Duke of Wellington, the victor over Napoléon at the Battle of Waterloo in 1815, was the Tory prime minister under whom the Reform Bill was first proposed, and he opposed it mostly because he was opposed to anything that threatened the status quo. Such reactionary conservatism was typical of many Tories. Lord Grey, the Whig who replaced Wellington in 1831 when the latter realized that he did not have the votes in the House of Commons to sustain a government, largely shared the duke's political outlook but had the wisdom to realize that to resist reform was to invite the violent overthrow of the government—which had already happened in France in 1830 when the particularly stupid King Charles X refused too long to bend before middle-class opinion. As Brock analyzes the state of public opinion during the debate over reform, it seems clear that violence of some sort would have broken out had the political elite dominating Parliament refused to accept the bill. The fact that wisdom finally prevailed set the tone for the moderate course of British politics through the rest of the nineteenth century.

S ome attempt must now be made to summarize the most important arguments used in Parliament for and against the [Reform] Bill. The parliamentary debates represented a discussion within the governing class to which other classes were allowed to listen. Of course, there could be no complete correspondence between arguments used publicly and views held privately. But there was some frank parliamentary speaking, particularly in the Lords.

It was not seriously disputed that a Reform Bill of some sort had been necessary when [Lord] Grey formed his government. Except for . . . a few ultra tories everyone recognized that an anti-Reform administration had become an impossibility by then. But the opposition had no truck with the view that it was social and economic changes which had necessitated the Bill. They maintained that the old system had been adaptable to such changes. Everyone had accepted it until the spring of 1830. Its unpopularity by November had been created by the irresponsible and office-hungry whigs, whose attacks on the constitution had unfortunately coincided with a trade depression and with revolutions in Paris and Brussels. This part of the opposition's case was unconvincing, though the suspicion that the whigs had introduced the Bill for reasons of party advantage gave it a certain force for tory partisans. Moderate people realized, however, that most of the cabinet had done very little to discredit the old system during 1830 whereas . . . Wellington had done a great deal. Moreover, there must have been something unstable about a system which required for its continuance that no one should attack it, and that there should be neither fluctuations in the economy nor disturbances in Europe.

Admitting the necessity of some Reform involved arguing that the government's best course would have been to introduce a moderate Bill. Peel and most of the opposition front bench [the tory leadership] in the Commons took this line, and so had to explain why they had not introduced such a Bill themselves. Peel justified his failure to do so on the ground that no moderate Reform could have been final. He had declined to sponsor one, he said, because: 'I was unwilling to open a door which I saw no prospect of being able to close.'

Even Peel had some difficulty in convincing his hearers that the whigs should be blamed for rejecting a solution which he had himself rejected. His speeches implied that the right policy in face of the agitation was to make the smallest possible change at the last possible moment. This argument has been mentioned in connexion with the July revolution and the 1830 election. The Reform agitation, it ran, had been aroused by temporary circumstances. Grey's surgery was the wrong treatment. The fever should have been allowed to die down, a mild dose of Reform being administered during convalescence. The [whig] government's contention was more convincing. They argued that a moderate measure might have succeeded if produced quickly. It was the long delay during 1830 which had made their sweeping Bill unavoidable. . . .

The imperative necessity for a Reform Bill to settle the question provided a rock-like foundation for the government's case. That case was strong even if all their expectations about the new voters were discounted. Relying on ten pounders might be disastrous in the end.

Clinging to the rotten boroughs would be disastrous at once. It was better to grant Reform and endure unstable governments than to refuse it and be left with an unstable system. . . . The cost of refusing the concession looked so high that granting it could scarcely be more costly on the worst forecast.

It was not possible for government speakers to keep this point before their hearers all the time. As the period before 1 March 1831 receded, the dangers of refusing any substantial Reform faded a little from people's minds. The argument could be shifted to the drawbacks of the new system; and it could be implied that there must have been a way to avoid incurring these. This shift brought the opposition onto far better debating ground. They demanded to know how the reformed House would improve on the unreformed in composition and in the policies which it would adopt. This question naturally embarrassed the government and they did not give a convincing reply. Ministers could not admit that the new House was designed to be as like the old one as possible in outlook and class composition, and that they did not expect it to adopt any drastic policy changes. An answer on these lines would have displeased the Birmingham Union [middle-class reformers]. . . .

By contrast, the [tory] opposition were free to prophecy every kind of disaster from the Bill. It would destroy the mixed or balanced system whereby aristocratic and popular elements provided checks to each other. It would lead to clashes between Lords and Commons. It would make the country impossible to govern because, once all seats were under popular control, no government would command stable support. The anti-reformers' picture of the uses to which the ten pounder would put his vote presented inconsistencies. He was depicted alternately as persecuting the poor and as wishing to enfranchise them. There were similar inconsistencies in the opposition account of how governments would fare under the Act. One picture was of governmental weakness and instability: Reform would produce a succession of weak and short-lived ministries, since constituents would not allow their MP [Member of Parliament] to support a government unless it pandered to their particular local interests. This was based on the continuance of a more or less traditional pattern of politics. The other picture was more apocalyptic. It showed governments as powerful at least in destruction: they would despoil the rich ruthlessly at the behest of the new voters. However inconsistent these prophecies might be with each other, they carried a certain conviction. The hearer was as unclear as the speakers about the political habits and interests which the new system might engender. He was free to adopt whichever picture of ruin corresponded most closely to his own fears.

The opposition leaders suffered from certain difficulties in prophesying doom. They maintained that to abolish rotten boroughs was to deprive governments of a much needed facility. . . . It was also difficult for Peel to say exactly why he distrusted the new voters. He must have realized that he would soon be asking for their votes. The issue underlying the parliamentary debate was whether the poachers would be reliable as unpaid assistant gamekeepers. It was equally awkward for the opposition to accuse anyone of being a poacher, and for the government to disclose the subordinate nature of the poachers' future role.

One aspect of these opposition prophecies has been somewhat misunderstood. If the wilder predictions about the abolition of the monarchy and the peerage are discounted, most of what was foretold eventually came about, in the sense that a democratic regime was established in Britain within a century of the Act being passed. This has led to the suggestion that the prophecies were essentially correct, although they exaggerated the speed with which the results predicted would follow. This suggestion obscures the fact that the essence of the prophecies lay in the time-scale. The opposition were predicting, not merely that the Act would usher in a democratic regime, but that this regime would apply to the Britain which they knew. A few diehards apart, they would have conceded that improved education and communications might eventually make possible, and even safe, further enlargements of the electorate. What they feared was the confusion which might follow if the enlargements were made before these improvements even came into sight.

The predictions went farther than this. The opposition foretold that the new system would fail to produce even the shortest interval of stability. The ministers had started down the slide that led to anarchy. Each concession would elicit a fresh demand; and each demand would be harder to resist than the last. 'Others will outbid you,' Peel told the ministers when the debate began, 'not now, but at no remote period. They . . . will quote your precedent for the concession, and will carry your principles to their legitimate and natural consequences.' The result of the Act reaching the statute book, Peel added in July 1832,

> would be that apprehensions would prevail for the security of property—apprehensions which were likely to affect considerably . . . the productive powers of the country—and that the political excitement would continue as rife, and the political unions as flourishing and as noisy, as ever.

Strip the debating points away: add private admissions to public statements; and it may seem that no great difference remains between the views of one side in Parliament and those of the other. Both sides recognized the need for a Reform measure. Both dreaded that when the Act was passed disillusionment would set in almost at once. Agitation, it was feared, would then be renewed by political unions of formidable strength and experience until another step was taken towards manhood suffrage. Many easy hopes had disappeared by June 1831. The whigs now shared most of their opponents' forebodings. The cabinet still thought their £10 line defensible; but they recognized it to be even more arbitrary and anomalous than they had originally supposed. They no longer felt sure of achieving 'finality' for their time. Grey and his colleagues had all along known that resisting the Reform agitation would be too dangerous. They now knew that intensifying it with a sweeping Bill was far from safe. Wellington and Peel still preferred to rely on borough owners rather than on ten pounders. But they knew the shortcomings of each tory borough owner and his MPs more intimately with every month that passed.

Nonetheless the division between supporters and opponents of the Bill went to the roots of politics. It was not only that the tory bred in the government party refused to destroy a system which formed part of his life. . . . In essence much of the opposition to the Bill was a protest against the new and apparently unstable England of mechanics' [working men's] institutes and Brougham's 'godless academy'. The squire who looked for deference and no longer found it blamed this on the new fad for education and on the middle class of the growing towns. He refused to bring the constitution into line with these changes. He would not acknowledge their permanence and his defeat. If he could recognize facts at all he knew that the unreformed system no longer worked usefully. He knew that he was voting for something already broken beyond repair. This knowledge did not lessen his opposition to the Bill. His protest was not a matter of reason. The same could be said about some of the support for the Bill among the governing class. Its authors believed that recent advances in political knowledge had equipped the new electors to vote wisely; and there were some facts to back this belief. But these facts were not the real foundation for the Bill. Like many other liberal reforms it was based as much on indignation as on any assessment of the facts. To do nothing towards enabling men to rise from ignorance, and then to use that ignorance as an argument for keeping those men powerless, struck Russell and Althorp as monstrous injustice. They would accept great risks rather than allow the last word to proponents of that argument.

Among the governing class complete and sustained approval for the Bill came largely from people who had some inclination to welcome the 'march of mind', and who shared the whigs' general belief in bold but carefully limited concession. Those who held this belief regarded the ministers as setting up a barrier against further change. Those who did not hold it saw them as inviting further change. Nearly all the reform schemes of the 1830s raised the same question. Would state support for education tame the working class and reconcile them to their lot, or give them dangerous thoughts and make them discontented? Would it teach men how to subvert society, or how to rise in it? Would its tendency be to disrupt institutions, or to ensure that they developed in a civilized way? . . .

Popular protests against the loss of the Bill showed the usual variation in intensity. In Birmingham the bells were tolled all night after the news had been received; and 100,000 people are said to have attended [the] protest meeting. . . .

The vote in the Lords intensified the popular demand for Reform. A number of new political unions were formed. . . .

While the Lords' decision stimulated the growth of the political unions, it also presented the union leaders with problems of control. It was not possible to confine reformers to supporting the Bill when there was no longer a convincing prospect that it would be carried intact. It became harder than ever for leaders such as Attwood to keep the working class united with the bourgeoisie in the path of moderation. A gathering of 10,000 at Manchester on 12 October was flooded by radicals who chased the moderates from the ground and passed resolutions in favour of universal suffrage. The Bolton Political Union held its first meeting on 31 October. At the second on 28 November there was a bitter split between moderates and extremists, the former walking out. On November 17 a group of Leeds working men met . . . to inaugurate a radical political union dedicated to the attainment of manhood suffrage. . . .

The union leaders were thus faced not only with the appalling difficulty of maintaining the agitation at full strength for months more but with the imminent threat of splits. If they took a moderate, middle-class line and stuck to the Bill they were liable either to be outvoted or to lose their working-class support by secession. . . . If they turned to the full radical programme they would scare off the substantial middle-class element which provided their leaders and their money. Either way they would lose their effectiveness. A check to a popular movement naturally intensifies any extremist threat to the moderate leaders. When the suspicion grows for any reason that a [moderate such as] a Dr Martin Luther King cannot deliver the goods, [radicals such as] the advocates of Black Power are sure to make gains.

The problem came to a crisis over the proposal for a 'National Guard' on the lines of the one which had played a part in Paris during the July revolution. The news of the Nottingham and Derby riots brought this suggestion to the fore. If peers were not to be created at once, the *Globe* said on 12 October:

> it will be necessary for the middle classes to take steps to protect property. . . . Armed associations of householders must be formed. Let them be called loyal associations, national guards, or by what name we will,

some such organization will be necessary, should the Reform Bill be long delayed; or we shall have to choose between an increase in the military force and military government on the one hand, and the violence of the mob on the other.

At least one working-class leader had anticipated such a proposal. 'It is in contemplation among the "middlemen",' the *Poor Man's Guardian* warned its readers on 8 October,

> to establish a National Guard, seeing how successful and immediate a power it has been in France to suppress the people and to protect the established institutions of property. Friends, . . . such a guard would ensure your political thraldom unless you have a counter-force. . . . You too must form your millions into a guard . . . a 'Popular Guard'. Keep yourselves prepared . . . lay by as much as possible out of your scanty earnings for the purchase of a musket and accoutrements.

Divisive though the national guard proposals might be, the *Morning Chronicle* took them up, and, being friendlier than the *Globe* to the radicals, did so with less of a repressive, middle-class twist. On 26 October the *Chronicle* called for a National Guard which would unite 'the most respectable and efficient of the middle and labouring classes'. On the following day *The Times* demanded the formation of 'Conservative Guards' who were to be drawn from 'the whole mass of householders'. They 'should be drilled occasionally and taught the use of the firelock'.

The pleas for conservative guards might have died away had it not been for the Bristol riots which broke out on 29 October and raged for three days. Bristol was a turbulent port containing all the ingredients for a riot. The corporation was self-elected and of the weakest kind. Although it had contained a tory majority since 1812 the mayor was a reformer who had presided in the previous year at the Bristol meeting welcoming the July revolution. Neither side had confidence in him. The local anti-reformers thought him a trimmer. To the Bristol Political Union he personified a corrupt oligarchy. . . .

By 26 October three troops of regular cavalry, comprising 93 mounted men, had arrived in the Bristol area, their orders being 'to obey the commands of the magistrates' of the city. The Bristol Political Union, to whom the magistrates had appealed for help, publicly denounced this reliance on the army. 'If the magistracy of the city,' the Union's poster read, 'feel themselves incompetent to preserve the public peace without being supported by the military they should resign their offices.' A few days earlier an attempt to use the seamen in the port in a peace-keeping role had been frustrated by the anticorporation party. The magistrates now failed to enroll the special constables they needed and were obliged to resort to paid constables. Meanwhile the Bristol press announced the arrival of the regular cavalry and it became clear that this force, though possibly provocative, was far from large.

[But] on 29 October . . . a riot developed outside in Queen's Square. The sessions were postponed and he escaped over the roof. Next morning the Mansion House was stormed and sacked and the mobs increased until they were some thousands strong. The military commander, Lieutenant Colonel Brereton, failed to obtain support from the magistrates and withdrew two of his troops from the city. An appeal from the Political Union had no effect on the rioters. By daylight on 31 October two sides of Queen's Square, including the Custom House and Excise Office, together with the Bishop's Palace and several gaols and toll houses, had been pillaged and burned.

Brereton was court-martialled for his performance in the riots and shot himself before the case had ended. He seems to have been convinced beyond reason that the civil authorities would not uphold him in strong measures. Had he been more resolute and less humane he could perhaps have prevented the rioters from gaining control on 30 October. But this would have been difficult. His troops were tired and most Bristol people still resented their presence. Major Mackworth, a staff officer who was in Bristol on leave, advised, in his own words, 'that the cavalry should refresh during the night . . . painful as it was to leave the city at the mercy of the mob'. If Brereton had withdrawn his men, but kept them within the city, they might have been overrun in their quarters. If he had attacked and been worsted, the mob, as he later argued, 'flushed with their victory would have . . . fired the shipping'. His men had to open fire even to make good their withdrawal.

On the evening of 30 October about two hundred Bristol householders gathered in the Council House. The vice-president of the Political Union was asked, in Mackworth's words, 'whether he would get his Union together and try to save the town. He said he could not answer for it if the soldiers were employed'. Mackworth, 'much disgusted and disheartened' at the 'party spirit' displayed, told the meeting that it was plain to him

> there would be no union or energy among them until danger compelled it. . . . The burning and plundering a few private houses, which would inevitably follow the unchecked destruction of public property, would alone, and that soon, rouse the inhabitants of Bristol to a sense of their common danger.

This prophecy was soon fulfilled. On the following day (31 October) the troops were welcomed by all peaceable inhabitants. The rioters were exhausted, many being incapably drunk. Some, having broached the cellars, had been burned to death when buildings were fired. At dawn Mackworth persuaded Brereton to charge with the only cavalry troop still in the city, just as the mob was starting on the still unburned side of Queen's Square. The charge succeeded and the other two troops were summoned back to the city and brought into action. The streets were finally cleared at midday when cavalry reinforcements arrived from Gloucester. Many more were wounded than killed in the cavalry charges, though some rioters were driven back without hope of escape into burning buildings. The number of casualties in the riots was never known. It probably exceeded 400. Charles Kingsley, then a schoolboy in Clifton, saw, and did not forget, the charred corpse fragments in Queen's Square.

The Emergence of a Working Class

E.P. Thompson

The middle class was not the only interest group in Great Britain that demanded passage of the Great Reform Act in 1831–1832; artisans and factory workers also signed petitions, joined marches and rallies, and sometimes rioted for the cause of cleaning up political corruption and extending suffrage.

In his massive and greatly admired work *The Making of the English Working Class,* British historian E.P. Thompson builds a fascinating picture of the lifestyles, the work routines, and the political and social interests of England's working people from the 1780s to the 1830s. That these people ardently sought a voice in the politics of their country is readily apparent; indeed, a democratic movement among ordinary people was an important part of life throughout the English-speaking world in this period, and many common aspirations were shared by British and American workers. Thompson argues that it was the willingness of the British upper class to extend suffrage to most middle-class people, but not to the workers, that split the reform movement in the early 1830s and made the workers aware, as they had not been so clearly aware before, that they constituted a distinct social and economic class. Thereafter, liberalism (in its nineteenth-century phase of demanding personal liberty but the most limited power for government) became overwhelmingly a middle-class ideology, and the working class began to search for other ways of defining their interests. This class split, much more characteristic of Great Britain and continental Europe than of the United States (where today almost everyone defines themselves as "middle class"), dates from the early nineteenth century.

There is no mistaking the new tone [in British society] after 1832. In every manufacturing district a hundred experiences confirmed the new consciousness of class which the [Reform] Bill had, by its own provisions, so carefully defined. It was the 'reformed' House of Commons which sanctioned the transportation of the Dorchester labourers in 1834 ('a blow directed at the whole body of united operatives'), and who launched, with 'the document' and the lock-out, the struggle to break the trade unions, whose intensity and whose significance (in both political and economic terms) is still too little understood. Against the manifesto of the masters, the Yorkshire Trades Union issued its own:

> The war cry of the masters has not only been sounded, but the havoc of war; war against freedom; war against opinion; war against justice; and war without justifying cause . . .

'The very men,' declared one Leeds trade unionist, 'who had pampered Political Unions, when they could be made subservient to their own purposes, were now endeavouring to crush the Trades Unions'. . . .

The line from 1832 to Chartism is not a haphazard pendulum alternation of 'political' and 'economic' agitations but a direct progression, in which simultaneous and related movements converge towards a single point. This point was the vote. There is a sense in which the Chartist movement commenced, not in 1838 with the promulgation of the 'Six Points', but at the moment when the Reform Bill received Royal Assent. Many of the provincial Political Unions never disbanded, but commenced at once to agitate against the 'shopocrat' franchise. In January 1833 the *Working Man's Friend* was able to announce that the fortress of middle-class Radicalism had been stormed: '. . . in spite of all the opposition and chicanery of a RAG MERCHANT MONARCHY, the Midland Union of the Working Classes was formed by the brave, but, till then, misled people of that country'. The characteristic ideology of Birmingham Radicalism, which united employers and journeymen in opposition to the aristocracy, the Banks, the National Debt, and the 'paper-money system', was beginning to fall apart. . . .

But the content of this renewed agitation was such that the vote itself implied 'much more', and that is why it had to be denied. (The Birmingham of 1833 was not the Birmingham of 1831: it was now the home of an Equitable Labour Exchange, it was the headquarters of the socialist Builders' Union, it housed the editorial office of the *Pioneer*.) The vote, for the workers of this and the next decade, was a symbol whose importance it is difficult for us to appreciate, our eyes dimmed by more than a century of the smog of 'two-party parliamentary politics'. It implied, first *égalité*: equality of citizenship, personal dignity, worth. 'Instead of bricks, mortar, and dirt, MAN ought to be represented,' wrote one pamphleteer, lamenting the lot of 'the miserable, so-called "free-born" Englishman, excluded from the most valuable right that man can enjoy in political society.'. . .

The claim for the vote implied also further claims: a new way of reaching out by the working people for *social control* over their conditions of life and labour. At first, and inevitably, the exclusion of the working class provoked a contrary rejection, by the working class, of all forms of political action. . . . But in the post-1832 swing to general unionism, this anti-political bias was not quietist but embattled, militant, and even revolutionary. . . . Nor were these ideas canvassed among a limited intelligentsia only; building workers, potters, weavers, and artisans were willing, for a while, to risk their livelihood to put experiments to the test. The swarming variety of journals, many of which made exacting demands upon the readers, were addressed to an authentic working-class audience. . . .

Two themes only may be mentioned of those which arose again and again in these years. The first is that of internationalism. . . . The French Revolution of 1830 had a profound impact upon the people, electrifying not only the London Radicals but working-class reformers in distant industrial villages. The struggle for Polish independence was followed anxiously in the working-class press; while Julian Hibbert, in the Rotunda, carried a vote of sympathy with the Lyons weavers, in their ill-fated insurrection, likening them to the weavers of Spitalfields. . . . In 1833 a 'Manifesto of the Productive Classes of Great Britain and Ireland' was addressed to 'the Governments and People of the Continents of Europe and of North and South America', commencing: 'Men of the Great Family of Mankind . . .' By the end of the same year, the question of some common alliance between the trade unionists of England, France, and Germany had already come under discussion.

The other theme was that of industrial syndicalism. When Marx was still in his teens, the battle for the minds of English trade unionists, between a capitalist and a socialist political economy, had been (at least temporarily) won. . . . 'What is capital?' asked a writer in the *Pioneer.* 'It is reserved labour!' cries M'Culloch. '. . . From whom and what was it reserved? From the clothing and food of the wretched.' Hence the workers who had been 'insolently placed without the pale of social government' developed, stage by stage, a theory of syndicalism, or of 'Inverted Masonry'. 'The Trades Unions will not only strike for less work, and more wages,' wrote 'A Member of the Builder's Union',

> but they will ultimately ABOLISH WAGES, become their own masters, and work for each other; labour and capital will no longer be separate but they will be indissolubly joined together in the hands of the workmen and work-women.

The unions themselves could solve the problem of political power; a 'Parliament' of the industrious classes could be formed, delegated directly from workshops and mills: 'the Lodges send Delegates from local to district, and from district to National Assemblies. Here are Universal Suffrage, Annual Election, and No Property Qualification, instanter.' The idea was developed (in the *Pioneer*) of such a House of Trades:

> which must supply the place of the present House of Commons, and direct the commercial affairs of the country, according to the will of the trades which compose associations of the industry. This is the ascendancy scale by which we arrive to universal suffrage. It will begin in our lodges, extend to our general union, embrace the management of trade, and finally swallow up the whole political power.

This vision was lost, almost as soon as it had been found, in the terrible defeats of 1834 and 1835. And, when they had recovered their wind, the workers returned to the vote, as the more practical key to political power. Something was lost: but Chartism never entirely forgot this preoccupation with social control, to the attainment of which the vote was seen as a means. These years reveal a passing beyond the characteristic outlook of the artisan, with his desire for an independent livelihood 'by the sweat of his brow', to a newer outlook, more reconciled to the new means of production, but seeking to exert the collective power of the class to humanize the environment:—by this community or that cooperative society, by this check on the blind operation of the market-economy, this legal enactment, that measure of relief for the poor. And implicit, if not always explicit, in their outlook was the dangerous tenet: production must be, not for profit, but for use.

This collective self-consciousness was indeed the great spiritual gain of the Industrial Revolution, against which the disruption of an older and in many ways more humanly comprehensible way of life must be set. It was perhaps a unique formation, this British working class of 1832. The slow, piecemeal accretions of capital accumulation had meant that the preliminaries to the Industrial Revolution stretched backwards for hundreds of years. From Tudor times onwards this artisan culture had grown more complex with each phase of technical and social change. . . . Enriched by the experiences of the seventeenth century, carrying through the eighteenth century the intellectual and libertarian traditions, . . . forming their own traditions of mutuality in the friendly society and trades club, these men did not pass, in one generation, from the peasantry to the new industrial town. They suffered the experience of the Industrial Revolution as articulate, free-born Englishmen. Those who were sent to gaol [jail] might know the Bible better than those on the Bench, and those who were transported to Van Diemen's Land [Australia] might ask their relatives to send Cobbett's *Register* after them.

This was, perhaps, the most distinguished popular culture England has known. It contained the massive diversity of skills, of the workers in metal, wood, textiles and ceramics, without whose inherited 'mysteries' and superb ingenuity with primitive tools the inventions of the Industrial Revolution could scarcely have got further than the drawing-board. From this culture of the craftsman and the self-taught there came scores of inventors, organizers, journalists and political theorists of impressive quality. It is easy enough to say that this culture was backward-looking or conservative. True enough, one direction of the great agitations of the artisans and outworkers, continued over fifty years, was to *resist* being turned into a proletariat. When they knew that this cause was lost, they reached out again, in the Thirties and Forties, and sought to achieve new and only imagined forms of social control. During all this time they were, as a class, repressed and segregated in their own communities. But what the counter-revolution sought to repress grew only more determined in the quasi-legal institutions of the underground. Whenever the pressure of the rulers relaxed, men came from the petty workshops or the weavers' hamlets and asserted new claims. They were told that they had no rights, but they knew that they were born free. The Yeomanry rode down their meeting, and the right of public meeting was gained. The pamphleteers were gaoled, and from the gaols they edited pamphlets. The trade unionists were imprisoned, and they were attended to prison by processions with bands and union banners.

Segregated in this way, their institutions acquired a peculiar toughness and resilience. Class also acquired a peculiar resonance in English life: everything, from their schools to their shops, their chapels to their amusements, was turned into a battleground of class. The marks of this remain, but by the outsider they are not always understood. If we have in our social life little of the tradition of *égalité* [equality], the class-consciousness of the working man has little in it of deference. 'Orphans we are, and bastards of society,' wrote James Morrison in 1834. The tone is not one of resignation but of pride.

Again and again in these years working men expressed it thus: 'they wish to make us tools', or 'implements', or 'machines'. A witness before the parliamentary committee enquiring into the hand-loom weavers (1835) was asked to state the view of his fellows on the Reform Bill:

Q: Are the working classes better satisfied with the institutions of the country since the change has taken place?

A: I do not think they are. They viewed the Reform Bill as a measure calculated to join the middle and upper classes to Government, and leave them in the hands of Government as a sort of machine to work according to the pleasure of Government.

Such men met Utilitarianism in their daily lives, and they sought to throw it back, not blindly, but with intelligence and moral passion. They fought, not the machine, but the exploitive and oppressive relationships intrinsic to industrial capitalism. In these same years, the great Romantic criticism of Utilitarianism was running its parallel but altogether separate course. After William Blake, no mind was at home in both cultures, nor had the genius to interpret the two traditions to each other. It was a muddled Mr Owen who offered to disclose the 'new moral world', while Wordsworth and Coleridge had withdrawn behind their own ramparts of disenchantment. Hence these years appear at times to display, not a revolutionary challenge, but a resistance movement, in which both the Romantics and the Radical craftsmen opposed the annunciation of Acquisitive Man. In the failure of the two traditions to come to a point of junction, something was lost. How much we cannot be sure, for we are among the losers.

Yet the working people should not be seen only as the lost myriads of eternity. They had also nourished, for fifty years, and with incomparable fortitude, the Liberty Tree. We may thank them for these years of heroic culture.

The Communist Manifesto

Karl Marx and Friedrich Engels

Karl Marx (1818–1883) was no utopian; in fact, he denounced what he called "utopian socialists" as dreamers whose fantasies of a perfect world of peace, harmony, and generosity could never be achieved. Trained at the University of Berlin as a philosopher, Marx called himself a "scientific socialist" and claimed to have discovered the laws of history. Socialism, and eventually communism, would sweep the world, he said, because the capitalist-industrial order of the nineteenth century carried the seeds of its own downfall. Eventually the competition among capitalists would grow so fierce, he predicted, that they would end up transforming the market system into a series of monopolies. Meanwhile workers would see their wages cut and their misery grow, and eventually they would rise in revolt. Seizing the means of production—factories, railroads, mines, land, and everything else out of which goods are made—and creating a workers' dictatorship, the working class would establish a just social order at last. First would come socialism, a system in which the revolutionary state owned the means of production on behalf of the workers. But soon thereafter would come communism, in which everything would be owned in common based on the principle "from each according to his ability, to each according to his need." History, which up to then had been a product of class struggle, would truly come to an end; there would be no more struggle because antagonistic classes will have been abolished.

Marx worked out his system of thought primarily in the years 1843–1848, while he was living first in Paris and then in Brussels, exiled from his native Germany for his radical activities as a journalist. He formulated his ideas principally by reading voraciously and arguing vehemently with the many "utopian" socialists whom he encountered among his fellow exiles. There, too, he found his lifelong collaborator and patron, Friedrich Engels (1820–1895), the son of a wealthy German manufacturer who shared Marx's vision of a better world and his scorn for dreamy "utopians."

This selection is the opening section of the famous *Communist Manifesto,* which was largely the work of Marx and Engels although it was published (at the beginning of the tumultuous year 1848) in the name of a small group of revolutionaries who accepted Marx's leadership. The *Manifesto* attracted very little attention at the time, and the police did not even pay Marx and his friends the compliment of trying to suppress it. Yet as the first major public statement of Marx's mature revolutionary thought, the document is of great historical importance. Notice the powerful praise that the *Manifesto* lavishes on the bourgeoisie for having revolutionized the world—destroying traditional power and class relationships (all of which Marx scorns as outmoded "feudalism") and ushering in the tremendous potential of industrialization. The *Manifesto* is in fact one of the Western tradition's classic statements of the idea of progress.

Yet, Marx insists, the bourgeoisie has also prepared its own doom by unleashing the fury of the exploited working class—the "proletariat," in his terminology. The more powerful capitalism and the bourgeoisie become, the greater the counterforce that will be arrayed against it, in the form of the proletarian revolutionary movement. Eventually the bourgeois order of things will be overthrown and the proletariat will inaugurate a classless society. The *Manifesto* closes with a famous challenge: "Workers of all countries, unite! You have nothing to lose but your chains!"

Manifesto of the Communist Party

A specter is haunting Europe—the specter of communism. All the powers of old Europe have entered into a holy alliance to exorcise this specter: Pope and Czar, Metternich and Guizot, French radicals and German police spies.

Where is the party in opposition that has not been decried as communistic by its opponents in power? Where is the opposition that has not hurled back the branding reproach of communism against the more advanced opposition parties, as well as against its reactionary adversaries?

Two things result from this fact:

I. Communism is already acknowledged by all European powers to be itself a power.

II. It is high time that communists should openly, in the face of the whole world, publish their views, their aims, their tendencies, and meet this nursery tale of the specter of communism with a Manifesto of the party itself.

To this end, communists of various nationalities have assembled in London and sketched the following Manifesto, to be published in the English, French, German, Italian, Flemish, and Danish languages.

Bourgeois and Proletarians

The history of all hitherto existing society is the history of class struggles.

Free man and slave, patrician and plebeian, lord and serf, guild master and journeyman, in a word, oppressor and oppressed, stood in constant opposition to one another, carried on an uninterrupted, now hidden, now open fight, a fight that each time ended either in a revolutionary reconstitution of society at large or in the common ruin of the contending classes.

In the earlier epochs of history we find almost everywhere a complicated arrangement of society into various orders, a manifold gradation of social rank. In ancient Rome we have patricians, knights, plebeians, slaves; in the Middle Ages, feudal lords, vassals, guild masters, journeymen, apprentices, serfs; in almost all of these classes, again, subordinate gradations.

The modern bourgeois society that has sprouted from the ruins of feudal society has not done away with class antagonisms. It has but established new classes, new conditions of oppression, new forms of struggle in place of the old ones.

Our epoch, the epoch of the bourgeoisie, possesses, however, this distinctive feature: it has simplified class antagonisms. Society as a whole is more and more splitting up into two great hostile camps, into two great classes directly facing each other: bourgeoisie and proletariat.

From the serfs of the Middle Ages sprang the chartered burghers of the earliest towns. From these burgesses the first elements of the bourgeoisie were developed.

The discovery of America, the rounding of the Cape opened up fresh ground for the rising bourgeoisie. The East Indian and Chinese markets, the colonization of America, trade with the colonies, the increase in the means of exchange and in commodities generally, gave to commerce, to navigation, to industry an impulse never before known, and thereby, to the revolutionary element in the tottering feudal society, a rapid development.

The feudal system of industry, under which industrial production was monopolized by closed guilds, now no longer sufficed for the growing wants of the new markets. The manufacturing system took its place. The guild masters were pushed on one side by the manufacturing middle class; division of labor between the different corporate guilds vanished in the face of division of labor in each single workshop.

Meantime the markets kept ever growing, the demand ever rising. Even manufacture no longer sufficed. Thereupon steam and machinery revolutionized industrial production. The place of manufacture was taken by the giant, modern industry, the place of the industrial middle class by industrial millionaires, the leaders of whole industrial armies, the modern bourgeois.

Modern industry has established the world market, for which the discovery of America paved the way. This market has given an immense development to commerce, to navigation, to communication by land. This development has, in its turn, reacted on the extension of industry; and in proportion as industry, commerce, navigation, railways extended, in the same proportion the bourgeoisie developed, increased its capital, and pushed into the background every class handed down from the Middle Ages.

We see, therefore, how the modern bourgeoisie is itself the product of a long course of development, of a series of revolutions in the modes of production and of exchange.

Each step in the development of the bourgeoisie was accompanied by a corresponding political advance of that class. An oppressed class under the sway of the feudal nobility, an armed and self-governing association in the medieval commune*; here independent urban republic (as in Italy and Germany), there taxable "third estate" of the monarchy (as in France), afterwards, in the period of manufacture proper, serving either the semi-feudal or the absolute monarchy as a counterpoise against the nobility, and, in fact, cornerstone of the great monarchies in general, the bourgeoisie has at last, since the establishment of modern industry and of the world market, conquered for itself, in the modern representative state, exclusive political sway. The executive of the modern state is but a committee for managing the common affairs of the whole bourgeoisie.

Karl Marx

---

* "Commune" was the name taken, in France, by the nascent towns even before they had conquered from their feudal lords and masters local self-government and political rights as the "third estate." Generally speaking, for the economic development of the bourgeoisie, England is here taken as the typical country; for its political development, France. [Note by Engels to the English edition of 1888.]

The bourgeoisie, historically, has played a most revolutionary part.

The bourgeoisie, wherever it has got the upper hand, has put an end to all feudal, patriarchal, idyllic relations. It has pitilessly torn asunder the motley feudal ties that bound man to his "natural superiors," and has left remaining no other nexus between man and man than naked self-interest, than callous "cash payment." It has drowned out the most heavenly ecstacies of religious fervor, of chivalrous enthusiasm, of Philistine sentimentalism in the icy water of egotistical calculation. It has resolved personal worth into exchange value and, in place of the numberless indefeasible chartered freedoms, has set up that single, unconscionable freedom—free trade. In one word, for exploitation, veiled by religious and political illusions, it has substituted naked, shameless, direct, brutal exploitation.

The bourgeoisie has stripped of its halo every occupation hitherto honored and looked up to with reverent awe. It has converted the physician, the lawyer, the priest, the poet, the man of science into its paid wage laborers.

The bourgeoisie has torn away from the family its sentimental veil, and has reduced the family relation to a mere money relation.

The bourgeoisie has disclosed how it came to pass that the brutal display of vigor in the Middle Ages, which reactionists so much admire, found its fitting complement in the most slothful indolence. It has been the first to show what man's activity can bring about. It has accomplished wonders far surpassing Egyptian pyramids, Roman aqueducts, and Gothic cathedrals; it has conducted expeditions that put in the shade all former exoduses of nations and crusades.

The bourgeoisie cannot exist without constantly revolutionizing the instruments of production, and thereby the relations of production, and with them the whole relations of society. Conservation of the old modes of production in unaltered form was, on the contrary, the first condition of existence for all earlier industrial classes. Constant revolutionizing of production, uninterrupted disturbance of all social conditions, everlasting uncertainty and agitation distinguish the bourgeois epoch from all earlier ones. All fixed, fast-frozen relations, with their train of ancient and venerable prejudices and opinions, are swept away, all new-formed ones become antiquated before they can ossify. All that is solid melts into air, all that is holy is profaned, and man is at last compelled to face with sober senses his real conditions of life and his relations with his kind.

The need of a constantly expanding market for its products chases the bourgeoisie over the whole surface of the globe. It must nestle everywhere, settle everywhere, establish connections everywhere.

The bourgeoisie has through its exploitation of the world market given a cosmopolitan character to production and consumption in every country. To the great chagrin of reactionists, it has drawn from under the feet of industry the national ground on which it stood. All old-established national industries have been destroyed or are daily being destroyed. They are dislodged by new industries, whose introduction becomes a life and death question for all civilized nations, by industries that no longer work up indigenous raw material, but raw material drawn from the remotest zones; industries whose products are consumed not only at home, but in every quarter of the globe. In place of the old wants, satisfied by the productions of the country, we find new wants, requiring for their satisfaction the products of distant lands and climes. In place of the old local and national seclusion and self-sufficiency, we have intercourse in every direction, universal interdependence of nations. And as in material, so also in intellectual production. The intellectual creations of individual nations become common property. National one-sidedness and narrow-mindedness become more and more impossible, and from the numerous national and local literatures there arises a world literature.

The bourgeoisie, by the rapid improvement of all instruments of production, by the immensely facilitated means of communication, draws all, even the most barbarian, nations into civilization. The cheap prices of its commodities are the heavy artillery with which it batters down all Chinese walls, with which it forces the barbarians' intensely obstinate hatred of foreigners to capitulate. It compels all nations, on pain of extinction, to adopt the bourgeois mode of production; it compels them to introduce what it calls civilization into their midst, i.e., to become bourgeois themselves. In one word, it creates a world after its own image.

The bourgeoisie has subjected the country to the rule of the towns. It has created enormous cities, has greatly increased the urban population as compared with the rural, and has thus rescued a considerable part of the population from the idiocy of rural life. Just as it has made the country dependent on the towns, so it has made barbarian and semi-barbarian countries dependent on the civilized ones, nations of peasants on nations of bourgeois, the East on the West.

The bourgeoisie keeps more and more doing away with the scattered state of the population, of the means of production, and of property. It has agglomerated population, centralized means of production, and has concentrated property in a few hands. The necessary consequence of this was political centralization. Independent, or but loosely connected provinces, with separate interests, laws, governments, and systems of taxation, became lumped together into one nation, with one government, one code of laws, one national class interest, one frontier, and one customs tariff.

The bourgeoisie, during its rule of scarce one hundred years, has created more massive and more colossal productive forces than have all preceding generations together. Subjection of nature's forces to

man, machinery, application of chemistry to industry and agriculture, steam navigation, railways, electric telegraphs, clearing of
whole continents for cultivation, canalization of rivers, whole populations conjured out of the ground—what earlier century had even a
presentiment that such productive forces slumbered in the lap of social labor?

We see then: the means of production and of exchange, on whose
foundation the bourgeoisie built itself up, were generated in feudal
society. At a certain stage in the development of these means of production and of exchange, the conditions under which feudal society
produced and exchanged, the feudal organization of agriculture and
manufacturing industry, in one word, the feudal relations of property, became no longer compatible with the already developed productive forces; they became so many fetters. They had to be burst
asunder; they were burst asunder.

Into their place stepped free competition, accompanied by a social and political constitution adapted to it, and by the economic and
political sway of the bourgeois class.

A similar movement is going on before our own eyes. Modern
bourgeois society with its relations of production, of exchange and
of property, a society that has conjured up such gigantic means of
production and of exchange, is like the sorcerer who is no longer able
to control the powers of the nether world whom he has called up by
his spells. For many a decade past, the history of industry and commerce is but the history of the revolt of modern productive forces
against modern conditions of production, against the property relations that are the conditions for the existence of the bourgeoisie and
of its rule. It is enough to mention the commercial crises that by their
periodical return put on its trial, each time more threateningly, the
existence of the entire bourgeois society. In these crises a great part
not only of the existing products but also of the previously created
productive forces are periodically destroyed. In these crises there
breaks out an epidemic that in all earlier epochs would have seemed
an absurdity—the epidemic of overproduction. Society suddenly
finds itself put back into a state of momentary barbarism; it appears
as if a famine, a universal war of devastation had cut off the supply
of every means of subsistence; industry and commerce seem to be
destroyed; and why? Because there is too much civilization, too
much means of subsistence, too much industry, too much commerce.
The productive forces at the disposal of society no longer tend to further the development of the conditions of bourgeois property; on the
contrary, they have become too powerful for these conditions, by which
they are fettered, and as soon as they overcome these fetters they bring
disorder into the whole of bourgeois society, endanger the existence of
bourgeois property. The conditions of bourgeois society are too narrow

to comprise the wealth created by them. And how does the bourgeoisie get over these crises? On the one hand, by enforced destruction of a mass of productive forces; on the other, by the conquest of new markets, and by the more thorough exploitation of the old ones. That is to say, by paving the way for more extensive and more destructive crises, and by diminishing the means whereby crises are prevented.

The weapons with which the bourgeoisie felled feudalism to the ground are now turned against the bourgeoisie itself.

But not only has the bourgeoisie forged the weapons that bring death to itself; it has also called into existence the men who are to wield those weapons—the modern working class—the proletarians.

The Great Exhibition

Margaret Drabble

Margaret Drabble describes the Great Exhibition of 1851, a collection of industrial products displayed in a specially built hall, the Crystal Palace. Margaret Drabble is the author of fourteen novels, including her 2001 *The Peppered Moth*, several plays, and critical editions about Jane Austen, Charlotte Brontë, and Thomas Hardy.

The Great Exhibition was an exhibition of science and manufacture, of design and raw materials, unprecedented in aim and achievement. Even the building which housed it, happily labelled The Crystal Palace by [the periodical] *Punch*, was a triumph of imaginative architecture. Designed by Joseph Paxton, after the model of the Great Conservatory at Chatsworth, it soared up, a glittering canopy of glass and steel; [writer Thomas Babington] Macaulay who was present at the opening came away enraptured, and wrote that it was 'a most gorgeous sight; vast; graceful; beyond the dreams of the Arabian romance. I cannot think that the Caesars ever exhibited a more splendid spectacle. I was quite dazzled. . . .'

The reference to the Caesars is revealing, for the Victorians showed a Roman determination to overcome obstacles. One of the objections to the building of the Palace in Hyde Park was that it would involve cutting down a clump of three tall elms on the site— the Victorians, too, could show concern for conservation, when it suited them. So Paxton incorporated the trees in his design, and an

Excerpted from *For Queen and Country* (New York: Seabury Press, 1979) by Margaret Drabble. Copyright © 1979 by Margaret Drabble. Reprinted with permission from the author.

immense transept was built to house them. They must have added to the exotic, fairy tale quality of the place. Paxton's whole concept was in fact based on nature; he is thought to have devised the rib structure from his study of the huge South American water lily, *Victoria Regina,* which he had seen at Chatsworth; its giant leaves were strong enough to bear the weight of Paxton's small daughter. Like so many of the great Victorians, Paxton was strictly an amateur, as he had no professional qualifications as architect, engineer or scientist; this was an age when the inspired amateur, his imagination unshackled by a narrow professional training or discipline, could achieve astonishing results.

Controversy Surrounded the Palace and the Exhibits

The elms were not the only excuse for opposition to [Queen Victoria's husband Prince] Albert's scheme. Some muttered that it would ruin Hyde Park, the only decent open space left in London; others feared the building, unorthodox by any standards, would collapse. A more natural fear, perhaps, was that the huge crowds it would attract might prove violent, and that it might provide an opportunity for a rekindling of the radical spirit of Chartism* which had inflamed the working classes in the previous decade. The Victorians were easily alarmed by the idea of a 'mob', and memories of the French Revolution lingered; more recently, Revolution had swept through Europe in 1848, and the English feared that it might be their turn next. The discontent of a badly-paid, badly-housed proletariat could not be totally ignored, many felt, though that was not how they expressed their alarm. 'I would advise those living near the Park to keep a sharp look over their silver forks and spoons and servant maids', wrote one angry colonel to *The Times.* But his fears were unfounded. The crowds were orderly and loyal, nobody took advantage of the situation to attempt to assassinate or even to shout abuse at Queen Victoria, and there was no drunken vandalism—perhaps wisely, the refreshments available did not include alcoholic beverages. The exhibits, ranging in scale from meat-paste pot lids to huge power looms, were generally considered wonderful, and the whole project, which had been financed entirely by private money, made a large profit.

But was it an artistic success? Did it not, rather, illustrate what we think of as typically Victorian 'bad taste'? One could argue either way. Sir Nikolaus Pevsner, an expert on design, writes: 'The attendance as well as the size of the buildings and the quantity of the products shown was colossal. The aesthetic quality of the products

* a movement by workers to gain suffrage

was abominable.' These are hard words. He goes on to argue that designers had not yet learned to cope with the newly invented processes of production, such as machine weaving and electroplating, and were applying the wrong techniques to the wrong materials. Certainly some of the objects indicate more pride in the fact that a thing *can* be done than interest in the use or beauty of the finished object—take, for example, the wonderful knife with eighty blades and other instruments, made by Rodgers and Sons of Sheffield. It was heavily decorated with gold inlay, etching and engraving—a remarkable piece of work, but neither use nor ornament. The Osler fountain of cut crystal glass was famed more for its size and weight than for its beauty; it weighed four tons. Designs for carpets and fabrics show, as Pevsner points out, a lack of restraint, a lack of plan, a picking from here and there of jumbled scraps of pattern, a confused eclecticism. Eclecticism is a word one cannot avoid long when talking of the Victorians, for it so perfectly describes their attitude to decoration; it is the art of borrowing from various sources, to suit oneself. The Victorians had a great deal to be eclectic about; easier travel and the spreading Empire, as well as new techniques, provided a vast range of new patterns—peacocks from India, carpet designs from Turkey and Persia, lace designs from France, even sphinxes from Egypt. The Victorian instinct was not to look for uniformity of style, but to jumble everything up together, at random;

The Great Exhibition of 1851 in London was housed in an unorthodox steel-and-glass palace designed by amateur architect Joseph Paxton.

even a room like The Indian Room at 7 Chesterfield Gardens, which at first sight looks as though it is trying to keep to some kind of Far Eastern plan, proves on closer inspection to combine Indian, Japanese, Chinese, and European bamboo chairs. Most interiors had even less coherence, and individual designs could show several separate influences.

So the Great Exhibition had, in the world of art, an immensely useful function; it drew attention to the chaos of taste and to the evils of 'Sheffield Eternal' and 'Brummagem Gothic'. From this chaos emerged art critics such as [John] Ruskin, and designers and artists such as William Morris. The artistic directors who had helped to set up the exhibition had already declared their desire for reform; Henry Cole and Owen Jones felt that 'ornament must be secondary to the thing ornamented', and that ornament should be fitted to the object's function. The Exhibition proved a focus for their theories and a breeding ground for new theories, as well as a display of the dangers and disasters of the age. Some of the new ideas were of course already in the air—the architect Augustus Welby Pugin was in charge of the medieval court, where he had scope to exhibit his highly original and influential views on design. He was of the opinion that

> All the mechanical contrivances and inventions of the day, such as plastering, composition, papier-mâché, and a host of other deceptions, only serve to degrade design, by abolishing the variety of ornament and ideas, as well as the boldness of execution, so admirable and beautiful in ancient carved works. . . .

We see here the growing revulsion against the new machine age of mass production and cheap imitation materials, and a new interest in the old arts of craftsmanship. (Today, some feel the same revulsion from plastic, nylon, and other 'unnatural' materials.) Professional designers were almost unknown in the early Victorian period; in the later half of the century, they were to flourish.

But the Great Exhibition offered far more than a spectacle of bad taste. Many of its visitors saw their first railway train there, and machinery of most kinds was still a novelty. A model diving bell, a lace machine, and a steam brewery attracted great attention. The Victorians may have liked over-decoration in luxury goods, but they had a strong sense of functional design; the sewing machine, the typewriter, the earthenware inhaler, and the gynaecological forceps remained unchanged for many years after their original conception. British engineering was the best in the world, encouraged by the efforts of men like James Nasmyth, the inventor of the steam hammer, and his pupil Joseph Whitworth, whose machine tools at the Great Exhibition were praised for 'their great beauty and power'. The nineteenth-century toolmakers have been acclaimed by modern art historians as a new race of artists, and even at the time, objects like lathes and microscopes were considered beautiful as well as useful; more significantly, many appreciated that they were beautiful because they were useful. The English, said [American writer Ralph Waldo] Emerson, love 'the lever, the screw and the pulley', and as early as 1759 the economist Adam Smith had stated that 'Utility is one of the principal sources of beauty.'

Over-decoration and embellishment never overwhelmed such inventions as the bicycle and the electric light bulb—the shape of the light bulb is so well adapted to its function that we accept it, says Herwin Schaefer in an excellent account of the functional tradition, 'as if it were a product of nature'. Significantly, more attempts were made to decorate the sewing machine and the typewriter, because they were primarily used by women, but even here the dignity of the basic design survived. Schaefer advises us, when looking for a good design, to concentrate not on luxury items such as the Osler fountain, but on ordinary objects in daily use, such as egg beaters, kitchen scales, scissors and coat hooks, bottles, pots and bell pushes. It is interesting to note that the American exhibits that most impressed the British were such things as sleighs, ice skates, racing sulkies, canoes and farm implements; necessity was proving the mother of invention and by the 1870s the Americans had taken over the world lead in machinery, as they demonstrated in 1876 at the Centennial Exhibition in Philadelphia.

The Function-Decoration Conflict Extends Beyond the Great Exhibition

The nineteenth-century conflict between function and decoration was nowhere better expressed than in the building of the railways. The telling contrast between the elaborate Gothic façade of St Pancras, more a cathedral than a railway terminus, and the austere simplicity of the roof and girders within is still eloquent. The Victorians themselves were conscious of such problems, and in 1852 Frederick S. Williams published a book, *Our Iron Roads,* which shows a spirited enthusiasm for the immense enterprise of the engineers, and for the beauty of their constructions. The railways have retained their excitement and glamour for some addicts, and Williams is one of their earlier admirers. Of the High Level Bridge at Newcastle, he writes:

> It is scarcely possible to imagine a more interesting and beautiful sight than it presents, with the huge span of arches diminishing in perspective, and the opening at the furthest end of the bridge showing only like a bright spot in the distance. The pillars, which carry the road, add greatly to the picturesque effect . . . such a combination of beautiful lines is seldom seen.

Here is a writer who does not despise the machine-made. He writes with equal lyricism of the Britannia tubular bridge across the Menai Strait:

> Could the reader stand upon the shores of the Isle of Anglesey, and view the entire spectacle, though but for a few moments, on some fine spring evening, he would retire with impressions of its magnificence that neither pen nor pencil can create. . . . Science and nature mingle in harmonious contrast, and receive the grateful homage of every rightly-constituted heart.

Williams clearly did not share the fears of [poet William] Wordsworth, who thought that the railways would ruin the scenery of the Lake District.

He is also impressed by sheer technical triumphs, such as the blasting of a tunnel through Shakespeare's Cliff between Dover and Folkestone, an event which attracted crowds of admiring sightseers, at the risk of their lives. It has been suggested that the fiery and dramatic paintings of John Martin, now restored to fashion after years of neglect, may have been partly inspired by the sight of the quarries and craters and scars that gashed Britain during the building of the railways; he was very fond of portraying caverns, tunnels, and falling rocks. His versions of Hell remind one of the fiery furnaces of industrial England, and his huge work, *Belshazzar's Feast,* distinctly resembles a vast railway station. Martin certainly appreciated the picturesque aspects of engineering feats, as well as their practical ones—significantly, he devoted a good deal of time not only to Biblical and classical subjects, but also to designing and drawing schemes for sewage and water supplies, embankments and colliery safety apparatus. Most Victorians were, like him, moved rather than appalled by the grandeur of the new engineering miracles, and Londoners watched the new cuttings slicing their way into the heart of the city with awe.

Yet efforts were made to landscape the railways; Williams had strong views on appropriate designs for tunnels and bridges. Tunnel entrances, he says, should show 'plainness combined with boldness, and massiveness without heaviness', which sounds sensible enough. But his book has illustrations which prove how difficult it was for the Victorians to find appropriate designs for wholly new concepts— there is a railway station that looks like a gothic chapel, a tunnel entrance with castellated towers modelled on a medieval castle, and the Britannia bridge, a triumph of modern engineering, was flanked by highly inappropriate sphinxes. Eclecticism at work, again. The bridges themselves dictated their own aesthetic laws, but when it came to decorating them, and blending them in with traditional ideas of the beautiful, the Victorians were less happy, and had less to guide them.

The Great Exhibition Inspires the Work Ethic

The Great Exhibition, which provided an opportunity for much debate on design, also created a new attitude to work, which was to prove equally significant. Work had become respectable; trade and manufacture were given the nation's blessing. Albert himself, who could have chosen to be little more than an idle and handsome figurehead, was much inspired by the romance of industry, and worked hard himself, contributing to the view that hard work is good even for the richest of us. In the words of *The Economist* of 1851, 'Labour is ceased to be looked down upon . . . the Bees are more considered than the Butterflies of society; wealth is valued less as an exemption from toil, than as a call to effort. . . .' The idea of a leisured class of wealthy parasites became less popular, as the work ethic and the virtues of self help took over. Sir Felix Carbury in [novelist Anthony] Trollope's *The Way We Live Now* is shown as even more contemptible than the unscrupulous Melmotte, because, although well-born, he is a complete idler and wastrel, who does nothing but play cards, hunt, borrow money, seduce poor girls, and plot to marry rich ones. The polite world of [novelist] Jane Austen, in which families lived without visible means of support, was on the way out. Religion placed itself firmly on the side of the worker; God would help those who helped themselves. Samuel Smiles published in 1859 a book called *Self Help,* which became the Bible of the self-made man; he also published glowing biographies of men like [railway engineer] George Stephenson, and praised the great industrialists who had started from humble origins.

Commerce had become respectable, and great buildings rose to celebrate the civic pride of the great commercial centres—Cuthbert Brodrick's Town Hall in Leeds, Bunning's Coal Exchange in London, Edward Walters' Free Trade Hall in Manchester. These, one could say, were the real cathedrals of Victorian England. Ruskin and Pugin were to look back nostalgically at the gothic cathedrals of a more spiritual age, but they could not stem the flow of pride in profit, in invention, in commercial daring. The Crystal Palace glorified the golden age of prosperity. In the official catalogue, Albert wrote 'We are living at a period of most wonderful transition', and went on to sing the praises of a unified world, in which 'thought is communicated with the rapidity and even by the power of lightning'. Science, industry and art together will, he said, help us to fulfil the sacred mission of man, helped on by the stimulus of competition and capital. Endless progress, sings *The Economist,* in a fine confident moment, is 'the destined lot of the human race'. And England was firmly in the forefront of that progress, a model to the world.

It is pleasing to note that the profits raised from the Great Exhibition went into educational projects which we can still enjoy today; again, the vision was Albert's, and the projects include the Victoria and Albert Museum, the Natural History Museum, and the Royal College of Music. Triumphant commerce did not neglect succeeding generations.

Chapter 3

The American Civil War

" The last, best hope of earth," Abraham Lincoln called the American democratic experience during the Civil War (1861–1865), and on the occasion of his Gettysburg Address (1863) he called on his fellow citizens to dedicate themselves anew to the Union cause, so that "government of the people, by the people, and for the people, shall not perish from the earth." Lincoln was well aware that he was raising the stakes in the American Civil War to global significance.

In the wartime years, the United States *was*, in fact, the only broadly based political democracy on earth. Although the Great Reform in Britain had somewhat widened political participation there, most working-class men and many people of the lower middle class still had no voice in government, and political decision making was still almost exclusively confined to members of the traditional elite. (One decision over which that elite agonized was whether to recognize the American slave states' decision to secede and form the Confederate States of America—an endorsement toward which the British government sometimes veered perilously close.) France at that time was a dictatorship ruled by Napoléon Bonaparte's nephew, Emperor Napoléon III, who used the opportunity of America's civil war to attempt to establish a satellite empire in Mexico under an Austrian prince, Maximilian. Germany was divided into many small and a few big monarchies, none of them remotely democratic. Italy was becoming unified, by force, by the armies of Sardinia's king, Victor Emmanuel, which were eclipsing the country's democratic-republican movement. Political participation, even in Western Europe's small, peaceful countries—Belgium, Holland, Switzerland, and the Scandinavian lands—was still narrowly based.

Russia, the largest country on earth, was in the 1860s going through an important reform process, but strictly from the top down. The czar still had unlimited power to do what he thought best, unchecked by a constitution, parliament, elections, political parties, or a free press. It is true that Czar Alexander II had the intelligence to realize that serfdom—the system of virtual slavery that put much of Russia's peasantry under the direct authority of their noble landlords—had become outmoded and inefficient. In 1861, just as the American Civil War was beginning, the czar issued his emancipation decree, freeing the serfs and paying off their former owners. In contrast to the United States, in Russia unfree labor was abolished without violence, and with compensation to the masters. And other reforms were also being enacted, such as the right of limited local self-government and greater freedom for the country's restless university students. But the czar had no intention of surrendering his autocratic power to rule by decree, or permitting national elections, or a legislature, or anything else that might have started Russia down the road toward eventual democracy.

In most Latin American countries, elites of "pure-blooded" landowners, high officials, and sometimes the Roman Catholic clergy by now exercised all political power. It is true that in Mexico a democratic nationalist movement had won significant support among the mestizo (mixed-race) and even the downtrodden Indian populations, but Mexicans were also having to fight for their independence against reactionary groups that were openly supported by an invading French army. The prospect of democracy, hitherto unrealized in Mexico, definitely looked hazy.

Canada, Australia, and New Zealand were in the early 1860s still basically British colonies, and India was ruled outright by the British government, which had recently suppressed (with great bloodshed) a national insurrection. China was engulfed in a vast and bloody civil war, the first stage of a long process of national disintegration and rebuilding that would culminate a century later in the tumultuous establishment of the communist People's Republic. Japan was also undergoing intense turmoil, but that would end with the creation of an efficient yet autocratic system of government presided over by an emperor whom most Japanese still regarded as a divine being. In the rest of what we would today call the Third World, the word *democracy* had generally not even been uttered or written.

Lincoln was right: in the 1860s, American democracy *was* a unique and fragile experiment, which could easily fail.

The United States was also—again in Lincoln's memorable words—like the biblical "house divided," half-slave and half-free. Irony lay in the fact that both freedom and slavery could be interpreted by the nation's dominant European-descended population as their democratic birthright. In the northern states, where slavery had been abolished after the American Revolution, "freedom" meant the right of white men to do what they wanted, to raise their voices freely about political matters, and to vote in the country's boisterous elections. It meant the freedom to go west and farm on cheap land, or to work at the trade for which they were trained. It meant that those who governed the nation must always submit themselves to the people's judgment, and carry out their will. And, for a growing number of women and a handful of men, the logic of "freedom" meant that women as well as adult males should have the vote.

Most of these definitions of freedom and democracy also held true in the southern states (although there was even less talk there of women's right to vote). But most southern whites added another right to their list of democratic freedoms—the right to own black slaves, and to buy and sell them as they saw fit, and to take their human property wherever they wanted.

In 1860 almost all northern whites agreed with southern whites that blacks were a degraded, alien race. Most northern states barred blacks from voting and severely restricted their rights in other ways. But almost all northerners agreed on one idea—that free labor should not have to compete with slave labor, and that the American West should not be opened to masters with their gangs of enslaved black laborers, robbing free white families of their chance for self-advancement.

A few northerners (and a handful of southern-born men and women) went further, arguing that slavery was a blight on the nation's democratic birthright, indeed a sin in the eyes of God, and must be abolished at once. The antislavery movement had roots in America's eighteenth-century revolution, and enlightened southerners like Thomas Jefferson had agreed that slavery should be ended if possible. But nowhere in the United States did voluntary abolition occur where slavery represented an important economic interest.

By the early 1830s, a second stage of the abolitionist movement emerged, first in Great Britain. By then, slavery within the British Isles had become an exotic novelty, but the situation in Britain's West Indian colonies was another matter. There, huge sugar plantations were owned by a tiny minority of Britain's wealthiest men, most of whom lived in luxury back home. Their influence in British politics seemed vastly excessive, and they were becoming intensely unpopular. The resurgent abolitionist movement was aimed at slaveowners such as these and it enlisted widespread popular support. Abolition, in fact, was part of the broader cluster of reform movements whose cumulative effect was to force enactment of the Great Reform Act of 1832.

The overriding issue connected with British abolition, however, was that of compensating the slaveowners. Increasingly, hardworking British workers questioned why their tax burden should be increased to pay off plantation owners who had already grown so rich from the slaves they owned. And rumors even began to spread that the slaves themselves might not have it so bad—their masters, after all, fed and clothed them (which no British factory owner did), and perhaps their work day was neither as long nor as arduous as that of working men and women at home. Just as in modern America there is talk of "welfare queens" taking it easy while honest taxpayers foot the bill, so in Britain in the early 1830s racial prejudice and bitter resentment undercut appeals to social justice and divided middle- from working-class reformers. As the first selection in this chapter explains, this issue became one more dividing line between Great Britain's social classes. The compensated abolition of slavery, which the newly reformed House of Commons finally enacted in 1834, did not evoke universal approval among ordinary Britons.

Nor did British abolition kindle enthusiasm for a comparable emancipation of slaves in the United States. Southerners generally reacted with horror, convinced that by whipping up talk of emancipation the British were pursuing an anti-American strategy, aimed at dividing Americans, cheapening the price of raw cotton (for which British textile mills had an endless appetite), and threatening race war in the United States. White southerners by the 1830s were convincing themselves, and telling the world, that slavery was not just a "necessary evil," but a "positive good." It ensured every white southerner a chance to get rich, and it was even (supposedly) good for Africans, who enjoyed the paternalistic care of kindly white masters and were being rescued from the pagan savagery of their native land. Northern whites may not have swallowed such propaganda (although some did), but most feared that abolishing slavery would bring a flood of newly freed blacks into their own communities, competing with white labor and driving down wages. Abolitionism in the northern United States would for these reasons remain the cause of a small, though militant, minority of idealists until well after the Civil War began.

Why did it take a civil war, which cost the lives of more than 600,000 combatants and must have cost billions of dollars in property losses, to destroy American slavery? One answer is suggested by the second selection in this chapter, a comparison of unfree labor in the United States and Russia. Russian serfdom was inefficient and, by 1861, clearly counter to the czarist government's interest in strengthening and modernizing the Russian state. Nor did the beneficiaries of serfdom, the landowning nobility, have any institutional means for registering their opposition to what the czar decided to do. American slavery, by contrast, was from an economic point of view relatively efficient, and it certainly represented a way for southern white families to prosper. And of course, southern whites had powerful means of defending their interests, including their political solidarity within the structure of nineteenth-century American democracy. The tragedy of the Civil War was that it represented the democratic will of both embattled sections of the nation, with the interests of the enslaved black minority hanging in the balance.

As early as 1820 the clashing interests of the American North and South had been apparent, when the western territory known as Missouri applied for admission to the Union as a slave state. Thomas Jefferson, old and largely retired from politics (and still a slave owner who had never freed any of his large force of bondspeople), heard amid the sectional conflict over Missouri "the death knell of the Union." After 1820, despite a political compromise that patched things up, the sectional cleavage only deepened, and the democratic political parties that soon emerged did their best to avoid any issue involving slavery.

When war finally erupted, after the northern candidate Abraham Lincoln was elected president in 1860 despite virtually unanimous southern opposition, the basic issues of the conflict were states' rights and whether the federal government could restrict the expansion of slavery into the American West. Lincoln and his new Republican Party firmly opposed slavery's further expansion, though they promised not to interfere with it in the states where bondage already existed. Most slaveholding states seceded and fought for independence because they did not trust such pledges, and because southerners believed that they must expand slavery's territorial reach if their section and its "peculiar institution" were to survive over the long run. Abolitionist sentiment existed in the North, of course—and nowhere did it burn more strongly than among northern free blacks—but it did not dominate northern opinion. The Democratic Party, appealing to northern white racism, adamantly opposed emancipation. Lincoln was willing to leave slavery untouched if doing so would convince the South to lay down its arms and rejoin the Union.

The last three selections in this chapter all address the question of how and why emancipation finally became a northern war aim, and with what ultimately global significance the war ended slavery. By late 1862, the North was beginning to feel frustrated and war-weary. The South had raised large, well-armed armies and possessed several superb military commanders, who far outshone the bumbling generals that the North had so far produced. Northern losses were mounting, and the northern public was grumbling; some Democrats were willing to let the South go its way if only the bloodshed would stop. This was exactly what Confederate leaders hoped would happen.

Lincoln, many Republicans, and a growing section of the northern public saw another way to prevail: to turn the war into a revolutionary war against slavery. This might well forestall European (and especially British) intervention on the Confederacy's side, and it would open the way to bringing black men into the Union army to fight for the liberty of their enslaved kin in the South, while at the same time threatening southern slave owners with the heightened resistance of their own bondspeople. By mid-1862, Lincoln had decided to use this strategy, holding back only because he did not want to appear to be acting in desperation. The bloody yet inconclusive Battle of Antietam, in September 1862, gave him the occasion he needed to announce his intention publicly. If the South did not end the rebellion by New Year's Day 1863, he would declare all the slaves in the rebel states forever free. This was a wartime measure, and for political reasons Lincoln did not promise to emancipate slaves in the border states that had remained loyal to the Union, or even in southern districts that Union armies already occupied. In those places, he was hoping to negotiate a compensated end to slavery, perhaps similar to what the czar of Russia had already carried out. The Confederacy, of course, ignored Lincoln's deadline, and on January 1, 1863, the president issued the Emancipation Proclamation, abolishing slavery in all states currently in rebellion against the United States. A Union victory was required to ensure slavery's downfall, and only after military victory had been won (and Lincoln had been assassinated) was the Thirteenth Amendment to the Constitution adopted, banning "slavery or involuntarily servitude" forever in the United States.

The United States was not the last Western nation to abolish slavery. The institution lingered in Cuba (then a Spanish colony) until 1886 and in Brazil until 1888. In both countries abolition was effected without bloodshed, although there was a long tradition of slave rebellion in Brazil and an ever-present threat of violence.

The final selection in this chapter, by a distinguished American economic historian, assesses the significance of slavery's abolition in global terms.

British Abolitionists Attack Slavery

Seymour Drescher

The enslavement of Africans was a fact of life in eighteenth-century Europe and in Europe's American colonies. Until the middle of the century practically no white voices questioned the institution, let alone demanded its abolition. Enormous fortunes were generated by the sugar plantations that a relatively few Europeans owned in the West Indian and Brazilian colonies, as well as by the rice plantations of Britain's overseas provinces of South Carolina and Georgia, and more modest success came to the planters of the Chesapeake region who raised tobacco for European markets.

The first significant Western critics of slavery were religious leaders in Britain and North America during the mid–eighteenth century. These men represented the Protestant religious resurgence known as the First Great Awakening, out of which such modern denominations as the Methodists and Baptists were born. Although they did not call for slavery's abolition, these reformers did recognize the slaves' humanity, tried to convert them to Christianity, and criticized masters for abusing their human character. By the time of the American Revolution, many Baptist and Methodist preachers were denouncing slavery and slave owners, and an abolitionist movement was rising in Britain as well. After the American Revolution, all states north of Delaware passed laws abolishing slavery, either immediately or over a span of years, and some American slave owners (like Thomas Jefferson) deplored the institution as morally embarrassing, even if they could not bring themselves to emancipate their own bondspeople.

The first large-scale antislavery movement began in Great Britain in the 1790s. It was driven partly by the religious conviction that it was wrong for one human being to hold another in bondage, partly because antislavery fit the wider context of political and social reform that was rampant in Britain at the end of the eighteenth century, and partly because the extremely wealthy and powerful "West India interest"—the plantation owners and merchants who had grown rich from the sugar trade—were perceived as corrupt abusers of their political clout in Parliament. During lulls in the Napoleonic wars, antislavery agitation kept surfacing in Britain, and in 1807 the movement became sufficiently influential to persuade Parliament to ban the transatlantic slave trade, a ban that the Royal Navy was empowered to enforce. (In 1808, the U.S. Congress took the parallel step of outlawing the importing of slaves from overseas.) These measures significantly reduced, if not totally eliminated, the infamous traffic of slaves over the dreaded "Middle Passage" from Africa to the New World. But of course slavery remained legal in both the American South and the British West Indies. Only in the French sugar colony of Saint Domingue (today, Haiti) was slavery actually abolished, and that because of a massive, bloody, and ultimately successful slave uprising that began in 1792.

Actually abolishing slavery proved easier in Great Britain during the first three decades of the nineteenth century than in the United States. The main reason was that the West India interest was a small, isolated, and unpopular minority in Great Britain itself, whereas in the American South slave ownership was widespread among whites, even those of relatively modest wealth. In this age of rising democracy, southern whites defended their right to own human property as their privilege as free men. Overt racism—the idea that liberty was the only appropriate status for whites and bondage for blacks—became an important part of the justification for slavery. American slavery was becoming entrenched by its very profitability and expansive energy, just as the suppression of the Atlantic slave trade sent the British West Indian sugar plantation economy into a deep tailspin.

In this selection, American historian Seymour Drescher analyzes the early-nineteenth-century British antislavery movement. Drescher examines the assertions that the British antislavery movement was propelled by industrial capitalists' desire to overthrow the corrupt political power of the West India interest and to supplant slavery with a labor system in which supply and demand kept wages as low as possible. While acknowledging that some British capitalists indeed were antislavery for these reasons, Drescher contends that abolitionism attracted increasing support in Great Britain because it was moralistic and religious, and because it fit closely with the ambitions of a growing segment of the public to root out all manifestations of corruption from British life. Abolitionism, in other words, was part of the same reform impulse that in 1831–1832 forced Parliament to reform its worst abuses and broaden suffrage to include many more respectable middle-class adult males. It is no accident that the final abolition of slavery throughout the British Empire was one of the first enactments made by the reformed Parliament in 1834.

Abolition of the ancient institution of slavery was one of the nineteenth century's most significant achievements. The process was not easy, for many entrenched interests, fears, and habits of thought supported the status quo. Working-class people were especially ambivalent toward slavery: They could be stirred by the claim that exploited workers and enslaved plantation hands were equally the victims of injustice, but they could also be frightened that freed slaves, if added to the labor market, would depress their own low wages. Similar difficulties faced the American abolitionist movement, which—partly inspired by the British example—grew more vocal and uncompromising in the 1830s. In the United States, where human bondage was profitable, white racism was rampant, and southern whites were convinced that their right to enslave blacks was the key to their upward mobility, it would take a civil war to destroy slavery.

From the very outset, abolition was a double-edged sword confronting the authorities of the metropolis. On the one hand its petitions affirmed [mother-countries, such as Britain and France]. . . . British civil liberty and the Constitution, Christianity, European mores and customs, and more occasionally, the market economy and free labour. There is no reason to doubt that on this general level the subscribers 'endorsed' their society. On the other hand abolitionism demonstrably heightened the sense of national shortcomings, and the possibility of actively changing those defects. . . .

The relationship of abolitionism to politico-economic cycles in Britain seems to sustain the hypothesis that mass abolitionism was activated in periods of relative prosperity and declined or was even suspended at moments of deepest economic or political crisis. The second abolitionist wave of 1791–2 was terminated by the counter-mobilization against radical reform and France. The more limited abolitionist mobilization of 1806 again occurred early in a new cycle of radicalism which lasted until after the passage of the abolition of the slave trade in 1807. The fourth abolitionist mobilization in 1814 came in the brief interlude of British prosperity between the crumbling of the Continental system and the onset of the post-war cycle of depression, mass discontent and governmental repression. There was as little appeal to popular abolitionism in the years from the Hampden clubs to Peterloo as there had been in the anti-Jacobin crusade of the later 1790s. For four decades after 1788 mass abolitionism was not quite the stalking horse of revolution envisioned by conservatives. It was, however, the crocus of reform movements. Its periodicity therefore indicates that abolitionism was a harbinger or catalyst of other popular mobilizations, rather than a deflector of social conflict.

With the final two campaigns of 1830–1 and 1832–3 there was a shift in the relationship between abolitionist mobilization and the social reform cycle. While abolitionism appeared to be stronger than ever in its climactic moments of maximum mobilization, it was bidding for support within increasingly polarized as well as politicized constituencies. Emancipation in 1833, unlike abolition of the slave trade in 1806–7, came only *after* a restructuring of the distribution of metropolitan religious and political privilege. In the political arena, repeal of the Test and Corporation Acts, Catholic Emancipation and Parliamentary reform all preceded slave emancipation. The abolitionist petition campaign of 1830–1 was itself displaced by the political reform crisis of 1831. The mass petitions of 1830–1 and 1832–3 did not occur during the worst points in British economic cycles, but it would be difficult to describe them as coinciding with moments of confident prosperity such as 1787–8, 1791–2, or 1814.

On the contrary, the campaign of 1830–1 triggered a fundamental ideological challenge to abolitionism's social justice credentials in its very core. The mass factory movement of Yorkshire arose directly out of a sharp division over factory reform among abolitionists. The final petition campaign and, even more clearly, the passage of the Act of 1833 intensified this ideological challenge. Abolitionism retained its cross-class and cross-denominational constituency through emancipation, but under increasing cross-pressures from competing social mobilizations. In other words the heightened multiclass mobilization of antislavery proceeded coincidentally with an intensified class mobilization.

One may illustrate this point by considering the relationship between political reform, slave emancipation, and factory child labour at the end of the age of abolition. The struggle for Parliamentary reform between 1830 and 1832 had mobilized large numbers of the working class and left many with an even sharper sense of exclusion from the political process. At the same time, as the class lines sharpened after 1830, the factory operatives found allies among strong abolitionists willing to transfer the ideology of antislavery from the abolitionist to the factory movement. If old radical campaigners who attempted to force working-class grievances into abolitionist rallies were ruled out of order, abolitionist spokesmen in Yorkshire were attracted, for the first time, into a popular movement against factory child labour. The interweaving of the rhetoric of the two campaigns has been detailed elsewhere. The important point is that antislavery

The abolition of slavery in the British Empire in 1834 served as an inspiration to American abolitionists.

was being used as the ideological point of departure for a sustained demand of factory workers in the old abolitionist heartland.

The burgeoning working-class press and leadership of the early 1830s was also more divided in its approach to antislavery than the older radical press. Before the end of the Napoleonic wars William Cobbett [a Radical spokesman] stood virtually alone in his denunciation of the 'negrophile' hypocrisy of British abolitionism. By 1830 London working-class radicals, distant from both the deep abolitionist traditions of the industrial North and the social realignment of the Factory Movement, tended to treat abolitionism in the old Cobbett style, as a diversion from the real miseries of white slaves at home in favour of remote and even comfortable colonial slaves abroad.

In the North [of England], however, antislavery did not lose its popular base. William Cobbett himself had to cross over into abolitionism as the campaign for emancipation entered its final phase. Cobbett, who for 30 polemical years had opposed every abolitionist initiative, finally pledged himself to immediate emancipation when he ran for Manchester's new seat in Parliament in 1832. He did so only in explicit deference to his working- and middle-class constituents, refusing to withdraw from his assessment of the comparative comfort of black slaves and British workers. He still only wished to God that 'all working people were as well fed, as lightly worked and . . . as civilly treated as the negro slaves. But it is the general wish of the people in these great towns of the north that the slaves should be totally emancipated; and I am for no half emancipation.' Cobbett concluded his pledge with a touch of a Freudian slip: 'if any one will bring forward a motion for the total and complete abolition of the slaves at once, I would be for that measure'. . . .

The electoral, petition and ideological evidence all indicate that the worker component of abolitionism held fast in its old industrial heartland. But it was clearly operating under a new set of pressures. One bit of evidence of both the new social context and its impact on abolitionism may be found in the open effort by the antislavery movement to adjust its propaganda to growing working-class interest in factory reform. The most widely distributed antislavery tract of the final campaign of 1833 was Henry Whitely's *Three Months in Jamaica, in 1832*. No less than 200,000 copies were distributed in two weeks. Extensive excerpts were published in newspapers and read aloud at public meetings. . . . Most significantly, *Three Months in Jamaica* ended with a joint plea for slave emancipation and factory reform.

For the antislavery movement this represented a striking change of policy. For 50 years abolitionist leaders had carefully preserved their autonomy from political parties and other social movements. As the most consensual cross-class and cross-denominational movement in England, and as the most successful from the late 1780s to the mid-1820s, this strategy made good political sense. By 1832, however, the terms of the 'movement' trade were clearly shifting. Some incorporation and recognition of the planter-factory analogy was becoming necessary to avert a major loss of abolition's social base. It was becoming as difficult for the movement to tack between the polarized currents of class as of religious and political conflict.

How is one to measure the impact of the contemporary denunciations of abolitionism as a class-based political displacement (now reconceptualized by historians as a psychological displacement of reforming energies)? At the level of popular mobilization neither the calls for rejection of the movement by most of the radical working-class press of London nor the more sympathetic perspective of Robert Owen in *The Crisis* appear to have played an important role in the national campaigns of 1832–3. . . .

There was, of course, a more subtle tactic available to antiabolitionists than outright repudiation. In towns with large working-class populations those hostile to the 'diversionary' influence of emancipation petitions were free to move amendments at popular antislavery meetings, demanding equal action on behalf of wage slaves or of factory children. . . .

But the fact that [the one known] 'linked' petition had no recorded imitators among the more than 5000 antislavery petitions presented in [1833] indicates this novel formulation of antiabolitionism was exceptional.

The stress of the factory movement was only one source of pressure. The final emancipation formula worked out by the government was a greater tax on abolitionist unity than the factory movement. Instead of 'immediate' emancipation, the country was confronted with a six-year intermediary stage and huge liquidation costs. The petitioners had not been led to expect either. If the abolitionist élite was most disturbed by the length of apprenticeship, the radical press was clearly more outraged by the size of the bill. Denunciations of the antislavery 'humbug', which had been muted during the height of the mass petition campaign, were now intensified by the 'swindle' of 'English tax-ridden slaves'. Cobbett, true to his pledge, had supported emancipation solely on the grounds of the wishes of his Oldham supporters, maintaining all the while that the slaves were better fed than his constituents. With the introduction of compensation he could return to his more comfortable role of abolition baiting: 'When the 187,000 females were signing their pretty names, they little thought that they were petitioning to have the bread taken from the mouths of their children!'

There was clearly a crisis of confidence, even in antislavery's Northern heartland. Since compensation alone assured passage of the Bill through the House of Lords, the Parliamentary abolitionists made no attempt to launch community-wide protests against the monetary terms of the Act. The *Voice of the West Riding* [a radical paper in Yorkshire] now taunted that an anticompensation petition meeting was held at a 'hole-and-corner' Wesleyan chapel for fear of unleashing the full backlash of public indignation against the terms assented to by the Parliamentary abolitionists. A special canvass was necessary among the Methodist poor to keep them from deserting the abolitionist ranks. . . .

Popular anger against compensation to planters sometimes spilled over into anger against blacks. London workers, who had fed for 30 years on Cobbett's images of blacks lolling in luxury, did not always draw a sharp line between the lazy white planter and the lazy black slave who worked 'only 55 hours and had everything provided for his comfort (hear, hear . . .)' while 'the mechanic of England procured a bare subsistence by 84 hours hard work'. Such words did not go unchallenged, but they lingered ominously. Lacking a means of measuring the relative influence of radical working-class editors it has been assumed only that they represented a substantial proportion of politicized workers in the early 1830s. At the very minimum one can conclude that class tensions were far more salient in the final preemancipation campaign than they had ever been before.

To say that abolitionism reflected class tensions in Britain during the early 1830s is not to say that it succumbed to them. Those with a metropolitan socialist perspective could be quite sympathetic to antislavery. . . .

Popular antislavery survived a withering drumfire even from radical working-class spokesmen until the end of apprenticeship. At the great Birmingham Chartist rally of 1838, launching the first national petition, the resolution's mover was the working man, Henry Sansum. Sansum began his speech by adverting, amidst cheers, that he had attended Birmingham town hall to 'celebrate the emancipation of the blacks in Jamaica' and now he was joining 'to work out the emancipation of the whites at home'. Two weeks later a correspondent from Birmingham also sought out the same common ground for women. This correspondent ignored Cobbett's taunt that 187,000 ladies of England had petitioned for black freedom in exchange for their children's food. Calling for a petition of 50,000 in favour of universal suffrage, she evoked not the cost of female abolitionism but its potency. The agency of women had 'redeemed the slavery of the negroes . . . and it shall now secure the most glorious and perfect of victories'.

Abolitionism, far from deflecting attention away from metropolitan grievances, delivered a message of long-term popular power. This was not merely a case of what Brian Harrison has called the spur of 'reciprocal rebuke', with one reform constituency storming into action against the misplaced efforts of another. Whatever room or necessity there was at the top of the abolitionist heap for telescopic vision, those who spoke at Birmingham to launch the great Chartist crusade considered it not only reasonable but natural for someone to march from a slave emancipation rally one day to a universal suffrage rally the next. Despite Cobbett's decades of denunciation of abolition as a humbug, despite years of infuriating comparisons of the hours of British workers and Caribbean blacks, despite cries of fraud against the staggering cost of compensation and the postponed liberation of apprenticeship, the pages of the Northern Star eloquently reiterated the ability of its audience to distinguish between means and ends.

Russian Serfdom and American Slavery Compared

Peter Kolchin

Informed comparative studies of similar institutions in different societies are fairly rare in modern historical scholarship, mainly because such studies demand that a writer have a command of complex issues that cross the barriers of academic specialization as well as the language skills to deal with a wide range of specialized source material.

Peter Kolchin is an American historian specializing in slavery and antebellum American society, but he has also mastered the intricacies of the history of serfdom in Russia. As a result, he has been able to produce a much-acclaimed study comparing "unfree labor" in both countries, excerpted here.

As Kolchin's account reveals, Russia and the United States were both similar and very different in dealing with their institutions of unfree labor. Before 1861, the majority of Russia's huge peasant population were serfs, legally bound to the soil and compelled to work for their masters—even in some cases liable to being sold to another master. Legally and practically, their position was not very different from that of American slaves. But there was no racial basis to Russian serfdom, and economically it was a very inefficient institution. Most educated Russians knew that serfdom must be abolished before their country could be modernized in other respects; the problem was how to accomplish abolition without damaging the interests of Russia's large landowning class. In the end, serfdom was ended by a decree from Czar Alexander II in 1861.

Such a peaceful outcome was impossible to achieve in the United States. Slavery was profitable, southern whites defended it as part of their God-given liberty, and no one in the free-labor North was willing to compensate southern slave owners for the immense capital losses that abolition would entail. In the end, there was no other way to sweep slavery out of American life than to fight a civil war that cost six hundred thousand lives and destroyed property on a scale even more vast than the cost of compensated emancipation.

A merican slavery and Russian serfdom served similar socioeconomic functions. Emerging under conditions of labor scarcity on the periphery of a modernizing Europe, they constituted productive systems designed to support landholding elites. As such they shared ambiguous economic characteristics that have spawned considerable historical confusion.

On the one hand, both had strong commercial components. From the beginning American—indeed all New World—slaveholders formed a preeminently market-oriented class, living off the sale of goods produced by their chattel. Although the commercial orientation of most Russian serfowners was less pronounced and many small landowners lived in semi-impoverished autarchy, as a system serfdom too was predicated on the masters' appropriation and sale of goods produced by their bondsmen. Except on the smallest holdings, barshchina, which remained the dominant form of labor exploitation, implied seigneurial production for market. In the broadest sense both slavery and serfdom were labor systems that served to maximize the master class's access to market.

At the same time, slavery and serfdom were fundamentally noncapitalist productive systems, increasingly antagonistic to the emerging bourgeois world order, because they lacked capitalism's basic ingredient: a market for labor-power (that is, labor hire). The two systems of forced labor were thus marked by an essential contradiction between the commercial orientation of the masters with respect to the *distribution* of their product and the noncapitalist nature of its *production*. This contradiction produced in both slavery and serfdom an incongruous mixture of characteristics, some of which engendered a distinctly capitalist tone; certainly, to take one example, slaveowners and serfowners were intensely interested in the price their crops would bring. Overall, however, the mode of production was more influential than that of exchange in shaping the nature of society in Russia and the United States South. The master-bondsman relationship was fundamentally different from that between employer and employee; so too was the social outlook of the master at odds with that of the bourgeois. In both countries bondage fostered distinctive societies that were increasingly out of step with the dominant course of the Western world. . . .

There were thus major differences between American slavery and Russian serfdom, differences that were based on specific demographic, socioeconomic, political, and cultural attributes of the two societies. (These differences were not, it should be clear by now, primarily based on the systemic distinction between slavery and serfdom, because in most respects Russian serfdom must be seen as a particular variety of slavery rather than a fundamentally distinct labor system.) Southern slaveowners were able to develop a far more cohesive civilization of their own than were Russian pomeshchiki [noble landlords who owned serfs]. The rural South constituted a slaveholder's world in a way that rural Russia was not a serfholder's world; indeed, the Russian countryside belonged largely to the peasantry. Although slaves had their own lives, which did not entirely conform to the ideal prescribed for them by their masters, they were rarely able to develop the kind of economic, social, and even political autonomy enjoyed by most serfs.

An integral relation existed between the character of the bondsmen's lives and that of the masters'. The relative lack of communal autonomy among American slaves was in part a product of the slaveowners' cultural dominance: resident owners who took an active interest in running their estates and who maintained political and cultural hegemony within southern society impinged pervasively on the lives of their slaves and acted both consciously and unconsciously to undermine their communal independence. In Russia, not only did the absentee orientation and weak local ties of the nobility enable serfs to exercise much greater control over their lives than was enjoyed by the slaves; that autonomy in turn further undercut the nobility's interest in becoming a rural aristocracy. Just as Jamaican slaveowners felt uncomfortable among their slaves, who represented a culturally alien group that vastly outnumbered them, so too did Russian pomeshchiki; in very much the same way, they were outsiders in their own villages. There was thus an inverse relation between the dominance of the masters' culture and the autonomy of the bondsmen's. . . .

Ultimately, therefore, despite many similar features of Russian serfdom and southern slavery, there was a contrast in their viability. By the middle of the nineteenth century, as southern slavery was flourishing as never before, Russian serfdom constituted a bankrupt system widely recognized as on its last legs. The vitality of antebellum slavery was evident in the dynamic growth of the southern economy, the daily behavior of resident owners, and the burgeoning efforts of southern spokesmen to defend slavery as a noble institution essential to the preservation of a virtuous and harmonious society. This growing commitment to slavery, both as a practical way of life and as an abstract system, stands in stark contrast to the withering of noble support for Russian serfdom. Most pomeshchiki never really "lived" serfdom as southern planters did slavery; it served more as an investment for them . . . than as an indispensable way of life. After the 1820s, when southerners were elaborating with increasing frequency and forcefulness their arguments in defense of the "peculiar institution," public defense of serfdom in Russia virtually disappeared. Informed noblemen realized that its demise was simply a matter of time.

So too did most serfs. Although bondsmen in both countries hated their servitude, most southern slaves saw little hope for an imminent end to slavery and continued to strive to make their lives as tolerable as possible within it (or to escape from it on an individual basis). In Russia, however, a spreading expectation of imminent emancipation fueled a growing unwillingness of serfs to tolerate continued bondage. The diminished provocation needed to ignite volneniia [freedom] was a telling sign of a breakdown in the serfs' acceptance of the social order

By midcentury, in short, Russian serfdom, unlike American slavery, was a system in internal crisis. It was not, in a literal sense, collapsing; it conceivably could have been maintained for years, perhaps even decades, but it had lost its long-term social viability. Informed noblemen, serfs, and government officials all expected its abolition. The question that remained to be determined was not whether emancipation would occur, but when and how.

A telling sign of the viability of unfree labor is provided by differing patterns of growth of the bound population. Historians of both New World slavery and Russian serfdom have recently paid considerable attention to demographic questions, and although they have not reached total agreement concerning the causes of variations in patterns of growth, they have established the existence of these variations. They are of interest to us here because of their indication of the general long-term health of unfree labor systems: a sharp decline in the proportion of bondsmen in the total population almost always signified serious problems for such a system and was followed within about a generation by its abolition.

In most New World slave societies slaves failed to reproduce themselves. . . . [But] slavery in the United States constituted a major exception to this pattern. Although in the early colonial period the number of slaves increased only because of importation from Africa, in the eighteenth century slaves experienced natural population growth, with annual births continually exceeding deaths. There was some variation in the timing of this transition to natural population growth, which occurred earlier in the Chesapeake region than farther south; in all the southern colonies, however, slaves were more than reproducing themselves by the outbreak of the American Revolution, well before the end of the legal slave trade in 1808. During the half-century after that, the number of American slaves more than tripled, from 1,119,354 in 1810 to 3,963,760 in 1860; with high birth rates (in excess of 50 per 1,000) and relatively low death rates (about 30 per 1,000), the black population—most of which was slave—grew naturally at an annual rate of more than 2 percent.

Several specific factors, whose relative importance is still disputed by scholars, contributed to the unique natural population growth of American slaves. . . . On a more general level, however, it is hard to avoid the conclusion that the relatively good material conditions under which most American slaves lived were central to their rapid population growth. The strength of their family life made possible a high birth rate, and it is surely no accident that the transition to natural population growth in the southern colonies coincided with the emergence of Afro-American families among second-generation slaves. An abundance of food and the determination of resident owners to look after the welfare of their "people" was equally important in promoting the slaves' health and longevity. (In the Caribbean, by contrast, life was cheap and slaves were driven mercilessly, especially during boom times on the sugar islands. In Jamaica, pregnant women typically labored in the field even in their ninth month, a practice that both reduced the number of live births and increased the female mortality rate.) On the whole, slaves were simply healthier in the American South than elsewhere in the New World. . . .

The growth pattern of the Russian serf population fell between the two extremes shown by American and Caribbean slaves. Births generally exceeded deaths, although by substantially smaller margins than among American slaves, and the number of serfs grew rapidly—primarily from natural increase but also from enserfment of state peasants and territorial expansion—in the eighteenth and early nineteenth centuries. The failure of the bound population to grow during the last years of serfdom, however, suggested a system unlikely to endure much longer.

The population of Russia, which was about 90 percent peasant, grew at a moderately rapid pace throughout the eighteenth and first half of the nineteenth century. . . . For most of the serfdom era serfs seem to have reproduced themselves at a rate at least as high as the population at large. With a high death rate which . . . was thus on the same order as that among Caribbean slaves and an even higher birth rate . . . , the serf population grew rapidly in the eighteenth century. Swelled by the continuing enserfment of state peasants, the number of serfs increased as a proportion of both peasants and the total population.

This situation changed in the nineteenth century: after peaking in 1795, the proportion of serfs declined steadily during the last half-century of serfdom; by 1858 serfs constituted only 39.2 percent of the population and a minority even of the peasants. . . .

A decline in the peasants' standard of living was apparently responsible for a decrease in the overall rate of population growth that was especially pronounced among serfs. . . . Evidence for an increase in mortality rates is more clear-cut: during the 1830s, 1840s, and 1850s growing population pressure combined with a series of poor harvests to create widespread hunger, malnutrition, and disease. . . . State peasants suffered too, but because serfs in general lived more precarious lives, anything that tipped the balance even a little toward insufficiency was bound to affect them more seriously. The serfs were in no sense "dying out," but their natural growth rate slowed to a crawl. . . .

Many serfs did escape from bondage. These included those drafted into military service as well as their families. . . . Also escaping serfdom were those who through self-purchase, owner manumission, government confiscation, and successful flight entered the ranks of state peasants. . . .

With the low rate of natural increase and the substantial transfer of serfs to nonserf status, the serf population could not have continued to expand during the prereform period without a steady supply of new recruits. Like Caribbean slavery after abolition of the African slave trade, Russian serfdom on the eve of emancipation was a system of labor living on borrowed time. . . .

The absence of public defense does not mean that most pomeshchiki supported abolition; almost certainly the great majority—(especially the less-educated small-scale landowners in the provinces) would have welcomed any delay in emancipation. Once the government made public its commitment to abolition in 1857, however, noblemen recognized the inevitability of change (and, equally important, were both unwilling and unable to take the kind of decisive action southern slaveholders were contemplating to prevent it). . . .

The slave South did not face an internal crisis similar to that of prereform Russia. . . . [R]ecent research . . . has cast grave doubt on the idea that slavery as a system was in serious trouble in the late-antebellum South.

In contrast to the widespread expectation of imminent emancipation in Russia, in the southern United States the 1850s was a time of general confidence among slaveholders. The southern economy, as a result of surging foreign demand for cotton, was booming, with per capita production actually increasing at a slightly faster pace than in the industrializing North. The recession that struck most of the United States in 1857 bypassed the South, where the price of cotton and other agricultural staples remained high, and planters strove to put as much land as possible under cultivation. Although the number of slaves continued to increase rapidly, demand for them grew at an even faster pace, leading to a sharp increase in slave prices and a vigorous although controversial movement to reopen the African slave trade. In short, although slavery impeded southern industrialization and mechanization, there is little evidence that as of 1860 it was producing the devastating effects on the southern economy that free-labor advocates insisted were inevitable.

If objective conditions in the slave South suggested a healthy society, the subjective attitudes of slaveowners indicated widespread satisfaction with those conditions. Of course, rising slave prices represented an indirect vote of confidence by slaveholders in the system, but more direct testimony of that confidence may be seen in the pervasive celebration of the system by leading southern spokesmen. The militant proslavery movement, with its concomitant defense of the virtues of southern civilization and assault upon the alien values of the free-labor North, expressed the basic sanguinity of white southerners in a slave system that seemed to be flourishing. Southern whites were increasingly committed to their "peculiar institution," and all that it entailed. Unlike Russia (or other New World slave societies after the abolition of the slave trade), the South in the mid–nineteenth century did not face the imminent collapse of its labor system.

The South did, however, face a very real crisis. Unlike that of Russian serfdom, it was an externally generated crisis, because the slave South was increasingly a society different from and at odds with the rest of the world, including (most importantly) the northern United States. The crisis that this conflict created was ultimately as fatal to the social order of the South as was the internally generated crisis to that of Russia.

In the seventeenth and eighteenth centuries the South was simply one of numerous unfree societies, but by the second quarter of the nineteenth century it stood more and more isolated in the Western world, a bastion of slavery and conservatism in an era that celebrated liberty, fraternity, and equality. The triumph of the Haitian revolution in 1804, the winning of independence by the Spanish mainland colonies in the early nineteenth century, the abolition of slavery in the northern United States during the half-century following the American Revolution, and the British emancipation of 1833–38 left Brazil and Cuba as the only major slave societies in the New World aside from the United States South. During the generation preceding the Civil War southern whites were increasingly conscious that they lived in a distinctive society whose most salient features were shaped by the "peculiar institution."

Distinctiveness alone need not have produced a crisis for the slave South, but the multipronged massive assault on the very fabric of southern society that this distinctiveness generated could not fail to do so. From the 1820s on, abolitionists in the North and abroad condemned southerners as moral lepers who could only redeem themselves by the immediate and complete abandonment of slavery. More influential still, especially from the 1840s, were the free-labor spokesmen who painted the South as a backward and degraded land where slavery corroded everything it touched. The vigor of the proslavery movement during these years was a sign not just of an increasing commitment to slavery but also of the degree to which southerners felt themselves under attack. A siege mentality pervaded the late antebellum South.

This mentality was by no means paranoid, because the South *was* under attack. History itself seemed on the side of the antislavery advocates, for the free-labor North was clearly pulling apart from and ahead of the slave South. Although the southern economy was expanding rapidly, it was not going through the kind of basic structural transformation that was occurring in the North . . . ; as a result the South increasingly lagged behind the North not just in industrialization and urbanization but in many other indices of modernization, from transportation to mechanization, literacy, scientific endeavor, and education. Because relatively few immigrants wanted to settle where slavery prevailed, the southern population grew much more slowly than that of the North. . . . Southerners had varying explanations for their section's backwardness: some turned it into a virtue, insisting that the South lacked the crude mercenary traits of the Yankees, others blamed the North for stealing the fruits of southern labor, and a few hardy souls . . . saw slavery as the culprit. They were, however, acutely aware of the problem.

The political assault on the South was most alarming of all. From 1789 to 1860 southerners dominated the federal government. Eight of the fifteen presidents who served during these years were southern slaveholders, and of the remaining seven, three were "doughfaces," northern men with southern principles. . . . Southern dominance of the executive branch of the government translated into southern ascendancy in the federal judiciary as well. . . . Southern interests were secure in the Senate too, because until 1850 half or more of the states (and hence of the senators) were southern, and even after 1850 southerners and doughfaces together formed a majority. Only in the House of Representatives, where the increasing northern majority of the population produced a corresponding northern majority of congressmen, were southerners not in command, and even there southern fears were assuaged until the mid-1840s by the gentlemen's agreement among Democrats and Whigs that agitation of the slavery issue was off limits; from 1836 to 1844, under the "gag rule," the House refused even to receive antislavery petitions. In short, southerners had come to expect the federal government to protect their interests—the most basic of which was slavery—from any and all attack; as long as it did so, it was performing an invaluable function and deserved full and enthusiastic support.

That situation began to change dramatically during the 1840s and 1850s, when the prospect loomed that the federal government might soon challenge rather than safeguard southern interests. Whereas the abolitionists of the 1830s had seemed dangerous fanatics to most northerners as well as southerners, from the mid-1840s an increasingly vociferous free soil movement, grounded on the free-labor argument that slavery was a backward and inefficient system of labor, threatened to bar slavery's expansion into new western territories and thus consign it to gradual but ultimate extinction. The gentlemen's agreement to refrain from agitating the divisive issue of slavery broke down under this pressure, and by the mid-1850s, with the emergence in the North of the antislavery Republican party, national politics was hopelessly divided along sectional lines. Not only did the South face a new assault from without, but the changing balance of population held out the terrifying likelihood that this assault would soon be victorious. To the growing free-state majority in the House of Representatives was added, after 1850, that in the Senate, as well as the prospect of a "black Republican" president. It was this last prospect that was the most frightening, and with Abraham Lincoln's election to the presidency in 1860 the South's general crisis became the nation's secession crisis.

The social isolation of the South and the economic, intellectual, and political assault upon it led, of course, to civil war and the overthrow of slavery. But it is not only because of this momentous objective change that one can legitimately assert a southern crisis, by taking advantage of historical hindsight to superimpose a theoretical construct upon the past. Abundant evidence suggests that politically aware southerners subjectively felt this crisis as well. It was not a narrowly defined economic (or cotton) crisis—the southern agricultural economy was booming in the 1850s and gave every indication that it would continue to do so in the immediately foreseeable future—but a general crisis of an entire social system. Southerners recognized that slavery—and with it their entire way of life—was under powerful attack from without; their increasingly shrill defense of it and the siege mentality that they exhibited during the last years of the old regime were indications of precisely how seriously they took this attack. As John C. Calhoun put it in 1850, the northern onslaught had already disrupted "the equilibrium between the two sections" and threatened the very existence of the Union, forcing the

South soon "to choose between abolition and secession." Eloquently he concluded, "The South asks for justice, simple justice, and less she ought not to take." It was a sentiment that southerners widely shared.

In both Russia and the United States South unfree labor systems were abolished in the 1860s. Because of differences in the internal viability of those systems, however, as well as in the nature of their crises, there were also fundamental differences in the course of abolition. Both slavery and serfdom were abolished from above, by governmental decree rather than popular upheaval. Nevertheless, the immediate consequences of the transformation were more far-reaching in the South than in Russia.

In the United States slavery died violently, as the result of northern military victory over a planter-led rebellion. Because southern slaveholders staked everything on preserving slavery—and lost—they were in a poor position to influence the terms of the new settlement. Viewed as traitors by an indignant northern population, they suffered an immediate, uncompensated emancipation of their slaves (the only large-scale confiscation of private property in American history), and they were powerless to prevent the federal government from imposing on the South a series of increasingly sweeping measures designed to bring freedom in fact as well as in name to the ex-slave population. Although historians continue to debate the degree to which "Radical" Republicans controlled the postwar Reconstruction process, in comparison with developments in most other ex-slave societies there can be little doubt about the radical nature of American Reconstruction. Through the Thirteenth, Fourteenth, and Fifteenth Amendments to the Constitution as well as the Reconstruction Acts of 1867 and innumerable measures passed by the individual southern states, a major effort was undertaken to extend to the freedmen the full rights of citizenship—redefined to include such new features as suffrage (at least for males) and education—and indeed to make the ex-slaves the backbone of political power in the South. The attempt was halting, half-hearted, and ultimately unsuccessful, but even so the overthrow of slavery constituted a revolution that brought fundamental changes to southern life. In short, the continued internal viability of southern slavery and the unique commitment to it of the master class produced an emancipation that proved unusually radical in its social consequences.

Emancipation in Russia, while momentous, represented less of a break with the past. Abolition of serfdom occurred internally (although from above) rather than by imposition of outside force; unlike southern planters, Russian pomeshchiki did not see their power and influence crushed by military defeat. Indeed, once the inevitability of change was clear to them, they played a major role in drafting and implementing the provisions of the emancipation set-tlement. As a result, emancipation, although representing a signifi-cant new departure for Russia, occurred within a broad framework of continuity. There was no radical attempt to give sudden equality to the ex-serfs or to break the social and economic hegemony of the pomeshchiki; peasants were still peasants and noblemen still noble-men in a highly stratified society. Russian emancipation, unlike southern, was undertaken with the interests of the masters at heart and involved both financial compensation to owners and measures to ensure their continued authority in the countryside. In this respect the Russian experience was typical of the emancipation process in most slave societies, from the British West Indies and Brazil to the northern United States; the unusual vehicle of southern emancipation—Civil War—brought with it unusual revolutionary potential as well.

But there was a common legacy of forced labor that Russia shared with the United States and with all other former slave societies as well. New forms of dependency that provided the ex-bondsmen with at best semifreedom became the rule. Exploitation, poverty, and bit-terness endured, even as the freedmen struggled to take advantage of changed conditions. It proved far easier to abolish slavery and serfdom than to remove their influence: the "peasant question" in Russia and racial issues in the United States persisted as grim re-minders of an earlier era.

The Missouri Compromise of 1820

Roger L. Ransom

Historian Roger L. Ransom provides an account of the background, enactment, and legacy of the 1820 Missouri Compromise. This first major
slavery-related political crisis that the United States faced in the 1800s
centered on slavery in the western territories. Congress had first dealt with
this problem shortly after the American Revolution when it passed laws
that divided up the western lands ceded by Great Britain into slave and
free regions. By prohibiting the introduction of slavery in territory north
of the Ohio River and permitting it south of the river, a numerical balance
between slave and free states was maintained as territories were settled
and became states. President Thomas Jefferson's 1803 purchase of the
Louisiana Territory from France doubled the size of the country, but left
open the question of whether slavery would be introduced into the newly
acquired area. In 1819 Congress deadlocked over whether Missouri—part
of the Louisiana Territory—should be admitted to the Union as a slave
state. The following year a compromise was narrowly approved in which
Missouri was admitted as a slave state and the rest of the Louisiana Territory was officially divided into future free and slave territory. Ransom, a
professor of history at the University of California at Riverside, argues that
because Americans were not ready to "go to the wall" on slavery, they
were willing to fashion a compromise that put to rest the issue of slavery
in the territories for the next three decades.

Excerpted from *Conflict and Compromise: The Political Economy of Slavery, Emancipation, and the American Civil War,* by Roger L. Ransom. Copyright © 1989 by Cambridge University Press. Reprinted with permission from Cambridge University Press.

The issue of slavery remained relatively quiet for the three decades following the ratification of the Constitution. The slave trade was banned in 1809 with relatively little opposition from North or South. As [Thomas] Jefferson had observed in 1776, only two states—South Carolina and Georgia—really favored a continuance of the trade at that time; in the rest of the South, a growing number of slaveholders favored putting an end to the flow of slaves from abroad. The question of allowing importation of slaves had always produced some ambivalence among slaveholders. Although imported slaves obviously represented a cheap source of labor for those wishing to purchase slaves, their presence also depressed the price of slaves. Those owning slaves realized that the value of their investment would be depressed by continuing imports. On balance, the slave interests were content to let the external slave trade disappear.

With the arrival of what promised to be a lasting peace in Europe and the settlement of our quarrel with England [following the War of 1812], the United States turned its attention with renewed vigor toward economic expansion. That meant western settlement. The years immediately following 1815 witnessed the first great land boom in the United States. Settlers pushed westward into both the Northwest Territory and the Southwest Territory. With the admission of Alabama in December 1819, nine new states had been formed and admitted into the Union. That brought the total to twenty-two states, evenly balanced between eleven slave and eleven nonslave. All this was in accordance with the guidelines of the Ordinance of 1787; each of the slave states had been south of the Ohio River, and each had been regarded as a slave territory from the outset of settlement. Thanks to the agreement of 1787, the process of settlement and organization had proceeded peacefully. That was about to change. As the Sixteenth Congress of the United States convened in the spring of 1820, the question of slavery and the western territory had suddenly been thrust to the forefront of national politics once again.

Crisis over Missouri

The immediate source of the problem was a difficulty in Congress over the request of Missouri to be admitted as a slave state. The roots of controversy went back to 1803, when President Thomas Jefferson obtained the Louisiana Purchase. At the time, it seemed a masterful stroke. For a mere $15 million, the nation's land area was almost doubled and the use of the Mississippi was secured for Americans. The issue of settling the new land (with or without slavery) was hardly on anyone's mind. Apart from New Orleans, most of the Louisiana Purchase was far beyond the limits of settlement in 1803. But as people began to think more seriously about settling in the new territory, they realized that most of that land lay north of the area defined in the

Northwest Ordinance as being free from slavery. Of the land west of the Mississippi River, only Louisiana (admitted as a state in 1812) and the Arkansas Territory were clearly marked as territories that would have slavery if the boundaries implicitly laid down by the compromise of 1787 were to be applied to the Louisiana Purchase.

The problem that arose in 1819 began in 1817 with the establishment in Missouri of a territorial government in preparation for statehood. The situation is evident in Map 1. The proposed state of Missouri lay only slightly south of Illinois; the Ohio River joins the Mississippi River in the southeastern corner of the territory. By the terms of the compromise of 1787, the new state would clearly be free territory. Slaveholders, however, were determined that Missouri would have slaves, and a substantial number of settlers pushed north into the territory bringing their slaves with them. In November 1818, the Legislative Council and the House of Representatives of Missouri petitioned Congress for statehood. Speaker of the House Henry Clay presented the memorial from the citizens of Missouri to the House on December 18, 1818. There was no question but that Missouri would eventually enter as a slave state under the arrangements existing in 1818.

Just prior to the Missouri request, Illinois and Alabama had each petitioned Congress for statehood. Although there was little controversy over the admission of these two states, Representative James Talmadge of New York created a minor crisis when he argued that the petition of Illinois to form a government should be rejected on the grounds that the proposed constitution of that state did not explicitly prohibit slavery. Talmadge's opposition did not carry the day, but his efforts signaled a warning that the case of Missouri might not be so simple.

The Talmadge Amendments

Missouri's petition for statehood represented the first attempt to allow slavery in a state that lay north of the implicit line of the Ohio River established by the Land Ordinances of 1787 and 1790. On February 13, 1819, as the House took up the bill for Missouri statehood, Talmadge renewed his efforts to exclude slavery north of the Ohio. He offered the following amendment to the bill admitting Missouri to the Union: "That the further introduction of slavery or involuntary servitude be prohibited . . . and that all children of slaves, born within the said state, after the admission thereof into the Union, shall be free, but may be held to service until the age of twenty-five years."

The House split Talmadge's amendment into two parts. The clause dealing with prohibition of slavery passed by a vote of 87 to 76; the clause for gradual emancipation passed by 82 to 78. The amended bill was then sent to the Senate. By a rather substantial margin, that body refused to accept Talmadge's clause and passed a bill admitting Missouri with no restrictions regarding slavery. Efforts to resolve differences between the bills passed by the House and the Senate failed, and the Fifteenth Congress adjourned without acting on Missouri's application for statehood. Talmadge had created a crisis in Congress that reached a critical juncture just as Congress adjourned.

The votes on the Talmadge amendments made it clear that opponents of slavery in the House of Representatives had enough votes in the House to hold up statehood for Missouri indefinitely. Encouraged by their success, antislavery forces redoubled their efforts during the Congressional recess to solidify the opposition to the admission of Missouri with slavery. Two issues were at stake here. The first was the importance of maintaining a balance between slave and nonslave states. This was largely a problem of timing and was clearly of greater concern to the South than to the North. Everyone could see that at least two more free states were going to be formed from existing territories in the Old Northwest, and there was the added possibility that Congress would act on the application of the newly formed territory of Maine [previously part of Massachusetts] for statehood. The second issue was more difficult: How could the territories of the Louisiana Purchase be kept free from slavery in the future?

The Compromise of 1820

As the Sixteenth Congress began debate on the Missouri question, it became apparent that the Senate would continue to oppose the Talmadge amendment adamantly and that the House was equally determined to force the issue of eliminating slavery in Missouri. The resolution of this stalemate is known as the Compromise of 1820. It was ultimately fashioned by tying together three related actions:

1. Admit Missouri as a slave state in accordance with the initial request for statehood.
2. Approve the application for statehood of Maine as a free state.
3. Define the territories in the Louisiana Purchase, which henceforth would be free and slave.

The first two parts of the compromise "package" were obvious enough; the applications for statehood from Maine and Missouri were combined into an omnibus bill. The third part of the bargain was the crucial element to get passage in the House. The solution, offered by Senator Jesse Thomas of Illinois, was to take the language used in the Northwest Ordinance of 1787 and apply it to the Louisiana Territory. What became known as the Thomas Proviso was attached to the bill approving statehood for Missouri and Maine:

> That, in all that territory ceded by France to the United States, under the name of Louisiana, which lies north of thirty-six degrees and thirty minutes north latitude, excepting only such part thereof as is included within the limits of the State contemplated by this act, slavery and involuntary servitude . . . shall be and is hereby forever prohibited: *Provided always,*

That any person escaping into the same, from whom labor service is law-fully claimed in any State or Territory of the United States, such fugitive may be lawfully reclaimed and conveyed to the person claiming his or her labor or service as aforesaid.

In the Senate there was little problem putting the pieces together, although the vote on the omnibus Missouri-Maine bill with the Thomas Proviso was uncomfortably close: 24 in favor and 20 opposed. In the House the task was not so easy. As [historian] Glover Moore observes, "One of the noticeable things about the passage of the Missouri Compromise was that the House never voted yea or nay on the compromise as a whole." Instead, Speaker Henry Clay masterfully guided the various parts of the package through the legislature piece by piece. The closest call came on the vote to eliminate the Talmadge clause from the Missouri bill and allow slavery in the new state, an action that passed by only 3 votes. The Thomas Proviso was then approved by an overwhelming majority, 134 to 42. The result of the compromise can be seen in Map 1, which shows the demarcation line established by the Thomas Proviso.

A Significant Achievement

Although it has received relatively little attention from historians in recent years, the Missouri Compromise was a pathbreaking achievement on the part of those who fashioned it. The narrowness with which it passed suggests a fragility that belies the robustness of the contract once it was struck. In fact, for the next three decades, the line defined in the Missouri Compromise clearly established the limits of slavery in the United States. One reason it worked so well was that it was based on the precedent established by the Northwest Ordinance in 1787. A majority of Southerners actually favored the Thomas Proviso when it came to a vote in the House. Although Northerners were more truculent in agreeing to the admission of Missouri as a slave state, it is easy to exaggerate the force of their opposition. Slavery, after all, was firmly established in Missouri by the time the issue came to a head in Congress. However distasteful opponents of slavery might find this fact, they could not reverse the pattern of settlement. Moreover, by the time the issue came to a vote, the outcome was assured. This meant that those strongly opposed could vote negatively so long as their vote did not jeopardize the agreed-upon outcome. They then overwhelmingly approved the Thomas Proviso. This was a compromise in the classic sense of the term: Each side got something and each side gave up something they deemed important. The slave interests got approval of Missouri as a slave state; opponents succeeded in permanently extending the ban on slavery in the Louisiana Territory north of the line thirty-six degrees thirty minutes.

Over the long term, the most important development of the Missouri Compromise turned out to be even more basic than the details of the bargain itself. The Missouri Compromise established the right of Congress to pass legislation allowing or prohibiting slavery in the western territories. This was not universally applauded; indeed a few people saw in the Thomas Proviso a threat to their long-term interests. Nathaniel Macon of North Carolina was one of only two southern senators to vote against the omnibus bill in the Senate. "To compromise," he wrote a friend shortly before the vote, "is to acknowledge the right of Congress to interfere and to legislate on the subject, this would be acknowledging too much." Future generations of southern representatives in Washington would tend to agree with Macon's assessment, while Northerners, many of whom resisted the compromise, gradually came to see the limitations to slavery contained in the Thomas Proviso as the cornerstone upon which a resistance to expansion of slavery could be built.

Emotions ran high during the debates over slavery in Missouri and the Louisiana Territory. Yet almost as quickly as it arose, the tension subsided. The country, as it were, heaved a collective sigh of relief and went back to work. Why was the compromise so successful? In part, because it reflected the fact that both sides could point to tangible gains from the legislation. But in a larger sense it was because, despite the rhetoric that proclaimed a willingness to fight for the principles at stake, the fact remained that most Americans were not prepared to "go

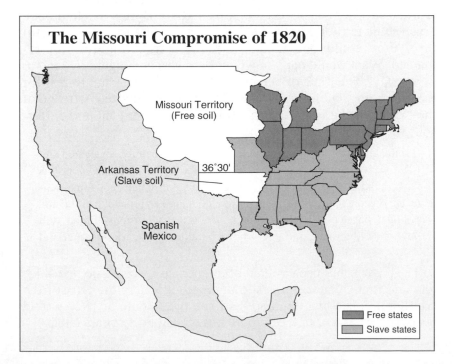

The Missouri Compromise of 1820

Missouri Territory (Free soil)

Arkansas Territory (Slave soil)   36°30'

Spanish Mexico

Free states

Slave states

to the wall" on the slavery issue in 1820. The specter of a slave system that was a genuine threat to northern interests had not yet appeared on the political scene. Slavery was a moral indignity; and some Southerners had pressed a step too far in allowing slavery to take hold in Missouri. But for most people living outside the south in 1820, slavery was a distant and relatively quiescent institution. Patience, not force, was needed to deal with the problem. The slave trade had been eliminated and a clear line of demarcation between slave and free territory had been established by the terms of the Thomas Proviso. Even if it could not be eradicated, slavery had been contained.

The political situation added to the sense of consensus rather than sectionalism. "Republicanism," the political movement launched by Thomas Jefferson with his presidential victory in 1800, was just reaching its zenith at this point. There was, for all practical purposes, only one effective political party. In the elections of 1820 the Federalists [a rival political party] captured only 7 of 42 seats in the Senate, and 27 of 183 seats in the House. The absence of party rivalries made the quest for a compromise much easier. The other side of that coin was that the crisis over slavery between 1819 and 1821 had a profound effect on the development of the two-party system that was to emerge a decade later.

Unresolved Issues

That was all in the future. For the time being, the deal that had worked in 1787 had worked again in 1820. Both sides had been given some territory; both sides had some assurances about the future. A few could look ahead to see that a troubling question remained: What would happen when there was no longer any land to give away? The issue of slavery and territories was put to rest for the time being, but for how long? The man who drafted Article 6 of the Northwest Ordinance thirty-four years earlier [Thomas Jefferson] was uneasy over the solution of 1820:

> But this momentous question, like a fire bell in the night, awakened and filled me with terror. I considered it at once as the knell of the Union. It is hushed, indeed for the moment. But this is a reprieve only, not a final sentence. A geographical line, coinciding with a marked principle, moral and political, once conceived and held up to the angry passions of men, will never be obliterated; and every new irritation will mark it deeper and deeper.

The passage has been quoted often, perhaps because no one since has said it any better. Jefferson understood where the crux of the conflict lay. The line that had resolved the dispute of 1820 would become the basis of an even more bitter fight thirty years later.

Abraham Lincoln and the Emancipation Proclamation

James M. McPherson

James M. McPherson, a Pulitzer Prize–winning Civil War historian and Princeton University professor, describes the events that led President Abraham Lincoln to issue the Emancipation Proclamation on January 1, 1863. Lincoln, who personally opposed slavery, had previously hesitated in taking such a step because of political and constitutional concerns. However, as the Civil War dragged on, abolishing slavery in the Confederacy emerged as an attractive way of furthering the Union war effort. McPherson writes that although the decision to issue the Emancipation Proclamation had limited legal impact—its declarations of freedom applied only to slaves in parts of the Confederacy not under control of the Union army—it still marked a turning point that transformed the Civil War into a war against slavery.

President Abraham Lincoln hated slavery, but before the Civil War he believed he had no constitutional power to interfere with the institution in the Southern states. Then, when war broke out, the slaves became the property of the Union's enemies, and as commander in chief of the United States armed forces and with his wartime power to take away the enemy's property, the president now had the right to free the slaves. Still, for political reasons, Lincoln hesitated. Four slave states—Kentucky, Maryland, Missouri and Delaware—had remained loyal to the Union, and Lincoln feared that hasty action against slavery might drive them into the Confederacy. Also, the president at first hoped that the war would be short and that the Confederate states could quickly be persuaded to return to the Union. Because they would never come voluntarily if the government declared an intention to abolish slavery, Lincoln was reluctant in the early months of the war to do anything that could be interpreted as unfriendly to slavery.

Even as late as August 1862, in a letter to newspaper editor Horace Greeley, who had urged Lincoln to free the slaves, the president stated, "My paramount object *is* to save the Union, and *is* not either to save or destroy slavery. . . . What I do about slavery, and the colored race, I do because I believe it helps to save the Union; and what I forbear, I forbear because I do *not* believe it would help to save the Union."

Views of Frederick Douglass

But many in the North, both white and black, thought the Union could not be saved without overthrowing slavery. One of the most articulate abolitionists was Frederick Douglass, an orator and editor who became the most prominent African-American of the Civil War period. A former slave who had escaped North, self-educated and now in a position of eminence, Douglass' words carried weight. From the beginning of the war, he wrote dozens of editorials and speeches asserting that slavery was the cause of the conflict and that victory was impossible without emancipation. After the fall of Fort Sumter, Douglass wrote in his newspaper, *Douglass' Monthly:*

> At last our proud Republic is overtaken. Our National Sin has found us out. . . . Slavery has done it all . . . We have sown the wind, only to reap the whirlwind. . . . Could we write as with lightning, and speak as with the voice of thunder, we should write and cry to the nation, REPENT, BREAK EVERY YOKE, LET THE OPPRESSED GO FREE, FOR HEREIN ALONE IS DELIVERANCE AND SAFETY! . . . Fire must be met with water, darkness with light, and war for the destruction of liberty must be met with war for the destruction of slavery. . . . This war with the slaveholders can never be brought to a desirable termination until slavery, the guilty cause of all our national troubles, has been totally and forever abolished.

One of the best arguments of Douglass and other abolitionists was that slavery was a source of strength to the Confederacy. Slaves worked in the fields and factories; slaves dug trenches and drove wagons for the Confederate army. Without their labor, the South would collapse, and the North could win the War. A proclamation of emancipation, said Douglass, would cripple the South by encouraging slaves to flee their masters and come over to the Northern side where freedom awaited them.

> The slaveholders . . . boast that the slave population is a grand element of strength, and that it enables them to send and sustain a stronger body of rebels to overthrow the Government that they could otherwise do if the whites were required to perform the labors of cultivation; and in this they are unquestionably in the right, provided the National Government refuses to turn this mighty element of strength into one of weakness. . . . Why? Oh! why, in the name of all that is national, does our Government allow its enemies this powerful advantage? . . . The very stomach of this rebellion is the negro in the condition of a Slave. Arrest that hoe in the hands of the negro, and you smite rebellion in the very seat of its life. . . . The negro is the key of the situation—the pivot upon which the whole rebellion turns. . . . Teach the rebels and traitors that the price they are to pay for the attempt to abolish this Government must be the abolition of slavery. . . . Henceforth let the war cry be down with treason, and down with slavery, the cause of treason.

As soon as Union forces occupied the border states and invaded the Confederacy, slaves from the surrounding countryside, sensing that the Northern army meant freedom, began to come into Union lines. But, as fugitives, they presented Northern generals with a problem. Should they be returned to their masters under the terms of the Fugitive Slave Law of 1850, or not? Some generals returned them, but in most cases their masters were Confederates and to return property to rebels seemed foolish. The Fugitive Slave Law could hardly be applied to slaveholders who had seceded from the United States.

Contraband of War

General Benjamin E. Butler went to the heart of the matter. Butler commanded a Union army base at Fortress Monroe, near Hampton, Virginia. In May 1861 three fugitive slaves who had escaped from a Confederate labor battalion entered the base. Butler, a former lawyer, labeled them "contraband of war" (enemy property subject to seizure) and gave them shelter and work with the Union army. By the end of July, there were almost 1,000 such "contrabands" at Fortress Monroe and many hundreds at other Union camps.

On August 6, the United States Congress passed a Confiscation Act providing for the seizure of all property, including slaves, used "in aid of the rebellion." However, the bill applied only to those slaves who had actually worked on Confederate military fortifications and naval vessels. It did not *emancipate* such slaves—it merely provided for their seizure as enemy property. Nevertheless, it was an important step: In spite of the Lincoln administration's efforts to keep slavery as an issue out of the war, the fugitive contrabands, by their own actions, were making it impossible.

Another way of dealing with the fugitives who flocked to Union lines was tried by General John C. Frémont, a former Republican presidential candidate and now commander of the Union forces in Missouri. On August 30, 1861, he issued a proclamation declaring that the slaves of every Confederate in the state were free. Black people and many white people in the North applauded, but Lincoln was afraid the proclamation would "alarm our Southern Union friends and turn them against us." So, on September 11, the president modified Frémont's order in such a way that it freed only a few slaves in Missouri.

Blacks were disappointed, and some criticized the president bitterly. But Harriet Tubman, the former slave whose secret trips into the South before the war to help other slaves escape had made her the "Moses" of her people, was hopeful that Lincoln would see the light. "God's ahead ob Massa Linkum," she said at the end of 1861, as reported by a white abolitionist in a letter to a friend that tried to capture Tubman's dialect.

> God won't let Massa Linkum beat de South till he do de right ting. Massa Linkum he great man, and Ise poor nigger; but dis nigger can tell Massa Linkum how to save de money and de young men. He do it by setting de niggers free. S'pose dar was awful' big snake down dar, on de floor. He bite you. Folks all skeered, cause you die. You send for doctor to cut de bite; but snake he rolled up dar, and while doctor dwine it, he bite you agin. De doctor cut out dat bite; but while he dwine it, de snake he spring up and bite you agin, and so he keep dwine, till you kill him. Dat's what Massa Linkum orter know.

In 1862, the government finally began to attack the "snake" of slavery. Congress passed a bill to abolish slavery in the territories and a second Confiscation Act declaring all slaves of Confederate masters "forever free" as soon as they entered Union lines. On April 16, 1862, Congress abolished slavery in the District of Columbia. The next day, a black resident of Washington wrote joyfully to a friend in Baltimore:

> This indeed has been a happy day to me sights have I witnessed that I never anticipated one of which I will relate The Chambermaid at Smith's (my former place) . . . is a slave so this morning I went there to inform her of the passage of the Bill when I entered The cook and another Slave woman who has a slave son were talking relative to the Bill expressing doubts of its passage & when I entered they perceived that something was ahead and emeadiately asked me "Whats the news?" The Districts

free says I pulling out the "National Republican" and reading its editorial when I had finished the chambermaid had left the room sobbing for joy. The slave woman clapped her hands and shouted, left the house saying "let me go and tell my husband that Jesus has done all things well" While the cook who is free retired to another room to offer thanks for the blessing sent. Should I not feel glad to see so much rejoicing around me? Were I a drinker I would get on a Jolly spree today but as a Christian I can but kneel in prayer and bless God for the privilege I've enjoyed this day. . . . Would to God that the Law applied also to Baltimore but a little patience and all will be well.

The Emancipation Proclamation

In the summer of 1862 Lincoln began to think about issuing an emancipation proclamation. Several reasons had brought him to this position. His former hope that a short and easy war would show the Confederates their mistake and persuade them to return to the Union had not been fulfilled. Things had been going badly for the Northern armies; they had suffered major defeats at the First Battle of Bull Run in July 1861, the Seven Days' Battles in June and July 1862 and the Second Battle of Bull Run in August 1862. The prospect of weakening the Confederacy and at the same time strengthening the Union by emancipating the slaves and encouraging them to come over to the Union side was thus more attractive now than at the beginning of the war.

Abraham Lincoln

The inconsistency of fighting a government based on slavery without striking against slavery was also becoming more obvious each day. The Confederacy hoped to enlist European support for its cause, and Lincoln believed that an emancipation proclamation might discourage England and France from aiding the South, by showing that the North was fighting for liberty as well as Union. Finally, more and more Northerners were becoming convinced—by the deaths of friends and relatives in the war—that slavery was vicious as well as immoral and that emancipation was the best way to win the war and secure a peace based on justice.

But Lincoln did not want to issue his proclamation in the midst of Northern defeat, when it might be interpreted as "our last *shriek* on the retreat." He waited until after the Union victory at the Battle of Antietam on September 17, 1862, and then, on September 22, he issued a preliminary Emancipation Proclamation. The final proclamation came on January 1, 1863. By virtue of his wartime power as commander in chief, the president proclaimed all slaves in the rebellious Southern states "thenceforward, and forever free."

Black People Celebrate

Black people hailed the Emancipation Proclamation with joy. All over the North they held meetings of celebration on that first day of January 1863. One such meeting took place in the Israel Bethel Church in Washington, D.C. The pastor of the church was Henry M. Turner, freeborn black who had migrated from his native South Carolina to Baltimore and finally to Washington. He became a leader in the black community and was eventually elected a bishop in the African Methodist Episcopal Church. He was still living on January 1, 1913, the 50th anniversary of the Emancipation Proclamation, and at that time he gave his recollections of the events in Washington 50 years earlier.

> Seeing such a multitude of people in and around my church, I hurriedly went up to the office of the first paper in which the proclamation of freedom could be printed, known as the "Evening Star," and squeezed myself through the dense crowd that was waiting for the paper. The first sheet run off with the proclamation in it was grabbed for by three of us, but some active young man got possession of it and fled. The next sheet was grabbed for by several, and was torn into tatters. The third sheet from the press was grabbed for by several, but I succeeded in procuring so much of it as contained the proclamation, and off I went for life and death. Down Pennsylvania Avenue I ran as for my life, and when the people saw me coming with the paper in my hand they raised a shouting cheer that was almost deafening. As many as could get around me lifted me to a great platform, and I started to read the proclamation. I had run the best end of a mile, I was out of breath, and could not read. Mr. Hinton, to whom I handed the paper, read it with great force and clearness. While he was reading every kind of demonstration and gesticulation was going on. Men squealed, women fainted, dogs barked, white and colored people shook hands, songs were sung, and by this time cannons began to fire at the navy-yard, and follow in the wake of the roar that had for some time been going on behind the White House. . . . Great processions of colored and white men marched to and fro and passed in front of the White House and congratulated President Lincoln on his proclamation. The President came to the window and made responsive bows, and thousands told him, if he would come out of that palace, they would hug him to death. . . . It was indeed a time of times, and a half time, nothing like it will ever be seen again in this life.

The proclamation actually freed no slaves: the slaves in the slave states loyal to the Union, and in the portions of the Confederacy under control of the Union army, were not included in Lincoln's proclamation. And it could obviously have no immediate effect in parts of the South still under Confederate control. This led some critics to jeer at the Emancipation Proclamation as a mere scrap of paper. But it was more than that. It was a declaration by the president of the United States that the North was no longer fighting only for Union; it was now fighting for the establishment of a new Union without slavery. The course of the war after January 1, 1863, and the final Northern victory put the proclamation in force, and on January 31, 1865, Congress passed the Thirteenth Amendment to the Constitution abolishing slavery throughout the United States. President Lincoln played a crucial role in persuading Congress to pass the Thirteenth Amendment. The amendment was ratified by the necessary three-fourths of the states 10 months later.

On February 4, 1865, blacks and whites in Boston celebrated congressional passage of the Thirteenth Amendment at a mass meeting. Several speakers entertained and inspired the crowd, and the celebration ended with the Reverend Mr. Rue, pastor of a Negro Methodist church, singing the hymn "Sound the Loud Timbrel." On the second chorus a few members of the audience seated near the platform began to sing along with Mr. Rue, and in each succeeding chorus more and more of the huge throng joined in, swelling the refrain to triumphant heights of joyfulness. A white member of the audience, William Lloyd Garrison Jr., described the meeting in a letter to his wife:

> It was a scene to be remembered—the earnestness of the singer, pouring out his heartfelt praise, the sympathy of the audience, catching the glow & the deep-toned organ blending the thousand voices in harmony. Nothing during the evening brought to my mind so clearly the magnitude of the act we celebrated, its deeply religious as well as moral significance than "Sound the loud timbrel o'er Egypt's dark sea, Jehovah has triumphed, His people are free."

The Emancipation Proclamation Is a Significant Achievement

Frederick Douglass

Abraham Lincoln issued a preliminary Emancipation Proclamation on September 22, 1862, shortly after the partial Northern success in the Battle of Antietam. The proclamation stated that on January 1, 1863, all slaves residing in every part of the South still in rebellion would be declared "then, thenceforward, and forever free." The following viewpoint expresses the elated reaction of Frederick Douglass, an escaped slave who had gained national and international fame as an abolitionist, lecturer, and writer. Douglass viewed the Civil War as a moral crusade against slavery and was an early advocate of both emancipation of the slaves and enlistment of black soldiers for the Union. In the October 1862 issue of *Douglass' Monthly*, a newspaper Douglass published and edited, he criticizes Lincoln for acting too slowly to free the slaves, but praises the proclamation and calls for renewed efforts to defeat the Confederacy.

Common sense, the necessities of the war, to say nothing of the dictation of justice and humanity have at last prevailed. We shout for joy that we live to record this righteous decree. *Abraham*

Excerpted from *The Emancipation Proclamation Is a Significant Achievement,* by Frederick Douglass, 1862.

Lincoln, President of the United States, Commander-in-Chief of the army and navy, in his own peculiar, cautious, forbearing and hesitating way, slow, but we hope sure, has, while the loyal heart was near breaking with despair, proclaimed and declared: *"That on the First of January, in the Year of Our Lord One Thousand, Eight Hundred and Sixty-three, All Persons Held as Slaves Within Any State or Any Designated Part of a State, The People Whereof Shall Then be in Rebellion Against the United States, Shall be Thenceforward and Forever Free."* "Free forever" oh! long enslaved millions, whose cries have so vexed the air and sky, suffer on a few more days in sorrow, the hour of your deliverance draws nigh! Oh! Ye millions of free and loyal men who have earnestly sought to free your bleeding country from the dreadful ravages of revolution and anarchy, lift up now your voices with joy and thanksgiving for with freedom to the slave will come peace and safety to your country. President Lincoln has embraced in this proclamation the law of Congress passed more than six months ago, prohibiting the employment of any part of the army and naval forces of the United States, to return fugitive slaves to their masters, commanded all officers of the army and navy to respect and obey its provisions. He has still further declared his intention to urge upon the Legislature of all the slave States not in rebellion the immediate or gradual abolishment of slavery. But read the proclamation for it is the most important of any to which the President of the United States has ever signed his name.

Reactions

Opinions will widely differ as to the practical effect of this measure upon the war. All that class at the North who have not lost their affection for slavery will regard the measure as the very worst that could be devised, and as likely to lead to endless mischief. All their plans for the future have been projected with a view to a reconstruction of the American Government upon the basis of compromise between slaveholding and non-slaveholding States. The thought of a country unified in sentiments, objects and ideas, has not entered into their political calculations, and hence this newly declared policy of the Government, which contemplates one glorious homogeneous people, doing away at a blow with the whole class of compromisers and corrupters, will meet their stern opposition. Will that opposition prevail? Will it lead the President to reconsider and retract? Not a word of it. Abraham Lincoln may be slow, Abraham Lincoln may desire peace even at the price of leaving our terrible national sore untouched, to fester on for generations, but Abraham Lincoln is not the man to reconsider, retract and contradict words and purposes solemnly proclaimed over his official signature.

Lincoln Will Take No Step Backward

The careful, and we think, the slothful deliberation which he has observed in reaching this obvious policy, is a guarantee against retraction. But even if the temper and spirit of the President himself were other than what they are, events greater than the President, events which have slowly wrung this proclamation from him may be relied on to carry him forward in the same direction. To look back now would only load him with heavier evils, while diminishing his ability, for overcoming those with which he now has to contend. To recall his proclamation would only increase rebel pride, rebel sense of power and would be hailed as a direct admission of weakness on the part of the Federal Government, while it would cause heaviness of heart and depression of national enthusiasm all over the loyal North and West. No, Abraham Lincoln will take no step backward. His word has gone out over the country and the world, giving joy and gladness to the friends of freedom and progress wherever those words are read, and he will stand by them, and carry them out to the letter. If he has taught us to confide in nothing else, he has taught us to confide in his word. The want of Constitutional power, the want of military power, the tendency of the measure to intensify Southern hate, and to exasperate the rebels, the tendency to drive from him all that class of Democrats at the North, whose loyalty has been conditioned on his restoring the union as it was, slavery and all, have all been considered, and he has taken his ground notwithstanding. The President doubtless saw, as we see, that it is not more absurd to talk about restoring the union, without hurting slavery, than restoring the union without hurting the rebels. As

Frederick Douglass

to exasperating the South, there can be no more in the cup than the cup will hold, and that was full already. The whole situation having been carefully scanned, before Mr. Lincoln could be made to budge an inch, he will now stand his ground. Border State influence, and the influence of half-loyal men, have been exerted and have done their worst. The end of these two influences is implied in this proclamation. Hereafter, the inspiration as well as the men and the money for carrying on the war will come from the North, and not from half-loyal border States.

The effect of this paper upon the disposition of Europe will be great and increasing. It changes the character of the war in European eyes and gives it an important principle as an object, instead of national pride and interest. It recognizes and declares the real nature of the contest, and places the North on the side of justice and civilization, and the rebels on the side of robbery and barbarism. It will disarm all purpose on the part of European Government to intervene in favor of the rebels and thus cast off at a blow one source of rebel power. All through the war thus far, the rebel ambassadors in foreign countries have been able to silence all expression of sympathy with the North as to slavery. With much more than a show of truth, they said that the Federal Government, no more than the Confederate Government, contemplated the abolition of slavery.

But will not this measure be frowned upon by our officers and men in the field? We have heard of many thousands who have resolved that they will throw up their commissions and lay down their arms, just so soon as they are required to carry on a war against slavery. Making all allowances for exaggeration there are doubtless far too many of this sort in the loyal army. Putting this kind of loyalty and patriotism to the test, will be one of the best collateral effects of the measure. Any man who leaves the field on such a ground will be an argument in favor of the proclamation, and will prove that his heart has been more with slavery than with his country. Let the army be cleansed from all such pro-slavery vermin, and its health and strength will be greatly improved. But there can be no reason to fear the loss of many officers or men by resignation or desertion. We have no doubt that the measure was brought to the attention of most of our leading Generals, and blind as some of them have seemed to be in the earlier part of the war, most of them have seen enough to convince them that there can be no end to this war that does not end slavery. At any rate, we may hope that for every pro-slavery man that shall start from the ranks of our loyal army, there will be two anti-slavery men to fill up the vacancy, and in this war one truly devoted to the cause of Emancipation is worth two of the opposite sort.

Two Necessary Conditions

Whether slavery will be abolished in the manner now proposed by President Lincoln, depends of course upon two conditions, the first specified and the second implied. The first is that the slave States shall be in rebellion on and after the first day of January 1863 and the second is we must have the ability to put down that rebellion. About the first there can be very little doubt. The South is thoroughly in earnest and confident. It has staked everything upon the rebellion. Its experience thus far in the field has rather increased its hopes of final success than diminished them. Its armies now hold us at bay at all points, and the war is confined to the border States slave and free. If Richmond were in our hands and Virginia at our mercy, the vast regions beyond would still remain to be subdued. But the rebels confront us on the

Potomac, the Ohio, and the Mississippi. Kentucky, Maryland, Missouri, and Virginia are in debate on the battlefields and their people are divided by the line which separates treason from loyalty. In short we are yet, after eighteen months of war, confined to the outer margin of the rebellion. We have scarcely more than touched the surface of the terrible evil. It has been raising large quantities of food during the past summer. While the masters have been fighting abroad, the slaves have been busy working at home to supply them with the means of continuing the struggle. They will not [back] down at the bidding of this Proclamation, but may be safely relied upon till January and long after January. A month or two will put an end to general fighting for the winter. When the leaves fall we shall hear again of bad roads, winter quarters and spring campaigns. The South which has thus far withstood our arms will not fall at once before our pens. All fears for the abolition of slavery arising from this apprehension may be dismissed. Whoever, therefore, lives to see the first day of next January, should Abraham Lincoln be then alive and President of the United States, may confidently look in the morning papers for the final proclamation, granting freedom, and freedom forever, to all slaves within the rebel States. On the next point nothing need be said. We have full power to put down the rebellion. Unless one man is more than a match for four, unless the South breeds braver and better men than the North, unless slavery is more precious than liberty, unless a just cause kindles a feebler enthusiasm than a wicked and villainous one, the men of the loyal States will put down this rebellion and slavery, and all the sooner will they put down that rebellion by coupling slavery with that object. Tenderness towards slavery has been the loyal weakness during the war. Fighting the slaveholders with one hand and holding the slaves with the other, has been fairly tried and has failed. We have now inaugurated a wiser and better policy, a policy which is better for the loyal cause than an hundred thousand armed men. The Star Spangled Banner is now the harbinger of Liberty and the millions in bondage, inured to hardships, accustomed to toil, ready to suffer, ready to fight, to dare and to die, will rally under that banner wherever they see it gloriously unfolded to the breeze. Now let the Government go forward in its mission of Liberty as the only condition of peace and union, by weeding out the army and navy of all such officers as the late Col. [Dixon] Miles, whose sympathies are now known to have been with the rebels. Let only the men who assent heartily to the wisdom and the justice of the anti-slavery policy of the Government be lifted into command; let the black man have an arm as well as a heart in this war, and the tide of battle which has thus far only waved backward and forward, will steadily set in our favor. The rebellion suppressed, slavery abolished, and America will, higher than ever, sit as a queen among the nations of the earth.

Now for the work. During the interval between now and next January, let every friend of the long enslaved bondman do his utmost in swelling the tide of anti-slavery sentiment, by writing, speaking, money and example. Let our aim be to make the North a unit in favor of the President's policy, and see to it that our voices and votes, shall forever extinguish that latent and malignant sentiment at the North, which has from the first cheered on the rebels in their atrocious crimes against the union, and has systematically sought to paralyze the national arm in striking down the slaveholding rebellion. We are ready for this service or any other, in this, we trust the last struggle with the monster slavery.

The Significance of America's Civil War and the Abolition of Slavery

Robert W. Fogel

Robert W. Fogel is director of the Center for Population Economics at the University of Chicago and the author of several influential books on American slavery. Fogel argues that a peaceful abolition of slavery in the American South was impossible at the time the Civil War began. He concludes that the Confederacy's defeat in the Civil War and the end of slavery in the United States had significant global ramifications; a victorious Confederacy would have strengthened the forces of slavery and aristocracy and demoralized antislavery and democracy reform movements worldwide.

For more than a century historians have been engaged in an intense debate about the causes of the Civil War. Although some scholars have held that slavery was *the* cause, others have developed complex analyses that draw distinctions between immediate and ultimate causes and that explore a variety of ways other than war that could have settled or at least contained the issue of slavery. They have also analyzed a wide range of economic, political, and cultural issues between the sections other than slavery that promoted antagonisms and that rival slavery (some believe they dominate it) as an explanation for the war. Among the most nagging of the moral questions to emerge from these debates is the one posed by David M. Potter, who, until his death in 1971, was one of the most respected historians of his generation.

In totaling up the balance sheet of the Civil War, Potter concluded: "Slavery was dead; secession was dead; and six hundred thousand men were dead." So one soldier died for six slaves who were freed and for ten white Southerners who were kept in the Union. In the face of so bloody a war, a "person is entitled to wonder," said Potter, "whether the Southerners could have been held and the slaves could not have been freed at a smaller per-capita cost." When he posed this problem it was still widely believed that slavery was an economically moribund system and the proposition that economic forces would eventually have solved the problem of slavery was tenable. Even so, there was a question of how soon. And if not, there was a question of when, if ever, southern slaveholders would have peacefully acceded to any scheme for emancipation, no matter how gradual, no matter how full the proffered compensation.

Prospects for Peaceful Abolition

Whatever the opportunity for a peaceful abolition of slavery along British lines before 1845, it surely was nonexistent after that date. To southern slaveholders, West Indian emancipation was a complete failure. It provided undeniable proof, if any was needed, of the malevolent designs that the abolitionists and their allies harbored for their class. They could plainly see that the economy of the West Indies was in shambles, that the personal fortunes of the West Indian planters had collapsed, and that the assurances made to these planters in 1833 to obtain their acquiescence to compensated emancipation were violated as soon as the planters were reduced to political impotency. Given such an assessment of the consequences of compensated emancipation, a peaceful end to slavery could only have been achieved if economic forces made slaves worthless or, more compelling, an absolute drain on the income of their owners.

From the mid-1840s on, however, the slave economy of the South was vigorous and growing rapidly. Whatever the pessimism of masters during the economic crises of 1826–1831 and 1840–1845, during the last half of the 1840s and most of the 1850s they foresaw a continuation of their prosperity and, save for the political threat from the North, numerous opportunities for its expansion. The main thrust

Historians speculate that nothing short of civil war could have brought about the emancipation of slaves in the cotton South.

of cliometric research[1] has demonstrated that this economic optimism was well-founded; it has also undermined the competing thesis that slavery was gradually expiring of its own internal economic contradictions. Although he presented it in a political rather than an economic context, [historian Kenneth] Stampp's rejoinder to Potter is equally germane here. A "person is also entitled to ask," he said, "how many more generations of black men should have been forced to endure life in bondage in order to avoid its costly and violent end."

After the [1860] election of Lincoln the choices open to northern foes of slavery no longer included the moderate strategy—which was to restrict and gradually undermine the slave economy as the British abolitionists had done between 1812 and 1833, and as the Brazilian abolitionists were able to do in the 1880s. Once the cotton states of the South moved on to the secessionist path, peaceful restoration of the Union was no longer possible merely by returning to the status quo of c. 1850, even if the rights of slaveholders everywhere below 36°30' and of their property rights in fugitives were embodied in new, irrevocable amendments to the Constitution, as was proposed in the Crittenden Resolutions.[2] The majority of the Senate and House members from these states rejected all such compromises. They were con-

1. applying economic and statistical methods to the study of history 2. Senator John J. Crittenden of Kentucky introduced several resolutions in December 1860 in an effort to placate southern concerns about preserving slavery and thus prevent secession.

vinced that northern hostility to slavery precluded a union that would promote the economic, political, and international objectives that had become predominant among politicians of the cotton South. As the votes for the delegates to the state convention indicated, by early 1861 majority opinion in the deep South held that a future in the Union "promised nothing but increasingly galling economic exploitation by the dominant section and the rapid reduction of the South to political impotence."

So the central moral problem of the Civil War is not the one posed by Potter but the one posed in Stampp's response to him. By early 1861 maintenance of peace required not merely northern acquiescence to the status quo of c. 1850, but acquiescence to the existence of an independent confederacy dedicated to the promotion of slavery. It follows that assessment of the dilemma posed by Stampp requires more than weighing the sin of slavery against the sin of war. It requires also a consideration of the likely chain of events that would have unfolded if the South had been unshackled from northern restraint and allowed to become a worldwide champion of slavery and of aristocratic republicanism.

What Would Have Happened?

Consideration of what might have happened if the Confederate states had been allowed to secede peacefully is an excursion into beliefs about a world that never existed. Even if these beliefs are based on patterns of behavior during the years leading up to the war, patterns of behavior that provide a reasonable basis for prediction, the best predictions are necessarily shrouded in uncertainty and open to debate. Yet there is no way of dealing with the moral issues of the Civil War that avoids these "counterfactual propositions" (as philosophers call them). Every historian who has set out to deal with the causes of the Civil War (certainly all those who have debated its necessity or avoidability) has implicitly or explicitly presumed what would have happened to slavery if some events had unfolded in a way that was different from the actual course. Indeed, much of the voluminous literature on the causes of the Civil War is nothing more or less than a marshaling of evidence on the events leading up to the Civil War that is dictated by different visions of this counterfactual world.

Peaceful secession, I believe, would not only have indefinitely delayed the freeing of U.S. slaves but would have thwarted the antislavery movement everywhere else in the world. It would also very likely have slowed down the struggle to extend suffrage and other democratic rights to the lower classes in Europe, and it might have eroded whatever rights had already been granted to them in both Europe and North America. Since the forces of reaction everywhere would have been greatly encouraged, and those of democracy and reform demoralized, it is likely that the momentum for liberal reform would have been replaced by a drive for aristocratic privilege under the flags of paternalism and the preservation of order.

Such a vision of events may seem fantastic to those accustomed to the rhetoric and conventions of modern (plebeian) democracy. We live in a world in which the underprivileged regularly contend for power: abroad, through labor and socialist parties; at home, through such influential organizations as the AFL-CIO, NOW, and the Rainbow Coalition.[3] However, during the 1850s and 1860s democracy as we now know it, and lower-class rights generally, hung in the balance throughout the Western world. In Great Britain the great majority of workers were disfranchised, trade unions were illegal, strikes were criminal acts, and quitting a job without an employer's permission was a breach of contract punishable by stiff fines and years of imprisonment. The legacy of serfdom was heavy in Portugal, Spain, Italy, eastern Prussia, Russia, Hungary, the Balkans, Turkey, and much of South America, while slavery flourished in Cuba, Brazil, Surinam, Africa, the Middle East, and numerous other places. Even in the North, strikes were proscribed, property qualifications for voting were widespread until the 1820s (and were still enforced against free blacks in New York and other states in the 1860s), and vagrancy laws were a powerful club against workers. The movement for the disfranchisement of the foreign born was partially successful in some northern states during the 1850s, and in Virginia a referendum to reinstitute a property qualification for voters was approved on the eve of the Civil War.

The fact that the liberals who dominated politics in the North and in Britain rejected slavery as a solution to the menace posed by an unconstrained lower-class "rabble" does not mean that they were oblivious to the menace. Reformers such as Lord [Thomas B.] Macaulay remained adamant in the opinion that the franchise had to be restricted to men of property and that a large police force and army were needed to keep the lower classes in check. Even such a celebrated champion of the propertyless masses as [newspaper publisher] Horace Greeley supported the use of military force to put down strikes.

Potential Power of the Confederacy

If the Confederacy had been allowed to establish itself peacefully, to work out economic and diplomatic policies, and to develop international alliances, it would have emerged as a major international power.

3. The American Federation of Labor-Congress of Industrial Organizations (AFL-CIO) is one of the nation's oldest and largest labor union organizations. The National Organization for Women (NOW), founded in 1966, is a prominent women's rights group. The "Rainbow Coalition" refers to political supporters of the 1984 and 1988 presidential bids of black civil rights leader Jesse Jackson.

Although its population was relatively small, its great wealth would have made it a force to be reckoned with. The Confederacy would probably have used its wealth and military power to establish itself as the dominant nation in Latin America, perhaps annexing Cuba and Puerto Rico, Yucatán, and Nicaragua as well as countering Britain's antislavery pressures on Brazil. Whether the Confederacy would have sought to counter British antislavery policies in Africa or to form alliances with the principal slave-trading nations of the Middle East is more uncertain, but these would have been options.

The Confederacy could have financed its expansionist, proslavery policies by exploiting the southern monopoly of cotton production. A 5¢ sales tax on cotton not only would have put most of the burden of such policies on foreign consumers, but would have yielded about $100 million annually during the 1860s—50 percent more than the entire federal budget on the eve of the Civil War. With such a revenue the Confederacy could have emerged as one of the world's strongest military powers, maintaining a standing army several times as large as the North's, rapidly developing a major navy, and conducting an aggressive foreign policy. Such revenues would also have permitted it to covertly or overtly finance aristocratic forces in Europe who were vying with democratic ones for power across the Continent.

Shrewd manipulation of its monopoly of raw cotton would have permitted the Confederacy to reward its international friends and punish its enemies. Embargoes or other restrictions on the sale of raw cotton could have delivered punishing blows to the economies of England and the Northeast, where close to 20 percent of the non-agricultural labor force was directly or indirectly engaged in the manufacture and sale of cotton textiles. The resulting unemployment and losses of wealth would have disrupted both the labor and capital markets in these regions, and probably speeded up the emergence of a large textile industry in the South. The West would also have been destabilized economically, since the decline of the Northeast would have severely contracted the market for western agricultural products. As the Confederacy shifted more of its labor into manufacturing, trade, and the military, it would probably have developed an increasing deficit in food, making it again a major market for the grain, dairy, and meat surpluses of the Northwest.

Such economic developments would have generated strong political pressures in the North for a modus vivendi with the Confederacy. Northern politics would have been further complicated by any border states, such as Maryland, Kentucky, and Missouri, that might have remained inside the Union. Attempts to appropriate their slave property would have run a high risk of further secessions. The Republicans not only would have borne the responsibility for the economic crisis created by the rise of the Confederacy, but would have lost the plank on which the party had risen to power. With the bulk of slaveowners prohibited from entry into northern territories because of secession, the claim that the victory by the Republican party was the only way of saving these lands for free labor would have been an empty slogan to farmers and nonagricultural workers who were suffering from the effects of a severe and extended depression. Moreover, the failure of the North to act against the slaveholders who remained within the Union would have undermined its credibility with democratic forces abroad. Such developments would probably have delivered both a lasting blow to antislavery politics and an enormous fillip to nativist politics.

I do not maintain that the preceding sketch of what might have happened in the absence of a civil war is the only plausible one. However, it is a credible sketch of the likely train of events, one that is consistent with what we now know about the capacity of the slave economy of the South as well as with current knowledge of the political crosscurrents in the South, the North, and the rest of the world. At the very least, it points to reasons for doubting that there was a happy, relatively costless solution to the moral dilemma posed by Stampp.

I have not, it should be emphasized, put forward the gloomiest view of the alternative to the Civil War. The preceding sketch suggests an indefinite but more or less peaceful continuation of slavery. It would not be difficult to make a case for the proposition that peaceful secession would merely have postponed the Civil War and that the delay would have created circumstances far more favorable to a southern victory. In that case aristocratic proslavery forces would have gained unchallenged control of the richest and potentially the most powerful nation in the world. Such an outcome not only would have greatly increased the likelihood of rolling back the movement for working-class rights everywhere, but might have led to a loss of human lives far greater than the toll of the Civil War.

What the Civil War Achieved

As pacifists, [abolitionist William Lloyd] Garrison and his followers had to confront the dilemma posed by a violent confrontation with the Confederacy. They reluctantly came to the conclusion that bloody as it might be, the Civil War was the only realistic way of ridding the world of slavery. [Unitarian clergyman] William E. Channing, who had hoped against hope that slavery could be ended by moral suasion alone, explained why the destruction of slavery was the moral imperative of his age. "Slavery must fall," he said, "because it stands in direct hostility to all the grand movements, principles, and reforms of our age, because it stands in the way of an advancing world."

What the Civil War achieved, then, was more than just inflated wealth for northern capitalists and "half" freedom for blacks ("the shoddy aristocracy of the North and the ragged children of the South"). It preserved and reinforced conditions favorable to a continued struggle for the democratic rights of the lower classes, black and white alike, and for the improvement of their economic condition, not only in America but everywhere else in the world. The fall of slavery did not usher in the millennium, it produced no heaven on earth, but it vitalized all the grand movements, principles, and reforms of Channing's age and of our own.

Modernization and Its Strains

The seemingly ordinary word *modernization* is loaded with subtle connotations. Essentially it means not just "bringing things up to date," but also encouraging and effecting the kind of change that advances a goal that seems desirable. It can also refer to the kind of change that seems desirable or inevitable, but that many people resist because it is too disruptive.

History is by definition the study of change—its causes, its agents, its beneficiaries, its victims, its effects. For most of the past, people's general attitude toward change has been negative. Change has seemed to be something threatening, destructive, bad—a movement away from all that was orderly, stable, and familiar. Generally speaking, in the West (and indeed throughout the world), until the 1700s such were the basic instincts not only of ordinary people but of the elite: those who held political power, those who defined proper religious beliefs, those who wrote books and educated the young. But during the great intellectual and cultural movement known as the eighteenth-century Enlightenment, a more positive attitude toward change began to gain a foothold at the upper end of European society (including its overseas outposts in the Americas). In this new view, it was "the modern" that was desirable; "progress" should be the goal; change, at least if it was directed by those who were intelligent and educated, could be positive, and not merely a degeneration from all that was comfortable and entrenched. The idea of positive change as a realization of modernity had been born. Change, in other words, could be welcomed as "modernization."

Such attitudes were born before the Industrial and French Revolutions, and at first they were confined to the intellectual and political elite. But in the course of the Dual Revolution that dominated nineteenth-century Western life, expectations that change could be for the best spread more widely among the general population. The growing legitimacy of democracy fed such expectations: If "the people" were the ultimate source of sovereignty, if the voting public should exercise a decisive role in public affairs, then it followed that ordinary individuals need no longer accept their traditional fate as mere passive objects of change from above. And if the advance of science and industry—whose glories the defenders of the new capitalist economy so fervently saluted—was visibly augmenting the national wealth, then should not ordinary workers and consumers expect significant material gain as their birthright? Progress—change for the better and not a decline from some supposedly happier "good old days"—became the nineteenth century's standard by which the experiences of everyday life were to be measured. "Modern," in short, was good.

Of course, not all the change that occurred during the nineteenth century was painless. Change was often wrenching, and for all the progress that undoubtedly occurred, individuals suffered. Cherished beliefs were discredited, and not all those—whether individuals or groups—who claimed a share of the age's prosperity or of its expanding rights succeeded.

The selections in this chapter focus on different aspects of the modernizing drives that were at work in nineteenth-century public life. One with dramatic and far-reaching effects was what historians call the "Darwinian Revolution," the subject of the first selection. No scientific hypothesis has ever had so devastating an impact on traditional ways of thinking as Charles Darwin's theory that all species (including human beings) evolve through a process known as natural selection—and that thus they are not the separate and distinct creations of God. Darwinism continues to be an explosive idea at the beginning of the twenty-first century, especially in the United States. Yet, at least among the educated elite of nineteenth-century Britain, Darwin's ideas gained a rapid and largely uncontroversial acceptance.

Russia's Era of Great Reforms, which historians date to the first decade of Czar Alexander II's rule (1856–1865), and which culminated in the emancipation of the Russian peasantry from serfdom, represented the enactment of one of nineteenth-century Europe's most important modernizing programs. Yet, as the chapter's second selection shows, its greatest success may well have been its least intended outcome—the radicalization of Russia's younger-generation elite, its student population. Frustrated by the incomplete process of reform that the czarist government set in motion, radical students from that point on became a constant, and thoroughly alienated, presence in Russian life; eventually they provided the nucleus of a succession of revolutionary political movements, all of them impatient to push modernization far beyond limits that czarism could tolerate.

No nation in the nineteenth-century West prided itself more than did Great Britain on being "progressive," yet the British Isles experienced both a terrible failure of policy and a resounding success. These are described in the third, fourth, and fifth selections in this chapter. The disastrous failure was the Irish Potato Famine of the mid-1840s, undoubtedly the consequence of Britain's political and economic elites' failing to take seriously the vital interests of a subject population under British rule. The success was the enactment—

without any degree of forethought, and largely as a result of compromises between rival viewpoints—of two Reform Acts (1832 and 1867) that brought the United Kingdom from a basically aristocratically ruled nation to one on the verge of modern mass democracy. Perhaps surprisingly, in view of the monarchy's deep unpopularity in the 1830s (when probably a majority of the population viewed it as corrupt and amoral), the advent of British political democracy was accompanied by the elevation of Queen Victoria to the stature of the land's supreme symbol of respectability and stability.

Modernization conspicuously failed to achieve a breakthrough in the United States in one highly significant sphere. When the century opened, under Thomas Jefferson's presidency, only a handful of women (namely, property-owning widows) had the right to vote in one state, New Jersey, and this right was soon taken away. By the mid-nineteenth century, a formidable women's rights movement had emerged in the United States, demanding significant legal reforms in women's favor and, crucially, the same access to the ballot that adult white male citizens enjoyed. Although American laws were reformed in the course of the century to remove some of the worst discriminatory provisions against women, female suffrage was still a rarity in the United States in the 1890s. Men simply refused to relinquish their political monopoly—a refusal that may have much to do with the way in which rough-and-tumble political debate and deal making (often centered in saloons or otherwise lubricated by the consumption of alcohol) constituted a kind of male-bonding sport. ("Politics ain't bean bag," observed the fictional "Mr. Dooley," an Irish saloonkeeper who was the creation of American political humorist Finley Peter Dunne in the 1890s. "Wimen an' childher do well to keep out of it.") By 1900, only a few American states, all in the thinly populated West, accorded women the right to vote. As the last two selections in this chapter make clear, nineteenth-century "modernization" succeeded only in putting urgent issues on the agenda for public debate—not for effecting far-reaching reforms. That agenda would continue to be debated, and only partly realized, throughout the twentieth century.

The Reception
of Evolution

Michael Ruse

This selection focuses on the appearance in nineteenth-century Europe of a sense of belonging to a different kind of community—that of the human race as a species that has evolved through natural selection. Charles Darwin (1809–1882), the scientist who first proposed this theory, was one of the most influential thinkers of all time. The theory itself remains not only one of the foundations of biology but also a subject of debate.

The times were ripe in the mid–nineteenth century for Darwin to propose a mechanism for biological evolution. For a generation, it had been known, both in scientific circles and among the educated public, that the earth's geological history was enormously long. Convictions were growing among naturalists that plant and animal species evolved rather than remained fixed. Such ideas were rooted in scientific data, but they resonated with a lay public that was quite interested in the evolution of *human* affairs. By the mid-1850s Darwin had developed his theory, but only when he learned that another eminent naturalist, Alfred Russel Wallace, was about to propose a similar theory did he rush into print with his great book *On the Origin of Species,* in 1859.

According to Darwin's theory, individuals in all plant and animal species vary slightly, and some of these variations are more conducive to the individual's survival than others. Those individuals better suited for survival tend to reproduce more readily; among animals, for example, those with better survival prospects are selected by potential mates, while those less well equipped (and therefore less attractive) die out without progeny. Over vast spans of time, this process of "natural se-

Excerpted from *The Darwinian Revolution: Science Red in Tooth and Claw,* by Michael Ruse. Copyright © 1979, 1999 by The University of Chicago Press. Reprinted with permission from The University of Chicago Press and Michael Ruse.

lection" (Darwin's phrase) causes new species to emerge and less adaptable or efficient ones to become extinct. True, Darwin did not know the biological ways in which more or less adaptable traits are expressed and transmitted to progeny; discovering how this happens was the lifework of the Austrian monk Gregor Mendel (1822–1884), who was working out the basic laws of genetics but whose findings did not become widely known in the scientific community until around 1900. But what Darwin had proposed was an application to biology of the familiar nineteenth-century idea of progress—the same concept that was the dominant mode of thinking about human communities, the rise and fall of nations, and the development of individual potentials.

This selection is taken from a book by American scholar Michael Ruse, *The Darwinian Revolution: Science Red in Tooth and Claw.* Ruse documents the strong resistance that Darwin's hypothesis generated among many (but not all) Christian believers who insisted on the literal truth of the Bible's account of human origins. The inaccurate notion that Darwin had claimed that human beings were descended from apes and monkeys* repelled many believers—believers not just in Christianity but in human dignity in general—but what most disturbed Christians was Darwin's implicit denial that God had created the human species and that instead humanity had simply evolved through natural selection.

But Ruse's book also shows that powerful forces favored acceptance of Darwin's ideas among the educated public and the scientific community. One such factor was the very respectability and moderation of Darwin himself and such outspoken defenders as T.H. Huxley. Another was the broader familiarity with change and evolution in nineteenth-century culture. In particular, the phrase "survival of the fittest," actually coined by the social philosopher Herbert Spencer in defending Darwin, pleased Darwin so much that he incorporated it into later editions of *On the Origin of Species.* "Survival of the fittest" was the principle nineteenth-century Westerners were to apply to all aspects of life: to business and economics, to ideas and culture, to social classes, to nationalities and states. The new communities and new nations that were taking shape throughout Europe and North America were highly energized, highly competitive environments; it was easy to think of them as almost biological entities, just as the natural world could be conceived as an extension of human beings' ceaseless struggle for advantage. Darwinism turned all of nature into one gigantic, swarming ant heap—a supercommunity that engulfed all other communities.

---

*What Darwin actually argued in his later book, *The Descent of Man,* was that human beings evolved from a common ancestor that they shared with other primates.

About 1830, . . . the argument from design centered on adaptation, the "utilitarian" argument. . . . There were a few minor difficulties like male nipples, but most things were taken to show direct purpose. In the thirty years following, . . . that argument came under fire and was somewhat displaced by other natural theological arguments that, because they did not center on adaptation, posed less of a threat to evolutionary hypotheses, if they did not positively invite them. The weakening of the utilitarian argument was surely one reason for the incredible speed with which the biological community converted to evolutionism. On the other hand, in Britain in the 1860s the utilitarian argument still had considerable force and was no doubt a factor in many people's reluctance to accept natural selection, other than to a very limited extent. Selection, working through blind law, claims to explain adaptation, and there remained a strong feeling that unguided law could not lead to intricately complex organic adaptation. Therefore, people felt that scientifically Darwin's theory must be wrong, and religiously they often found it offensive, because by denying or downplaying adaptation one cuts away at the foundations of natural theology.

For some of the older . . . [biologists], this was the end of the matter. Darwin's book is "*utterly false*" because "it repudiates all reasoning from final causes; and seems to shut the door upon any view (however feeble) of the God of Nature as manifested in His works." Others, though they felt strongly about adaptation and final causes, tried to go some way with Darwin. Almost invariably these were the same people who had thought Darwin's theory needed an extra push for man; so they simply introduced more pushes through the course of evolution—law-bound, yet directed, saltations introducing adaptations. . . . Herschel [a scientist who could not accept Darwin's hypothesis] made it clear that he himself favored some kind of saltatory evolutionary theory, with occasional law-bound jumps from one species to another, where adaptation-causing design could take effect, presumably aided by the backup action of natural selection. He spoke of the "idea of *Jumps* . . . as if for instance a wolf should at some epoch of lapine history take to occasionally littering a dog or a fox among her cubs.". . . He added that such a process would introduce "*mind, plan, design,* and to the . . . obvious exclusion of the haphazard view of the subject and the casual concourse of atoms."

We have here another point at which science and religion came together and ought not be considered as separate. We know there were scientific reasons why many favored saltationism. Now we see religious reasons, and though for many they may have been more basic, those wanting designed saltations could legitimately turn to science to strengthen their case. . . .

Darwin disagreed with those who wanted to explain adaptation through guided laws. But he agreed that adaptation is important and must be explained. Therefore we have one more reason why Huxley was not totally committed to natural selection. For Huxley the utilitarian argument never had great charm, and so he downplayed the importance of adaptation. He went so far as to deny that the color of birds and butterflies or the color and shape of flowers could have any adaptive value. . . .

The Darwinians and Their Society

So far we have been dealing with the reception of Darwinism at the intellectual and emotional level—at the level of thought, loosely construed. But there was a more tangible level involved—a world of human relations and of social and political factors. For all the reservations we must draw, it is clear that Darwin's ideas scored some striking successes—especially if we consider matters from the viewpoint of the scientific community. . . . If we are to understand fully why Darwin achieved such success, we must go beyond pure ideas and look at the scientists in their human settings.

At the most general level, the period we are considering—the fifteen years from 1860 to 1875—was a time of stability and prosperity in Britain, at least until the agricultural depressions started in 1873. This was true despite great political developments, including the Reform Bill of 1867. When Darwin published the *Descent of Man* (1871), one reviewer chided him for "revealing his zoological conclusions to the general public at a moment when the sky of Paris was red with the incendiary flames of the Commune"; but in general one does not get this reaction. . . . Undoubtedly this is partly because the 1860s were a very different time from the 1840s. In the 1840s, many people justifiably thought that revolution was just around the corner. In the 1860s, many started to conclude that God was a middle-class Englishman after all. Hence evolutionism was less threatening than it had been, apart from the fact that ideas one has been living with for years are less worrisome than fresh heretical ideas.

The "respectability" that evolutionism gained after the *Origin* was in large part due to the respectability of the Darwinians themselves. [Earlier,] people claimed that evolutionism leads to atheism, which is immoral and threatening to the stability of society. But the Darwinians gave the lie to this. To a man, they were exemplars of the most boring Victorian respectability—hardworking to the point of neurosis . . . , earnest, and good family men of impeccable sexual propriety. They were not outsiders. Conversely, they shared many of the values and norms of their contemporaries. . . .

Their attitude toward women illustrates the conventionality of the Darwinians. [Darwin's supporter T.H.] Huxley, to his great credit, was much concerned with upgrading women's education, but he was still convinced that women are by nature men's intellectual inferiors. He blocked their attendance at the Geological Society, and though in theory he had no objection to a man's marrying his dead wife's sister (a much-debated Victorian topic, involved with the threat an unmarried sister might pose to the unity of the home), when his own daughter married her dead sister's husband, he did not approve. Darwin was even more a child of his time. In the *Descent of Man,* with all the emphasis on sexual differences as determined by sexual selection through male combat and female choice, one can well imagine the status of women. "Man is more courageous, pugnacious, and energetic than woman, and has a more inventive genius." In compensation, woman has "greater tenderness and less selfishness." Shades of [English geologist and professor Adam] Sedgwick and [Scottish physicist Sir David] Brewster here! The Darwinians may have been rebels in some respects—in other respects, they were anything but.

Moreover, the Darwinians were not merely respectable members of Victorian society; in important ways they were positive and valued forces in that society. For instance, this was a time of great concern about education at all levels, from the elementary level, where the children of the working classes were getting virtually none, to the university level, where the British seemed so anachronistic compared with the Germans. Huxley was incredibly active and useful here and was recognized as rendering invaluable service. . . . At Kew [Gardens, in London], botanists were classifying plants sent from all over the empire and experimenting to see what could be grown where: Could new commercially valuable crops be raised in different parts of the world? Thanks to their work, in 1861 cinchona (quinine) was introduced from South America to India and Ceylon, and in the 1870s rubber trees were transplanted from South America to the East Indies. Although much of this work was done under the rubric of humanitarian benefits to mankind in general, it was critical to British imperialism, which was of increasing economic importance as the growing industrialization of Europe and America threatened Britain's preeminence. Quinine permitted white men to function in tropical areas despite malaria, and rubber transformed the Malay Peninsula.

Hence, quite apart from the fact that these latter projects depended on principles important to Darwinism, men like Huxley . . . carried weight in Victorian society. . . . One might not like the Darwinians' ideas; but their example went a long way to counter the argument that those concepts were antisocial or otherwise corrupting.

Emergence of the Student Movement in Russia

Abbott Gleason

If the United States was the only truly democratic nation on earth in the middle of the nineteenth century, the Russian Empire was the most rigidly autocratic, at least in the Western world. Under Czar Nicholas I (reigned 1825–1855), the police and the imperial bureaucracy maintained the tightest possible control. There was no constitution, no elections, no legislature, no political parties, and no appeal possible after the czar's decisions. Justice was apt to be arbitrary, and educated people suspected of harboring opposition ideas could be summarily jailed, sent to Siberian penal camps or mental institutions, or driven into exile abroad. Possible reforms were simply not discussed, and universities were watched closely for signs of dissent. In 1849 the great writer Fyodor Dostoyevsky was —at the czar's personal order—subjected to a horrifying mock execution and then dispatched to years of penal service in Siberia merely for having belonged to a mildly "subversive" student group.

Nicholas I died in the midst of the Crimean War, which he had helped precipitate by his excessively aggressive moves toward extending Russia's sphere of influence in the Balkan peninsula. The war, which largely consisted of British and French armies invading Russia's Crimean peninsula and subjecting the great naval base of Sevastopol to a lengthy, bloody siege, revealed the desperate backwardness of the Russian army and bureaucratic state. It became obvious that further modernization was impossible unless serfdom was abolished and something approaching a Western-style rule of law established. The new czar, Alexander II, firmly refused to consider creating a constitutional monarchy on the West European model.

The years roughly 1855–1865 are known in Russian history as the Great Reform Era. Serfdom was abolished in 1861, the court system was overhauled, and laws and legal procedures were made more humane and less arbitrary. Elected councils called *zemstvos,* dominated by the nobility but with middle-class and even peasant participation, were given considerable latitude in local government. The press became somewhat freer of censorship, and more critical. And the rigid controls on university life characteristic of Nicholas I's day were generally relaxed, so that Russian campuses became lively centers of discussions about what more ought to be done. Radical critics of existing society, such as Nikolai Chernyshevsky and Nikolai Dobroliubov, gained wide respect among young people. Some educated youths even began to entertain the idea of "going to the people"—that is, mingling with the peasantry in the hope of stirring up unrest.

The American historian Abbott Gleason, a specialist in nineteenth-century Russian history, describes the rise of a student movement in the Great Reform Era. Some of the participants in this movement would go on to become active (though ineffectual) revolutionaries in the 1870s. In the excerpt from his book *Young Russia* that follows, Gleason draws explicit contrasts and parallels to the student movement that emerged in the United States a century later, in the 1960s.

A s in so many other areas of Russian life, the Crimean defeat quickly convinced the government that "improvements" were necessary: the quality of education had to be improved and the quantity of educated men increased. So the new era began quickly in the universities, and a stream of decrees and administrative changes were launched after 1855. The universities were opened up to all those who could pass the qualifying examinations, and a dramatic increase in enrollment resulted. Between 1854 and 1859, the population of the universities increased by more than half. St. Petersburg almost tripled in size. Formerly proscribed subjects were reintroduced. Travel restrictions and the ban on the importation of scholarly materials were relaxed. Many of the military bully boys who had occupied the crucial posts of curators and inspectors were replaced by milder men with civilian backgrounds, and even more important was a general relaxation of "supervision." After 1858, student inspectors were relieved of their supervisory responsibilities except within the walls of the university.

The response of the rapidly growing student body to these changes—and to the feeling of liberal drift that accompanied them—was rapid and pronounced. Students seem to be particularly sensitive to the inner strength and self-confidence of the authorities whom they "confront." So it is no wonder more and more Russian students sensed that neither Alexander nor his subordinates had a clear sense of what they wanted to achieve, beyond the broadest possible commitment to "improvement." Indecision at the top translated itself down the chain of command. Curators, inspectors, rectors, and the older professors lost their sense of the situation and some of their self-confidence. And the students were not slow to take advantage of this development. Beards, mustaches, and long hair—formerly strictly forbidden—made their appearance, then as now symbols of liberation. . . .

If a propensity for messianic elitism is characteristic of able young people, a number of factors in the Russian situation contributed to its luxuriant development. One was that there were so few students—still fewer than five thousand in 1860–61. Then there was the importance the new Tsar clearly ascribed to the university and its personnel. To be a student was to be in the vanguard of progress, to be the hope of the nation; to the students from lower-class backgrounds, there was the additional feeling that they were joining this new elite, rather than merely assuming their natural place within it. And around them they perceived an inchoate or articulated sympathy; *obshches-tvo* [society] wanted to "believe in youth," especially in university youth, especially at the dawn of the new era.

No other social forces could contest the students for their self-assumed role as the nation's hope. The government had been disastrously defeated in war, and [the reactionary Tsar] Nicholas [I] was dead. A substantial modern middle class was still decades away; the Great Reforms had yet to do their work. And the students were geographically concentrated; their developing *esprit de corps* could easily assume tangible and organized forms.

Until very recently, it has been customary to rely heavily on social factors to explain the growing radicalism of Russian students in the latter 1850s and 1860s. Alexander's measures to democratize the universities, so the argument runs, brought plebeian elements into *obshchestvo* (or at least into its vicinity), resulting in quite substantial changes in the quality and texture of Russian culture within a surprisingly brief period. These people—the children of priests, doctors and medical functionaries, marginal landowners, and lower bureaucrats—received the now-famous label of *raznochintsy* (literally, "the people of various ranks"), those who could not or did not fit into Russia's disintegrating caste system. . . .

That much of the intellectual leadership in Russian radicalism in the 1850s and 1860s was in the hands of *raznochintsy* cannot be denied. In such an aristocratic culture as Russia was, the appearance of so many sons of priests on the social and intellectual scene could not fail to make a deep impression, and it is perhaps not surprising that historians often characterize the entire period as *raznochintsy*. . . . Certain of the seminarians pioneered a militant and uncompromising style and image that proved deeply attractive to several generations of Russian radicals. With the broadening of the social base of the universities, upper-class students came to be more immediately aware of the poverty of their lower-class confreres, and in the atmosphere of the period diluted their snobbery with a volatile mixture of compassion and admiration. This opening up of the university, despite periodic attempts by the government to limit or even reverse the policy, proved irresistible, and it undoubtedly hastened the demise of the educated gentry's virtual monopoly over Russian intellectual life.

Still, . . . there is little evidence to suggest that *raznochintsy* students as a group were decisive in the growth of student dissatisfaction and radicalism. . . . Despite the appearance of a number of *raznochintsy* in prominent positions, the evidence suggests that most lower-class students were simply trying to "make it" in the upper world of Russian society, whose doors were now at least ajar.

The two great Russian novels about the radical politics of the 1860s, Ivan Turgenev's *Fathers and Children* and Fyodor Dostoevsky's *The Possessed,* suggest opposite answers to the question: Were the young radicals of the 1860s rebelling *against* the values of their "parents" (the gentry liberals of the 1840s) or simply acting out those values in a more vigorous, extreme, and uncompromising fashion? Turgenev stressed rebelliousness, and his version of the generation gap has been more generally accepted. It is certainly true that in any period of impending social change or upheaval, generational conflicts are exacerbated, which is one reason why Turgenev's vivid portrayal of those differences has always seemed so compelling.

But it might be argued that Dostoevsky's view of the situation was more profound, however idiosyncratic his demonic portrayal of 1860s radicalism. . . . What Dostoevsky saw less clearly is that the Slavophile [nationalistic] ideas that affected him so powerfully had themselves contributed to the satanic social doctrines against which he fought so hard.

The fact is that we do not know enough about the backgrounds of individual radicals to generalize as to whether they were rebelling against the personal values of their families or putting those values into practice in a more consequent and militant fashion, a question that has often been raised with respect to more recent "young radicals.". . .

An unquestionable precondition of the growing student radicalism of the late 1850s was the mood of "liberal" reformism unleashed by Alexander II's educational reforms and most of all by the coming of Emancipation. In general, this link between student attitudes and broader and more diffuse social moods seems characteristic. A determined radical minority can pursue its activities for some time without broad social sympathy, but a large-scale student movement depends on its participants feeling that they have substantial—if halting or inarticulate—support outside the walls. When the social mood changes drastically, as Americans have recently had occasion to observe, student attitudes are likely to alter correspondingly. Perhaps it is best of all to be able to feel that you are doing the right thing, that most people know you are, and that they admire you and wish you well, although they are too timid or socially encumbered to join you, despite the belief, shared by all thoughtful parties, that the future is on your side. For a time in the late 1850s, Russian students— or at least an activist minority—were in that happy position.

Student movements also need non-student figures with whom they can identify—members of the faculty or other individuals within the university, or figures from the larger world of journalism or politics. Russian students, in fact, had both. There were the remote but glamorous figures of [the exiled radicals Alexander] Herzen and [Nikolai] Ogarëv in London, and the increasingly influential group around the [radical journal] *Contemporary*—above all, Chernyshevsky. Nearer at hand were sympathetic and popular "liberal" professors, like Konstantin Dmitrievich Kavelin, professor of law at the University of St. Petersburg. . . . Kavelin was probably the most influential of the activist, reform-minded professors of the late 1850s, but at the climax of student unrest and disorders in 1861–62 he ran into trouble. His was the basic dilemma of all moderate progressives in periods of acute disorder. He did not provide the kind of uncompromising support the most militant students demanded, while the more moderate and conservative authorities held him responsible for the breakdown of order. Kavelin always prided himself on being able to communicate with people of radically different persuasions: the Slavophiles, conservative bureaucrats, [and radicals]. In that respect he belonged to the 1840s, not the 1860s. And when the political situation polarized beyond a certain point, he ended by being acceptable to no one.

The relationship between what one might call "campus issues" and the dramatic development of reform at the national level was complex. Undoubtedly, most student activists focused on local rather than national concerns, although the excitement of the Emancipation drama had a catalytic effect. What people seem to have noticed first was that students seemed to be thinking and feeling more as a group, that class and regional differences seemed to be diminishing, and that the students who arrived at the universities in 1858 seemed to be distinctly more interested in politics than their predecessors had been.

Soon the greater cohesion of the students began to create "we-they" situations. Since the attitude of the university authorities—the curators and rectors—was now uncertain or even sympathetic, student organizations began to spring up: libraries, scholarship funds (financed by the richer students for their poorer colleagues), social clubs, and a spectrum of periodicals. . . . As student corporatism developed, clashes with the police began to be more serious, if not actually more frequent. In the old days, these clashes seldom had had serious consequences. Increasingly, after 1856, students viewed the beating or maltreatment of one of them as an offense against the entire body, and they met, often in large numbers, to seek redress. Sometimes they succeeded, particularly at first, as neither the university nor the civil authorities were accustomed to dealing with crowds of determined students. Under Nicholas the educational bureaucracy would automatically have had recourse to Draconian measures. Now its officials hesitated—either because they simply had lost their bearings, or because the signals they received from above were confusing, or because elements among them were touched with the sympathy toward reform, so common to *obshchestvo* in general. . . .

Incompetent, indifferent, or authoritarian professors (some were all three), who were regarded as holdovers from the bad old days of Nicholas, were frequent targets. To achieve their removal was not merely educationally desirable but took on a political coloring as well: it was part of the task of reforming Russia. Students answered back to these professors in class, petitioned against them, boycotted their lectures, or resorted to systematic harassment (clapping, whistling, and so on). These incidents, too, were likely to escalate, and the administration frequently found itself in the middle, between an outraged and defensive faculty majority and an aroused student body. . . .

Although the primary focus of the students' discontent was on their own position in a university badly in need of reform, a few were getting more interested in radical solutions to national problems; after 1858, the loose congeries of ideas that would become known as Populism was more and more attractive to a minority of the students, although not necessarily to the most militant. Everyone had something to say about Herzen's *Bell*. Newssheets and "journals," some printed and some handwritten, began to make their appearance in the universities during and after 1858. . . . Most of the students' own newspapers were largely oriented toward what was taking place on campus, but there was a distinct subcurrent of interest in national politics, and the hostility toward local figures spilled over into criticisms of the government and Alexander himself.

Toward 1860, on most university campuses, groups were forming who cared only about the national arena and who utilized campus issues primarily to radicalize the student body. . . . A decision was grandly taken to extirpate the imperial family, although no one actually did anything.

What is the best way to get at the relationship between student discontent within the university, spilling over into national politics, and the larger question of the development of Russian radicalism? Was the radical literature, to which the students had access in the late 1850s, actually important in their development? An even harder question to answer: What was the nature of the radicalizing experience that many of the Russian students underwent in the five-year period following the death of Nicholas?

To the first question, Soviet scholarship has given a fairly simple and unequivocal answer: student discontent was an important part of the larger upheaval that brought about Emancipation in 1861 and inaugurated the "capitalist period" of Russian historical development. . . . But this "explanation" is quite inadequate. Perhaps the notion of "reflection" is never adequate to explain the relationship between ideas and an economic substructure. . . . [Belief in an imminent peasant uprising] was basically a fantasy of the disenchanted portion of the Russian elite, and it often was more a function of their own powerlessness than anything else. The largely self-generated excitement that animated *obshchestvo,* and the students in particular, had more to do with their own altered situation than with any frightening or challenging upheaval from below. The government and many of the landowners certainly worried, among other things, about a peasant uprising, but the students saw themselves bestowing a full humanity on the peasants; their attitude was generous and rather patronizing.

The significance of literature and ideas as radicalizing agents has been much discussed. . . . Certainly the cluster of ideas, feelings, beliefs, and prejudices that eventually became known as Populism has a genuine intellectual content, and as the 1860s went along, people spoke and wrote in this vocabulary. But one should not exaggerate the direct, unmediated role of books and ideas. The ground must be prepared and the times right. [German writer Georg] Büchner's *Force and Matter,* which seems to have shattered so many Russians' faith in revealed religion, now seems to educated readers, even to radicals, not only a cramped and pedestrian tract but a new form of metaphysics. Even in Russia its vogue was brief, if powerful. The books that "influence" us this year may fail to move us two years hence. Intellectuals, and students in particular, are notably susceptible to fashion or, to employ a more complimentary term, to "the intellectual currents of the day." To say this is not to deny the sincerity of the commitment of the radical minority, but merely to stress their vanguard role; the commitment of most students to the "intellectual currents of the day" was "broad, rather than deep.". . .

Very rapid and at least superficially "extreme" shifts in political allegiance were common in the late 1850s. Many students who had never really had any political views at all became "radical" quite quickly. But this characteristic of the period, attested to both by contemporaries and historians, should not be exaggerated. The movement of some students to the left was gradual and rather hard fought. . . . Moderate, vaguely "liberal," and Westernizing journals . . . also had student adherents. The *Annals,* in particular, appealed to students who retained a pronounced bureaucratic mentality, who wanted orderly reform from above, and who continued to dream of brilliant careers within the limits of *obshchestvo* Russia as it then seemed to be evolving. Such students, who were likely to regard [radicals] as rabble-rousers, were in a real sense not "typical" of the times, but they, too, applauded the Emancipation. . . .

Nor is it anachronistic to discuss the matter of "image," so important in American politics today, not least in student and radical politics, in the Russian radicalism of the 1850s and 1860s. Men like P.N. Rybnikov and especially P.I. Iakushkin helped by their lives and examples to create the figure of a Populist-ethnographer, wandering among the people and becoming part of them. That this image is not an adequate rendering of these men does not matter to the student of the 1860s. What matters is to understand how an influential minority of their contemporaries regarded them.

Part of the declining appeal of Herzen to Russian youth and his replacement by Chernyshevsky has more to do with the two men's images than with the ideas they put forward. The "younger generation" of Russian radicals in the late 1850s and 1860s was powerfully attracted to Chernyshevsky's puritanism, asceticism, deliberate lack of charm, and social ease. His whole bearing was an affront to the existing order, and he conveyed the impression that he would not make the slightest social concession: to smile and murmur a few ceremonial words to put an interlocutor at his ease would be, somehow, to betray his whole position. Sincerity was everything. He insisted on being accepted exactly as he was. Herzen, on the other hand, was a "gentleman." even an aristocrat. He loved good food, good wine, and brilliant conversation. He was charming—or could be—and however much he might criticize the existing order, he was clearly a product of it and was bound to it by myriad tangible and intangible ties—not least the substantial sum of money he arranged to have brought out of Russia when he emigrated. Chernyshevsky conveyed none of this sense of attachment to the old. Both he and [Nikolai] Dobroliubov embodied the most militant rejection of the old and the determination to create something new. . . .

Few, if any, students of the late 1850s and early 1860s consciously modeled themselves any longer on Herzen, while Chernyshevsky was personally fascinating to many. Leo Tolstoy thought that "a bilious, spiteful man is not normal," but increasing numbers of radical students did not agree. In an aristocratic society like that of Russia, smelling of bugs was an excellent way of proclaiming one's disaffection. Good manners and reasonableness not only bound one indirectly to the established order, they were among the essential guarantors of liberal impotence

Many contemporaries and historians noticed the intellectual shallowness of the radicalism of students (and some older people) in the late 1850s. In one sense they were correct. Very few of the students had really mastered Büchner [or other radical Western writers], and their radical impulses most often found expression in sloganizing. (The arguments of their opponents, one might add, were not ordinarily on a higher level.) But intellectual influences are a secondary consideration here. Most people do not become radicals because of the books they read—although they may appeal to books and draw sustenance from them. To understand the radicalizing experience that students underwent in the late 1850s, one must look instead to the sharp break with the past that occurred in 1855–56 and the *consciousness* it helped induce, a consciousness that men were not wholly impotent with respect to their environment, that things might be changed, ought to be changed—and were about to be changed. One must look to the special qualities of youth and adolescence, and to the privileged and isolated position of Russian university students. Various Western intellectual currents helped to provide a language for expressing these feelings of mission: German materialism; the utilitarianism of [English writer Jeremy] Bentham and [James] Mill; the socialism of [the French writers] Saint-Simon and Fourier. And many of the ideas and preoccupations that had animated both the Slavophiles and the Westerners in the 1840s were reappearing now as guiding motifs of the new radicalism, although not in a form that was intelligible to the older generation.

Some students understood these ideas, made a deep commitment to them, and contributed in turn to their development. For others they remained satisfyingly shocking slogans that corresponded to the emotional needs of the moment and gave them an important but fleeting sense of themselves and their generation. Some students went on to a deeper involvement with radicalism and the revolutionary movement; for others, radicalism was merely their kind of wild oats. But those whose radicalism could survive the withdrawal of the inchoate, "liberal" support of the late 1850s were a minority.

The view that institutions of higher education became, from here on out, the nursery of Russian radicalism is a theme of recent Western scholarship on this period. But which students were likely to be radicalized at the university? Behind this question of university radicalism lies the larger general question of secondary education in

Russia. The seminaries, the gymnasia, and the military schools were all harsh in their discipline, primitive in their pedagogical methods, and notably lacking in creature comforts. Most memoir literature that tells about these schools in the time of Nicholas is bloodcurdling. . . . But until much more systematic study has been made of secondary education under Nicholas, no serious discussion will be possible.

In fact, no background discussion of causal factors and circumstances can take us very far in analyzing what went on in Russian universities in the late 1850s and early 1860s. What happened there had a rhythm of chronological development that was determined in part by national politics and in part by the logic of events within each university. These patterns were similar in a rough kind of way, but there were many local variants. . . .

Soviet historians generally employ the term "student movement" as if there had been some kind of coordinated leadership and formally agreed-upon program—as if the students' encounters with the authorities were an organized political movement. But despite a good deal of interuniversity contact, the ferment and the disturbances developed autonomously. One crucial difference between the Russian student movement of the 1850s and 1860s and the student radicalism in America a hundred years later has to do with the means of communication. Geographical mobility and in particular the electronic media gave American student politics of the 1960s a national and even supranational unity that was far removed from anything possible in the nineteenth century. The spread of radical politics on American campuses was often abetted by the gnawing feeling of inferiority that many students began to feel if their campus had remained relatively tranquil, while nightly news programs showed building seizures at Stanford and Columbia and a bombing at Wisconsin. Russian students simply could not be anything like so aware of what their confreres elsewhere were up to.

But one should not treat each university as a separate and unrelated story: the drama was far too similar. The national excitement and the government's attitude were unifying factors; and students moving from one university to another did help push the movement along. Fundamentally, however, structural similarities, rather than "influence" of one institution upon another, made for similarities in their histories during this period.

The Irish Potato Famine Brings National Tragedy

Don Nardo

In 1845, a terrible blight hit the Irish potato crop. The potatoes rotted in the fields, and people began to starve. In all, more than 1 million Irish died of starvation or hunger-related diseases in the great potato famine. Millions more fled the country. In the following excerpt, Don Nardo details the advance of the famine, as well as the British Parliament's heartless refusal to help the Irish. Nardo is an award-winning author of over a hundred books.

In July 1845 Irish farmers had every reason to believe that the soon-to-be-harvested potato crop would be one of the best in years. They inspected their growing potatoes and found them unusually large and plentiful. On July 23, an Irish newspaper, the *Freeman's Journal,* reported, "The poor man's property, the potato crop, was never before so large and at the same time so abundant." On July 25, another paper, the *Times*, announced, "An early and productive harvest is everywhere expected."

But the bountiful harvest never came. The mysterious blight that destroyed potato crops in North America in 1843 and 1844 was on the move. With frightening speed, the disease attacked potato fields in country after country. By August the blight appeared in Holland and France, and in September potatoes in Britain began to die. News of British potato losses quickly reached Ireland, and fearful Irish farmers prayed the pestilence would not descend upon them next.

On September 13, the Irish magazine *Gardener's Chronicle* stopped its presses and printed a special report:

> We stop the Press with great regret to announce that the potato Murrain has unequivocally declared itself in Ireland. The crops about Dublin are suddenly perishing . . . where will Ireland be in the event of a universal potato rot?

Within a few weeks, the disease spread into the central sections of the island. The potatoes became soft and gave off a putrid odor. Then they decayed into a rotten, slimy mass. The Irish were used to crop failures. But those of the past were caused by climatic factors: too little rain or too much, frosts, and so on. This new episode was entirely different. Perfectly healthy potatoes spoiled and melted away before people's eyes. As the deadly blight swiftly moved from farm to farm, from county to county, a wave of fear swept through the Irish countryside.

Suggestions and Theories

What could be the cause of the plague, people asked? The farmers and peasants had numerous suggestions and theories. Some thought static electricity was the culprit. Others were sure that puffs of smoke from train locomotives had poisoned the air. This pollution, they said, sank into the ground and choked the spuds. Another explanation claimed that vapors rose from "blind volcanoes" located deep inside the earth. In this explanation, the pollution attacked the lumpers from below. Still another proposal suggested that bird droppings caused the blight. Proponents of this theory could not account for the fact that bird droppings had landed on the island for centuries with no ill effects.

Little Scientific Knowledge

So many theories about the nature of the blight abounded because, at the time, there was little scientific knowledge available to explain the causes of disease. Members of the scientific community scoffed at the farmers' theories but were unable to offer any better explanations. For instance, Dr. John Lindley, a well-known botany professor, believed that the blight came from too much rain. He said the spuds had absorbed so much water that a "wet putrefaction" had taken hold of them. Another plant expert also blamed the weather. He declared that "the season has been so ungenial and the absence of sunshine so remarkable during the last two months that the potatoes have imperfectly ripened." But even the uneducated farmers knew that there had been adverse weather conditions many times in the past. Nothing before had produced such a strange and devastating blight. The sad fact was that no one had a satisfactory explanation for the cause of the disease.

Days Without Food

As the blight raced through Irish fields, people went for days without food. When days of hunger stretched into weeks, many desperate farmers dug up their seed potatoes, small supplies of spuds set aside to plant future crops. To their horror, the farmers found that the plague had reduced their seed potatoes to a sticky rotten heap. After months without food, people began to starve to death. W.E. Forester, a British traveler in Ireland who witnessed the starvation, reported:

> When we entered a village, our first question was, "How many deaths?" "The hunger has been here" was everywhere the cry, and involuntarily we found ourselves regarding this hunger as we should an epidemic, looking on starvation as a disease. In fact, as we went along, our wonder was not that the people died but that they lived. . . . Like a scourge of locusts the hunger daily sweeps over fresh districts, eating up all before it: one class [of people] after another is falling into the same abyss of ruin.

John Mitchel, an Irish patriot, toured the Irish countryside during the winter. He too witnessed the mounting death toll and saw the effects of prolonged hunger on the living. Mitchell said:

> In the depth of winter we travelled to Galway, through the very centre of that fertile island, and saw sights that will never wholly leave the eyes that beheld them—cowering wretches, almost naked in the savage weather, prowling in turnip-fields, and endeavoring to grub up roots . . . sometimes I could see in front of the cottages little children leaning against a fence . . . for they could not stand—their limbs fleshless, their bodies half naked, their faces bloated yet wrinkled, and of a pale greenish hue—children who would never, it was too plain, grow up to be men and women.

In despair, the starving peasants asked what could be done to stop the blight. Was there a way to treat the infected spuds? Dr. Lyon Playfair, a respected chemist, suggested, "It might be possible to mitigate the evil of the potato disease by some chemical application." But he admitted he was not at all sure what chemical should be used. Others proposed salvaging the rotten potatoes. The *Freeman's Journal* called for the building of a machine that would extract the starch from spuds. This starch, the newspaper suggested, might be mixed with flour to make pies and puddings. But no one was sure if it was possible to build such a machine. In any case, health experts pointed out that starch is not the most nutritious ingredient in potatoes. People who lived only on starch would eventually starve to death anyway.

The Plague Raged On

The newspaper the *Nation* printed a recipe for treating diseased potatoes. "Cut off the diseased parts," the recipe instructed, "and steam or boil into a mash with bran and salt." Those who tried this method found it did not work. Other suggested treatments called for soaking the potatoes in bog water or exposing them to poisonous gas. And some advocated baking the spuds until the foul-smelling "blackish matter" oozed out. None of these methods worked. No one knew where the blight came from or how to stop it, and the plague raged on through the countryside.

By the spring of 1846, the Irish peasants were desperate. Some resorted to eating diseased potatoes. They became ill and vomited. Fever spread, as did dysentery, an infection of the intestines that causes severe diarrhea. Increasing numbers of tenants even risked punishment or eviction and ate some of their rent crops. The landlords' agents checked these crops often and reported shortages. After eating their rent crops, many poor tenants could not pay their rents. The landlords were well aware that their tenants were suffering. Yet many landlords cared only about making money and cruelly evicted any families that failed to pay rent. As a result, the number of evictions in Ireland increased dramatically during the blight.

During the worst days of the famine, the heartlessness of the landlords caused shameful evictions in every county in Ireland. Witnessing such events, John Mitchel wrote, "Pity and Terror! What a tragedy is here—deeper, darker than any *bloody* tragedy even yet enacted under the sun. . . . Who will compare the fate of men burned at the stake, or cut down in battle . . . with this?" Mitchel said that British landlords and government officials should do something to stop such abuses and help alleviate the misery of the Irish. W.E. Forester agreed, saying that only the British could end the suffering. Ireland, he said, must look "to England . . . to save the lives of her children."

At first, the British government did nothing about the blight in Ireland. Reports about the crisis that reached Britain were often sketchy and contradictory. Most British held the opinion that the situation in Ireland was not all that bad. After all, the Irish had suffered crop failures before and survived. Many British cautioned against making too much of a fuss over a minor problem. The blight, they said, would go away on its own, and Ireland would be the same as before.

But the British prime minister, Sir Robert Peel, knew better. As early as the fall of 1845, he sent officials to study the problem. They predicted the possibility of a large-scale disaster in Ireland. One official wrote, "Famine must be looked forward to and there will follow, as a natural consequence, as in former years, typhus fever, or some other malignant pestilence." Unlike many British people at the time, Peel was genuinely concerned about the Irish. He believed that since the Act of Union had made Ireland a part of Britain, the Irish should be treated like other British citizens. Peel's opinions about Ireland were unpopular with many British people.

A Substitute Had to Be Found

To save the Irish from starvation, Peel realized that a substitute had to be found for the potato. Shipping large amounts of wheat, barley, and other grains to Ireland seemed the only realistic solution to the problem. But where would the grain come from? The British consumed most of the grain grown in Ireland and Britain. Grain for famine relief would have to come from other countries. But mass importation of foreign grain was forbidden by trade rules called the Corn Laws. Peel decided on a bold and controversial plan. He would try to convince British lawmakers to repeal the Corn Laws.

The Corn Laws were first established to protect British farmers. The laws placed very high import taxes, called duties, on cheap grain and other foodstuffs from foreign countries. This prevented most foreign grain from entering Britain. As a result, British farmers did not have to compete in the marketplace against the suppliers of cheaper foreign grain. British farmers could keep their prices high and still make large profits. Most people in Britain believed that the strength of the British economy depended on the Corn Laws. They feared that repealing the laws would allow a flood of cheap foreign foods into the country, which, they argued, would cause British farmers to go bankrupt. The economy would collapse, and the social structure of the country would be destroyed. Since Ireland was now a part of Britain, the Corn Laws also applied to grain entering Ireland.

Peel knew that repealing the Corn Laws was a highly emotional issue, one that might ruin his career. But he felt it his duty to try to avoid a catastrophe in Ireland. Courageously, he went ahead with his plans to repeal the laws. He called emergency meetings of the British cabinet and made his case for eliminating the laws. But the other cabinet ministers insisted that repeal would ruin Britain, and they outvoted Peel.

Tens of Thousands Starving

Meanwhile, Lindley and Playfair issued a detailed report of their study of the blight in Ireland. They informed Peel that the situation was dangerous, that tens of thousands of people were already starving. Other eyewitnesses told of seeing entire villages abandoned. John Mitchel called such ghost towns "Places of Skulls" and described returning to a once-prosperous village he had visited two years before.

As Mitchel and his companions approached the town, they saw no animals, no children playing, no smoke rising from the chimneys of the cottages. "There is a horrible silence," Mitchel wrote. "Grass grows before the doors, we fear to look in any door . . . for we fear to see yellow chapless skeletons grinning there." Mitchel did enter some of the houses and, to his horror, found dogs, themselves crazed from hunger, devouring human corpses. As the dogs ran away "with doleful howling," Mitchel and others realized "how they had lived, after their masters died." Finding the house of his former host, Mitchel called out a greeting. But there was "no answer—ghastly silence, and a mouldy stench, as from the mouth of burial vaults." Mitchel found the remains of his friends. "They are all dead," he wrote later. "The strong man and the dark-eyed woman, and the little one . . . they shrunk and withered together . . . their horrid eyes scowled on each other with a cannibal glare."

Similar gruesome and heartrending stories continued to reach Robert Peel in London. Agonized with concern, Peel took matters into his own hands. Deciding that the Irish needed grain immediately, he secretly ordered a large shipment of Indian corn from the United States. This food later helped many Irish peasants survive the winter of 1845 and 1846.

Disapproved of Irish

Peel ordered the American corn without getting permission from the head of the British treasury, Charles Edward Trevelyan. In accordance with British law, Trevelyan had the final say over spending of government money. This included funds for famine relief—extra food, clothes, medical supplies, and loans to the poor. The problem was that Trevelyan, like so many other well-to-do British, disapproved of the Irish. And he did not get along with Peel, who wanted to help them. When Trevelyan found out about the shipment of American corn, he was furious.

Trevelyan angrily informed Peel that the British government followed the principles of laissez-faire, an economic theory that holds that the government should stay out of private business affairs as much as possible. According to the theory, a strong economy is a free economy in which individual landowners can buy and sell whatever and whenever they please. Almost every British politician and government official firmly believed in the laissez-faire philosophy and ran the government according to its principles. Trevelyan told Peel that if the government left the landlords and the food distribution system alone, the landlords would feed their own tenants and the famine would end.

British People Disliked Irish

But Peel doubted that many of the landlords would deal fairly with their tenants. He knew that most British people disliked the Irish. The common belief was that too much aid would only make the Irish more lazy and dependent on the British. Many British openly expressed the opinion that an Irish famine might actually be a good thing. Many agreed with the poet Alfred Lord Tennyson, who said about the Irish:

> They live in a horrible island and have no history of their own worth the least notice. Could not anyone blow up that horrible island with dynamite and carry it off in pieces—a long way off?

Peel ran up against such prejudice at every turn, but he continued in 1846 to push for repeal of the Corn Laws.

The Stench of Rotting Spuds

That spring, the Irish potato crop failed again. The stench of the rotting spuds drifted relentlessly across the countryside. Trevelyan's relief efforts were small and poorly managed. He set up a few medical clinics, soup kitchens, and homeless shelters, but they were equipped to serve only a tiny percentage of the hundreds of thousands of sick and starving people. Demonstrations and riots broke out in Ireland.

While people starved, huge quantities of food bound for England left the docks of Belfast and other Irish ports. John Mitchel told how he stood on the docks and wept. "During all the famine years," he wrote, "Ireland was actually producing sufficient food and flax, to feed and clothe not nine, but eighteen millions of people." But British landlords and merchants continued to ship the food and cloth to British markets. Vessel after vessel left Ireland, carrying loads of wheat, oats, cattle, pigs, butter, and eggs.

Mitchel was not the only person to see the food ships departing. Each day, hundreds of starving peasants gathered near the docks and watched helplessly as the food they so desperately needed headed for British dinner tables. Isaac Butt, an Irish politician, described how these impoverished city slum dwellers wandered aimlessly through the streets. They were thin and pale, said Butt, with "emaciated forms. . . . The strong and hale . . . peasant of a few years ago, is now wasted to the weak, and miserable, and half-starved pauper, that sits listless and idle on the flags of Dublin streets." Both Mitchel and Butt saw the wagons that each morning collected the bodies of those who had died on the streets during the night. The wagons carried the corpses into the countryside for burial in mass graves.

On June 25, 1846, after a fierce political battle, Robert Peel finally managed to push a repeal of the Corn Laws through the British Parliament. But the repeal came too late and did little good. Some foreign grain did reach Ireland. But the flood of goods leaving the island for Britain overshadowed the small amount of relief grain. In a sense, Peel himself now became a casualty of the famine. Angry politicians and adverse public opinion forced him out of office, and the suffering Irish lost their only important British supporter.

Lord John Russell followed Peel as prime minister. Russell did not pressure Trevelyan about relief efforts as Peel had done. So Trevelyan closed down many of the small-scale Irish relief operations he had installed. He did not want the Irish to become too dependent on British aid and bleed the British treasury.

The winter of 1846 and 1847 brought more devastation to Ireland. The justice of the peace of County Cork reported seeing people dying in ditches everywhere. He watched a feverish woman drag the naked corpse of her twelve-year-old daughter to a ravine and cover it with stones. A local doctor found seven people lying in the ruins of a tumbled cottage. One lice-infested cloak covered all seven, one of whom had been dead for several hours. The people were so weak from hunger they could not move.

John Mitchel described how a starving farmer wandered the countryside for weeks, searching for roots and leaves to feed his family. Finally, unable to find the strength to go on, the man went home to die. Mitchel reported that the man and his wife barely recognized each other: "There is a dull stupid malice in their looks: they forget that they had five children, all dead weeks ago and thrown coffinless into shallow graves . . . and at last, in misty dreams of drivelling idiocy, they die utter strangers."

One Brief Harvest

In 1847, there was one brief harvest of edible potatoes. This fed many people during the winter and offered them hope that the blight was over. But it proved to be a false hope. The pestilence returned stronger than ever in 1848 and 1849. Starvation, disease, and eviction once more took their terrible toll in Ireland.

In the winter of 1849 and 1850, the potato blight finally subsided. But the suffering of the Irish people did not end. In the five years of famine, families were shattered and children orphaned. Over one million people died, and millions more fled the country. And Irish hatred for the British reached a new high. The land known around the world as the beautiful Emerald Isle became a wasteland of desolation and human misery. The famine drained the energies and hopes of the survivors. One Irish woman from County Cork said, "After the famine . . . there was no spirit left in the people."

Death and Flight—Ireland Depopulated

An estimated one and one-half million Irish died of starvation and disease during the great famine. Medical experts estimated that more than half a million people died from disease in the famine years.

There were no official figures for the number of evictions, but contemporary historians believe that they occurred at a rate of about 150 per week. That adds up to more than 38,000 evictions over the five years of famine. In all, at least half a million people lost their homes. Most of these homeless people eventually died of starvation, disease, or exposure to the elements. A majority of the dead were children.

Over the years, much of the blame for this frightening death toll has been placed on the British. Historian Cecil Woodham-Smith said, "The treatment of the Irish people by the British government during the famine has been described as genocide—race murder.

The British government has been accused, and not only by the Irish, of wishing to exterminate the Irish people." But, as Woodham-Smith and other scholars point out, the British did not have a specific plan to destroy the Irish.

"It is not characteristic of the English to behave as they behaved in Ireland. As a nation, the English have proved themselves to be capable of generosity, tolerance . . . but not where Ireland is concerned," said Woodham-Smith. There was a prejudice "felt by the English towards the Irish . . . rooted far back in religious and political history." This prejudice, along with a strong belief in the idea of laissez-faire, compelled the British government to neglect the Irish during the great famine.

White Slaves

Much of the suffering of the Irish during the famine was caused by the absentee British landlords. The British Parliament later blamed these wealthy landowners, saying they were "very much like slaveholders with white slaves." One member of Parliament said that the landlords had abused "the great powers entrusted to them by the law." They had brought a "whole people to the brink of starvation . . . the landlords had not done their duty." The government punished many landlords by charging them high fines. Some were imprisoned, and many others suffered public disgrace.

But disciplining some of the landlords did nothing to ease the suffering of the Irish people. In addition to the great numbers who died, many more fled their homeland in search of better living conditions. During the winter of 1847, for example, Irish emigration to other countries increased dramatically. That year, more than 215,000 people embarked for foreign lands from the Irish ports of Sligo, Baltimore, Westport, and Killala, and others.

Coffin Ships

The ships leaving these ports were almost always overcrowded. Such vessels did not have adequate food and water to sustain the number of people on board. These dangerous boats became known as "coffin ships." Sometimes, overcrowding caused the bottoms of the vessels to scrape underwater rocks, which could cause a ship to capsize. One ship that sailed from Westport in 1847 sank within sight of the town. Relatives who had just said good-bye to the emigrants watched helplessly as everyone on board the ship drowned.

A typical coffin ship, the *Elizabeth and Sarah,* sailed from Killala to Canada in 1846. The vessel was supposed to carry 12,500 gallons of water but carried only 8,700 gallons. There was not enough food for the 276 passengers, who had to share thirty-two sleeping berths.

There were no bathrooms or other sanitary facilities on board. One passenger later described the state of the ship as "horrible and disgusting beyond the power of language to describe." During an eight-week voyage, forty-two people died of hunger and thirst. It is estimated that more than five thousand Irish died on the way to other countries during the famine years.

Prejudice and Hatred

Most of the 1847 emigrants went to North America, 110,000 to Canada alone. Unfortunately, these emigrants faced the same prejudice and hatred in their new country that they experienced in Ireland. One reason the Canadians reacted inhospitably was that they feared the Irish would bring disease to Canada. In fact, thousands of Irish suffering from fever and dysentery did arrive in Canadian ports in 1847. On May 31, forty ships lined up on the St. Lawrence River. Many of those on board were sick. They waited for days, even weeks, to get permission from Canadian officials to disembark.

Worried Canadian authorities eventually passed a law that eliminated cheap tickets on ships crossing the Atlantic Ocean. As a result, most of the poorest Irish could not afford the trip and had no choice but to stay in Ireland. Thus, the Canadians accomplished their goal of keeping at least some of the Irish out.

To escape the famine, Irish peasants also fled to the United States. In fact, more Irish emigrated to the United States than to any other country. More than 800,000 came in the 1840s. And another 900,000 came in the 1850s. Like the Canadian authorities, U.S. officials were worried about the extreme poverty of the incoming Irish. There was a general feeling that the United States might become "the poorhouse of Europe." People were afraid that the British and other foreigners would try to get rid of their paupers by sending them to the United States. This unreasonable fear caused the U.S. Congress to pass two Passenger Acts in March 1847. These acts reduced by one-third the number of passengers a British ship could carry to the United States. Authorities also greatly increased the price of passage in hopes of discouraging the poor from making the trip.

At first, the Irish had a difficult time living in the United States. Most were afraid to try farming again. So they settled in northeastern cities like Boston, New York, and Philadelphia. Work was hard to find, and most Irish occupied overcrowded, filthy slums. And they constantly had to deal with prejudice. Many Americans feared that Irish Catholics would multiply, overrun the country, and take orders from the Catholic pope in Rome instead of the American president. Anti-Catholic riots rocked New York and other American cities. Often, members of anti-Irish organizations and even the police chased and beat up Irish-Americans for no reason.

The Irish Endured

But the Irish endured the abuses they received in the United States. They remembered the terrible conditions they had escaped in Ireland and vowed to succeed in their new homes no matter what the cost. And they worked hard. Irish men labored for low wages building canals and railroads. Many of the women found jobs as housemaids and seamstresses. They saved their money, sending some of it back to Ireland to pay for ship passages for relatives and friends. Eventually, Irish-Americans rose to positions of power in the United States. They became police officers, fire fighters, municipal clerks, politicians, and government officials.

Emigration from Ireland continued throughout the rest of the nineteenth century. By 1890, three million Irish lived in foreign countries, nearly as many as lived in Ireland itself. Of the "overseas" Irish, 84 percent resided in the United States, 8 percent in England, and 7 percent in the British Commonwealth nations of Canada, Australia, and New Zealand. By the early 1900s, there were about four million people living in Ireland.

In addition to population loss through emigration, the potato famine had other long-term effects. Widespread poverty continued in Ireland for generations and remains common today. British mistreatment during the crisis left a legacy of deep hatred of the British. Many Irish people could not forget the accusations of Lord John Russell, the British prime minister during most of the famine years. When the potato crop failed in 1848, and the plight of the Irish poor worsened, Russell blamed the Irish themselves. He said the British government had spent great sums of money in 1847 to help the Irish get back on their feet. He insisted that the money had been wasted on the Irish who were lazy and refused to find a replacement for the potato. "How can such people be assisted?" he asked angrily. Many British shared Russell's anti-Irish bias. The mutual dislike of the Irish and British continues into the twentieth century, and much resentment between the two peoples still exists.

The Reform Acts Expand Democracy in Britain

Norman Gash

Norman Gash argues that England gradually extended voting rights to a larger percentage of its people without clashes and violence among the social classes. Widespread unemployment among the workers had instigated reformers to organize in the early part of the century and in the 1840s. Consequently, politicians in Parliament passed the three reform acts of 1832, 1867, and 1884 because they feared losing their seats if they did not. Ironically, men who neither saw universal suffrage as an ideal nor trusted the illiterate to have power greatly expanded democracy even though still short of one person one vote. Norman Gash has been lecturer in modern history at the University of London and the University of Leeds in Yorkshire. He is the author of *Politics in the Age of Peel, Reaction and Reconstruction in England,* and *The Prime Ministers.*

It could be said with reasonable assurance that the three British nineteenth-century parliamentary reform acts established the broad principle of political democracy, leaving the finer details and the separate problem of female suffrage to be solved in the twentieth century by the legislation of 1918, 1928 and 1948.

What this generalization obscures, however, is the odd circumstance that the acts of 1832, 1867 and 1884 were passed by men who had no belief in the kind of political democracy implicit in universal suffrage and equality of electoral districts and who feared that the introduction of such a system would lead to the tyranny of the illiterate many over the cultured few and of a numerical majority over the interests of minorities. For the greater part of the century the view of most politicians, and indeed of most educated people, was that the parliamentary vote was a trust and that the proper exercise of that trust called for a certain degree of education and social responsibility. Direct advocates of democracy—the radical reformers of the early part of the century, the Chartists[1] of the 1840s, and the extreme radicals of the age of [liberal William] Gladstone and [radical liberal MP Joseph] Chamberlain—never found much substantial support in the House of Commons.

There is another difficulty in accepting parliamentary reform as a smooth evolutionary process moving in successive stages towards a clearly defined goal. It is this. The three acts were carried by sharply contrasting methods and with sharply contrasting motives. . . .

This rather mundane reflection, if it is to be persuasive, needs to be established in a wider context. In 1831 it was clear that Lord [Charles] Grey's ministry (the first in which the Whigs as a party had held office for a quarter of a century) would have to bring forward a parliamentary reform measure if it was to survive. It had no guaranteed majority in either House of parliament and whatever it did, reform was certain to be raised early in the first session as one of the more important political issues. That the country generally had expectations of reform in the winter of 1830–1 is a commonplace. Yet it is worth noting that these expectations did not amount to a large degree of popular pressure until the cabinet had actually put their proposals before parliament. The contemporary charge that Grey first created public excitement by his bill and then used that excitement to justify the bill had an element of truth. . . .

Grey, of course, had been identified with the cause of parliamentary reform ever since the 1790s. The boldness of the 1831 bill, however, arose from his conviction that the reform question could only be settled for his generation if the public was offered as full and generous a measure as possible. Grey did not miscalculate the degree of public fervour he was able to rouse on behalf of his bill. What he underestimated was the degree of opposition he would encounter in parliament and from the king. . . .

The fierce contest over this first great reform of the electoral system not surprisingly produced a debate on fundamentals unmatched

---

1. a party of political reformers, chiefly workingmen who advocated universal suffrage, secret ballots, annual elections, payment of members of parliament, no property qualifications for members, and equal electoral districts

by any of its successors. It was, if one may use the phrase, the most 'principled' of the three nineteenth-century reform acts. It was fought out by a determined but unhappy cabinet which had gone too far to withdraw and a determined but often despairing opposition which was never able to offer a satisfactory alternative reform of their own. A paradox of the whole reform process was that the violence of the party battles was in inverse proportion to the extent of the actual changes proposed. Though no precise statistical calculation is possible, the probable result of the first Reform Act was to add about 300,000 to the existing electorate of about 500,000. Some estimates make the increase even smaller. In any case it was substantially less than in 1867 or 1884.

What caused the bitter debate in 1831–2 was, of course, the fact that this was the first successful attempt by any British government to carry out a major change in the electoral system. It was a crucial event because it set a precedent. Even so, what was intended by the cabinet was no more than a pruning, purification and enlargement of the existing electoral structure. The motive behind the measure was to strengthen the aristocratic constitution by widening its political basis. It was emphatically *not* a democratic measure. It was, as Lord Grey insisted, a conservative measure in the truest sense. . . .

The reform crisis of 1866–7 offers an almost total contrast to that of 1831–2. In the first place the great precedent had been set; the principle that it was proper for the legislature to review the system by which it was elected had been given respectability. Since 1832 in fact there had been many discussions in parliament on the need for further reform, if only to remove the imperfections left or even created by the act of 1832. Bills had been introduced by successive ministries of opposed political complexion in 1859 and 1860, only to founder on opposition or apathy. There did not, however, seem any strong feeling in the country on the question. . . .

What decided the timing of the next instalment of parliamentary reform were personal and party considerations. Of these the most important were the death in 1865 of the veteran Liberal prime minister Lord [Henry] Palmerston who had been a consistently conservative influence in domestic politics; the desire of the elderly Lord John Russell, who had personally introduced the 1831 reform bill (the only political triumph he had ever enjoyed), to atone for the frustrations of his subsequent career; and Gladstone's somnambulistic intuition that parliamentary reform was a popular cause he ought to take up.

The bill these two Liberal leaders produced, though moderate, split their party and brought about the entry to office of a Conservative ministry which lacked a majority in the House of Commons. . . .

The ultimate determination of the Conservative cabinet to pass a reform bill of their own was based less on what was happening in the country than on a calculation of party advantage. Three motives seem to have been operating. First, to settle the reform question now that it had been inconveniently raised by their opponents. Next, to remain in office as long as possible—a natural desire in a party which had been almost uniformly in opposition since 1846. Lastly, to demonstrate to the public that parliamentary reform was not a party issue and that the Conservatives as well as the Liberals were entitled to take up the question. To this must be added a determination, particularly strong in [Benjamin] Disraeli (the ministerial leader in the Commons) to discredit his personal rival Gladstone and keep the Liberal party divided. There was, on reflection, little to be lost and perhaps something to be gained by changing an electoral system which only once since 1832 had returned a Conservative majority— and that perhaps in exceptional circumstances.

Nevertheless, to embark on legislation without control of the legislature is a hazardous business. The cabinet's policy involved them in abrupt and sometimes contradictory changes in their detailed proposals and a steady surrender to chance majorities in the House of Commons. The end result was an act more extensive than had ever been intended by either party and one whose precise effects could only be a matter of guesswork. It resulted from a process of constant and extraordinary improvisation on the part of a few ministers. Their bemused followers scarcely knew to what they were committing themselves other than it was a measure recommended by their own leaders rather than one introduced by the hated Gladstone. . . .

In its final form a genuine household suffrage, freed from any restrictions such as the payment of rates, became the basis of the new borough² franchise. The practical results were startling. Over a million new voters were added to the electorate, representing for the whole United Kingdom an increase of 80 per cent and for England and Wales an increase of 88 per cent. The increase was all the more dramatic for being concentrated in the boroughs, where the electorate more than doubled. . . .

The character of the 1867 act, at once drastic and lopsided, made a further adjustment within the foreseeable future almost inevitable. The exclusion of the country dweller from the household franchise was logically indefensible; and the inadequacy of the 1867 redistribution of seats threw into sharper relief the steady growth of urban and industrial population outside the parliamentary boundaries of the borough constituencies. . . .

The third Reform Act has in general received far less scrutiny from historians than its two predecessors. Yet it was in many ways a

2. a town that sends a representative to Parliament

remarkable measure. The delay in bringing it forward was its first curious feature. Certainly there was no great demand in the country for yet another instalment of electoral reform. . . . The justification for Gladstone's bill lay in wider considerations—the unbalanced state of the franchise and the changed attitude of Victorian public opinion towards another downward extension of the electorate. Whatever their private misgivings, politicians now had to show a proper deference to the fashionable view that the mass of the British people had shown themselves worthy of political responsibility. What Gladstone called 'the enfranchisement of capable citizens' became a piece of conventional wisdom against which it was morally indecent and politically dangerous to argue—a political cliché elevated above rational criticism. Even the Conservative peers in the House of Lords only threw out Gladstone's first bill on the argument that it should have been accompanied by a suitable measure for redistributing the constituencies. The real parliamentary struggle did not come therefore over the extension of the franchise, even though the bill as eventually passed added another 80 per cent to the already enlarged electorate created by the 1867 act. It came over what was to the parliamentary parties the more important tactical issue of the new parliamentary constituencies.

A second oddity about the act was that the whole interparty dispute was settled rapidly, secretly, and authoritatively by the two party leaders, Gladstone and Lord [Robert] Salisbury. They then pushed the bill through parliament in a quite astonishing demonstration of party discipline—or, as some might unkindly say, party subservience. The House of Commons, which had debated at such length the 1831–2 bills, and almost dictated the form of the 1867 act, was in 1884–5 little more than a rubber-stamp. What counted were the decisions arrived at privately by six men, of whom only three really mattered—Gladstone, Lord Salisbury, and the Liberal electoral expert [Sir Charles] Dilke. . . .

Certainly Gladstone's insistence, against all precedent, on a unified reform measure for the whole United Kingdom, was in sharp contrast to the tepid and conventional remarks he made about the 'peasantry' of England and Wales (whereby he meant the landless rural labourers) as 'capable citizens' who should now be admitted to the franchise. It was precisely the inclusion of Ireland in the government's bill which aroused greatest unease in the Liberal ranks. There had been no mandate for it at any of the party conferences and it produced the most powerful and prophetic passages of the reform debates in parliament. . . .

As for Lord Salisbury, the considerations which governed his actions were almost entirely tactical. Though he did not like the extension of the suffrage, he knew it could not be prevented and as party leader he declined to tie his followers to a losing cause. What Gladstone had oratorically described in 1866 as 'the great social forces which move onward in their might and majesty' could not be stopped in 1884 if the Liberal government of the day was determined to advance their progress. . . .

The moral to be drawn from these three reform episodes is not perhaps an elevated one. In all three crises party and personal advantages played a considerable part: an underlying one in 1831–2, a dominant one in 1866–7, and a large one in 1884–5. Yet one must distinguish between motives and consequences. British political evolution in the nineteenth century has incurred the reproach that democratic reform came too slowly and lagged behind social progress. There is much to support this view. Large as the additions to the electorate had been between 1832 and 1884, they still left Britain with something perceptibly short of full democracy. Only two adult males in three in England and Wales, three out of five in Scotland, five out of ten in Ireland, had the vote. It was the second, third and fifth decades of the present century, within the lifetime of many still living, which saw the establishment of the principle of one man, one vote, together with the admission of women to the franchise on equal terms with men, which is commonly held to mark the perfected political democracy.

The first three reform acts now regarded as milestones along the road to that achievement were then no more than—and were intended by their authors to be no more than—modifications of the traditional pre-1832 system. . . .

Yet there is a case also for the contrary view: that this slow and piecemeal approach towards democracy proceeded at least as fast as, if not faster than, social development. Much of the conventional justification among late-Victorian politicians for extensions of the franchise rested on little more than a string of comfortable assumptions. They talked of 'the respectable working-man' (to mention the disrespectable 'residuum' soon became unfashionable), of 'capable citizens' (with little attempt to define 'capability'), of 'trusting the people' (though they did not say with what). This vocabulary was based on not much evidence other than the absence of violent popular disorders after the middle of the century (with Ireland always the admitted exception) and on the practical continuation in power of an aristocratically dominated ruling class. It was this apparently remarkable social stability, even more striking when contrasted with the continent of Europe, which made it possible for each of the two great political parties in turn to propose, or at least not vociferously oppose, substantial additions to the electorate on which they both depended for parliamentary office. . . .

It would in fact be difficult to show that the newly enfranchised masses had either exhibited their fitness for the vote or were qualified for its exercise on any previously accepted criteria. Nor did the rise of a cheap, sensational national newspaper press under such new-style proprietors as [Alfred] Harmsworth Northcliffe hold out much encouragement for the future. Robert Lowe's famous remark after the 1867 legislation, that 'we must educate our masters' (more accurately 'compel our future masters to learn their letters') applied with even more force to the 1884 act. The first compulsory education act was passed in 1870, three years *after* the second Reform Act had created a working-class majority in the boroughs. In the rural areas the early inefficiencies of the educational system and the notorious difficulties of enforcing attendance of country children needed for small jobs on farms, made it unlikely that the new electorate was much affected by formal state education until the generation after 1900. One of the more reflective British prime ministers, Stanley Baldwin, who had been born in the year of the second Reform Act and had watched all this process as he grew up, said in 1928 that 'democracy has arrived at a gallop in England and I feel all the time that it is a race for life. Can we educate them before the crash comes?'

Even so, there was probably some advantage in the course taken by parliamentary reform in Victorian Britain, narrow, selfish, short-sighted and muddled though the process had been. It is often a charge against aristocratic or oligarchic societies that they rarely surrender power until they are forced and that then it is too late for the concession to produce any benefits. In an oblique fashion the British reform acts, specially those of 1867 and 1884, had the merit of coming when there was no particular demand for them by those who stood to be enfranchised. As Professor Norman McCord has suggested in one of the more perceptive articles on the nineteenth-century reform acts which have appeared in recent years, not only were those acts typically English in their untidy 'muddling-through', on no discernible basis of principle, but *because* of that, they avoided any direct class conflict of the kind which has damaged the stable evolution of democracy in other countries.

If that point is accepted, one further comment may be allowed. Political parties do not as a rule earn much praise from political theorists. Yet in their pursuit of self-regarding ends, it may be that the Liberal and Conservative parties of the Victorian age contributed more than they intended to the general good.

Queen Victoria: Stability Within an Era of Change

Asa Briggs

Asa Briggs describes the influence Queen Victoria and her husband, Prince Albert, had on the era identified by the queen's name. Crowned at eighteen, from the start she insisted on moral and dignified behavior. Her husband, though less popular, promoted intellectual endeavors and causes that helped common people. Asa Briggs, a lecturer at the University of Oxford and the University of Leeds in England, was a member of the Institute for Advanced Study in Princeton, New Jersey. He is the author of *History of Birmingham, Victorian People,* and *Friends of the People.*

W hen Victoria came to the throne in 1837 at the age of 18 the monarchy was at a low ebb. There was little republican sentiment and much talk of 'altar, throne and cottage', but William IV's early popularity had withered away. Victoria's initial advantages were threefold—her youth, her sex, and her already clearly formed sense of duty. When George IV and William IV[1] ascended the throne they had a past behind them; Victoria, whose succession to the throne had been far from certain, had only a future. Her sex, which might in different circumstances have been a handicap, enabled her

1. kings of Great Britain and Ireland; George IV 1820–1830; William IV 1830–1837

Excerpted from *The Age of Improvement* (London: Longmans, 1959) by Asa Briggs. Reprinted with permission from Pearson Education Limited.

to make a special appeal not only to the public but to her prime minister, Melbourne.[2] He was fascinated by the 'girl-Queen' and she by him, and the first phase of their 'partnership' between 1837 and 1839 was stimulating and happy for both of them. Moreover, from the start the Queen displayed great strength of character and responsibility. She wrote in her journal on the day of her accession that she would do her utmost to fulfil her duty to her country, and despite her youth and lack of experience she immediately took it for granted that others would obey her. Her first triumph of character was over the experienced and worldly-wise Melbourne, whose occupations and habits she revolutionized. 'I have no doubt he is passionately fond of her as he might be of his daughter if he had one', Greville[3] wrote, 'and the more because he is a man with capacity for loving without having anything in the world to love. It has become his province to educate, to instruct, and to form the most interesting mind and character in the world.' He watched his language—usually 'interlarded with damns'—sat bolt upright rather than lounged in his chair, and greatly restricted the range of his anecdotes.

The Young Queen Sets Her Tone

Victoria's childish resolves 'to be good' were in harmony with a new spirit in society, and Melbourne was responding to pressures which even at the time were applied not only by the Queen but by 'respectable' opinion. He enjoyed the one form of pressure but hated the second. 'All the young people are growing mad about religion', he once lamented. As it was, he could scarcely protest when the etiquette of the Court was tightened up and the Queen revealed herself as a stern and self-determined moralist, on one occasion at least exposing herself to great unpopularity by wrongly 'suspecting the worst' of a member of her Court. Admission to the Court was made to depend on good character, and 'rakishness' which Melbourne thought 'refreshing' the Queen considered at best 'melancholy' and at worst 'bad'. Manners as well as morals changed. The relatively easy informality of 'drawing room' and 'levées', during which the King might talk frankly or even rudely to people he knew, gave way to far more restrained and dignified ceremonial. Victoria's own sense of dignity was prominently displayed in 1839 when after Melbourne's defeat in the House of Commons she quarrelled with Peel[4] about the party affiliations of the Ladies of the Bedchamber and prevented him from forming a new government. 'The Queen maintains *all* her ladies', she wrote to Melbourne (her dignity had been the surface defence of her warm affection for her old prime minister) 'and

2. Lord Melbourne, a British politician, served as prime minister in 1834 and again in 1835–1841.
3. Charles Cavendish Fulke Greville, author of *The Greville Memoirs* 4. Sir Robert Peel, a British politician, served as prime minister 1834–1835 and 1841–1846.

thinks her Prime Minister will cut a sorry figure indeed if he resigns on this'. Melbourne was back in office again for two more years and Peel, condemned simply because he did not share Melbourne's delightful qualities, was left with the cares of 'responsible opposition'.

The Queen Marries Prince Albert

The position was altered, however, as a result of the Queen's marriage in February 1840, and after the influence of her husband had established itself—almost at once—Melbourne was inevitably pushed more and more into the background. It had long been the ambition of King Leopold of the Belgians, the Queen's uncle and one of her earliest *confidants,* to marry his niece to her cousin, Prince Albert of Saxe Coburg Gotha, and there had been much gossip about the match from 1837 onwards. Fortunately for Victoria, the marriage which had been planned was also a marriage of love. Albert, in her own words, 'completely won my heart', and the wedding, celebrated quietly in St. James's Palace, with no signs of enthusiasm in the country, began the happiest period of her life. Her husband was still six months under the age of 21 in 1840 and he was a far from popular figure with the aristocracy, the crowds, or the House of Commons—by a majority of 104 votes the annuity of £50,000 the government proposed to pay him was reduced to £30,000—but he was just as resolved as Victoria to take the task of government seriously and willing in so doing to sink 'his own *individual existence* in that of his wife'. Stiff and conservative,

Queen Victoria on her wedding day

his first efforts were devoted to reinforcing the Queen's own desire to set an example of strict propriety at Court.

The difference between old ways and new was well brought out in an early clash of ideas with Melbourne about the nature of social morality. 'Character', Melbourne maintained, 'can be attended to when people are of no consequence, but it will not do when people are of high rank'. Albert cared far less about rank than industry and integrity, and besides being willing to work long hours with a Germanic thoroughness that Smiles could not have excelled, he displayed all those 'Victorian' virtues of character which Melbourne regarded as unnecessary in a man of his station. His 'seriousness' of purpose is witnessed by the causes to which he gave his full support. His first public speech was at a meeting on behalf of the abolition of slavery; he was a vigorous advocate of scientific research and education, of official patronage of art, and of reformed universities; he took an active interest in the work of the Society for Improving the Condition of the Labouring Classes, founded in 1844, and when criticized by Lord John Russell[5] for attending one of its meetings replied firmly that he conceived 'one has a *Duty* to perform towards the great mass of the working classes (and particularly at this moment) which will not allow one's yielding to the fear for some possible inconvenience'; he helped to design and plan the building of a block of houses known as Prince Albert's 'model houses for families'; and last, but perhaps most important of all, he played such an important part in organizing the Great Exhibition of 1851[6] that if it had not been for his efforts, it is doubtful whether the Exhibition would have been held. In all these efforts Albert met with resistance and opposition, much of it centred in the country houses and the universities, places where old prejudices were strong and suspicions difficult to break down.

Albert had perforce to follow the dictates of self-help as much as Stephenson or Paxton,[7] and on many doors which were open to them he had to knock loudly. Two years after the Queen had written in 1853 that the nation appreciated him and fully acknowledged what he had done 'daily and hourly for the country', he was being lampooned in the popular press and attacked in the clubs more than ever before. If there was any truth in the Queen's claim that he eventually succeeded in raising monarchy to 'the *highest* pinnacle of respect' and rendering it 'popular beyond what it *ever* was in this country', it was entirely as a result of his own exertions and courage. He had no deficiency of spirit. When times were blackest for him on the eve of the Crimean War, he could still write that he looked upon his troubles as 'a fiery ordeal that will serve to purge away impurities'.

Friendship with Peel was as important to Albert as friendship with Melbourne had been to Victoria, and it helped in itself to set the tone of mid-Victorian England. Between 1841 and 1846 the Queen and her husband came to put their full trust in their great prime minister and

---

5. British politician, served as prime minister 1846–1852 and 1865–1866 6. international exhibition of industry, science, and commerce held at Hyde Park, London, in the Crystal Palace; the exhibit was viewed by 6 million people 7. George Stephenson invented the railway and opened lines in 1825 and 1830; Joseph Paxton designed the Crystal Palace in Hyde Park that housed the Great Exhibition of 1851.

the causes for which he stood—sound administration, strong government, and free trade. As early as 1843 the Queen wrote to the King of
the Belgians praising Peel as 'a great statesman, a man who thinks but
little of party and never of himself'; after Peel's death she wrote that
Albert felt the loss *'dreadfully'*. He feels 'he has lost a second father'.

The Prince Consort's Unpopularity

There was something in common, indeed, between Peel and Albert,
not only in their dislike of the noisy clamour of party but in their desire for practical improvement and their resentment of unthinking
aristocracies. During the Crimean War Albert complained of the
'hostility or bitterness towards me' not only of the radicals but 'of
the old High Tory or Protectionist Party on account of my friendship
with the late Sir Robert Peel and of my success with the Exhibition',
and the bitterness certainly went deep. If in the case of Peel the main
taunt was one of betrayal of the landed interest, in the case of Albert
it was one of never having belonged to it, of being un-English, of
working by slow deliberation, not by instinct, of paying attention to
the wrong things in the wrong way. In such a context of criticism
even Albert's virtues could appear as vices. He was ridiculed in
Punch for trying to act twenty different character parts; he was criticized in army messes for his zealous interference; he was attacked
in Cambridge University for trying to do too much as Chancellor,
not too little. He had won a hotly contested election for the Chan-
cellorship in 1847, and it is easy to guess the reaction of Cambridge
dons to his earnest desire to look at 'schemes of tuition' and examination papers on subjects in which he was particularly interested. His
collection of information on every conceivable issue of public policy, his investigation of statistics, his preparation of memoranda, and
his considerable European correspondence were all activities calculated to alienate aristocratic holders of power. So too was his stern
insistence on the morality of the Court. There was an interesting incident in 1852 when the new prime minister, Lord Derby,[8] submitted his list of names for household appointments and Albert noted
with horror that 'the greater part were the Dandies and Roués of London and the Turf'. The Prince cared little for aristocratic company
or aristocratic pursuits—in 1861, the year of his death, for instance,
he described Ascot[9] as rendered 'much more tedious than usual by
incessant rain'—and he did not attempt to hide his preference for the
company of authors, scientists, social reformers, and pioneers of education. 'Culture superseded blood, and South Kensington became
the hub of the universe'. The result was that the Court stood aloof

8. Edward George Stanley Derby, prime minister of Great Britain in 1852, 1858–1859, and
1866–1868 9. the Royal Ascot horse races, held annually on Ascot Heath

from the rest of the London world, and had 'but slender relations with the more amusing part of it'.

The Queen's Popularity

Victoria did not share all Albert's enthusiasms or even understand them. She cared little for the company of scientists, showed no interest in royal patronage of art, and in only few of her letters referred to literature. She delighted, however, in the Exhibition of 1851 and thrilled to the bravery of British troops in the Crimea.[10] On thirty occasions she visited the Crystal Palace, noting in her *Journal* that she never remembered anything before that everyone was so pleased with as the Exhibition; during the war she wrote that 'the conduct of our *dear noble* Troops is *beyond praise*', said that she felt as if 'they were *my own children*', and objected to those critics of the military system who detracted from British victories by 'croaking'. Just because she genuinely shared such English sentiments and was not tempted, as Albert was, to seek for forms of intellectual expression, she was far more popular than he. She was not, of course, in any sense a democratic monarch responding to mass pressures or gaining publicity through the influence of mass communications, but she won loyalty and respect from the majority of the population, including the middle classes, many of whose qualities and limitations she shared. Perhaps the most vivid impression of her impact on English society can be gained from a perusal of newspaper reports of her visits to the provinces in the 1850s. In 1858 she visited both Birmingham and Leeds. Everywhere there were great crowds 'who behaved as well in the streets as could any assemblage of the aristocracy at a Queen's drawing room'. The local newspapers, while praising the interest of the Prince Consort in science and industry, reserved their loudest praise for a queen who 'is as it were partner with the great and multitudinous people who do gladly obey her, joins with them in legislation, shares with them in government, and makes them to a great extent their own rulers'. They extolled her combination of 'feminine grace and royal dignity' and her lofty eminence above all party faction, but above all they argued that 'what consummates the whole is, that she is a wife and a mother of so lofty a purity and discharging her duties so well that she forms the brightest exemplar to the matrons of England'. . . .

Not the least of the achievements of Victoria and Albert was to provide for the country a pattern of obviously happy domestic life which contrasted sharply with the pattern provided by all the Queen's recent predecessors. At her marriage ceremony the 'royal family' was a collection of aged and for the most part discredited minor personalities, better known for their defects than for their mer-

10. The Crimean War was fought in 1854–1856.

its. By 1861, there were nine royal children, the eldest of whom, the Princess Royal, had already produced a grandchild for the Queen, the future Emperor William II of Germany. On more than one state occasion in the '40s and '50s the royal children accompanied the Queen. In 1849, for instance, on the occasion of her first visit to Ireland (she went there again in 1853 and 1861) she took her four children with her. They were objects of universal attention and admiration. 'Oh, Queen, dear', screamed a stout old lady, 'make one of them Prince Patrick, and all Ireland will die for you.'

Victoria Mourns and Withdraws

The death of the Prince Consort from typhoid fever in 1861 was a tragic blow to the Queen from which she never fully recovered. 'The loss of her husband', wrote Lady Lewis to her brother, Lord Clarendon, 'has changed her from a powerful sovereign (which she was with the knowledge and judgement of her husband to guide her opinions and strengthen her will) into a weak and desolate woman with the weight of duties she has not the moral and physical power to support'. Conventional condolences meant nothing to her, and only those who could find the right words to demonstrate their understanding of the extent of her loss were likely to touch any chord in her heart. Strangely enough, it was Palmerston,[11] with whom both she and the Prince had had so many differences and had fought such hectic battles, who found the correct phrase and wrote to her of the Prince as 'that perfect Being'.

Victoria Resists Pressure to Be More Public

From 1861 to the end of the [nineteenth century] the Queen was in the deepest retirement, resolved irrevocably that Albert's 'wishes—his plans—about everything are to be my law'. Although she found some consolation in the affairs of her family and its network of associations with other European courts, and although she spent many peaceful days at Balmoral, her favourite home, she wore mourning, shrank from large crowds, and feared formal social gatherings. She hated the thought of appearing in public as a 'poor, brokenhearted widow' and declared that she 'would as soon clasp the hand of the poorest widow in the land if she had truly loved her husband and felt for me, as I would a Queen, or any other in high position'. It was natural, though hard for her to bear, that the public could not appreciate the reason for her social abdication. In 1865 *Punch* printed a famous cartoon in which Paulina (Britannia) unveiled the covered statue and addressed Hermione (Victoria) with the words 'Tis time! descend; be stone no more!' Two years later the

11. Henry John Temple Palmerston, British politician, served as prime minister 1855–1858 and 1859–1865.

Queen was still lost in an unfinished winter's tale and Bagehot[12] could dismiss her and the Prince of Wales in the tersest of phrases as 'a retired widow and an unemployed youth'.

In time the Queen's age and experience were to produce new waves of loyalty and admiration, but the comment of Bagehot is the epitaph on the mid-Victorian period. What would have happened had the Prince Consort lived is a speculative puzzle which has fascinated many specialists in historical 'ifs'.

12. Walter Bagehot, a political theorist and editor of the *Economist*.

The First Women's Rights Convention

Bill Severn

After women were barred from participating in the 1840 World Anti-Slavery Convention, Lucretia Mott and Elizabeth Cady Stanton vowed to hold a convention focused on women's rights. Mott and Stanton were not able to put this plan into action until 1848, but the convention that they and three other women organized in Seneca Falls, New York, created a firestorm of controversy. Most controversial of all was Stanton's speech demanding the right of suffrage for women. In the following reading, excerpted from his book *Free but Not Equal: How Women Won the Right to Vote,* Bill Severn explains that the Seneca Falls Convention gave birth to the women's suffrage movement. Despite the fact that most newspaper editorialists mocked the convention's participants and their goals, Severn writes, the news struck a chord with numerous American women, who quickly organized their own conventions and women's rights groups. A former news editor, Severn is the author of more than twenty-five books, including many biographies and popular social histories.

Five women got to talking things over around a tea table at the home of one of them in Waterloo, New York, in July 1848 and started something that stirred up almost as much of a sensation in the nation's newspapers as the discovery of gold in California. Two of them were Elizabeth Stanton and Lucretia Mott. Sharing tea with them at the home of Jane Hunt were Lucretia's sister, Martha Wright, and a neighbor, Mary McClintock. All but Elizabeth were Quakers.

Lucretia and her husband had come from Philadelphia to visit her sister and attend a Quaker meeting. Elizabeth had settled in nearby Seneca Falls. It was a chance to renew the friendship they had kept up by mail since those days in London when they had vowed to hold a convention to demand woman's rights. Both had been busy with their homes and families and in carrying on the battle against Negro slavery. Elizabeth's husband, Henry Stanton, had studied law and built up a successful practice, first in Boston and then in upstate New York, but the role of a small-town housewife filled her with restless discontent.

Her marriage was a happy one but Henry often was away from Seneca Falls on business and she was left in an isolated household with only the children for company and the boredom of routine housekeeping chores that were no challenge to her mind. "My experiences at the World Anti-Slavery Convention, all I had read of the legal status of women, and the oppression I saw everywhere, together swept across my soul," she later wrote, "intensified now by many personal experiences. I could not see what to do or where to begin—my only thought was a public meeting for protest and discussion."

Planning the Convention

The others at the tea party shared her feelings and the five of them decided something should be done then and there. They wrote out a public notice to be published in the next edition of the *Seneca County Courier,* announcing that a meeting would be held the following week in Seneca Falls "to discuss the social, civil and religious rights of woman." Ambitiously they advertised that it would be a two-day convention. "During the first day the meeting will be held exclusively for women, who are earnestly invited to attend," the notice said. "The public generally are invited to be present on the second day, when Lucretia Mott of Philadelphia and other ladies and gentlemen will address the convention."

Having made the public announcement, they began to wonder at their own courage. They had no experience in arranging conventions, no program planned, and only a short time to line up speakers and write resolutions. But, having gone that far, they couldn't back down so they met again at Mary McClintock's house. Gathering in her parlor, they drew chairs around Mary's antique mahogany center table and spent the whole day going through a stack of books and anti-slavery society pamphlets trying to find models for the resolutions they wanted to write. The table became one of the historic exhibits at the Smithsonian Institution in Washington years later because it was upon it that they wrote the first document to spell out women's grievances.

The Declaration of Sentiments

It was Elizabeth Stanton's idea to change the Declaration of Independence into their own Declaration of Sentiments. She found a copy of it in Mary's bookcase and began reading it aloud, substituting words that declared woman's independence from man in the same stirring language of rebellion that had inspired the nation to fight for its freedom from King George. Because the declaration of 1776 had listed eighteen grievances against the King they were determined that women should list as many against men.

Holding that "all men and women are created equal" and that "the history of mankind is a history of repeated injuries and usurpations on the part of man toward woman," they declared that "in view of this entire disfranchisement of one-half the people in this country . . . and because women do feel themselves aggrieved, oppressed and fraudulently deprived of their most sacred rights, we insist they have immediate admission to all the rights and privileges which belong to them as Citizens of the United States."

Demanding Suffrage

Elizabeth took on the job of drafting the final document and the resolutions to go with it. Entirely on her own she worked out one demand she considered the key to winning all other rights for women. None of her friends knew about it until later. It read: "Resolved, That it is the duty of the women of this country to secure for themselves their sacred right to the elective franchise." Her final version of the declaration also made the extravagant promise that "we shall employ agents, circulate tracts, petition the State and National legislatures, and endeavor to enlist the pulpit and the press in our behalf. We hope this convention will be followed by a series of conventions embracing every part of the country."

When she showed her resolution on voting rights to her husband, he was strongly against it. Henry told her it was far too revolutionary and that she would turn the whole meeting into a farce if she offered it. He was willing to go along with the rest of her ideas but not that. When she wouldn't listen to his protests he threatened to leave her on her own and have nothing more to do with the affair. Elizabeth refused to give in and Henry packed a bag and left Seneca Falls until the convention was over.

Even Lucretia Mott was worried when Elizabeth showed her the voting resolution. "Oh, Lizzie! If thou demands that, thou will make us ridiculous," Lucretia said. "We must move slowly."

"We must have the vote," Elizabeth answered.

Nobody, not her husband and not Lucretia, could change her mind. None of the others would publicly support her in it even though most of them agreed suffrage was a goal to work toward in the years ahead. They argued, as Henry had, that it would get them a lot of bad publicity. The whole country would make fun of them for demanding such a thing.

When Frederick Douglass, the former Negro slave who had become editor of an abolitionist paper in Rochester, New York, arrived to take part in the meeting, Elizabeth took it up with him. She asked him what the Negroes needed more than anything else to win their rights.

"The ballot," Douglass said.

"And isn't that what women need?" she asked. "Will you speak for it? I cannot alone."

He agreed that he would. But she was troubled about it as the first day of the convention came. Perhaps she had gone too far. Maybe people who read the little notice in the paper were already laughing and nobody would turn up for the meeting that they had so grandly called a convention. They had been granted permission to hold it in the Wesleyan chapel. Because none of them knew how to conduct a public meeting and they didn't want to show their ignorance of parliamentary procedure they asked Lucretia's husband, James Mott, to preside.

The Seneca Falls Convention

July 19, 1848, was a sunny summer day and the small crowd began to grow from early in the morning. Neighbors came from fifty miles around by horse and buggy, in farm wagons, and some on foot. Despite the fact that it was the busy haying season almost as many men showed up as women. Most of the men were tolerantly curious to find out for themselves what it was all about. Although Elizabeth and the others had planned to keep men out on the first day, they decided they couldn't turn them away.

But when they reached the chapel to start the meeting they found the door locked against them. They had been promised the use of it but the minister had become convinced that he was inviting trouble. He wouldn't go back on his word and refuse them the hall but he hoped that when they found the door locked they would take the hint and realize they weren't welcome. Elizabeth called to a young nephew, got him to climb through a window and open the door from the inside, and the crowd moved in.

Lucretia, who was more accustomed to public speaking than the rest, started things off by explaining the aims of the convention. Her sister, Martha Wright, read some newspaper articles she had written, and Mary McClintock spoke about the resolutions that would be offered. A young law student, Samuel Tillman, read some of the laws that were on the books to deny women equal rights with men and Ansel Bascom, a member of the state constitutional convention, spoke about the recently passed law to protect the property of married women. Even when the usually fiery Frederick Douglass spoke, his tone was mild and reasonable.

A Calm Rebellion

There was none of the hysterical ranting of rebellious women bent upon destroying the established rule of men that the newspapers later described. It was a quiet, orderly, and even somewhat dull meeting, with one speaker after another going on at great length. The reading of the wordy resolutions and grievances seemed endless. But for all of that, it was a rebellion, and women across the country would be inspired by what was said and done.

After two days of debate and decision, sixty-eight women and thirty-two men signed their names to the Declaration of Sentiments and adopted the resolutions. The first convention for woman's rights approved nearly all the basic demands the suffrage movement would make during the next seventy-two years.

They demanded equal rights in the churches and universities, in trades and professions, the right to share in all political offices and honors, equality in marriage, freedom of person, property and wages, the right to speak in public and to take an equal part with men in deciding the great moral questions of the day, to make contracts, to sue and be sued, and to testify in courts of justice. All those resolutions were agreed upon unanimously. Then Elizabeth Stanton took to the floor and voiced the first formal demand for woman's right to vote that had ever been made in the United States.

"I should feel exceedingly diffident to appear before you at this time, having never before spoken in public," she said, "were I not nerved by a sense of right and duty, did I not feel that the time had come for the question of woman's wrongs to be laid before the public, did I not believe that woman herself must do this work; for woman alone can understand the height, the depth, the length and breadth of her degradation."

For a maiden speech what she went on to say was surprisingly eloquent. Clear, scholarly, delivered in a firm voice that took courage from her belief in what she said and that drew upon the study and the thoughts which had so long filled her mind, it captured her listeners with the spirit that was to become familiar to her audiences for the next fifty years. Her cheeks were burning before she finished, but her eyes were shining. The vote on her resolution was not unanimous, as it had been on the others, but by a narrow margin the convention did agree "that it is the duty of the women of this country to secure to themselves the sacred right of the elective franchise."

Ridicule and Criticism

Because of Elizabeth Stanton's determined boldness, the village meeting that called itself a convention did arouse the press. It wasn't important news to the nation's editors that some women had gotten together for a discussion with their neighbors in Seneca Falls. Such an event hardly rated notice by the city newspapers. But a local reporter wrote it up as a humorous item and before long it became a national joke. Readers chuckled over the wit and ridicule editors were able to poke at the notion of a woman's Declaration of Independence. The demand for the right to vote made news, even if only as something for men to laugh about.

"Insurrection Among Women," was one headline. Another newspaper warned in jest against "The Reign of Petticoats." Joking comments were captioned: "Women Out of Their Latitude," "Bolting Among the Ladies," and "Petticoats vs Boots." Papers almost everywhere began to take up the subject.

The *Rochester Daily Advertiser* said women wanted to change the sexes around so they would "wear the breeches" and hold public office while men put on petticoats "to nurse the babies, or preside at the wash tub, or boil a pot." Albany's *Mechanic's Advocate* said that if women took on men's jobs "males must change their position in society to the same extent in an opposite direction" and that "the order of things established at the creation of mankind would be completely broken up."

Philadelphia's women would have no part of any move to turn them into Amazons who would "mount the rostrum, do all the voting and, we suppose, all the fighting, too," declared the *Public Ledger and Daily Transcript.* "A woman is nobody. A wife is everything. A pretty girl is equal to ten thousand men and a mother is, next to God, all powerful. The ladies of Philadelphia are resolved to maintain their (present) rights as Wives, Belles, Virgins, and Mothers, and not as women."

James Gordon Bennett of the *New York Herald* thought the "little convention" at Seneca Falls was "amusing," but wondered if the ladies were really eager to "doff the apron and buckle on the sword." He jokingly suggested that perhaps Lucretia Mott wanted to become President herself and added that she might make a better one "than some of those who have lately tenanted the White House."

As Henry Stanton had warned, newspaper humorists turned the whole thing into a laughing matter. It wasn't easy for Elizabeth and her friends to take. But the enormous publicity, even in jest, drew great attention to the issue of woman's rights. Here and there papers such as Horace Greeley's *New York Tribune* discussed it seriously. Gradually others treated the question with some greater respect. As for the fun-making editorials, Elizabeth wrote Lucretia, "That is just what I wanted. Imagine the publicity given to our ideas. It will start women thinking, and men too; and when men and women think about a new question, the first step in progress is taken."

The Movement's Rapid Spread

While some men were laughing, and maybe because they were, women did begin to take up the battle started in Seneca Falls. There was another woman's rights convention in Rochester, New York, that same year. Reports about it were widely circulated in newspapers from Maine to Texas, again mostly in ridicule, but women started thinking. They talked about it at their church and literary clubs and in their own parlors. Without any direction from the outside and without knowledge at first of what others were doing, new woman's rights groups began to spring up in towns and cities. Before long there were state organizations in Ohio, Indiana, Pennsylvania, Massachusetts and Kansas.

A group in Salem, Ohio, decided to hold a convention for women from all parts of that state. They announced it would be run entirely by women, without the help of a single man. Women would preside as its officers and no man would be allowed to speak, vote or sit on the platform.

"Never did men so suffer," the women gleefully reported afterwards. "They implored—just to say one word; but no; the president was inflexible—no man should be heard. If one meekly arose to make a suggestion he was at once ruled out of order. For the first time in the world's history, men learned how it felt to sit in silence when questions in which they were interested were under discussion."

Those planning the Ohio convention wrote to Elizabeth Stanton for advice about the rights and grievances they meant to include in a petition to the state. Her answer was firm:

"For what shall you first petition? For the exercise of your right to the elective franchise—nothing short of this. The grant to you of this right will secure all others; and the granting of every other right while this is denied is a mockery. It is our duty to assert and reassert this right, to agitate, discuss and petition, until our political equality be fully recognized. Depend upon it, this is the point to attack, the stronghold of the fortress—the *one* woman will find the most difficult to take; the *one* man will most reluctantly give up. . . . By her own efforts the change must come. She must carve out her future destiny with her own right hand."

The Declaration of Sentiments: A Landmark of Women's Rights

Elizabeth Cady Stanton, Susan B. Anthony, and Matilda Joslyn Gage

The Declaration of Sentiments that follows was written in July 1848 by the organizers of the first women's rights convention in Seneca Falls, New York. It is primarily the work of Elizabeth Cady Stanton, who modeled it closely on the Declaration of Independence. Its blistering condemnation of men's historical treatment of women became a rallying cry for the fledgling women's movement.

When, in the course of human events, it becomes necessary for one portion of the family of man to assume among the people of the earth a position different from that which they have hitherto occupied, but one to which the laws of nature and of nature's God entitle them, a decent respect to the opinions of mankind requires that they should declare the causes that impel them to such a course.

We hold these truths to be self-evident: that all men and women are created equal; that they are endowed by their Creator with certain inalienable rights; that among these are life, liberty, and the pursuit of happiness; that to secure these rights governments are

Excerpted from *History of Women Suffrage,* edited by Elizabeth Cady Stanton, Susan B. Anthony, and Matilda Joslyn Gage (Rochester, NY: Charles Mann, 1889).

instituted, deriving their just powers from the consent of the governed. Whenever any form of government becomes destructive of these ends, it is the right of those who suffer from it to refuse allegiance to it, and to insist upon the institution of a new government, laying its foundation on such principles, and organizing its powers in such form, as to them shall seem most likely to effect their safety and happiness. Prudence, indeed, will dictate that governments long established should not be changed for light and transient causes; and accordingly all experience hath shown that mankind are more disposed to suffer, while evils are sufferable, than to right themselves by abolishing the forms to which they were accustomed. But when a long train of abuses and usurpations, pursuing invariably the same object evinces a design to reduce them under absolute despotism, it is their duty to throw off such government, and to provide new guards for their future security. Such has been the patient sufferance of the women under this government, and such is now the necessity which constrains them to demand the equal station to which they are entitled.

The history of mankind is a history of repeated injuries and usurpations on the part of man toward woman, having in direct object the establishment of an absolute tyranny over her. To prove this, let facts be submitted to a candid world.

He has never permitted her to exercise her inalienable right to the elective franchise.

He has compelled her to submit to laws, in the formation of which she had no voice.

He has withheld from her rights which are given to the most ignorant and degraded men—both natives and foreigners.

Having deprived her of this first right of a citizen, the elective franchise, thereby leaving her without representation in the halls of legislation, he has oppressed her on all sides.

He has made her, if married, in the eye of the law, civilly dead.

He has taken from her all right in property, even to the wages she earns.

He has made her, morally, an irresponsible being, as she can commit many crimes with impunity, provided they be done in the presence of her husband. In the covenant of marriage, she is compelled to promise obedience to her husband, he becoming, to all intents and purposes, her master—the law giving him power to deprive her of her liberty, and to administer chastisement.

He has so framed the laws of divorce, as to what shall be the proper causes, and in case of separation, to whom the guardianship of the children shall be given, as to be wholly regardless of the happiness of women—the law, in all cases, going upon a false supposition of the supremacy of man, and giving all power into his hands.

After depriving her of all rights as a married woman, if single, and the owner of property, he has taxed her to support a government which recognizes her only when her property can be made profitable to it.

He has monopolized nearly all the profitable employments, and from those she is permitted to follow, she receives but a scanty remuneration. He closes against her all the avenues to wealth and distinction which he considers most honorable to himself. As a teacher of theology, medicine, or law, she is not known.

He has denied her the facilities for obtaining a thorough education, all colleges being closed against her.

He allows her in Church, as well as State, but a subordinate position, claiming Apostolic authority for her exclusion from the ministry, and, with some exceptions, from any public participation in the affairs of the Church.

He has created a false public sentiment by giving to the world a different code of morals for men and women, by which moral delinquencies which exclude women from society, are not only tolerated, but deemed of little account in man.

He has usurped the prerogative of Jehovah himself, claiming it as his right to assign for her a sphere of action, when that belongs to her conscience and to her God.

He has endeavored, in every way that he could, to destroy her confidence in her own powers, to lessen her self-respect, and to make her willing to lead a dependent and abject life.

Now, in view of this entire disfranchisement of one-half the people of this country, their social and religious degradation—in view of the unjust laws above mentioned, and because women do feel themselves aggrieved, oppressed, and fraudulently deprived of their most sacred rights, we insist that they have immediate admission to all the rights and privileges which belong to them as citizens of the United States.

In entering upon the great work before us, we anticipate no small amount of misconception, misrepresentation, and ridicule; but we shall use every instrumentality within our power to effect our object. We shall employ agents, circulate tracts, petition the State and National legislatures, and endeavor to enlist the pulpit and the press in our behalf. We hope this Convention will be followed by a series of Conventions embracing every part of the country.

Europeans and the United States Dominate the Globe

No effect of the Dual Revolution reached farther or had more last-ing effect than the expansion of Western power and ideas around the globe in the course of the nineteenth century. For better or worse, the interdependent, technology-dependent world in which we live today is ultimately the product of the imperial systems that the European great powers and the United States constructed in the nineteenth century.

The building of the Western empires was not a pretty process; it was riddled with violence, arrogance, greed, corruption, and conde-scension. It was exploitative; it bred in Westerners a sense of racist superiority that to this day has not wholly vanished, and it inculcated into millions of non-Western peoples a volatile mixture of fear, re-sentment, self-doubt, and vengefulness that also survives today. Nor were all the ideas that the West taught its non-Western dependents always the best lessons to learn. Exclusionary nationalism, statist so-cialism, and the supposed "efficiency" of one-party dictatorship— all fruits of nineteenth-century Western ideas, and all exports from Europe to what we call today Third World societies—proved disas-trous when applied in twentieth-century European nations like Ger-many and Russia, and their bankruptcy has been equally apparent in the former Western colonies during the past fifty years.

Modern Americans do not usually think of their country's west-ward expansion as part of the process of nineteenth-century Western empire building. And in some respects the realization of "manifest destiny" (an electric phrase invented by an American journalist in the 1840s) was an experience vastly different from European na-tions' acquisitions of overseas colonies. The United States was, in Thomas Jefferson's phrase, "an empire of liberty," seemingly an open land across which settlers were free to move, establishing new self-governing communities and achieving political equality with the rest of the Union.

Yet there was a darker side to the growth of this "empire of lib-erty." Native American nations had to be swept aside, deprived of their lands and eventually driven onto squalid reservations. A war of aggression had to be launched against Mexico to secure the annex-ation of the southwest, from Texas to California. The railroad, min-ing, and other corporations that were soon extracting the West's natural resources were politically ruthless, often corrupt, and always exploitive of their workforces. Realizing America's manifest destiny was a process as brutal as the parallel experience of nineteenth-century czarist Russia extending its borders in Central Asia and Siberia, or of the British colonies of Australia and New Zealand expanding at the expense of those lands' indigenous populations, the Aborigines and the Maoris.

In the short run, the non-Europeans whom the expanding Western empires encountered and usually dominated simply did not have the technological resources, nor often the organizational strength, to withstand the invaders. Africa, whose interior Europeans penetrated and subjugated between the 1860s and 1880s, could offer very little resistance once the Westerners had learned to cope with indigenous diseases like malaria and yellow fever. India, a vast land of diverse cultures and competing religious traditions, failed to expel the British, who had been entrenching themselves in the subcontinent since the 1700s. After a bloody revolt (1857–1858) was suppressed, India became the "crown jewel" of the British Empire, dramatically symbolized in 1877 when Queen Victoria took the title "Empress of India." The ancient and extremely populous land of China, to which the nineteenth century brought all manner of disasters, was simply too huge for any one Western power to take over, and a partition plan too complex a problem for the imperialist powers to agree on, so it managed to retain a nominal independence. Only Japan, among all the non-Western nations of the globe, successfully modernized itself along European lines, by 1900 adopting Western-style imperialist ambitions of its own.

The selections in Chapter 5 address various aspects of the nineteenth-century European and American drive for global dominance. The first selection details, the sordid steps by which the East India Company—then the ruler of British India—recouped its fortunes by exporting opium to China and, when that country's officials tried to stop the traffic, induced Great Britain's government to go to war to open the Chinese empire to British merchants. The second selection discusses the social and cultural world of the native soldiers who served the British authorities in mid-nineteenth-century India, and analyzes the reasons why they finally led the "great mutiny" against British rule in 1857–1858. The third selection focuses on the most tumultuous and—in human terms—most costly civil war of the nineteenth century, the Taiping Rebellion in China. What did this epic upheaval signify for China's internal condition during the era of Western encroachment, and what responsibility did the West assume in supporting China's decaying Qing dynasty against the nation's internal forces of renewal?

The fourth and fifth selections present what may be the starkest contrasts of the experiences of non-Western peoples who were subjected to the West's global reach. The Congo River basin, in the heart of equatorial Africa, with its rich stores of rubber and mineral wealth, attracted the greed of one of the most ruthless men of the century, King Leopold II of Belgium. A virtually powerless crowned figurehead in his increasingly democratic homeland, Leopold had tyrannical instincts that he could fully indulge by setting up a privately run colony called the Congo Free State and staffing it with profit-seeking adventurers from all over Europe and even the United States. Leopold's "Free State," which endured from 1885 until scandals and managerial incompetence forced the Belgian government to take it over as a state colony in 1908, probably was the most viciously exploitative of the many colonial regimes—none of them remotely benevolent—that the imperialist powers created, and the psychological and social damage that it inflicted on the people of central Africa still lingers.

The spread of the United States across the North American continent and beyond is the subject of the chapter's final three selections. In the first, James K. Polk, the expansion-minded southern slave owner who served as president from 1845 to 1849, tells Congress in 1846 why he believes that war with Mexico is necessary—an aggressive war, essentially precipitated by the White House, that will result in America's acquisition of a huge stretch of southwestern territory by 1848. Next, a contemporary American historian explains why and how the American military, at the bidding of the White House and with the full support of the southern state governments, carried out a thorough "removal" of the Cherokee and other Indian nations from Tennessee, Georgia, Alabama, and Mississippi in the late 1830s. These territories were then cleared so that whites (often with workforces of enslaved blacks) could claim them for cotton cultivation. This so-called Trail of Tears, whose tragedies aroused the sympathy of only a few whites at the time, has become one of the great blots on American history, fully comparable to the most drastic actions taken against native peoples by any European colonizing power in the nineteenth century. And finally, in the chapter's last selection, another modern historian discusses how, in 1898, amid a surge of self-righteous enthusiasm, the American public enthusiastically embraced the short, glorious war against a beleaguered, decrepit Spanish empire, seizing for the United States the new colonies of the Philippines and Puerto Rico, and turning Cuba into the American satellite state that it would remain for sixty years until Fidel Castro's revolution. The Spanish-American War of 1898, as this selection makes clear, brought the United States out of the single-minded absorption with continental expansion that had been its goal since Jefferson's acquisition of Louisiana in 1803 had made it possible to conceive of North America as an "empire of liberty," and started the nation on the path toward world power that would be its fate in the dawning twentieth century.

Great Britain Forces Opium on China

Jonathan D. Spence

China became the richest and often the best-governed part of the world beginning in the Middle Ages. When the thirteenth-century Venetian traveler Marco Polo reached China, he was awestruck by the contrasts in wealth and sophistication that he noticed between Europe and East Asia—and at the time of his visit, China had recently been devastated and conquered by the Mongols, whose policy it now was to encourage reconstruction. Medieval China relied on many things that contemporary Europeans considered marvels: paper, printing, paper money, gunpowder, firearms, and a bureaucracy staffed by men chosen for their ability in national competitions. In addition, Chinese medicine and Chinese understanding of the natural world considerably surpassed that of medieval Europeans.

Even as late as the middle of the eighteenth century, China and Europe were roughly equivalent in terms of their relative prosperity and power. But in the course of the eighteenth century, that relationship changed. The Industrial Revolution, under way in Great Britain by the 1760s, greatly widened the possibilities for human beings to generate energy from natural resources (first water power, then coal-fired steam engines) and therefore to increase output to meet the demands of a growing population. At the same time Great Britain ousted its principal European rival, France, from imperial power in India and accelerated the extension of its sphere of influence on that vast subcontinent. China, on the other hand, experienced no Industrial Revolution and therefore, with productivity stagnant, faced increasing difficulty in providing for a population that had begun to grow at least as fast as Europe's. Unlike Britain, the Chinese government made no attempt to extend its sway farther into Asia, but rather looked for ways to close off contacts with the outside world and increase "the Middle Kingdom's" self-sufficiency.

In the early nineteenth century the expanding British Empire and the inward-looking Chinese Empire collided. The occasion for this clash was a sordid one, especially from our present-day perspective. One of British India's principal exports was opium, and one of the principal markets in which this narcotic could be sold profitably was China. (Great Britain itself was another potential destination for the drug, for opium was frequently used by early-nineteenth-century Westerners, but this market was far smaller than that of China.) The East India Company, the charted joint-stock company through which Britain ruled India, saw a golden opportunity to offset it chronic losses by boosting its opium exports to China. Almost all of this trade passed through the port of Canton (today, Guangzhou), where by treaty a community of British and other Western merchants were permitted to operate. The business involved a great deal of corruption, but so popular did imported opium prove that southern China in particular experienced a net drain of silver to pay for the drug. Chinese officials were outraged, partly because this silver drain cut into the taxes that they would otherwise collect from the population and also because of the social demoralization and crime that the drug trade produced.

In this selection, Jonathan D. Spence, a distinguished American historian of modern China, examines the Chinese government's response to the East India Company's blatant sponsorship of the opium trade and to the British government's unswerving endorsement of the company's practice. In 1839–1842, the Anglo-Chinese collision over British drug pushing in China produced the so-called Opium War. Superior British naval power forced China to capitulate, to legalize the drug trade, to grant British merchants and missionaries extensive access to China, and to cede the island of Hong Kong to Great Britain. From our present-day perspective, Britain's sponsorship of the opium trade in China is morally indefensible, and it represented one of the most humiliating defeats that China experienced in its thousands of years of history as a civilized nation.

[T]he] political complexities of relations with the West were slowly becoming apparent to Qing [the ruling dynasty] officials. One indication of this was the growing importance that began to attach to Canton and to the officials who governed the Guangxi-Guangdong region. The sums of money circulating in the southeast because of the opium trade and the stockpiling of silks and teas for export in turn brought heightened official corruption and a rise in state revenues from transit dues and from taxation of legitimate foreign trade. The Cohong merchants were forced to make immense "donations" to the court and to local officials in order to assure continued imperial favor. . . . It is likely that the Cohong system lasted as long as it did because of the establishment of a mutual guarantee system known as the "Consoo fund," into which each major Hong merchant paid 10 percent of his trading profits, to be used as a cushion in times of emergency. Initially a secret shared only by the merchants, the fund was publicly supported by the Qing after 1780 with a 3 percent surcharge on foreign imports. By 1810, payments to the Qing government out of the Consoo fund reached a level of around 1 million taels a year.

As Canton became a major financial center, scholars were attracted there and academies began to proliferate. Ruan Yuan, the influential governor-general of the region from 1817 to 1826, founded the Xuehai Tang, the name literally meaning "Sea-of-Learning Hall." The academy became a famous center of scholarship. . . . Ruan Yuan also took a hard line against the opium trade. In one show of strength in 1821, he rounded up a number of opium dealers in Macao and tried to stop opium smoking in Canton.

The taking of a hard or soft line on the problem of opium addiction now became a central issue in China's foreign affairs and domestic economy. Moreover the controversy began to affect the formation of factions and alliances within the metropolitan and the provincial bureaucracy. Jiaqing's successor, Emperor Daoguang, who reigned from 1821 to 1850, seems to have been a well-meaning but ineffective man. . . . The strict prohibitions that Jiaqing had imposed on opium dealing in 1800 and 1813 had not been effective, and Daoguang now sought a more successful alternative.

By 1825, Daoguang was aware from censors' reports that so much Chinese silver was going to pay for Western opium that the national economy was being damaged. Although this phenomenon was still mainly restricted to the southeast coastal regions of China, its effects were being felt far inland. A scarcity of silver meant that its price rose in relation to copper; since peasants used copper currency in their everyday transactions but still had to pay their taxes to the state in silver, a rise in the value of silver meant that the peasants were in fact paying steadily higher taxes, and that unrest was sure to follow. The situation worsened in 1834 when the British Parliament ended the East India Company's monopoly of trade with Asia. The action threw open the China trade to all comers, with a predictable rise in opium sales and in the numbers of foreign traders from elsewhere in Europe and from the United States. The crisis for China was exacerbated by a worldwide silver shortage that caused foreigners to use specie less frequently when buying Chinese goods. . . .

The 1834 arrival in Canton of Lord Napier, the British government's first superintendent of trade in China following the end of the East India Company monopoly, led to new misunderstandings. Napier refused to conduct relations through the Cohong merchants, but wished to deal directly with the governor-general of the region. After the Qing pointed out to him that "the great ministers of the Celestial Empire are not permitted to have private intercourse by letter with outside barbarians," Napier forced his fleet up the Bogue to Canton; only his death from malarial fever prevented the outbreak of serious fighting. Opium imports meanwhile continued to rise, passing 30,000 chests in 1835 and 40,000 in 1838.

In 1836 the emperor Daoguang asked his senior officials to advise him on the opium issue. The advice was split. Those who advocated legalization of the opium trade pointed out that it would end the corruption and blackmailing of officials and bring in a steady revenue through tariffs. It would also allow domestically grown Chinese opium—believed to be of better quality than Indian opium and cheaper to market—gradually to squeeze out that of the foreigners. Many officials, however, considered this view pernicious. They argued that foreigners were cruel and greedy, and that the Chinese did not need opium, domestic or foreign. They thought the prohibitions made by Emperor Jiaqing, far from being abandoned, should be pursued with even greater rigor.

In 1838, after evaluating the evidence, Emperor Daoguang made his decision. The opium trade must be stopped. To enforce this decree he chose a Fujian scholar-official of fifty-four named Lin Zexu, and ordered Lin to proceed to Canton as a specially appointed imperial commissioner to end the practice of the opium trade. On paper, the choice was a fine one. Lin . . . had served in the Hanlin Academy—the prestigious government center for Confucian studies in Peking—and in a wide range of posts in Yunnan, Jiangsu, Shaanxi, and Shandong provinces. As governor-general of Hubei and Hunan, he had launched vigorous campaigns against opium smokers. One of his confidants was the outspoken scholar Gong Zizhen, who wrote in a letter to Lin that he believed all smokers of opium should be strangled, while pushers and producers should be beheaded. . . .

To stamp out opium, Commissioner Lin (as the English came to call him) tried to mobilize all the traditional forces and values of the Confucian state. In public proclamations, he emphasized the health dangers of opium consumption and ordered all smokers to hand over their opium and pipes to his staff within two months. Educational officials were ordered to double-check whether any degree holders were opium smokers; all those who smoked were to be punished, and the rest were to be organized into five-man mutual-responsibility teams . . . pledged to guarantee that no one in the group would smoke. In an ingenious adaptation of the traditional examination system, Lin summoned over 600 local students to a special assembly. There, in addition to being asked conventional questions on the Confucian classics, they were asked to name—anonymously, if they so chose—the major opium distributors and to suggest means of stopping their trade. Similar groups were formed among military and naval personnel. Lin also mobilized the local Confucian gentry, who formed an expanded version of the *baojia* system to spot addicts in the community. By mid-May 1839, over 1,600 Chinese had been arrested and about 35,000 pounds of opium and 43,000 opium pipes had been confiscated; in the following two months, Lin's forces seized a further 15,000 pounds of the drug and another 27,500 pipes.

With the foreigners, Lin used a similar combination of reason, moral suasion, and coercion, and we know from numerous statements of his that he did not wish his policies to lead to armed conflict. He moved first against the Chinese Cohong merchants, interviewing them personally in March. Lin scolded them for posting false bonds in which they stated that certain prominent British merchants . . . were not opium traders, when everyone knew they were. He ordered the merchants to pass on a command to the foreigners to hand over the thousands of chests of opium they had stored . . . and to sign pledges that they would cease all further trade in opium. Foreign residents in Canton were also told to state in writing the number of weapons they owned. Lin did not wish to move rashly against foreign ships with the weak navy at his disposal, but felt he could bring enough pressure to bear on the local foreign community to force them to yield. He did not offer compensation for the opium they were to hand over.

Lin also tried to reason with the foreigners, urging them to stick to their legitimate trade in tea, silk, and rhubarb (he believed this last to be essential to the health of foreigners) and to desist from harming the Chinese people. The Guangxi-Guangdong governor-general, with whom Lin cooperated closely, had already optimistically told the Westerners that "the smokers have all quit the habit and the dealers have dispersed. There is no more demand for the drug and henceforth no profit can be derived from the traffic." In a carefully phrased letter to Queen Victoria, Lin tried to appeal to her moral sense of responsibility. "We have heard that in your honorable nation, too," wrote Lin, "the people are not permitted to smoke the drug, and that offenders in this particular expose themselves to sure punishment.

. . . In order to remove the source of the evil thoroughly, would it not be better to prohibit its sale and manufacture rather than merely prohibit its consumption?" Opium in fact was *not* prohibited in Britain and was taken—often in the form of laudanum—by several well-known figures, Samuel Taylor Coleridge among them. Many Englishmen regarded opium as less harmful than alcohol, and Lin's moral exhortations fell on deaf ears.

Although they were begged to yield by the panic-stricken Hong merchants, the foreign traders first explained that they handled opium on consignment for others and so were not empowered to hand it over, and then offered to give up a token 1,000 chests. Lin, furious, ordered the arrest of Lancelot Dent, one of the leading British opium traders. When the foreign community refused to yield up Dent for trial, on March 24, 1839, Lin ordered the Hoppo to stop foreign trade completely. All Chinese staff and servants were ordered to leave foreign employ; and the 350 foreigners in Canton, including the senior British official, Superintendent Elliot, were blockaded in their factories. Although food and water were available to the foreigners, and some extra goods and messages were smuggled in, it was a nerve-wracking time for them, made worse by the din of gongs and horns that Chinese troops kept up throughout the nights. After six weeks, when the foreigners had agreed to give up over 20,000 chests of opium and Commissioner Lin had taken delivery, the blockade was lifted and all but sixteen foreigners were allowed to leave.

Lin had carefully supervised the transfer of the foreign opium to Chinese hands. . . . He was now faced with the remarkable challenge of destroying close to 3 million pounds of raw opium. His solution was to order the digging of three huge trenches, 7 feet deep and 150 feet long. Thereafter, five hundred laborers, supervised by sixty officials, broke up the large balls of raw opium and mixed them with water, salt, and lime until the opium dissolved. Then, as large crowds of Chinese and foreigners looked on, the murky mixture was flushed out into a neighboring creek, and so reached the sea.

In a special prayer to the spirit of the Southern Sea, "you who wash away all stains and cleanse all impurities," Lin brooded over the fact that "poison has been allowed to creep in unchecked till at last barbarian smoke fills the market." . . . As to the foreigners who had lived through the blockade and now watched the solemn proceedings. Lin wrote in a memorial to Emperor Daoguang, they "do not dare show any disrespect, and indeed I should judge from their attitudes that they have the decency to feel heartily ashamed."

Britain's Military Response

Commissioner Lin Zexu and Emperor Daoguang were conscientious, hard-working men who had fully internalized the Confucian structures of hierarchy and control. They seem to have believed that the citizens of Canton and the foreign traders there had simple, child-like natures that would respond to firm guidance and statements of moral principles set out in simple, clear terms. The reality was unfortunately more complex, as plenty of their contemporaries saw. Even before the opium had been washed out to sea, one Chinese official had dared to point out that Lin had not really solved the opium problem, just one of its immediate manifestations. And a British opium trader, reflecting on his experiences during the blockade, noted dryly to a friend that the blockade "is even fortunate as adding to the account for which we have to claim redress."

The buildup toward war between China and Britain was now gaining momentum. Some of the broader causes [included] . . . the social dislocations that began to appear in the Qing world, the spread of addiction, the growth of a hard-line mentality toward foreigners, foreign refusal to accept Chinese legal norms, changes in international trade structures, and the ending of Western intellectuals' admiration for China. Other elements were more precisely tied to the background of Lin's negotiations and had ramifications that he did not understand. . . .

A second contributing factor was that the new British post of superintendent of foreign trade in China was held by a deputy of the British crown, not by an employee of the East India Company. If the Chinese crossed the superintendent, they would be insulting the British nation rather than a business corporation, a distinction they did not fully see. The superintendent, in turn, lacked clear legal powers over the British traders and had no control over nationals from other European nations or from the United States. He could, however, call directly on the aid of British armed forces and the Royal Navy in times of serious trouble.

The third element in the picture on the British side was a crucial combination of these previous two: British opium dealers, suffering from a glut of the unsold drug, had handed their supply over to Charles Elliot, Napier's successor as the superintendent of foreign trade, and Elliot, in turn, had handed it over to Lin Zexu. Thus, far from being properly "ashamed" as their opium drifted out to sea, the merchants could anticipate putting pressure on the British government to make sure that they got financial recompense.

The unfolding events in China were monitored as closely in England as time and distance allowed. . . . [The] foreign secretary, Lord Palmerston, initially unsympathetic to British merchants who would not abide by Chinese laws, now swung in their favor. As Palmerston wrote in a letter addressed to "The Minister of the Emperor of China," he had heard "with extreme surprise" that Chinese officers had "committed violent outrages against the British Residents at Canton, who were living peaceably in that city, trusting to the good faith of the Chinese Government." Although the queen did not condone opium selling, she "cannot permit that her subjects residing abroad be treated with violence, and be exposed to insult and injustice."

After news of the blockade and opium seizures reached England, China trade interests and chambers of commerce in the larger manufacturing areas launched intensive lobbying efforts to pressure Parliament into taking retaliatory action. The wealthy opium merchant William Jardine even traveled back to England from China to add his voice to the chorus, and to ensure that the moral objections to the opium traffic being raised by various Protestant missionary societies did not gain too wide an influence. China merchants had raised $20,000 for his lobbying expenses, and he was promised more if necessary, "as the magnitude of the object can well bear any amount of expense that may be considered necessary or desirable." He was also told "to secure, at a high price, the services of some leading newspaper to advocate the cause." Parliament did not, however, declare war on China. It merely authorized the dispatch of a fleet and the mobilization of further troops in India in order to obtain "satisfaction and reparation" and, if necessary, to "hold in custody the ships of the Chinese and their cargoes." The total force . . . consisted of 16 warships carrying 540 guns, 4 newly designed armed steamers, 28 transports, and 4,000 troops, along with 3,000 tons of coal for the steamers and 16,000 gallons of rum for the men.

Lin Zexu, meanwhile, continued his cleansing of Guangdong province. Arrests and investigations of addicts and dealers went on apace, with opium now commanding "famine prices" of up to $3,000 a chest instead of the usual $500. When the British merchants refused to sign bonds pledging that they would not indulge in any opium traffic under penalty of Chinese law, Lin had them ousted from Macao as they had been from Canton. It was in response to this expulsion order that [the British representative in Canton,] Charles Elliot, inaugurated a new phase in cast east Asian history by settling his group on the almost deserted rocky island of Hong Kong. Trade in Canton by no means came to a standstill, since the Americans especially were delighted to profit from the new opportunity to operate as middlemen for the British. . . .

But even as the trade continued, Lin was fortifying the waterways into Canton, buying new cannon for the forts and immense chains to block the channel, and commencing the training and drilling of his forces. The British who had retreated to Hong Kong were harried by the local Chinese, who poisoned many wells and refused to sell the foreigners food. Armed clashes between British and Chinese war junks in Hong Kong harbor and in the Bogue outside Canton occurred in September and October 1839, with casualties on both sides. Chinese ships were sunk, and the possibilities of further negotiation faded. In a surprising gesture for Qing officials usually so wary of popular manifestations, Lin even encouraged mobilization of local "braves" against the British, who had grown even more unpopular since a group of drunken seamen had killed a Chinese villager on Kowloon, across from Hong Kong island, and Elliot had refused to hand the accused over to the Chinese courts. "Assemble yourselves together for consideration," ran one proclamation; "Purchase arms and weapons; join together the stoutest of your villagers and thus be prepared to defend yourselves."

The full British fleet under George Elliot arrived off Canton in June 1840. To Lin's chagrin they did not try to storm his new defenses, but contented themselves with leaving four ships to blockade the entrance to the harbor and sailing north with the bulk of their force. In July, the British blockaded Ningbo with two ships and seized the main town on the island of Zhoushan (Chusan) off the Zhejiang coast, from which they could interdict sea traffic to the Yangzi delta region. Leaving a garrison force on Zhoushan with a missionary-interpreter standing in for the Qing magistrate who had committed suicide, the fleet sailed on unopposed to the mouth of the Bei He (North River), near the Dagu forts that guarded the approaches to the city of Tianjin. Here, in August and September 1840, serious negotiations began with Qishan, the governor-general of the region, a senior Manchu, and a grand secretary trusted by Emperor Daoguang. Qishan persuaded the British to leave north China and return to Canton to complete the negotiations, for which he was lavishly praised by the emperor and named governor-general of Guangxi and Guangdong. Lin Zexu, who had been named to that post earlier in the year, was now dismissed for his inadequate policies and banished. . . .

In January 1841 Qishan reached an agreement with the British in which he ceded up Hong Kong, agreed to pay $6 million in indemnities, allowed the British direct official contacts with the Qing state, and promised to reopen the Canton trade to them within ten days. This so enraged Daoguang when he heard of it that he ordered Qishan dismissed and executed, a sentence later commuted to banishment.

Lord Palmerston was equally furious with Charles Elliot for not exacting *better* terms from the Chinese. . . . [The war continued, and a new British commissioner, Sir Henry Pottinger, was sent to China.]

In late August 1841, Pottinger proceeded north with the British fleet, seizing Xiamen (Amoy) and Ningbo, and recapturing Zhoushan. When reinforcements reached him from India in late spring 1842, he launched a campaign to force Qing capitulation by cutting China's main river and canal communications routes. The British captured Shanghai in June and took Zhenjiang in July, even though the Manchus fought with savage desperation. Scores of Qing officers committed suicide with their families when defeat was certain. The traffic on the Grand Canal and lower Yangzi was now blocked. Pottinger, ignoring Qing requests for a parley, pushed on to the great city and former Ming dynasty capital of Nanjing, taking up attack positions outside the walls on August 5. The Qing quickly sued for peace, and on August 29 the terms of the Treaty of Nanjing, translated into Chinese, were signed. . . . Daoguang accepted the treaty in September, and Queen Victoria ratified it at the end of December.

Before turning to the precise stipulations of this treaty and its supplements, it is worth re-emphasizing that in military terms the Opium War of 1839–1842 marked an important historical moment. It was not only the most decisive reversal the Manchus had ever received, it also saw innovations in Western military technology and tactics. The emergence of the steam-driven vessel as a considerable force in naval battles was perhaps the most important of these. . . .

The Qing, however, were not merely passive targets of Western technology and fire power. While still in Canton, Commissioner Lin had deputed a special task force of scholars to furnish him with all the information they could on Western nations, culled mainly from foreign publications in Canton and Singapore. He had also asked an American missionary to translate some brief passages of international law for him. Moreover, as the British proceeded with their campaigns in 1842, they found much evidence of the speed with which the Qing officials were trying to respond to the West's new technology. . . . At least some people in China had clearly found the barbarian challenge to be a stimulus as well as an outrage.

The New Treaty System

The Treaty of Nanjing was signed on August 29, 1842. . . . It was the most important treaty settlement in China's modern history. The treaty contained twelve main articles that cumulatively had significant ramifications for China's ideas of commerce and society:

Article 1. Stipulated peace and friendship between Britain and China, and "full security and protection for their persons and property within the dominions of the other."

Article 2. Determined the opening of five Chinese cities—Canton, Fuzhou, Xiamen, Ningbo, and Shanghai—to residence by British subjects and their families "for the purpose of carrying on their mercantile pursuits, without molestation or restraint." It also permitted the establishment of consulates in each of those cities.

Article 3. "The Island of Hong Kong to be possessed in perpetuity" by Victoria and her successors, and ruled as they "shall see fit."

Article 4. Payment of $6 million by the Qing "as the value of the opium which was delivered up in Canton."

[Articles 5–7 provided for Chinese financial compensation to the British.]

Article 8. Immediate release of any prisoners who were British subjects, whether Indian or European.

Article 9. An unconditional amnesty for all Chinese subjects who had resided with, dealt with, or served the British.

Article 10. At the five treaty ports listed in Article 2, all merchants should pay "a fair and regular Tariff of Export and Import Customs and other Dues." Once those fees were paid, only fair and stipulated transit dues should be paid on goods conveyed to the interior of China.

Article 11. Instead of terminology such as "petition" or "beg" that foreigners had previously been forced to use, nonderogatory and nonsubordinate terms of address such as "communication," "statement," and "declaration" were to be used in future official correspondence between Britain and China.

Article 12. On receiving the first installment of the indemnity money, British forces would leave Nanjing and the Grand Canal, and "no longer molest or stop the trade of China." Troops would continue to hold Zhoushan until all money was paid and the "opening [of] the Ports to British merchants be completed.". . .

The clauses of the Treaty of Nanjing and its supplements were studied carefully by other powers. In 1843, President John Tyler acted on behalf of the United States and its considerable China-trade interests by dispatching Caleb Cushing—a congressman from coastal Massachusetts, where many of America's wealthiest China merchants lived—to China as minister plenipotentiary. [Cushing negotiated similar concessions for the United States in early 1844.] . . .

In October 1844, the French followed with their own treaty, modeled closely on the American agreement. . . . Yielding to French pressure, . . . full toleration [was granted] to the Catholics; . . . in a supplementary proclamation of 1845, . . . same rights [were extended] to Protestants.

So within six years of Lin Zexu's appointment as imperial commissioner, the Qing, instead of defending their integrity against all comers, had lost control of vital elements of China's commercial, social, and foreign policies. A host of other nations followed where Britain, the United States, and France had shown the way. The British did not have to worry about these other negotiations, because any new concessions offered up by the Chinese came also to them. In an ingenious article—number 8—to their own supplementary treaty of 1843, they had stipulated a "most-favored nation" clause: "Should the Emperor hereafter, from any cause whatever, be pleased to grant additional privileges or immunities to any of the subjects or citizens of such foreign countries, the same privileges or immunities will be extended to and enjoyed by British subjects." The Qing had agreed to this clause in the belief that it would limit foreign pressures. But in fact this clause prevented the Qing from forming alliances or playing one foreign power against another, seriously hampering China's foreign-policy initiatives. . . .

Canton had held the promise of enormous profits once the Cohong monopoly was abolished and trade was thrown open to all, but so strong was the local antipathy to the British and other foreigners that the Westerners found it impossible to establish residence and to conduct business or open their consulates in the city. The 1840s and early 1850s were marked by constant rioting and a bitter cycle of anti-British attacks by rural militias and urban mobs that were met by British reprisals and reciprocal atrocities. The Qing court condoned the anti-British violence since it could not afford to alienate Cantonese sensibilities any further.

Of the five new treaty ports, only Shanghai became a boom town when extensive "concession" areas of marshy and largely uninhabited countryside were made available for British, French, and other foreign settlements. By 1850, with the land drained and the river banks shored up, there were over one hundred merchants in residence there, supported by consular staffs, five physicians, and seventeen missionaries, many of whom were married. Whereas 44 foreign ships had entered the port in 1844, the number for 1849 was 133, and by 1855 it was 437. The silk trade expanded prodigiously, reaching a value of over $20 million by the mid-1850s. Opium, still illegal, was coming in at a rate of at least 20,000 chests a year.

Roots of the Sepoy Mutiny in British India

Christopher Hibbert

In 1857 the most serious revolt against a nineteenth-century European colonial power broke out in India. To Westerners, the immediate occasion for the revolt seemed trivial: the British army's introduction of a new type of cartridge, which soldiers had to bite before ramming it into their muskets. The cartridge was greased with animal fat, and despite British denials it was rumored that the fat came from hogs and cattle—the former an unclean animal to Muslims, and the latter a sacred animal to Hindus. The overwhelming majority of troops in the British army in India were sepoys—native recruits, both Muslim and Hindu—and a mutiny by both these elements was bound to dangerously challenge British rule. Indeed, it required the introduction of a massive new military force from outside India, as well as heavy fighting and savage reprisals, before the British were able to restore their control.

Yet greased cartridges were not the only reason for the revolt. British historian Christopher Hibbert explores, in the selection that follows, the many factors that were putting India's British masters on a collision course with both the Hindu and the Muslim populations of the subcontinent. Eighteenth-century British willingness to accommodate India's diverse cultural patterns was giving way, by the mid–nineteenth century, to a more abrasive British style of rule. For example, Britons in India tended to take their Christian values more seriously, stirring Indian suspicions that religious conversion was the ultimate British aim.

Excerpted from *The Great Mutiny: India 1857,* by Christopher Hibbert (New York: The Viking Press, 1978). Copyright 1978 by Christopher Hibbert. Reprinted with permission from David Higham Associates.

The introduction of British technology, especially the railroad and the telegraph, also challenged traditional Indian ways of life. Modernization and Westernization, in other words, were the key issues. The issue of whether sepoys would be required to bite into cartridges greased with animal fat was simply the last straw.

T he living quarters of the native soldiers [in India], although exceedingly primitive, were far less unpleasant than those of the British. Most native troops in all three of the East India Company's armies were married, and were permitted to live on the station with their wives and children, their widowed mothers, aged grandmothers and any other relations for whom they cared to provide. Each man was allotted a small piece of ground on which he was expected to build his own hut, a simple edifice of bamboo, matting and mud, thatched with straw. A married man's hut was usually about fifteen feet long, nine feet high and eleven wide; a single man's about two-thirds that size. . . .

Sanitary conditions in the native lines were little better than they were in the bazaar; and in most stations the huts were built much closer together than they need have been. But for most of the year the men slept in the open air in front of their huts . . . , and their general health was a good deal better than that of the white troops.

The sepoys were also of more imposing physique than the European soldiers since there was never a shortage of recruits, and commanding officers were able to choose only the strongest, tallest and most presentable-looking men, while medical officers felt justified in rejecting all those with physical defects. In the Bengal Army most soldiers, both Muslim and Hindu, were . . . generally taller than the white soldiers, few being less than five feet eight inches. Three out of four were Hindus, and of these most were high-caste Brahmins or Rajputs, the profession of arms being considered by Hindus worthy and honourable, like the calling of a poet.

Their pay of seven rupees a month was scarcely a third of that earned by European troops, but even so—though reduced by various fees and deductions—it was far more than they could have hoped to earn as civilians. Admittedly they were frequently in debt, for not only did numerous relations consider themselves entitled to their support, but also there were certain Hindu *dustoors* [customs] which could not be ignored. Europeans might consider the laying out of two or three hundred rupees on a marriage as an unwarranted extravagance for a private soldier. To a self-respecting Hindu, however, it was a *dustoor* imposed by a tradition as compelling to him as a law. In debt or not, when they returned to their villages—where many of their fathers were landholders—they were treated as men of consequence to whom every respect was due.

A high proportion of these Hindus were vegetarians, eating little other than chupatties [bread], dhal [a grain], and rice; and while the smoking of opium and the consumption of *ganja* and bhang [hashish and hemp] were common, the higher classes of Hindus never drank intoxicating spirits, believing that, like the eating of meat and fish, it was a defiling practice to be left to Mohammedans, to low-caste Hindus and to the 'so-called Christian dummers' who were often Eurasians of partly Portuguese stock.

Although it was virtually impossible to gain promotion by merit, a native soldier did at least have the satisfaction of knowing that, provided he could read and write and had a record of good conduct, he would be promoted when his turn eventually came, even though he might have to wait twenty years before he became a havildar [sergeant], was unlikely to be commissioned until he was within a year or two of being pensioned off, and would never rise higher in rank than the most junior European subaltern [lower-ranking officer], however young and inexperienced the subaltern might be.

This system of promotion by seniority—even if it sometimes resulted in native soldiers becoming officers only when they were . . . 'worn-out imbeciles unfit for command'—did not appear to worry the sepoys any more unduly than did their debts. Nor did their uniforms of thick, unyielding European cloth. They never looked, nor ever felt, entirely comfortable in these uniforms. . . .

The sepoys rarely wore their uniforms when not on parade. As soon as they returned to their huts, they would discard their tunics and trousers, and, having indulged in those ritual ablutions imposed upon them by their faith, put on instead a dhoti [loincloth] or a pair of linen trousers before sitting down to eat the meal prepared for them by their families. The sepoy might then, like the British soldier, settle down to sleep, or to smoke, or to indulge with his neighbours in the gossip of which they never tired, or play with his children, or make love with his wife, or go over to the gymnasium with which every native regiment—in significant distinction to every British regiment in India—was supplied. To most observers, indeed, the sepoy seemed, as he seemed to an English officer in the Bengal Artillery, 'perfectly happy with his lot, a cheerful, good-natured fellow, simple and trustworthy'. He might have some odd ideas and strange habits, to be sure; but then the Englishman's taste for beef and brandy must seem strange, even disgusting to the sepoy. This did not prevent them feeling a respect, even affection for each other. . . .

Although apparently content with their present lot, the sepoys did, however, have fears for their future. And these fears were shared by the people in the towns and villages from which they came. . . .

[I]ntensive efforts had been made [by the British authorities] to establish the rights of landholders to the property which they claimed to own and the amount of money which ought to be received from it. Several great landowners had been dispossessed of large parts of their estates. Thousands of lesser landlords had been dispossessed entirely. And many, relatively poor, who let out small parcels of land while ploughing other pieces themselves—the kind of men from amongst whom most sepoys were recruited—had also been deprived of the lands which they had inherited. So they, too, felt deeply aggrieved by the Government's reforms, apprehensive as to what further deprivations their British rulers might have in mind. Nor were the peasants as pleased with the reforms as the Government had expected. They preferred their own old ways to the strange ones being imposed upon them by the foreigners. As one of them told an English inquirer, they did not understand the new rules and regulations; they did not trust the new law courts whose native officials were notoriously corrupt and whose procedure was quite incomprehensible; they would much rather have been governed by their former native masters, unpredictable and violent though they sometimes were. 'The truth, Sir, is seldom told in [the English] courts,' a Brahmin told William Sleeman, whom [the British governor-general] sent on a tour through one of those few remaining semi-independent states in India to help him decide whether the incompetence of its government justified him in annexing it. 'There they think of nothing but the number of witnesses, as if all were alike. Here, Sir, we look to the quality. When a man suffers wrong, the wrongdoer is summoned before the elders, or most respectable men of his village; and if he denies the charge, and refuses redress, he is told to bathe, put his hand on the peepul tree, and declare his innocence. . . . A man dares not, Sir, put his hand upon that sacred tree and deny the truth. The gods sit in it and know all things; and the offender dreads their vengeance.'. . .

This threat to . . . Hindu custom . . . was seen by Indians as part of a concerted attack upon their religions as a whole. Muslims shared with Hindus this fear for their religion. Indeed, the Commissioner of Patna reported that there was a 'full belief' among even 'intelligent natives', especially 'the better class' of Mohammedans, 'that the Government was immediately about to attempt the forcible conversion of its subjects'. The Lieutenant-Governor of Bengal considered that the suspicion had taken such deep root that he must issue a proclamation denying it, which, far from subduing the people's fears, served merely to aggravate them.

There had been no such widespread fear in the eighteenth century. The British had been far more tolerant then. Their officials had contributed to Mohammedan processions; they had administered Hindu temple funds and supervised pilgrimages to holy places; their officers had piled their swords, next to their soldiers' muskets, round the altar at the Hindu festival of *Dasehra,* to be blessed by the priests. It had been perfectly well understood that the obligations and restrictions that caste imposed upon a Hindu soldier's behaviour were all-important to him, that he would have to throw away his food if the shadow of a European officer passed over it, that it would be better to die of thirst—as some soldiers did die—than to accept a drink from a polluted hand or vessel. But since then all had changed. Indian culture was less inclined to be respected than to be mocked by British officials who agreed with Lord Macaulay that it consisted of nothing better than 'medical doctrines that would disgrace an English farrier—Astronomy, which would [be laughed at by] girls at an English boarding school—History, abounding with kings thirty feet high, and reigns thirty thousand years long—and Geography, made up of seas of treacle and butter'.

Rarely scrupling to pull down temples that might stand in their way, the British had brought the so-called wonders of science to India, the electric telegraph, the railway and those steam-engines which, so some villagers [thought] were driven by the force of demons trying to escape from the iron box in which the *Firinghis* (the foreigners) had imprisoned them—demons who were, perhaps, precursors of those devils that, as ancient prophecies foretold, were to rule the world in an accursed age soon to dawn. The railways, the electric telegraph and the steam-vessel would bring all men closer, the British said; but that in itself was a threat. For bringing men closer might eventually put an end to caste; and without caste how could a man be rewarded for his acts in a previous incarnation?

There were more obvious threats to religion than railways. Missionaries, prohibited from working in India in the eighteenth century, now spoke openly of the day when all men would embrace Christianity and turn against their heathen gods; and, though it was claimed that the missionaries were not paid by the Government—as the chaplains who cared for the British soldiers and civilians were—their activities were approved of, and in many cases supported by, the Government. So what really was the difference?

Moreover, as the Indians went on to argue, there were plenty of British officers and officials who behaved as though they were missionaries themselves. Colonel S.G. Wheler, commanding officer of the 34th Native Infantry, openly admitted in 1857 that he had endeavoured to convert sepoys and others to Christianity, that he conceived this to be the aim of every Christian, that it was certainly his own object in life, that he always hoped that 'the Lord would make him the happy instrument of converting his neighbour to God or, in other words, of rescuing him from eternal destruction'. Colonel

Wheler, in Lord Canning's opinion, was 'not fit to be trusted with a regiment'. But he continued to command it; and his opinions were far from uncommon amongst army officers, many of whom shared his views that the entire Bible, the Old Testament as much as the New, was the inspired word of God. Even in the 7th Dragoon Guards, so Trooper Quevillart recorded in his journal, 'a religious mania sprang up and reigned supreme'. 'The adjutant and sergeant-major having become quite sanctimonious and attending religious meetings every morning. . . . In consequence a vast number of men . . . also muster strongly at these meetings.' If the number of conversions amongst the men in native regiments was negligible, no one denied that Colonel Wheler and the adjutant of the 7th Dragoon Guards were far from being alone in their anxiety to see many more.

Proselytizing civilians were even more common. . . . 'The missionary is truly the regenerator of India,' announced one of many similar and widely circulated tracts. 'The land is being leavened, and Hindooism is everywhere being undermined. Great will some day, in God's appointed time, be the fall of it. The time appears to have come when earnest consideration should be given to the question whether or not all men should embrace the same system of religion.'

The Government's determination to convert Indians to Christianity seemed evident too in a variety of small ways. In certain areas *patwaris* [village scribes], sent to mission schools to learn the Hindi script, were presented on the completion of their course with copies of the New Testament. In other areas the Christian gospel was preached to prisoners in the local gaol [jail]. Indeed, it was widely rumoured that the Government were making a special effort to interfere with religion in gaols where the prisoners were at their mercy. . . . Ostensibly for the purpose of cleanliness, Muslim prisoners were required to shave off their beards, symbols of their faith. And ostensibly because they could be used as weapons, brass *lotas* [pots] had to be replaced with earthenware drinking vessels which were much less easy to cleanse were they to be touched by polluted lips. . . .

In hospitals, too, Indian susceptibilities were ignored in the accommodation of patients. 'Sick men or women, high or low, "purdah nisheen" (those who never go out in public) and others' were all required to share the same wards, a Sikh subahdar [officer], complained. 'People imagined in their ignorance that it was the intention of the British to take away the dignity and honour of all.'

While the virtues of Christianity were praised by missionaries in gaols, the evils of the native religions were condemned and lamented outside them. 'There is something very oppressive in being surrounded by heathen and Mohammedan darkness, in seeing idol-worship all around,' wrote Honoria Lawrence, wife of the Chief Commissioner of Oudh. 'When we see the deep and debasing hold these principles have on the people, it is difficult to believe they can ever be freed from it.'

Some primitive practices, suttee, for example, had been forbidden by law, to the satisfaction of the more progressive and enlightened [Hindus] but to the dismay of the orthodox. The orthodox were similarly outraged when Hindu widows, no longer permitted to burn themselves to death on their husbands' funeral pyres, were allowed to remarry. Perhaps even more obnoxious, both to the old-fashioned Hindu and the Muslim, was an earlier law which enabled a son who had changed his religion to inherit his father's property. This was inevitably interpreted as an attempt to remove at least one possible obstacle to a child's conversion to Christianity.

The fear of forcible conversion to Christianity became stronger than ever in the army in 1856 with the passing of the General Service Enlistment Act. This stipulated that all recruits to the seventy-two battalions of the Bengal Army . . . must agree to serve overseas if required to do so. Previously only six battalions of the Bengal Army had been available for foreign service, it being considered impossible for a faithful Hindu to go to sea as he could not, in a wooden ship, have his own fire to cook his food which his faith obliged him to do himself; nor could he properly perform the prescribed rituals of daily ablution even if water butts, filled by men of the same caste and never approached by others, had been available. Hindu sepoys who had gone overseas or crossed the Indus [River] were likely to be spurned by their comrades when they returned home. After the Afghan War 'none of the Hindoos in Hindostan would eat with their comrades who went to Afghanistan', wrote [an Indian officer], 'nor would they even allow them to touch their cooking utensils. They looked upon them all as outcasts, and treated them accordingly.'. . .

But these grievances were . . . paltry compared with the alarm aroused by rumours about a new rifle cartridge which was gradually being introduced into the Bengal Army.

The army was then mainly equipped with a smooth-bore musket which was quicker to load than the few rifles at that time in use but was less accurate over long ranges. After lengthy experiments at Enfield in England a new rifle had been developed which effectively combined long-distance accuracy with a less protracted method of loading. It had consequently been decided to bring this Enfield rifle into general use throughout the army.

Rifles of the old pattern had two grooves in their bores. They were loaded by ramming a charge of powder down the muzzle followed by a bullet which, to ease its way down the rifling, was wrapped in a patch of cloth lubricated with a mixture of wax and vegetable oil. The new rifle had three grooves, and the powder and bullet were made up together in a single cartridge—like the cartridge for a musket. To load the rifle, the end of the cartridge containing the powder had to be bitten or nipped off so that the charge would ignite; the cartridge was then pushed down the rifled bore of the muzzle. To make its passage easier, the paper of which the cartridge was composed was heavily greased. The grease was tallow which, so experiments had shown, lasted longer as a lubricant than the wax and vegetable oil used with the bullets for the old rifle. But the problem with tallow, as the Adjutant-General of the Bengal Army had realized, was that, whereas it was entirely unobjectionable to European troops, it was certainly not so to native troops for if it contained beef fat it would be degrading to Hindus and if it contained pig fat it would be offensive to Mohammedans. It was suggested, therefore, that the new cartridges should be issued only to British troops in India. The suggestion was ignored. Some cartridges greased with tallow had been sent out from England in 1853 to test the suitability of the new lubrication to the climate. These found their way into the hands of Indian soldiers before being returned to England in 1855. At that time no outcry had been raised against them. Since then, however, the greased paper having proved suitable for the climate, further cartridges had been sent out from England; and manufacture of them had begun in India where no specification for the composition of the tallow was given to the contractors. Since beef and pig fat were the cheapest animal fats available, the sepoys' suspicion that these were used instead of mutton or goat fat was far from unreasonable.

So far none of the new cartridges had been issued. But consignments of Enfield rifles had reached the various musketry depots in India where detachments from selected native regiments were, at the beginning of 1857, being given preliminary training in their use. There had been no objections yet; but suspicions about the cartridges which would have to be used with the new rifles were deepening, and rumours were spreading fast.

All the sepoys' fears, suspicions and grievances might even so have been overcome, had there remained the same sympathy and understanding between them and their officers as had existed in the earlier years of the century and in the century before. . . .

In a few native regiments, indeed, the British officers did not merely ignore their men when they could but actually abused them on parade, swearing at them in 'the most insulting language imaginable'. According to a British resident in India

> the sepoy is [regarded as] an inferior creature. He is sworn at. He is treated roughly. He is spoken of as a 'nigger'. He is addressed as 'suar' or pig, an epithet most approbrious to a respectable native, especially the Mussulman, and which cuts him to the quick. The old [officers] are less guilty. . . . But the younger men seem to regard it as an excellent

joke, as an evidence of spirit and a praiseworthy sense of superiority over the sepoy to treat him as an inferior animal.

The lack of understanding between the British officers and the sepoy was aggravated by regimental life in India being considered by many officers as a kind of purgatory to be endured while waiting to pass on to a higher calling. . . .

In his young days at the beginning of the century, in contrast to the 1850s, the colonel of [a typical] regiment was a familiar figure to everyone, responsible for discipline, not forbidden, as he subsequently was, to award a punishment more severe than five days' drill without obtaining higher authority. He was 'well known all around' as well as in the regiment . . . and 'the villagers came from as far as thirty miles away to inform him where the game was' when he wanted to organize a tiger hunt to which he would, perhaps, invite a local landholder. Contemporaries . . . , who appear in other memoirs of the time, wrestled with their men or fenced with them or took them out hawking. One colonel is described as sending a non-commissioned officer ahead of him on the march to discover the best chess players in the village nearest his camping-ground. Another, who knew 'how to treat the sepoys in their own way', who was not one 'of your pipe-clay rigid disciplinarians who would utterly extinguish the native in the soldier', could make his men roar with laughter or shake in their shoes as he pleased. Like most British officers in India then he had a native mistress, and made no attempt to interfere with her ancient faith which he was prepared to respect until God saw fit to change it. It was not until the 1830s and 1840s, when marriage to white women became more common, that living with a native mistress was considered to be rather disreputable. By then it was 'fashionable to admire what came from England and to eschew everything "black."'

The Taiping
Rebellion in China

Jean Chesneaux

Two currents reappear in the vast river that is China's history: the tendency for the crises of ruling dynasties to take the form of peasant unrest, and the tendency for peasant unrest to breed not only antigovernment violence but also new religious movements, sometimes tinged with foreign influences. This pattern recurred in the mid–nineteenth century.

The Qing, or Manchu, dynasty that had ruled China since 1644 was of non-Chinese origin. Originally efficient, by the nineteenth century Manchu rule was growing corrupt, and the Opium War demonstrated its inability to defend China against foreign incursions. The missionaries and merchants from Europe who began moving into China in large numbers after the Opium War ended in 1842 made themselves deeply unpopular among ordinary Chinese people, and blame fastened on the ruling dynasty.

Paradoxically, elements of Christianity can be found in the ideas preached by Hung Hsiu-ch'üan, the leader of the most formidable of all the anti-Manchu and antiforeign movements that swept through China after 1842. Hung had spent enough time in a Christian mission to be impressed by the potential that European inventions had for making China stronger, and he learned enough about Christianity to proclaim himself Jesus Christ's younger brother, sent to redeem China. But the aim of the Taiping movement, which he led and which probably would have toppled the Manchus had the European powers not seen it as dangerous and lent crucial aid to the Manchus, was not to introduce superficial resemblances to European ways into the ancient Middle Kingdom. Rather, the Taipings must be seen as the first wave of the great peasant revolutionary movement that, having adapted elements of Marxism rather than of Christianity from the West, would attempt to make China "stand up" (in Mao Zedong's words) against imperialism.

In this selection, Jean Chesneaux, a French historian of East Asia, tells the story of how the Taipings came close to revolutionizing China in the mid–nineteenth century.

Partly as a result of the increase in population and a whole series of natural disasters, but above all because of a dynastic crisis of power, agrarian unrest, which had been muted in the seventeenth century, broke out again all over the country after the beginning of the nineteenth, with local incidents, secret society activities and armed risings. They were no more, however, than dispersed and marginal expressions of peasant discontent, and gave way, between 1850 and 1870, to a major wave of peasant rebellions of exceptional size. Several million peasants were involved; nearly all the eighteen provinces were affected; many of them, between 1855 and 1860, were totally or partially out of the control of the central government. Rebellions continued for almost twenty years, and constitute what was probably the greatest wave of peasant wars in history. But once more [these] rebellions . . . were separate movements, incapable of effectively coordinating their efforts. Consequently the Manchu dynasty was able . . . to make an unexpected recovery.

It was no mere coincidence that this powerful peasant outburst occurred in the period of the Opium Wars and the 'opening' of China by the Western powers. The age-old contradictions between the peasants and the feudal holders of power, land and learning were deepened and brought to a climax by a combination of exceptional circumstances. The political and social crisis, which had been fermenting in the Chinese countryside since the beginning of the nineteenth century, was brutally exacerbated by the First Opium War and the Treaty of Nanking (1842). The Manchu [Qing] dynasty was discredited by its readiness to give in to Western demands. The opium traffic, illicit before the war, and then legalized, drained China of a large part of her reserves of silver, and changed, to the disadvantage of the peasants, the exchange rate between silver and copper. The opening of other ports in the east of the country deprived Canton [Guangzhou] of much of the commerce which had been concentrated there when it had been the only port open to foreign trade. Hundreds of thousands of boatmen and porters in central and southern China were thrown out of work, and it was from among this army of unemployed that several of the leaders of the Taiping rebellion emerged.

This most spectacular and exceptional of the great peasant move-

ments of the mid–nineteenth century was more profoundly 'precon-
ditioned' than peasant risings in general throughout the history of
China. It occurred at the point when the traditional social crisis coincided with the penetration of China by the Western powers. This
fusion of archaic and modern elements is shown in the geographical
area where the movement originated and in the personality of its
founder. Though Kwangsi may seem to have been no more than a
typical province of old China, where for centuries peasants, gentry
and secret societies confronted each other, it constituted the hinter-
land of Canton—the point of contact for more than a century between China and the West, the port frequented by Western merchants
and missionaries. This influence was felt as far as Kwangsi. Hung
Hsiu-ch'üan, the Taiping leader, shows the same combination of influences. He was an educated man from a family of poor peasants,
who had not succeeded in gaining admission to the ranks of the ruling class. He had also been a pupil of a Protestant missionary in Canton. He had visited the great port and had experienced the historical
'gap' which existed between China and the 'barbarians'. In about
1845 Hung Hsiu-ch'üan began to preach a new faith in the mountains of Kwangsi. Into the 'Society of God-worshippers' which he
formed, he welcomed landless peasants, coolies, miners, charcoal
burners and disbanded soldiers. Initially his movement enjoyed the
assistance of [secret society] lodges which were very powerful in this
area, and were the traditional meeting points for dissident elements.
But he soon broke with the secret societies for ideological reasons:
they refused to follow his attempted Christian syncretism. For his
part, he disapproved of their dream of restoring the Ming dynasty,
and in 1851 founded his own dynasty—'The Celestial Kingdom of
Great Peace' (*T'ai-ping T'ien-kuo*). Soon the Taiping armies, swelled
by thousands of rebellious peasants, began their march to the northeast, and in 1853 arrived at Nanking, which remained the rebel capital for eleven years.

The Taiping movement was fundamentally an agrarian one, a revolt of the peasants against their 'natural' enemies within Chinese
society, against landlords, gentry and officials. But at the same time
it had a strong colouring of nationalism or proto-nationalism, and
shows certain unique elements of modernization.

Its peasant character is reflected in the personality of its leaders,
who gave themselves the archaic title of *wang* (king); many of them
came from the poor peasantry of the south-west. As they advanced
through central China and the Yangtze valley, the Taiping troops
were supported by spontaneous peasant risings; officials, wealthy
and unpopular landlords were put to death, tax registers, land registers and loan receipts were burned, government offices sacked. A
contemporary chronicler wrote, 'Each time they entered into a rich

house, or into that of a great family, they would dig three feet into the ground [to find buried treasure]. But not only did they not plunder the peasants, on the contrary, wherever they passed they distributed clothes and other things they had taken to the poor, and announced a remission of taxes for three years, thus winning the gratitude of the villagers.'

In the same year that they set up their capital at Nanking, the Taipings promulgated their 'Land System of the Celestial Dynasty', the primitive collectivism of which places it in the direct tradition of Chinese peasant utopianism.

> All lands under Heaven shall be farmed jointly by the people under Heaven. If the production of food is too small in one place, then move to another where it is more abundant. All lands under Heaven shall be accessible in time of abundance or famine. If there is a famine in one area move the surplus from an area where there is abundance to that area. . . . Land shall be farmed by all; rice, eaten by all; clothes, worn by all; money, spent by all. There shall be no inequality, and no person shall be without food or fuel. No matter whether man or woman, everyone over sixteen years of age shall receive land.

The same primitive collectivism, never widely enforced, however, was to govern industrial production, by means of 'artisans' battalions', the products of which went into 'state treasuries' and were shared among all.

The elements of proto-nationalism in the Taiping movement linked it with peasant revolts of the past, with the risings against Mongol power in the fourteenth century, for instance, led by the peasant Chu Yuan-chang, the founder of the Ming dynasty. The Taipings wished to liberate China from the domination of the Manchus. They accused the dynasty of being incapable of governing China, of wanting to drain the country of its wealth, of being responsible for the internal and external misfortunes of China. Symbolically the Taipings cut off their queues, imposed upon the Chinese in the seventeenth century as a sign of humiliation, and allowed their hair to grow—hence the contemporary epithet 'long-haired rebels' (ch'ang-mao tsei). This nationalistic element explains the recruitment by the Taipings of a number of educated and relatively wealthy people who had no particular reason to support the social struggle of the peasantry, but whose anti-Manchu patriotism gave them some sympathy for the rebel cause. They helped to draw up proclamations, undertook administrative functions, and made possible the creation of a real rebel state which survived for eleven years and controlled extensive territories.

The activities of the Taipings took place in a context which was no longer purely Chinese, for the shadow of the West had lain over

China since the humiliating defeat in 1842. The Taipings were not indifferent to the challenge of the West; for instance, they adopted a semi-solar calendar in place of the old lunar calendar; they envisaged modern reforms, the construction of a network of railways, a postal service, hospitals and banks. Above all they attempted to penetrate the 'secret' of the Westerners in borrowing elements of their religion. They professed a militant monotheism; they accepted the Ten Commandments and the divinity of Christ, whose younger brother Hung Hsiu-ch'üan claimed to be; they practised baptism and gave the Old and New Testaments a place among their canonical books. These Christian elements were combined with popular traditional religions, with peasant cults and with Buddhist and Taoist elements. The Taipings thus created a complete politico-religious system, which combined spiritual salvation and obedience to the will of God with the political and military defence of the rebel state.

Like many other peasant rebels in history, the Taipings were subject to the contradictions inherent by definition in a rebel order. Should they be content with harassing the enemy, exposing its decadence, fighting and overthrowing the imperial regime, or should they, as others had done, attempt to construct new social machinery with its own forms of subordination and obligation? Could the revolt transform itself into a stable social structure without becoming a prisoner of the exigencies of such a structure? The Taipings began by conducting mobile warfare, all the way from the mountains of Kwangsi to the city of Nanking. This was a real people's war, and the peasants rose in response. But once established in Nanking, the Taipings created the apparatus of government, with a capital, a political system, a bureaucratic administration and a group of leaders which soon became a privileged class. Many of the leaders had large harems, though in the army the Taipings preached monogamy and the separation of the sexes. To make this governmental machinery work involved increasing demands upon the peasantry, who ceased to be the motive force of a movement and became the subjects of a government. They had to pay taxes, suffer requisitions and give corvée [unpaid labor] services. This is why the peasantry became increasingly disaffected in the last years of the Celestial Kingdom of Great Peace. The rebel dynasty suffered the same withdrawal of allegiance in the rural areas under its control as had undermined the regime it sought to replace.

The disaffection of the peasantry, the main cause of the failure of the Taipings, was accompanied by certain other unfavourable factors. The movement never succeeded in controlling more than a fairly limited region. It was restricted in the first instance to the south-west, from which it detached itself soon after 1850, and then established more durable roots in . . . the lower Yangtze valley. Two expeditions against Peking, sent out in 1853 and 1854, did not succeed in mobilizing the peasants of the north and were utterly defeated. Moreover, the Taipings were weakened by dissension between ruling cliques. The two principal colleagues of Hung Hsiu-ch'üan, together with thousands of their followers, were killed in an outbreak of mutual slaughter in Nanking in 1856. Another gifted leader, Shih Ta-k'ai, preferred to flee Nanking with his troops and campaign on his own in the south-west. In 1859 the rebel king's cousin, Hung Jen-kan, a former catechist of Protestant missionaries in Canton and a capable administrator, arrived in Nanking. But he was soon ousted by powerful military men or incapable courtiers who had the fickle favour of Hung Hsiu-ch'üan.

In contrast to the weakening of the rebel regime, its enemy proved capable of vigorous recovery. From the beginning of the rebellion, imperial generals had been easily defeated. Since then, the gentry and landlords of the provinces had taken over the defence of their own economic interests. They organized disciplined and well-paid provincial militia and gradually established a blockade of rebel territory. The imperial government was also assisted in the reconquest of the empire by the Western powers, France and England, who, having once again imposed their will upon the Manchu dynasty in the Second Opium War and the Treaty of Tientsin (1858–60), preferred to maintain a conservative and docile government in Peking rather than see it swept away by rebels. Western aid, though not decisive, contributed to the defeat of the Taipings; Western officers helped to train imperial troops, steamships were put at their disposal for the transport of armies to the front in the lower Yangtze, foreign detachments sometimes even engaged directly in the hostilities and capable foreign officers, such as C.G. Gordon, commanded certain mixed units. Nanking was finally taken in the summer of 1864, and thousands of Taipings killed themselves with their leaders.

A Reign of Terror in the Congo Free State

Adam Hochschild

By the mid-1880s, the European powers' race for the control of Africa's territory and resources was in full swing. In 1885 an international meeting of European foreign ministers convened at Berlin with the ostensible purpose of suppressing Africa's internal slave trade but with the more important aim of dividing up the map of Africa and, hopefully, forestalling wars among European claimants.

One of the parties represented at Berlin was Leopold II, king of the Belgians. A monarch whose power was limited by Belgium's increasingly democratic constitution, Leopold was at heart an ambitious and ruthless autocrat, and he saw in the unfolding scramble for Africa an opportunity to indulge his restless personal ambitions. Using his personal financial resources, Leopold had already been subsidizing the American journalist Henry Stanley and his well-publicized explorations of central Africa. Now he conceived the idea of creating not a Belgian colony (for the parsimonious Belgian parliament wanted nothing to do with the scheme) but a large, theoretically independent territorial entity under Leopold's personal control, to be called the "Congo Free State." Supposedly it was to be free of slavery, was to serve as a kind of buffer zone between the colonial empires that France, Great Britain, Germany, and Portugal were building in the heart of Africa, and was to be open to the commercial activities of citizens of all nations, including the United States (for that reason, the U.S. government gave its blessing to Leopold's scheme).

Actually, the Congo Free State was a private empire for Leopold II. The Belgian government took no official role in governing it, and a company that Leopold set up recruited officials and employees from all over the Western world to administer the Free State. To meet expenses—which included the supposed cost of suppressing the slave trade—Leopold and his company licensed private entrepreneurs to set up rubber plantations and to hunt for ivory. In practice, no one could do business in the Congo without Leopold's consent, and without giving him a generous share of the profits.

As might be expected in this era of rampant racism and ruthless greed, Leopold's Congo Free State quickly became a land in which, one observer opined, "there aren't no Ten Commandments." The exploitation of the Congolese peoples reached horrible proportions—probably worse than in any other European colony because no government officials could be called in to account for what was going on. Any vacant land in this vast country (almost a million square miles) of hunter-gatherers could be declared Leopold's personal property and leased to European exploiters. Virtually the entire indigenous population could be drafted for forced labor, and whole villages were given quotas for ivory or rubber to gather, on pain of having hostages killed or mutilated. Far from suppressing traditional slavery, the Congo Free State became a virtual slave labor camp for the benefit of Leopold and the entrepreneurs whom he chose—for a price—to favor.

American historian Adam Hochschild describes Leopold's regime in the Congo in the following extract from his 1998 book *King Leopold's Ghost: A Story of Greed, Terror, and Heroism in Colonial Africa.*

Leopold established the capital of his new Congo state at the port town of Boma, just upriver from the Atlantic, where Stanley had finished his epic trans-African trek in 1877. As the 1890s began, Boma was complete with a narrow-gauge trolley—a steam engine pulling a couple of cars—that linked the bustling docks and trading-company warehouses to a cooler plateau above. There stood the government offices and houses for the Europeans who worked in them. Boma also boasted a Catholic church made of iron, a hospital for Europeans, a post office, a military base whose cannon fired a salute to any newly arriving VIP, and a two-story hotel. Three times a day—at 6 A.M., 11:45, and 6:30 P.M.—about seventy-five white officials took the trolley down the hill and through a plantation of banana trees for meals in the hotel dining room. The only European who ate elsewhere was the governor general, who took his meals in his dignified Victorian mansion, complete with a cupola, French windows, and covered porches. Every year, the king's birthday was celebrated with such events as a ceremonial review of troops, a target-shooting contest, and a concert by a Catholic black children's choir.

Despite his impressive mansion, guarded by African sentries with blue uniforms and red fezes, the Congo's governor general had far less power than did a British, French, or German colonial governor. More than any other colony in Africa, the Congo was administered directly from Europe. The real headquarters of the État Indépendant du Congo [Congo Free State] were not in Boma but in suites of offices in Brussels, one on the grounds of the Royal Palace, the others next door or across the street. All the Congo's high- and middle-level administrators were picked and promoted by the king himself, and a mini-cabinet of three or four Belgians at the top, in Brussels, reported to Leopold directly.

His one-man rule over this huge territory was in striking contrast to Leopold's ever more limited power at home. Once, in his later years, while he was talking in his study with several Cabinet ministers, his nephew and heir apparent, Prince Albert, opened a window, and a draft blew some papers onto the floor. Leopold ordered Albert to pick them up. "Let him do it," the king said to one of the ministers, who had hastily offered to do so instead. "A future constitutional monarch must learn to stoop." But in the Congo there was no stooping, Leopold's power was absolute.

At the lowest level, the king's rule over his colony was carried out by white men in charge of districts and river stations throughout the vast territory; some of them were not visited by steamboats for months at a time. Far in the interior, practice often lagged behind theory, but on paper, at least, even the humblest station chief was allotted a bottle of red wine per day and a plentiful supply of English marmalade, Danish butter, canned meats, soups and condiments, and *foie gras* and other pâtés from Fischer's of Strasbourg.

For these functionaries there was a plethora of medals, whose grades reflected the burgeoning hierarchy of imperial rule. For holders of the Order of the African Star, for instance, there were six classes, ranging from *grands-croix* and *commandeurs* down to mere *médaillés*. The Royal Order of the Lion, created by Leopold to "recognize merit and acknowledge services rendered to Us": also had six classes. For African chiefs who collaborated with the regime, there was a special medal—bronze, silver, or gold-plated, depending on the degree of "service" rendered. It bore Leopold's profile on one side and, on the other, the Congo state coat of arms and the words LOYALTY AND DEVOTION.

The white officials in Leopold's Congo were usually single men, many of whom took on one or more African concubines. But by the turn of the century a few officials began to bring their wives, and some of those who didn't turned to an enterprising British matchmaking agency that supplied mail-order brides from Europe.

Photographs of remote Congo posts from the 1890s generally show the same pattern. From the long shadows, it appears to be late afternoon. The two or three white men in the picture wear suits and ties and elongated sun helmets, like a London bobby's cap in white. They are seated on wicker chairs, a dog at their feet, in front of a tent or simple thatched-roofed building, smiling. Behind them stand their unsmiling African servants, holding some emblem of their status: a serving tray, a towel draped over an arm, a bottle ready to pour. Wine glasses or tea cups rest on a table, symbols of the comforts of home. The white men are always dressed in white.

Underpinning such scenes were a number of royal decrees from Brussels. The first and most important had been issued on the very day in 1885 that the existence of the Congo state was formally proclaimed; it declared that all "vacant land" was the property of the state. There was no definition of what made land vacant. All over the world, of course, land that *looks* vacant has often been deliberately left to lie fallow while crops are planted somewhere else—especially in the tropics, where heavy rainfalls leach nutrients out of the soil.

Leopold was after whatever could be quickly harvested. In that sense, he treated both vacant and nonvacant land as his property, claiming a right to all its products. He made no distinction between the tusks of an elephant roaming wild or villagers' vegetables that could feed his soldiers; it was all his.

He did not, however, have the resources to exploit the entire territory, so another set of decrees carved parts of the Congo into several giant blocks, whose "vacant land" was leased out for long periods as concessions to private companies. These concession companies had shareholders—largely, though not entirely Belgian—and interlocking directorates that included many high Congo state officials. But in each of them the state—which in effect meant Leopold himself—usually kept 50 percent of the shares. In setting up this structure, Leopold was like the manager of a venture capital syndicate today. He had essentially found a way to attract other people's capital to his investment schemes while he retained half the proceeds. In the end, what with various taxes and fees the companies paid the state, it came to more than half.

Unlike a venture capitalist in the marketplace, however, the king deployed troops and government officials as well as investment funds. He used them ruthlessly to shut out of the territory most businesses in which he did not have a piece of the action. [A] Dutch trading firm . . . found itself facing stiff competition for ivory from Congo state officials who stopped its boats, in one case with gunfire. Once, according to a history of the company, "a state of siege was proclaimed for a certain region which made it closed territory for traders. When the state of siege was lifted, all the ivory had disappeared."

The king, meanwhile, continued to claim that making a profit was the farthest thing from his mind. "I thank you for having done justice yesterday to the calumnies spread by enemies of the Congo state, to the accusation of secrecy and the spirit of gain," he wrote to the prime minister after a parliamentary debate in 1891. "The Congo state is certainly not a business. If it gathers ivory on certain of its lands, that is only to lessen its deficit."

And if Africans were made to help out in the ivory-gathering, why that too, Heaven forbid, was not to make a profit, but to rescue these benighted people from their indolence. Talk of the lazy native accompanied the entire European land grab in Africa, just as it had been used to justify the conquest of the Americas. To an American reporter, Leopold once declared, "In dealing with a race composed of cannibals for thousands of years it is necessary to use methods which will best shake their idleness and make them realize the sanctity of work."

As the 1890s began, the work whose sanctity Leopold prized most highly was seizing all the ivory that could be found. Congo state officials and their African auxiliaries swept through the country on ivory raids, shooting elephants, buying tusks from villagers, for a pittance, or simply confiscating them. Congo peoples had been hunting elephants for centuries, but now they were forbidden to sell or deliver ivory to anyone other than an agent of Leopold. A draconian refinement of the ivory-gathering method, which set the pattern for much that was to come, was a commission structure the king imposed in 1890, whereby his agents in the field got a cut of the ivory's

In the Congo Free State, enormous numbers of elephants were slaughtered to produce the ivory tusks demanded by King Leopold's officials.

market value—but on a sliding scale. An agent received only 6 percent of the value of any ivory purchased at eight francs per kilo, but the commission climbed, in stages, to 10 percent for ivory bought at four francs per kilo. The European agents thus had a powerful incentive to force Africans—if necessary, at gunpoint—to accept extremely low prices.

Almost none of these Belgian francs actually reached any Congolese elephant hunters. They received only small amounts of cloth, beads, and the like, or the brass rods that the state decreed as the territory's main currency. For Africans, transactions in money were not allowed. Money in free circulation might undermine what was essentially a command economy.

The commands were above all for labor. At the beginning, the state most wanted porters. Like Stanley, any official who ventured away from the river system and into the bush—to collect ivory, set up new posts, put down a rebellion—needed long columns of porters to carry everything from machine-gun ammunition to all that red wine and pâté. These tens of thousands of porters were usually paid for their work, if only sometimes the food necessary to keep them going, but most of them were conscripts. Even children were put to work: one observer noted seven- to nine-year-olds each carrying a load of twenty-two pounds.

"A file of poor devils, chained by the neck, carried my trunks and boxes toward the dock," a Congo state official notes matter-of-factly in his memoirs. At the next stop on his journey more porters were needed for an overland trip: "There were about a hundred of them, trembling and fearful before the overseer, who strolled by whirling a whip. For each stocky and broad-backed fellow, how many were skeletons dried up like mummies, their skin worn out . . . seamed with deep scars, covered with suppurating wounds. . . . No matter, they were all up to the job."

Porters were needed most at the points where the river system was blocked by rapids, particularly—until the railroad was built—for the three-week trek between the port town of Matadi and Stanley Pool. This was the pipeline up which supplies passed to the interior and down which ivory and other riches were carried to the sea. Moving dismantled steamboats to the upper section of the river was the most labor-intensive job of all: one steamboat could comprise three thousand porter loads. Here is how Edmond Picard, a Belgian senator, described a caravan of porters he saw on the route around the big rapids in 1896:

> Unceasingly we meet these porters . . . black, miserable, with only a horribly filthy loin-cloth for clothing, frizzy and bare head supporting the load—box, bale, ivory tusk . . . barrel; most of them sickly, drooping under a burden increased by tiredness and insufficient food —a handful of

rice and some stinking dried fish; pitiful walking caryatids, beasts of burden with thin monkey legs, with drawn features, eyes fixed and round from preoccupation with keeping their balance and from the daze of exhaustion. They come and go like this by the thousands . . . requisitioned by the State armed with its powerful militia, handed over by chiefs whose slaves they are and who make off with their salaries, trotting with bent knees, belly forward, an arm raised to steady the load, the other leaning on a long walking-stick, dusty and sweaty, insects spreading out across the mountains and valleys their many files and their task of Sisyphus, dying along the road or, the journey over, heading off to die from overwork in their villages.

The death toll was particularly high among porters forced to carry loads long distances. Of the three hundred porters conscripted in 1891 by District Commissioner Paul Lemarinel for a forced march of more than six hundred miles to set up a new post, not one returned.

Stanislas Lefranc, a devout Catholic and monarchist, was a Belgian prosecutor who had come to the Congo to work as a magistrate. Early one Sunday morning in Leopoldville, he heard the sound of many children screaming desperately.

On tracing the howls to their source, Lefranc found "some thirty urchins, of whom several were seven or eight years old, lined up and waiting their turn, watching, terrified, their companions being flogged. Most of the urchins, in a paroxysm of grief . . . kicked so frightfully that the soldiers ordered to hold them by the hands and feet had to lift them off the ground. . . . 25 times the whip slashed down on each of the children." The evening before, Lefranc learned, several children had laughed in the presence of a white man, who then ordered that all the servant boys in town be given fifty lashes. The second installment of twenty-five lashes was due at six o'clock the next morning. Lefranc managed to get these stopped, but was told not to make any more protests that interfered with discipline.

Lefranc was seeing in use a central tool of Leopold's Congo, which in the minds of the territory's people, soon became as closely identified with white rule as the steamboat or the rifle. It was the *chicotte*—a whip of raw, sun-dried hippopotamus hide, cut into a long sharp-edged corkscrew strip. Usually the *chicotte* was applied to the victim's bare buttocks. Its blows would leave permanent scars; more than twenty-five strokes could mean unconsciousness; and a hundred or more—not an uncommon punishment—were often fatal.

Lefranc was to see many more *chicotte* beatings, although his descriptions of them, in pamphlets and newspaper articles he published in Belgium, provoked little reaction.

The station chief selects the victims. . . . Trembling, haggard, they lie face down on the ground . . . two of their companions, sometimes four, seize them by the feet and hands, and remove their cotton drawers. . . .

> Each time that the torturer lifts up the *chicotte,* a reddish stripe appears on the skin of the pitiful victims, who, however firmly held, gasp in frightful contortions. . . . At the first blows the unhappy victims let out horrible cries which soon become faint groans. . . . In a refinement of evil, some officers, and I've witnessed this, demand that when the sufferer gets up, panting, he must graciously give the military salute.

The open horror Lefranc expressed succeeded only in earning him a reputation as an oddball or troublemaker. He "shows an astonishing ignorance of things which he ought to know because of his work. A mediocre agent," the acting governor general wrote in a personnel evaluation. In an attempt to quiet his complaints, Lefranc wrote, officials ordered that executions at his post be carried out in a new location instead of next to his house.

Except for Lefranc, few Europeans working for the regime left records of their shock at the sight of officially sanctioned terror. The white men who passed through the territory as military officers, steamboat captains, or state or concession company officials generally accepted the use of the *chicotte* as unthinkingly as hundreds of thousands of other men in uniform would accept their assignments, a half-century later, to staff the Nazi and Soviet concentration camps. "Monsters exist," wrote Primo Levi [an Italian Jew and Holocaust survivor] of his experience at Auschwitz. "But they are too few in number to be truly dangerous. More dangerous are . . . the functionaries ready to believe and to act without asking questions."

What made it possible for the functionaries in the Congo to so blithely watch the *chicotte* in action and, as we shall see, to deal out pain and death in other ways as well? To begin with, of course, was race. To Europeans, Africans were inferior beings: lazy, uncivilized, little better than animals. In fact, the most common way they were put to work was, like animals, as beasts of burden. In any system of terror, the functionaries must first of all see the victims as less than human, and Victorian ideas about race provided such a foundation.

Then, of course, the terror in the Congo was sanctioned by the authorities. For a white man to rebel meant challenging the system that provided your livelihood. Everyone around you was participating. By going along with the system, you were paid, promoted, awarded medals. So men who would have been appalled to see someone using a *chicotte* on the streets of Brussels or Paris or Stockholm accepted the act in this different setting, as normal. We can hear the echo of this thinking, in another context, half a century later: "To tell the truth," said Franz Stangl of the mass killings that took place when he was commandant of the Nazi death camps of Sobibor and Treblinka, "one did become used to it."

In such a regime, one thing that often helps functionaries "become used to it," is a slight, symbolic distance—irrelevant to the victim—

between an official in charge and the physical act of terror itself. That symbolic distance was frequently cited in self-defense by Nazis put on trial after World War II. Dr. Johann Paul Kremer, for example, an SS physician who liked to do his pathology research on human tissue that was still fresh, explained:

> The patient was put on the dissecting table while he was still alive. I then approached the table and put several questions to the man as to such details which pertained to my researches. . . . When I had collected my information the orderly approached the patient and killed him with an injection in the vicinity of the heart. . . . I myself never made any lethal injections.

I myself never made any lethal injections. Although some whites in the Congo enjoyed wielding the *chicotte,* most put a similar symbolic distance between themselves and the dreaded instrument. "At first I . . . took upon myself the responsibility of meting out punishment to those whose conduct during the previous day seemed to warrant such treatment," recalled Raoul de Premorel, who worked for a company operating in the Kasai River basin. "Soon . . . I found it desirable to assign the execution of sentences to others under my direction. The best plan seemed to be to have each *capita* [African foreman] administer the punishment for his own gang."

And so the bulk of *chicotte* blows were inflicted by Africans on the bodies of other Africans. This, for the conquerors, served a further purpose. It created a class of foremen from among the conquered, like the *kapos* in the Nazi concentration camps and the *predurki,* or trusties, in the Soviet gulag [labor camp system]. Just as terrorizing people is part of conquest, so is forcing someone else to administer the terror.

Finally, when terror is the unquestioned order of the day, wielding it efficiently is regarded as a manly virtue, the way soldiers value calmness in battle. This is the ultimate in "becoming used to it." Here, for instance, a station chief named Georges Bricusse describes in his diary a hanging he ordered in 1895 of a man who had stolen a rifle:

> The gallows is set up. The rope is attached, too high. They lift up the nigger and put the noose around him. The rope twists for a few moments, then *crack,* the man is wriggling on the ground. A shot in the back of the neck and the game is up. It didn't make the least impression on me this time!! And to think that the first time I saw the *chicotte* administered, I was pale with fright. Africa has some use after all. I could now walk into fire as if to a wedding.

Successful Westernization: Japan in 1900

Richard Perran

Between 1853 and 1869, Japan went through a sweeping political revolution, known in history as the Meiji Restoration. In the course of this revolution, the shogun—a kind of hereditary viceroy or supreme general ruling in the name of the sacred but powerless emperor—was swept aside and power was restored to Emperor Matsushito (known as the Meiji Emperor after his death in 1912). But this was no mere palace revolution. Not only the shogunate but also the whole complex system of Japanese feudalism disappeared. The men who carried out the Meiji Restoration mostly belonged to the samurai, a class of warriors roughly comparable to medieval European knights, who under the shogunate had gradually been transformed into government officials. Although the samurai deeply revered the emperor, the political and social system that they established was designed to adapt as many Western institutions and practices as were necessary. Since the early seventeenth century, the shogunate had attempted to seal Japan off from Western and even Chinese influence. But some educated Japanese (mostly of the samurai and merchant classes) knew what was happening in the West, particularly in the spheres of science and technology, and they understood that Japan could not keep its independence without selectively following Western models. The arrival of an American fleet commanded by Commodore Matthew Perry in 1853, which forced the shogunate to open Japan to Western commerce, set in motion the chain of events that led to the

Reprinted from "On the Turn: Japan, 1900," by Richard Perran, *History Today*, June 1992. Reprinted with permission from *History Today*.

shogun's fall by 1868 and the establishment of a new, imperial regime dominated by modernizers.

By the late 1870s, argues British historian Richard Perran, the adoption of Western technology, economic practices, and political structures, all of which began with the Meiji Restoration, had become irreversible. The ways in which Japan had been transformed by 1900 are described by Perran.

However, it is vitally important to understand that the transformation of Japan was not something that had begun abruptly in 1868, with the downfall of the shogunate. Japan had been developing capitalist institutions, including a sophisticated banking and commercial system, since the eighteenth century. Although the samurai continued to honor their medieval martial traditions, many of them had become urbanized officials long before the Meiji Restoration. Awareness of Western science and technology became widespread in the eighteenth and early nineteenth centuries as well, even though this knowledge had to come secondhand, through translated books, rather than through direct contact and emulation. Thus the Meiji Restoration must be understood not so much as a new departure—but rather as a clearing of the ground that permitted an *intensification* of Japan's adaptation of Western ways. Moreover, this adaptation was consciously designed to enhance Japan's position as a powerful nation-state that could vigorously assert its interests, including its desire to build an overseas empire in East Asia.

Following the Meiji Restoration in 1868, when rule by the emperor replaced the government of Japan by the Tokugawa shogun, the country embarked on a process of modernisation. In the next thirty years Western experts were imported to train the Japanese at home, selected Japanese were sent abroad to learn from the West, and Japan's new leaders embarked on a programme of radical reform. By these means they aimed at transforming a country that was weak and backward into a strong modern industrial nation. This new Japan would be capable of dealing with Western powers on equal terms and of throwing off the humiliating 'unequal treaties' they had imposed between 1858 and 1869.

When the Emperor Meiji died in 1912, control was concentrated in a highly centralised state whose functions were carried out through Western-style political, administrative and judicial institutions operating in the name of the emperor. Western-style armed forces upheld the position of the Japanese state at home and abroad. A modern and efficient education system served the aims of the state. Western-style economic and business institutions were in place, and factory-based industry firmly established. Japan had already been victorious in two major wars, against China in 1894–95 and Russia in 1904–5. She had not only achieved the much desired revision of the unequal treaties, but was a world power with an alliance with Britain, and a possessor of colonies. Yet the country still retained many traditional features, and had only adopted those characteristics of the West that were absolutely necessary to achieve its desired aims.

How far had the transformation process gone by 1900, and can the decade of the 1890s be described as a 'turning point'? To answer this we need to judge when Japan passed beyond that point in time when her modernisation could not have been reversed. Because the whole process of Japanese modernisation involved a complex interaction of social, economic, and political change it is not possible to ascribe a precise date to its completion. Nevertheless, there are a number of factors to suggest that by 1900 it had reached a stage where it was unlikely to be reversed.

It was the authorities that had to provide the necessary pump-priming and make strategic decisions about which areas of Japanese life needed to be transformed. It had become a traditional habit of the Japanese to look to officialdom for example and direction in almost everything, and this habit naturally asserted itself when it became necessary to assimilate a foreign civilisation which for nearly three centuries had been an object of national repugnance. This required the education of the nation as a whole and the task of instruction was divided among foreigners of different nations. The Meiji government imported around 300 experts or *yatoi*—a Japanese term meaning 'live machines'— into the country to help upgrade its industry, infrastructure and institutions. Before the Franco-Prussian War, Frenchmen were employed in teaching strategy and tactics to the army and in revising the criminal code. The building of railways, installing telegraphs and lighthouses, and training the new navy was done by Englishmen. Americans were employed in forming a postal service, agricultural development, and in planning colonisation and an educational system. In an attempt to introduce Occidental ideas of art, Italian painters and sculptors were brought to Japan. German experts were asked to develop a system of local government, train Japanese doctors and, after the Franco-Prussian War, to educate army officers. A number of Western observers believed that such wholesale adoption of an alien civilisation was impossible and feared that it would produce a violent reaction.

Although this did not occur, many early innovations were not really necessary to modernisation but merely imitations of Western customs. At that time the distinction between the fundamental features of modern technology and mere Occidental peculiarities was by no means clear. If it was necessary to use Western weapons there might also be a virtue in wearing Western clothes or shaking hands in the Occidental manner. Moreover, Meiji Japan had good reason to adopt even the more superficial aspects of Western culture. The international world of the nineteenth century was completely dominated by the Occident, and in view of the Western assumption of cultural superiority, the Japanese were probably correct in judging that they could not be regarded as even quasi-equals until they possessed not only modern technology but also many of the superficial aspects of Western culture. The resulting attempts in the 1870s and 1880s to borrow almost anything and everything Western may now seem to us to be amusingly indiscriminate, but it is perfectly understandable.

As the object of modernisation was to obtain equal treatment by the West many of the cultural innovations, besides being more than outward forms to the Japanese themselves, had an important psychological influence on Western diplomats and politicians. Under the shogun, members of the first Japanese delegation to the United States in 1860 wore traditional samurai dress with shaved pate and long side hair tied in a bun and carried swords. Under the emperor, Western-style haircuts were a major symbol of Westernisation. Soldiers and civilian functionaries wore Western-style uniforms, and politicians often adopted Western clothes and even full beards. In 1872 Western dress was prescribed for all court and official ceremonies. Meat eating, previously frowned on because of Buddhist attitudes, was encouraged, and the beef dish of *sukiyaki* was developed at this time. Western art and architecture were adopted, producing an array of official portraits of leading statesmen as well as an incongruous Victorian veneer in the commercial and government districts of the cities and some rather depressing interiors in the mansions of the wealthy.

Though the pace of change was hectic at first, and the adoption of Western forms seemed indiscriminate, it soon slowed as the Japanese became more selective about which aspects of their society they wanted to transform. Their adaptability meant the contracts of most Western experts and instructors only needed to be short-term, the average length of service being five years, and *yatoi* were less in evidence by the 1890s. The craze for Westernisation reached its height in the 1880s, but thereafter there was a reaction against unnecessary imitations and many of its more superficial features, like ballroom dancing, were dropped. Other social innovations subsequently abandoned were the prohibition of prostitution and mixed bathing, both of which were initially enforced to placate the prejudice of Western missionaries.

In reforming the legal system, Western concepts of individual rather than family ownership of property were adopted. But for purposes of formal registration of the population the law continued to recognise the old extended family or 'house', known in Japanese as the *ie*. This consisted of a patriarch and those of his descendants and collateral relatives who had not yet established a new *ie*. Within this structure the position of women was one of obedient subservience. In the 1870s the theme of liberation of women from their traditional Confucianist bondage was taken up by a number of Japanese intellectuals, influenced by Western writers on the subject. At the same time a number of women activists publicly engaged in politics. As both movements lacked public appeal they waned in the 1880s. In 1887 the Peace Preservation Ordinance, which remained in force to 1922, banned women from political parties and meetings. Women under the Civil Code of 1898 had no independent legal status and all legal agreements were concluded on a woman's behalf by the male to whom she was subordinate—either father, husband, or son. Women had no free choice of spouse or domicile and while they could in theory protest against this situation, they could do so only in a non-political manner. Such action posed a challenge to the whole social orthodoxy on which the Japanese state was founded, so in practice few women protested.

One Western institution whose adoption would have made a very favourable impression on the West, but which made next to no headway in Japan, was Christianity. Like the women's movement it had some impact among Japanese intellectuals, but prejudices against it ran too deep. In 1889 less than a quarter of 1 per cent of Japanese were Christians. The only religion that did flourish was Shinto which was one of the traditional faiths of Japan. Revived interest in it had been a key element in the intellectual trends that led to the imperial restoration. But there was little deep interest in religion among Japan's new leaders. Though the government continued to control and support the main Shinto shrines, the many cults that made up the faith lapsed into a traditional passive state forming no more than a ceremonial background to the life of the Japanese people.

There was greater enthusiasm for Westernisation over the matter of constitutional reform, and this dated back to the early 1870s when Meiji rulers realised change here was necessary to gain international respect. In the next decade the major tasks for building a modern political constitution were undertaken. In 1882 the statesman Ito Hirobumi led a study mission to several European capitals to investigate the theories and practices he believed were most appropriate for Japan. Before his departure he decided not to slavishly reproduce any Western system but that whatever example was taken as a model would be adapted to Japan's special needs. Most of his time was spent in Berlin and Vienna, and after his return to Japan work on the new constitution began in the spring of 1884. A new peerage was created, in December 1885 a cabinet type government was introduced, and to support it, a modern civil service with entry by examination was established. The Meiji constitution which took effect from November 1890 was essentially a cautious, conservative document which served to reinforce the influence of the more traditionally-minded elements in Japan's ruling class. While distinctively Japanese, it compared most closely with the German model of the monarchy.

This constitution, though nominally democratic, retained power in the hands of a small ruling élite with minimal interference from or responsibility to, the majority of the population. There was to be a bicameral parliament, called, in English, the Diet. The House of Peers was mostly made up from the ranks of the new nobility and the lower house chosen by an electorate limited to adult males paying taxes of fifteen yen or more. In 1890 this was limited to 450,000 persons or 5 per cent of adult males. Even when the taxation qualification was reduced to ten yen in 1902 it only increased the electorate to 1,700,000 males. The constitution's architects hoped that the provisions for democratic government it contained would be counterbalanced by other safeguarding provisions. Most important of these was the position of the emperor, who was accorded a position of primacy in the state. The imperial family were said to rule over Japan in perpetuity, and under the constitution the emperor was the repository of absolute and inviolable sovereignty. This was underlined by making cabinet and armed forces responsible not to political party, nor to the Diet, or the Japanese people, but to the emperor alone.

The emperor as an individual had little personal influence on events, and was not strong enough to unify the various factions that vied for political power. This was only possible by reference to pre-existing traditions of Japanese culture. These were invoked to stress the duties of loyalty and obedience to the sovereign, and through him to the state. As early as October 1890 the Imperial Rescript on Education, often seen as the basic tool for inculcating the orthodox philosophy of the state, showed the strong influence of the Confucian view that the state was essentially a moral order. This edict made only passing reference to education itself, but showed the revived influence of Confucian ideology in its stress on harmony and loyalty to the throne. Its central concept of mass indoctrination through formal education was an entirely modern emphasis. Intensive drilling of Japanese children with lessons in patriotism became possible when funds were available for universal compulsory education. In 1885 only 46 per cent of children of statutory school age were in school, though by 1905 this had risen to 95 per cent.

The purpose of educational reform, at its most basic level, was to turn out efficient recruits for the army, factory, and farm. This was because political and military modernisation, as well as industrialisation, depended on new skills, new attitudes and broader knowledge. Japan's leaders realised from the 1870s that social and intellectual modernisation was a prerequisite to success in other fields. But in the social and intellectual areas, as in economics, the responsiveness of thousands of individuals was more important than the exhortations of authority.

While political and social reform and cultural change were limited in extent and selective in their nature by the end of the 1890s, the same picture emerges in economic life. Industrial modernisation took two forms—the reorganisation of traditional industries, and the transplantation of new industries from the West. Some traditional industries, like cotton-spinning, experienced radical change and the introduction of factory production, while others made slower progress. Japan was an important exporter of raw silk but that industry was not dependent upon elaborate or expensive machinery. The production of cocoons was a labour-intensive industry, already carried out as a by-employment in peasant households. Gradually small factories equipped with improved but relatively simple and inexpensive power-driven machines were introduced. The investment in this industry was thus spread thinly over a great number of producers. Where large investments of capital were absolutely necessary, as with Japan's strategic heavy industries like iron and steel, armaments, and shipbuilding, the initial investment was made by the government. But even here success was not immediate and these early concerns were sold off to Japanese businessmen at low prices in the 1880s. In some of the new industries success came sooner than in others. In 1897–1906, 90 per cent of railway rolling stock was built in Japan but 94 per cent of locomotives were still imported, mainly from England and Germany. It was not until after 1900 that the basis of heavy industry in Japan was firmly established.

Indeed, the whole of Japanese economic and social life in 1900 was still firmly rooted in traditional forms with quite a small modern superstructure. But for Japan the term 'traditional' needs qualification because it does not necessarily mean that pre-modern Japanese economy and society was antagonistic to change. In spite of Japan's decision to isolate itself for almost 300 years, features evolved that could be built upon once the country was forced to accept Western influence. The growing volume of research on the period before 1868, in the form of local and regional studies, has reinforced the view that Japan was a relatively advanced pre-industrial economy. For an underdeveloped country it was already well provided with a basic infrastructure by the time the process of modernisation began in earnest. Agricultural output per head of the population was quite high and pre-modern Japan possessed a substantial degree of commerce. In the more backward northern regions, on the island of Hokkaido, and also parts of the extreme southern island of Kyushu, medieval forms of social and economic organisation persisted until quite late. But on the more advanced regions of the main island of Honshu, especially the Kanto Plain around Edo—the old name for Tokyo—and Osaka, there was a thriving urban-centred commercial economy. Merchants and traders supplied the wants of the towns of the region and production for exchange and not just subsistence, was carried on in the countryside.

Much of Japan's growth after 1868 was built upon the foundations of its pre-modern economy. Partly under the protection and encouragement of government most of the capital-intensive investments went into railways, steamships, and mechanised heavy industrial plants. But just as important in promoting development at that time were a vast number of small improvements and minor capital undertakings. Before 1940 the majority of roads were of unsurfaced dirt and bridges were simple wooden structures. Agricultural construction, represented primarily by irrigation works, changed little from Tokugawa times. Only after the turn of the century did most Japanese make Western products a part of their daily lives, and they were adapted to a traditionally Japanese life-style. In Tokyo in 1910 most of the dwellings were made of wood and only about an eighth used brick, stone, or plaster. Within the houses most furniture was still the traditional kind and most of the food eaten was of a traditional type. This meant that there was still an enormous market to be supplied by peasant farmers, village entrepreneurs, small businesses and traditional craftsmen. In 1890 nearly 70 per cent of Japanese investment was in the traditional sector and it still accounted for 45 per cent, fifteen years later.

But the success of Japan's modernisation efforts needs to be judged not only by what happened within the economy itself, or by the changes within Japanese society. Reform was undertaken as a means to an end and that end was recognition as an equal by the West. This was necessary before there was any chance of removing the unequal treaties of the 1850s and 1860s and contained two major restrictions on Japanese sovereignty. Firstly, there was the provision of 'extra-territorial jurisdiction'. Under this Westerners accused of crimes were not tried by Japanese courts, but by consular courts within the foreign settlements of the seaports of Japan set out in the treaties. The other restriction was the loss of tariff autonomy. Eager for markets, the Western powers placed severe limits on Japanese import and export duties. These measures were the usual way for nineteenth-century Western powers to regulate diplomatic and commercial relations with Oriental countries, the model being the treaties imposed on China after the Opium War of the 1840s. For Japan the actual consequences of the treaties were not particularly damaging. No great market for opium was developed, and the opening of Japanese industry to competition from the West forced the pace of economic change instead of allowing inefficient industries to shelter behind protective tariffs. Foreigners resident in Japan were restricted to the treaty ports and needed official permits to travel outside so were never a great intrusion into Japanese life. And the justice dispensed in the consular courts was generally fair to both Japanese and Westerners.

Nevertheless, the fact of these treaties' existence was rightly regarded as a great humiliation as they usurped functions which are the proper preserve of a fully independent state. They came up for renewal periodically and from 1871 onwards Japan asked for their revision. In that year refusal was a foregone conclusion, as even the Japanese could see that the conditions originally necessitating extra-territorial jurisdiction had not undergone any change justifying its abolition. In later years Western nations were reluctant to allow their citizens to come under the power of a legal system that was still not fully reformed, despite the abolition of torture as an accepted legal practice in 1876 and the introduction of a Code of Criminal Procedure, framed in accordance with Western ideas, in 1882. But this was the start of what the West wanted and when negotiations were reopened in 1883, Japan included as compensation for the abolition of consular jurisdiction a promise to remove all restrictions on trade, travel, and residence for foreigners within the country. These and subsequent discussions in the 1880s reached no definite conclusion, mainly because the Japanese refused to grant foreigners living in the country the right to own freehold property. It was not until 1894 that a final settlement of the consular question became a real possibility when Britain agreed to abolish consular jurisdiction by 1899.

The five-year delay was for two reasons. Before the new treaty came into force Japan had to fully implement a new legal code. The thorough recodification of the law this required was a slow and difficult task as most legal reforms were introduced piecemeal. This area is probably the strongest example of direct Western pressure being applied to change a fundamental feature of Japanese life. Drafts drawn up, largely under French influence, were submitted in 1881 and again in 1888, but a completely revised legal code only went into effect in 1896, removing the final impediment to ending extra-territorial jurisdiction in 1899. The other cause for delay was to allow Japan to renegotiate the rest of its treaties—of which there were over fifteen—with other Western powers, so that all nations were on an equal footing. This aspect was undoubtedly made possible by the successful outcome with Britain. Tariff autonomy was not finally restored to Japan until twelve years after 1899, but up to 1911 she was allowed to increase import and export duties.

The successful negotiations in 1894 were important as a turning point for the Japanese and for the West. The greatest opponents of the loss of extra-territorial jurisdiction were the few hundred foreign merchants and businessmen who lived and worked in the treaty ports. But for Japan this was a national political question that had provoked fierce debates in the Diet and in the press. The first treaties between Japan and the West were signed when the nation was still in a state of torpor from its long slumber of seclusion, and under circumstances of duress. The redemption of her judicial and fiscal authority had been, for thirty years, the dream of Japanese national aspiration, and both domestic and foreign policies had been shaped with this one end in view. For Japan's rulers, innovation after innovation, often involving sacrifices of traditional sentiments, were introduced for the purpose of assimilating the country and its institutions to the standard of Western civilisation. By 1900 Japan was still not regarded as a full equal by Western nations, but she was now accorded greater respect. In the next decade this was built upon with the Anglo-Japanese Alliance in 1902, the defeat of Russia in 1905, and the annexation of Korea in 1910. By 1912 there was no doubt that Japan had achieved 'Great Power' status.

The United States Must Go to War with Mexico to Defend Itself

James K. Polk

James K. Polk began his presidency in 1845 determined to add the Oregon and California territories to the Union, to go along with the recently annexed Texas. Negotiations with Great Britain were successful in resolving joint ownership claims of Oregon and attaining Polk's goal of a U.S. boundary at the 49th parallel; negotiations with Mexico proved more difficult. Mexico had broken off relations with the United States immediately after America's annexation of Texas in 1845. An attempt to purchase California from Mexico in 1845 failed when Mexico refused to receive American diplomat John Slidell.

In January 1846 Polk responded to Slidell's failed initiative by stationing American troops in Texas on the north bank of the Rio Grande, in territory south of the Nueces River that was claimed by both Mexico and the United States. Several months later, on April 25, Mexican troops crossed the Rio Grande and attacked two companies of American soldiers. News of the attack reached Washington on May 9, just *after* Polk and his cabinet had discussed and agreed on sending a war message to Congress. The attack was quickly incorporated into the message Polk sent to Congress on May 11. Congress responded to the message, excerpted here, by overwhelmingly voting to go to war with Mexico.

Excerpted from James K. Polk's message to Congress on May 11, 1846, as reprinted in *A Compilation of the Messages and Papers of the Presidents, 1798–1897,* edited by James D. Richardson (New York: 1896–1899).

*T*o *the Senate and House of Representatives:*

The existing state of the relations between the United States and Mexico renders it proper that I should bring the subject to the consideration of Congress. In my message at the commencement of your present session the state of these relations, the causes which led to the suspension of diplomatic intercourse between the two countries in March, 1845, and the long-continued and unredressed wrongs and injuries committed by the Mexican Government on citizens of the United States in their persons and property were briefly set forth. . . .

A Desire for Peace

The strong desire to establish peace with Mexico on liberal and honorable terms, and the readiness of this Government to regulate and adjust our boundary and other causes of difference with that power on such fair and equitable principles as would lead to permanent relations of the most friendly nature, induced me in September last [1845] to seek the reopening of diplomatic relations between the two countries. Every measure adopted on our part had for its object the furtherance of these desired results. In communicating to Congress a succinct statement of the injuries which we had suffered from Mexico, and which have been accumulating during a period of more than twenty years, every expression that could tend to inflame the people of Mexico or defeat or delay a pacific result was carefully avoided. An envoy of the United States [John Slidell] repaired to Mexico with full powers to adjust every existing difference. But though present on the Mexican soil by agreement between the two Governments, invested with full powers, and bearing evidence of the most friendly dispositions, his mission has been unavailing. The Mexican Government not only refused to receive him or listen to his propositions, but after a long-continued series of menaces have at last invaded our territory and shed the blood of our fellow-citizens on our own soil. . . .

The Government of Mexico, though solemnly pledged by official acts in October last to receive and accredit an American envoy, violated their plighted faith and refused the offer of a peaceful adjustment of our difficulties. Not only was the offer rejected, but the indignity of its rejection was enhanced by the manifest breach of faith in refusing to admit the envoy who came because they had bound themselves to receive him. Nor can it be said that the offer was fruitless from the want of opportunity of discussing it; our envoy was present on their own soil. Nor can it be ascribed to a want of sufficient powers; our envoy had full powers to adjust every question of difference. Nor was there room for complaint that our propositions for settlement were unreasonable; permission was not even given our envoy to make any proposition whatever. Nor can it be objected that we, on our part, would not listen to any reasonable terms of their suggestion; the Mexican Government refused all negotiation, and have made no proposition of any kind.

Defending Texas

In my message at the commencement of the present session I informed you that upon the earnest appeal both of the Congress and convention of Texas I had ordered an efficient military force to take a position "between the Nueces and the Del Norte [Rio Grande]." This had become necessary to meet a threatened invasion of Texas by the Mexican forces, for which extensive military preparations had been made. The invasion was threatened solely because Texas had determined, in accordance with a solemn resolution of the Congress of the United States, to annex herself to our Union, and under these circumstances it was plainly our duty to extend our protection over her citizens and soil.

James K. Polk

This force was concentrated at Corpus Christi, and remained there until after I had received such information from Mexico as rendered it probable, if not certain, that the Mexican Government would refuse to receive our envoy.

Meantime Texas, by the final action of our Congress, had become an integral part of our Union. The Congress of Texas, by its act of December 19, 1836, had declared the Rio del Norte to be the boundary of that Republic. Its jurisdiction had been extended and exercised beyond the Nueces. The country between that river and the Del Norte had been represented in the Congress and in the convention of Texas, had thus taken part in the act of annexation itself, and is now included within one of our Congressional districts. Our own Congress had, moreover, with great unanimity, by the act approved December 31, 1845, recognized the country beyond the Nueces as a part of our territory by including it within our own revenue system, and a revenue officer to reside within that district has been appointed by and with the advice and consent of the Senate. It became, therefore, of urgent necessity to provide for the defense of that portion of our country. Accordingly, on the 13th of January last [1846] instructions were issued to the general in command of these troops to occupy the left [northeast] bank of the Del Norte. This river, which is the southwestern boundary of the State of Texas, is an exposed frontier. From this quarter invasion was threatened; upon it and in its immediate vicinity, in the judgment of high military experience, are the proper stations for the protecting forces of the Government. In addition to this important consideration, several others occurred to induce this movement. Among these are the facilities afforded by the ports at Brazos Santiago and the mouth of the Del Norte for the reception of supplies by sea, the stronger and more healthful military positions, the convenience for obtaining a ready and a more abundant supply of provisions, water, fuel, and forage, and the advantages which are afforded by the Del Norte in forwarding supplies to such posts as may be established in the interior and upon the Indian frontier.

The movement of the troops to the Del Norte was made by the commanding general under positive instructions to abstain from all aggressive acts toward Mexico or Mexican citizens and to regard the relations between that Republic and the United States as peaceful unless she should declare war or commit acts of hostility indicative of a state of war. He was specially directed to protect private property and respect personal rights.

Mexican Attack

The Army moved from Corpus Christi on the 11th of March, and on the 28th of that month arrived on the left bank of the Del Norte opposite to Matamoras, where it encamped on a commanding position, which has since been strengthened by the erection of fieldworks. A depot has also been established at Point Isabel, near the Brazos Santiago, 30 miles in rear of the encampment. The selection of his position was necessarily confided to the judgment of the general in command.

The Mexican forces at Matamoras assumed a belligerent attitude, and on the 12th of April General [Pedro de] Ampudia, then in command, notified General [Zachary] Taylor to break up his camp within twenty-four hours and to retire beyond the Nueces River, and in the event of his failure to comply with these demands announced that arms, and arms alone, must decide the question. But no open act of hostility was committed until the 24th of April. On that day General [Mariano] Arista, who had succeeded to the command of the Mexican forces, communicated to General Taylor that "he considered hostilities commenced and should prosecute them." A party of dragoons of 63 men and officers were on the same day dispatched from the American camp up the Rio del Norte, on its left bank, to ascertain whether the Mexican troops had crossed or were preparing to cross the river, "became engaged with a large body of these troops, and after a short affair, in which some 16 were killed and wounded, appear to have been surrounded and compelled to surrender."

The grievous wrongs perpetrated by Mexico upon our citizens throughout a long period of years remain unredressed, and solemn treaties pledging her public faith for this redress have been disregarded. A government either unable or unwilling to enforce the execution of such treaties fails to perform one of its plainest duties.

Our commerce with Mexico has been almost annihilated. It was formerly highly beneficial to both nations, but our merchants have been deterred from prosecuting it by the system of outrage and extortion which the Mexican authorities have pursued against them, whilst their appeals through their own Government for indemnity have been made in vain. Our forbearance has gone to such an extreme as to be mistaken in its character. Had we acted with vigor in repelling the insults and redressing the injuries inflicted by Mexico at the commencement, we should doubtless have escaped all the difficulties in which we are now involved.

Instead of this, however, we have been exerting our best efforts to propitiate her good will. Upon the pretext that Texas, a nation as independent as herself, thought proper to unite its destinies with our own she has affected to believe that we have severed her rightful territory, and in official proclamations and manifestoes has repeatedly threatened to make war upon us for the purpose of reconquering Texas. In the meantime we have tried every effort at reconciliation. The cup of forbearance had been exhausted even before the recent information from the frontier of the Del Norte. But now, after reiterated menaces, Mexico has passed the boundary of the United States, has invaded our territory and shed American blood upon the American soil. She has proclaimed that hostilities have commenced, and that the two nations are now at war.

Vindicating Our Rights

As war exists, and, notwithstanding all our efforts to avoid it, exists by the act of Mexico herself, we are called upon by every consideration of duty and patriotism to vindicate with decision the honor, the rights, and the interests of our country. . . .

In further vindication of our rights and defense of our territory, I invoke the prompt action of Congress to recognize the existence of the war, and to place at the disposition of the Executive the means of prosecuting the war with vigor, and thus hastening the restoration of peace. To this end I recommend that authority should be given to call into the public service a large body of volunteers to serve for not less than six or twelve months unless sooner discharged. A volunteer force is beyond question more efficient than any other description of citizen soldiers, and it is not to be doubted that a number far beyond that required would readily rush to the field upon the call of their country. I further recommend that a liberal provision be made for sustaining our entire military force and furnishing it with supplies and munitions of war.

The most energetic and prompt measures and the immediate appearance in arms of a large and overpowering force are recommended to Congress as the most certain and efficient means of bringing the existing collision with Mexico to a speedy and successful termination.

Prepared to Negotiate

In making these recommendations I deem it proper to declare that it is my anxious desire not only to terminate hostilities speedily, but to bring all matters in dispute between this Government and Mexico to an early and amicable adjustment; and in this view I shall be prepared to renew negotiations whenever Mexico shall be ready to receive propositions or to make propositions of her own.

The Tactics and Impact of Indian Removal and Relocation

Peter Farb

One of the most devastating aspects of the American Indian wars was the forced removal of whole tribes from their ancestral lands and relocation to distant, often inhospitable regions. In this essay, Peter Farb, former curator of American Indian Cultures at the Riverside Museum in New York City, effectively explains the rationale and methods employed by whites during Indian removal. He then examines the horrendous impact removal and relocation had on Native American cultures, paying special attention to the sad plight of the Cherokee, whose suffering was particularly extreme.

Following the War of 1812, the young United States had no further need for Indian allies against the British, and as a result the fortunes of the Indians declined rapidly. By 1848, twelve new states had been carved out of the Indians' lands, two major and many minor Indian wars had been fought, and group after group of Indians had been herded westward, on forced marches, across the Mississippi River.

The 1830 Removal Act

As in other inhumane and deceitful chapters in the history of the United States, the justifications of God and civilization were invoked. To Senator Thomas Hart Benton of Missouri it was all very simple: The Whites must supplant Indians because Whites used the land "according to the intentions of the Creator." Some spoke of the benefits to the Indian of removing him from contact with Whites, which would give him the time to assimilate at his own pace the blessings of civilization. A senator from Georgia, hoping to expedite the removal of Indians from his state to what later became Oklahoma, glowingly described that arid, treeless territory as a place "over which Flora has scattered her beauties with a wanton hand; and upon whose bosom innumerable wild animals display their amazing numbers."

Such statements do not mean that the Indians lacked defenders, but the intensity of the indignation was in direct proportion to a White's distance from the Indian. On the frontier, the Indian was regarded as a besotted savage; but along the eastern seaboard, where the Spaniards, Dutch, English, and later the Americans had long since exterminated almost all the Indians, philosophers and divines began to defend the Red Man. In response to Georgia's extirpation [uprooting] of her Indian population, Ralph Waldo Emerson protested: "The soul of man, the justice, the mercy that is the heart's heart in all men, from Maine to Georgia, does abhor this business." Presidents such as Jefferson, Monroe, and Adams, who came from the East, occasionally displayed some scruples about the treatment the Indian was receiving. . . .

But President Andrew Jackson had been reared on the frontier and he was utterly insensitive to the treatment of the Indians. He denounced as an "absurdity" and a "farce" that the United States should bother even to negotiate treaties with Indians as if they were independent nations with a right to their lands. He was completely in sympathy with the policy of removal of the Indians to new lands west of the Mississippi. He exerted his influence to make Congress give legal sanction to what in our own time, under the Nuremburg Laws, would be branded as genocide. Dutifully, Congress passed the Removal Act of 1830, which gave the President the right to extirpate all Indians who had managed to survive east of the Mississippi River. It was estimated that the whole job might be done economically at no more than $500,000—the costs to be kept low by persuasion, promises, threats, and the bribery of Indian leaders. When U.S. Supreme Court Justice John Marshall ruled in favor of the Cherokee in a case with wide implications for protecting the Indians, Jackson is said to have remarked: "John Marshall has made his decision, now let him enforce it."

Becoming Historical Footnotes

During the next ten years, almost all the Indians were cleared from the East. Some like the Chickasaw and Choctaw went resignedly, but many others left only at bayonet point. The Seminole actively resisted and some retreated into the Florida swamps, where they stubbornly held off the United States Army. The Seminole Wars lasted from 1835 to 1842 and cost the United States some 1,500 soldiers and an estimated $20,000,000 (about forty times what Jackson had estimated it would cost to remove all Indians). Many of the Iroquois sought sanctuary in Canada, and the Oneida and the Seneca were moved westward, although fragments of Iroquois tribes managed to remain behind in western New York. The Sac and Fox made a desperate stand in Illinois against overwhelming numbers of Whites, but ultimately their survivors also were forced to move, as were the Ottawa, Potawatomie, Wyandot, Shawnee, Kickapoo, Winnebago, Delaware, Peoria, Miami, and many others who are remembered now only in the name of some town, lake, county, or state, or as a footnote in the annals of a local historical society.

All in all, an estimated seventy thousand Indians are believed to have been resettled west of the Mississippi, but the number may have been closer to one hundred thousand. No figures exist, though, as to the numbers massacred before they could be persuaded to leave the East, or on the tremendous losses suffered from disease, exposure, and starvation on the thousand-mile march westward across an unsettled and inhospitable land.

The "Civilized" Cherokee

Some of the Indians who were forced west of the Mississippi might with justification be regarded as "savages," but this cannot be said of the Cherokee. About 1790 the Cherokee decided to adopt the ways of their White conquerors and to emulate their civilization, their morals, their learning, and their arts. The Cherokee made remarkable and rapid progress in their homeland in the mountains where Georgia, Tennessee, and North Carolina meet. They established churches, mills, schools, and well-cultivated farms; judging from descriptions of that time, the region was a paradise when compared with the bleak landscape that the White successors have made of Appalachia today. In 1826 a Cherokee reported to the Presbyterian Church that his people already possessed 22,000 cattle, 7,600 houses, 46,000 swine, 2,500 sheep, 762 looms, 1,488 spinning wheels, 2,948 plows, 10 saw mills, 31 grist mills, 62 blacksmith shops, and 18 schools. In one of the Cherokee districts alone there were some 1,000 volumes "of good books." In 1821, after twelve years of hard work, a Cherokee named Sequoya (honored in the scientific names for the redwood and the giant sequoia trees in California, three thousand miles from his homeland) perfected a method of syllabary notation in which English letters stood for Cherokee syllables; by 1828 the Cherokee were already publishing their own newspaper. At about the same time, they adopted a written constitution providing for an executive, a bicameral legislature, a supreme court, and a code of laws.

Before the passage of the Removal Act of 1830, a group of Cherokee chiefs went to the Senate committee that was studying this legislation, to report on what they had already achieved in the short space of forty years. They expressed the hope that they would be permitted to enjoy in peace "the blessings of civilization and Christianity on the soil of their rightful inheritance." Instead, they were daily subjected to brutalities and atrocities by White neighbors, harassed by the state government of Georgia, cajoled and bribed by federal agents to agree to removal, and denied even the basic protection of the federal government. Finally, in 1835, a minority faction of five hundred Cherokee out of a total of some twenty thousand signed a treaty agreeing to removal. The Removal Act was carried out almost everywhere with a notable lack of compassion, but in the case of the Cherokee—civilized and Christianized as they were—it was particularly brutal.

After many threats, about five thousand finally consented to be marched westward, but another fifteen thousand clung to their neat farms, schools, and libraries "of good books." So General Winfield Scott set about systematically extirpating the rebellious ones. Squads of soldiers descended upon isolated Cherokee farms and at bayonet point marched the families off to what today would be known as concentration camps. Torn from their homes with all the dispatch and efficiency the Nazis displayed under similar circumstances, the families had no time to prepare for the arduous trip ahead of them. No way existed for the Cherokee family to sell its property and possessions, and the local Whites fell upon the lands, looting, burning, and finally taking possession.

Some Cherokee managed to escape into the gorges and thick forests of the Great Smoky Mountains, where they became the nucleus of those living there today, but most were finally rounded up or killed. They then were set off on a thousand-mile march—called to this day "the trail of tears" by the Cherokee—that was one of the notable death marches in history. Ill clad, badly fed, lacking medical attention, and prodded on by soldiers wielding bayonets, the Indians suffered severe losses. An estimate made at the time stated that some four thousand Cherokee died en route, but that figure is certainly too low. At the very moment that these people were dying in droves, President Van Buren reported to Congress that the government's handling of the Indian problem had been "just and friendly throughout; its efforts for their

civilization constant, and directed by the best feelings of humanity; its
watchfulness in protecting them from individual frauds unremitting."
Such cynicism at the highest level of government has been approached
in our own time by the solemn pronouncements by President Lyndon
B. Johnson about the Vietnam War.

Their Nation Has Ceased to Exist

One man who examined the young United States with a perceptive
eye and who wrote it all down in his *Democracy in America,*
[Frenchman] Alexis de Tocqueville, happened to be in Memphis during an unusually cold winter when the thermometer hovered near
zero. There he saw a ragged party of docile Choctaw, part of the
thousands who had reluctantly agreed to be transported to the new
lands in the western part of what was then the Arkansas Territory.
Wrote de Tocqueville:

> It was then the middle of winter, and the cold was unusually severe; the
> snow had frozen hard upon the ground and the river was drifting huge
> masses of ice. The Indians had their families with them, and they brought
> in their train the wounded and the sick, with children newly born and old
> men upon the verge of death. They possessed neither tents nor wagons,
> but only their arms and some provisions. I saw them embark to pass the
> mighty river, and never will that solemn spectacle fade from my re-
> membrance. No cry, no sob, was heard among the assembled crowd; all
> was silent. Their calamities were of ancient date, and they knew them to
> be irremediable.

De Tocqueville was a discerning observer of the methods used by
the Americans to deal with the Indians, and he described with restrained outrage how the Indians were sent westward by government
agents: ". . . half convinced and half compelled, they go to inhabit
new deserts, where the importunate whites will not let them remain
ten years in peace. In this manner do the Americans obtain, at a very
low price, whole provinces, which the richest sovereigns of Europe
could not purchase." Reporting that a mere 6,273 Indians still survived in the thirteen original states, he predicted accurately the fate
of the Indians in their new homes across the Mississippi:

> The countries to which the newcomers betake themselves are inhabited
> by other tribes, which receive them with jealous hostility. Hunger is in
> the rear, war awaits them, and misery besets them on all sides. To escape
> from so many enemies, they separate, and each individual endeavors to
> procure secretly the means of supporting his existence.

Long before the science of anthropology and the study of what today is politely called "culture change," de Tocqueville understood
how an entire culture might become raveled like some complexly
woven fabric:

The social tie, which distress had long since weakened, is then dissolved; they have no longer a country, and soon they will not be a people; their very families are obliterated; their common name is forgotten; their language perishes; and all traces of their origin disappear. Their nation has ceased to exist except in the recollections of the antiquaries of America and a few of the learned of Europe.

Indian Pitted Against Indian

The great removal was not the panacea that its advocates in Congress had maintained, in the names of God and civilization, it would be. Families had been separated, and many Indians had died en route. The new lands were much less hospitable to farming than those the Indians had been forced to evacuate, and the different game animals required new skills to hunt. To make matters worse, there was the hostility of the Plains Indians, who had been inveigled [enticed] into giving up some of their lands to make room for the eastern Indians. The Plains Indians asserted that the bison had been driven away by the newcomers, and clashes between various groups became increasingly common. The Chickasaw, who had dutifully agreed to removal, said they could not take up the land assigned to them because of their fear of the "wild tribes" already inhabiting it. The United States government no more honored its obligation to protect the Indians in their new territory than it had honored any of its previous obligations toward them. In 1834 fewer than three thousand troops were available along the entire frontier to maintain order and to protect the newcomers against the Plains tribes. The result was that the very Indians whose removal had been ordered ostensibly to pacify and to civilize them were forced once more to take up their old warrior ways to defend themselves. So the result of the great removal was that once again, as in earlier years of competition between French and English, Indian was pitted against Indian for the benefit of the Whites.

The Spanish-American War

Deborah Bachrach

Though the Spanish-American War lasted only ten weeks and very few lives were lost, it was a significant event for the United States. The new nation proved to the world and to itself that it could and would fight against foreign nations, especially when those countries interfered in the Western Hemisphere, as Spain had done. In the following selection, Deborah Bachrach summarizes the importance of the U.S. victory in the war. Bachrach holds a doctorate in history and has taught at the University of Minnesota and Queens College.

T he United States emerged from the Spanish-American War with a great deal more than American leaders expected. At war's end, the United States controlled Puerto Rico and Cuba in the Caribbean Sea and Guam and the Philippine islands in the Pacific Ocean.

Representatives of the United States and Spain then went to Paris to discuss peace terms. There, the United States demanded complete freedom for Cuba. It also demanded political control over the islands it had conquered during the war.

Spain had no choice but to agree to these terms. The American demands were incorporated in the Treaty of Paris that was signed by representatives of Spain and the United States on December 10, 1898. The Treaty of Paris marked the end of Spanish control of a once-great empire. It simultaneously marked the emergence of the United States as an imperial power, a country that controls the domestic and foreign affairs of other people.

As a result of the war, the United States took on an important role in managing the affairs of the western hemisphere. One of its goals was to keep the influence of European powers out of the region. During the nineteenth century, the United States produced the Monroe Doctrine but did not have the power to enforce it. In the aftermath of the Spanish-American War, the Monroe Doctrine became the guiding principle of U.S. foreign policy. And the United States could enforce its beliefs with a military force that was ready to fight.

The war also resulted in U.S. plans to build a canal linking the Atlantic and Pacific oceans across the country of Panama. One event during the Spanish-American War had indicated the need for such a canal. This was the spectacular voyage of the battleship *Oregon*.

The ship had been docked in Puget Sound, off the coast of Washington State, at the beginning of the crisis. It made the heroic sea voyage around the tip of South America and arrived in Key West, Florida, on May 26, in time to take part in the blockade of Cuba. That thirteen thousand mile voyage took the *Oregon* sixty-five days to complete. If a canal connecting the Atlantic and Pacific had existed, the trip would have been completed in one-third the time.

Supporters of an American canal used the voyage of the *Oregon* to support their campaign. They believed the canal would be a useful route during times of war and also an important trade route during peacetime. Chief among those supporters was Theodore Roosevelt, who became president of the United States in 1901. As president, Roosevelt began a lively campaign to alert the American people to the importance of a canal for military security. Roosevelt took an active role in assisting Panama, then a possession of Colombia, in gaining its independence in 1901. He then received permission to begin construction of a canal across the Isthmus of Panama, which connected North and South America. The efforts of Roosevelt and his supporters resulted in the opening of the enormously important ship canal linking the Atlantic and Pacific oceans in 1911. In future wars, the United States could move its troops around the world with greater speed.

Improving the Military

Construction of the Panama Canal was one of the many changes that resulted in a more powerful United States. Another of these changes—the establishment of a general military staff—affected the ability of the United States to wage a future war.

American military leaders realized that the country had won its first conflict with a European power only because of the enemy's weakness. These leaders knew that a war with another major country would have ended in defeat for the U.S. Army. There was an urgent need for a change in its organization. The Congress therefore began the development of a general staff.

A general staff acts as the brain of an army by directing, planning, and organizing all of the army's activities. Since the American people had feared the existence of any kind of standing army in peacetime, the United States was almost the only major country without a general staff. The consequence was the confusion in all branches of the national service, which had been painfully clear during the training and equipping of the troops at Tampa.

That confusion altered the attitude of the American people toward the development of an efficient military force. The first piece of legislation that resulted in the creation of a general staff was signed by Congress in 1903. The staff was in place by the beginning of World War I. When the United States entered that war in 1917, American soldiers at the front did not suffer from the same problems that afflicted the troops in 1898.

The Spanish-American War also brought about some changes in how Americans viewed the countries of Europe. The change in attitude toward Great Britain was the most dramatic. Until the end of the nineteenth century, Great Britain was disliked and distrusted by the people of the United States. This negative attitude was the result of the antagonism felt for the British during the Revolutionary War, the War of 1812, and during the American Civil War, when Great Britain aided the Confederacy. The behavior of Great Britain during the Spanish-American War helped to change this attitude.

The United States and Great Britain

During the Spanish-American War, Great Britain was the sole European power that sided with the United States. All the others openly befriended Spain. Only Great Britain was, in the phrase of historian Samuel Eliot Morison, "ready to cheer America down the path of imperialism." Great Britain's leaders encouraged the United States to take military action against the Spanish forces on the Philippine Islands and openly supported the American decision to keep the islands as imperial possessions at the conclusion of the war.

This staunch support for the United States ended the anti-British feelings in the youthful country. It led to the beginning of a mature friendship that has endured through many wars and that remains today.

On the other hand, events during the war led to the development of poor relations with Germany. German leaders did not like the fact that the United States was gaining an empire while Germany's foreign holdings remained small.

Soon after Admiral Dewey's great victory, German battleships appeared at Manila Bay. They attempted to interfere with American military operations. According to one newspaper, the Germans were there "not to protect existing German interests but to find new interests to protect." The bad feelings Americans had for Germany continued long after the end of the Spanish-American War. Dislike of Germany contributed to strong anti-German feelings at the beginning of World War I.

All of these changes were significant. They led to the development of a new view toward the rest of the world on the part of the United States.

During the nineteenth century, the United States had been content to look after its own interests. Most people wanted only to expand the country's frontiers to the Pacific Ocean. Now, with the development of the new steel navy and a growing army, the United States began to feel more self-assured. It saw itself as the guardian of the undeveloped countries it had acquired and as the natural protector of the peoples of South America.

That feeling led the country to annex Hawaii. The United States had long had a connection with the Pacific island chain and by the end of the nineteenth century, American sugarcane growers controlled the islands' economy. Now that the United States controlled the Philippine Islands and began to contemplate trade with China, Hawaii's harbors would be an important naval asset. So on July 7, 1898, Congress annexed the islands during the heat of the Spanish-American War.

A New Sense of National Unity

On the mainland, equally dramatic changes took place in the wake of the Spanish-American War. One of these was the development of a sense of national unity that had previously been shattered by the Civil War. In the minds of many Americans, the Civil War did not really end until the Spanish-American War. This was because until the 1890s, many people, particularly people in the South, were still divided by Civil War memories.

After 1865, many Northerners moved to the South and treated Southerners as if they were a conquered people. This domination of the political and economic affairs of the South left deep scars and anger between the two sections of the country. In many ways, North and South remained divided until 1898.

The Spanish-American War gave Northerners and Southerners a common enemy to hate. They stopped hating each other so they could cooperate in fighting Spain. This change was reflected in the difference in treatment given to the Sixth Massachusetts Regiment in 1861 and then in 1898. During the war in 1861, soldiers of the regiment were stoned as they passed through the Southern city of Baltimore on their way to war. But in 1898, hostilities had lessened so much that when this same military unit stopped near the capital on its way to Tampa, it was treated to a massive reception in Washington. One writer announced that the reception was "the most dramatic event of the war on American soil for it was not a mere reception and patriotic demonstration. It was the new national spirit rising Phoenix-like from the ashes of '61.''

President McKinley contributed greatly to this spiritual union of the nation. He selected generals from both Civil War armies to lead the units in Cuba. Former Confederate cavalry hero Joe Wheeler led a unit that fought near Santiago. When he was selected for service, Wheeler announced proudly that "a single battle for the Union flag was worth fifteen years of life." These were unusual words coming from the mouth of a Confederate officer who had spent more than four years trying to destroy the Union.

Northerners and Southerners served with great pride during the Spanish-American War. Their enthusiasm and love of country found expression in this poem by William Lightfoot Visscher:

> Blue and Grey are One
> Hurrah for the East and the West!
> The nation is one, individual and free,
> And all of its sons are the best.

Blacks and Whites

The Spanish-American War not only helped to overcome regional differences but also influenced relations between blacks and whites. The Civil War had freed the slaves, but it did not free people's minds of prejudice. The Spanish-American War was an opportunity for the country to move toward this goal.

There were four black regiments in the U.S. Army in 1898. The chaplain of one of these regiments, the Twenty-Fifth infantry, expressed the opinion of many black people when he said, "I believe that this war will very greatly help the American colored man of the South, and result in the further clearing of the national atmosphere."

Many American blacks showed their patriotism. In addition to the four regular army regiments, eight to ten thousand black men volunteered to serve in 1898. But they were still not integrated into the regular forces.

While the black volunteers, like most of the white volunteers, spent the war in American training camps, the experience of the regular army soldiers was very different. The four regular black regiments were involved in the fighting in Cuba. For the very first time in American history, these black soldiers served under the command of black officers.

The Ninth and Tenth Cavalry and the Twenty-fourth and Twenty-fifth Infantry units were sent to Tampa. They became an important part of the Fifth Army Corps, which fought in Cuba. They showed great valor at El Caney and at San Juan Hill, where their military abilities were noted by Theodore Roosevelt. The four black regiments served with great distinction in 1898 and were a credit to their country.

The people of the United States also benefited from the war in other ways. For example, there were many major advances in sanitation and medical treatments. Knowledge gained in the training camps led to better ways of disposing of and treating waste to prevent infection. Also, the Army Medical Corps was greatly enlarged as a result of the enormous medical deficiencies experienced during the Spanish-American War. In future conflicts, soldiers would receive quicker and better treatment.

Walter Reed

The most dramatic advances in the medical field were made by Maj. Walter Reed and his associates in the Army Medical Corps. Before the Spanish-American War, no one knew that the bite of an infected mosquito caused yellow fever. Reed and his staff conducted experiments in Cuba that led to this revolutionary discovery. His work with the *Stegomyia* mosquito led to the destruction of the mosquitoes' breeding grounds. As a result, yellow fever gradually ceased to be a problem.

Mass outbreaks of yellow fever had halted several attempts in the 1870s and 1880s to build a canal linking the Atlantic and Pacific oceans. Thousands of workers had died from the disease. Thanks to Reed, it became possible to build a canal in mosquito-infested Panama by destroying the breeding grounds of the insects.

Advances in medicine were not the only changes the war brought. Significant changes also took place in the field of politics. The role of the presidency, for example, was altered during the Spanish-American War. Many of McKinley's immediate predecessors had been colorless men, and the office of the presidency was in decline at the end of the nineteenth century. Several previous presidents had been elected only because of their Civil War experience. These presidents did very little for the country during their terms. William McKinley assumed responsibilities that many presidents had ignored in the past. McKinley was interested in and played a vital role in foreign affairs. Other presidents had been content to let Congress conduct foreign policy. He was assisted by technological advances that enabled him to exercise an effective, direct control never before possible.

McKinley had originally opposed the war, but once he understood the national mood, he stepped out to lead. He actively directed the war effort, filling in when his subordinates proved to be incompetent. Originally an anti-expansionist, McKinley came to believe that it was important for the United States to have an empire. So the president took his message to Congress and to the American people. He even went on several major speaking tours in order to gain support for this position. He made expansionism an acceptable principle of U.S. foreign policy.

William McKinley gave new life to the office of the presidency and set an example of activism for his successors. The outspoken and aggressive behavior of Theodore Roosevelt and the plunge into foreign matters taken by Woodrow Wilson were more easily accepted by the American public as a result of McKinley's work during the Spanish-American War.

These various developments were among the most significant consequences of the short war that the United States fought with Spain in 1898. Both domestically and in foreign affairs, great changes took place. The country could not return to its earlier, carefree attitude toward world matters. It had entered the ranks of the world's great powers. America was called upon to accept new responsibilities. During World War I, the United States emerged as the most important military and political power in the world.

Chapter
6

New Ideas

T he nineteenth-century West's preoccupation with "modernity," chiefly in the realm of politics and society, also extended to the realm of ideas and culture.

Art and ideas in the traditional West (and in traditional cultures all over the globe) had always seemed to look backward, toward the standards and the great accomplishments of the past. Even as they took what modern historians of art and ideas regard as innovative forward steps, the artists and thinkers of the West before the 1700s typically thought of themselves as restoring the styles, or recapturing the ideals, of the past. The present, in all traditional cultures, has been regarded at best as the worthy continuation of the past—and more commonly as an era of sorry degeneration from some bygone "golden age." The traditional ideal was to recapture the spirit and the accomplishment of that golden age, whether in artistic expression or in the clarity of ideas.

Such cultural aspirations found their parallel in the aspirations of premodern political and social thought to ensure continuity, tradition, and hierarchical authority. Change, in this view, was bad and was to be resisted if possible; it was stability and the absence of change that ought to be sought.

Just as the Dual Revolution of industrialization and political democratization had shaken the foundations of the traditional Western—and indeed global—social, economic, and political orders, so the eighteenth-century Enlightenment challenged the fundamental cultural ideas of all Western civilization. Now change—new ways of thinking, new questions, new answers—replaced the old assurances. The existence of God, the reality of our perceptions, the superiority of past to present, the value of civilization itself—all these and many other formerly self-evident propositions were called into question by the critical thinkers of the Enlightenment. And the answers that Enlightenment thinkers offered were, it was assumed, to be judged by a single standard: were they *reasonable?*

During the eighteenth and early nineteenth centuries, the arts experienced a fundamental reorientation, too. Painting, sculpture, music, and literature were no longer expected to reveal great spiritual truths, or to celebrate those who held power, or to teach some other moralistic lesson. Some important works of art continued to serve such ends, of course, but these purposes were not automatically assumed to be all that an artist sought to express. Art, in short, could now legitimately aim to give pleasure or to amuse; it could even criticize existing assumptions and ridicule those who wielded power. These new aims of, and assumptions about, the arts and ideas dominated the intellectual and cultural life of the nineteenth-century West.

By the late nineteenth century a term was coming into focus that summed up the new standards of art and culture: *modernism.* It is the word that best defines the varying cultural aims with which this chapter's readings are concerned. The artists and thinkers whom historians now label as modernist were quite explicitly aware that in their time major changes were under way, and their creativity was shaped by their determination to give voice to these forces of change and reevaluation. Innovation, in other words, was what they *sought,* not passively accepted. "Modern" is how they defined themselves. Today, we are so accustomed to the positive value of "modern" and "up-to-date" in describing everything from consumer goods to culture to ideas that it is easy to forget how surprising (and sometimes shocking) the modernist stance seemed to the public a little over a hundred years ago.

No figure in Western culture more strikingly speaks for modernism than the German philosopher Friedrich Nietzsche (1844–1900), the author of the first selection in this chapter. A corrosive critic of what he considered a complacent, materialistic middle-class society, Nietzsche called for a complete revaluation of morality. Himself a nonbeliever in religion, Nietzsche convinced himself that the science and the self-congratulatory attitudes of his times had killed the noble idea of a transcendent God, on which all other values of the culture depended. The religion of his own time Nietzsche condemned as a "slave religion"—a weak assurance that respectable people would get their heavenly reward because they conformed to the standards of "proper" behavior. It was his age's sense of progress—to Nietzsche, a pseudo-progress that masked the nineteenth century's loss of a sense of risk and danger—that had killed God. Little read and generally considered shockingly irreverent during his active career, Nietzsche became a world-famous (and often misunderstood) symbol of the modernists' critique of their own times after he himself had ceased to speak— ironically, the victim of insanity that destroyed his mind eleven years before his physical death.

Just as Nietzsche the thinker tried to reorient the way his generation intellectually comprehended the "progress" of his times, so the French painters known to history as the Impressionists tried to make people see anew the relationship between art and the world that we actually experience. Ever since the Renaissance (and before that, in Greek and Roman antiquity), the ideal in Western art had been to "imitate nature"—to capture on a surface or in stone, most likely in idealized form, exactly what we see. But the nineteenth-century invention of photography had destroyed forever the artist's function as the creator of an image of nature; moreover, the same complacency with "progress" that had aroused Nietzsche's scorn also put the Impressionists at odds with the bland idealism of the conventional art that the general public enjoyed. This chapter's second selection describes the advent of the Impressionist group in Paris in the 1870s, much to the initial scorn of the public and established critics. Yet art, as this new generation of creative painters insisted, should challenge our eyes and our imaginations, not play safe; it should (to borrow Nietzsche's terminology) force us to "revalue" what we see, not passively endorse accepted perceptions. And like Nietzsche, the modernist Impressionists of the late nineteenth century, abandoning conventional standards of "prettiness," set the tone for the creative aspirations of all the generations that followed during the twentieth century.

Not all modernist impulses were what the twentieth century has called "highbrow." In the last decade of the nineteenth century a new spirit swept through popular culture. To be sure, popular culture was becoming what it is today—essentially a consumer good, manufactured to make a profit—and thus it was often the object of modernist scorn. But the spirit of the new popular culture was fresh, brash, and by no means uncritical of all that was "proper," as the third selection here makes clear. In both senses, both as a frankly commercial product and as a breezy break with conventional proprieties, the new popular music of England in the 1890s represented the first step toward the "show" and rock music of the twentieth century, and it was breaking this new ground just as another crucial ingredient of coming styles—jazz—was being created in American popular culture. When, in the 1920s jazz and the Anglo-American vaudeville styles combined, linked with two other turn-of-the-century inventions, movies and the radio, modern popular culture would come into its own.

The chapter's final selection comes from the work of arguably the most influential modernist of them all, the Austrian psychologist Sigmund Freud. No one shocked his times more than did Freud. The basis of much of our psychological behavior, he claimed, was sex—especially our sexual feelings in childhood, which remain embedded in our subconscious throughout adulthood and continually rise up to create neuroses and irrational behavior. Freud's theories demolished the myth of childhood innocence that had been a bedrock conviction of conventional attitudes, and cast a spell to which every novelist, poet, and painter of the twentieth century had little choice but to respond.

The Death of God

Friedrich Nietzsche

German philosopher Friedrich Nietzsche (1844–1900) was not a typical representative of his profession. He resigned his teaching position (as a professor of Greek) while still young because of deteriorating health that included almost unbearable headaches, probably associated with his nervous, high-strung temperament. His writing style was flamboyant, indeed extravagant. During his lifetime he was more notorious than seriously read, but after his death he became a cultural icon for people whom he had despised while he lived, especially Germany's nationalists and anti-Semites. Eventually many considered him an intellectual precursor of the Nazis. He spent the last eleven years of his life hopelessly insane, most likely the consequence of having contracted syphilis as a young man.

Nietzsche, it is true, was contemptuous of virtually all the accepted ideas of late-nineteenth-century society. He rejected democracy, feminism, and socialism, and so profoundly did he repudiate Christianity that he called himself "the Antichrist." Yet he also denounced nationalism (particularly German nationalism), racism, and anti-Semitism. He believed that all the things his contemporaries found praiseworthy in nineteenth-century civilization—the idea of progress, middle-class values, humanitarianism, power politics—actually were "false values" that reflected the complacent smugness of people of his day. He called on people to reexamine their values, to move beyond self-serving concepts of good and evil, to master their own internal impulses. A man or woman who could transcend the false values of the times he considered an *Übermensch,* a word conventionally but misleadingly translated into English as "superman."* Such people, Nietzsche asserted, would be so

---

*The comic strip and movie character "Superman" is the ultimate vulgarization of this idea. It was also adopted by Nazi ideologues dreaming of creating an "Aryan" superrace. Such ideas are associated with Nietzsche only because he coined the phrase, but with an entirely different meaning in mind.

at peace with themselves that they could endure the thought of eternally reliving the same life, without fear and without resentment.

Another of Nietzsche's phrases—"God is dead"—has resonated through subsequent history in ways that he did not originally intend. Although he was an atheist, Nietzsche did not mean by this phrase either contempt or triumph. For him, the death of God was a tragedy. The pure idea of God, he thought, had been killed by the false values of his time—the mechanistic ideas of the science of his day, European notions of progress, the glib morality of conventional Christianity. Modern people, he thought, worshiped a God who really was a reflection of their own selfish greed and self-satisfaction. What would happen, he wondered, when modern people finally discovered for themselves that the God they had invented was truly dead, and they had nothing but their own shallow, rootless values to live by? It would, he feared, mean the unchaining of all the destructive impulses in modern society—repressed hatreds, racism, nationalistic and socialistic delusions—all of which rested on morally inferior people's resentments. In fact, Nietzsche feared precisely what the twentieth century would disclose: murderous and totally amoral mass movements on both political extremes, which would be let loose when the trammels of traditional religion were destroyed.

Nietzsche conveyed these thoughts in a disturbing parable called "The Madman," one of the many brief pieces collected in his 1882 book *The Joyous Science.*

The Madman. Have you not heard of that madman who lit a lantern in the bright morning hours, ran to the market place, and cried incessantly, "I seek God! I seek God!" As many of those who do not believe in God were standing around just then, he provoked much laughter. Why, did he get lost? said one. Did he lose his way like a child? said another. Or is he hiding? Is he afraid of us? Has he gone on a voyage? or emigrated? Thus they yelled and laughed. The madman jumped into their midst and pierced them with his glances.

"Whither is God" he cried; "I shall tell you. *We have killed him—* you and I. All of us are his murderers. But how have we done this? How were we able to drink up the sea? Who gave us the sponge to wipe away the entire horizon? What did we do when we unchained this earth from its sun? Whither is it moving now? Whither are we moving now? Away from all suns? Are we not plunging continually? Backward, sideward, forward, in all directions? Is there any up or down left? Are we not straying as through an infinite nothing? Do we not feel the breath of empty space? Has it not become colder? Is not night and more night coming on all the while? Must not lanterns be lit in the morning? Do we not hear anything yet of the noise of the gravediggers who are burying God? Do we not smell anything yet of God's decomposition? Gods too decompose. God is dead. God remains dead. And we have killed him. How shall we, the murderers of all murderers, comfort ourselves? What was holiest and most powerful of all that the world has yet owned has bled to death under our knives. Who will wipe this blood off us? What water is there for us to clean ourselves? What festivals of atonement, what sacred games shall we have to invent? Is not the greatness of this deed too great for us? Must not we ourselves become gods simply to seem worthy of it? There has never been a greater deed; and whoever will be born after us—for the sake of this deed he will be part of a higher history than all history hitherto."

Here the madman fell silent and looked again at his listeners; and they too were silent and stared at him in astonishment. At last he threw his lantern on the ground, and it broke and went out. "I come too early," he said then; "my time has not come yet. This tremendous event is still on its way, still wandering—it has not yet reached the ears of man. Lightning and thunder require time, the light of the stars requires time, deeds require time even after they are done, before they can be seen and heard. This deed is still more distant from them than the most distant stars—*and yet they have done it themselves.*"

It has been related further that on that same day the madman entered divers churches and there sang his *requiem aeternam deo* ["Grant the Lord eternal rest"]. Led out and called to account, he is said to have replied each time, "What are these churches now if they are not the tombs and sepulchers of God?"

Impressionism

Otto Friedrich

The word *Impressionism,* which refers to one of the most important styles in modern art, was meant to be insulting when it was coined by a French art critic in the late 1870s. The critic was dismissing the work of painters of this movement as vague "impressions" of the moment, seemingly unworthy of being captured by the artist on canvas. For this critic—and for most of the public of his day—art should be formal, elegant, highly polished, and edifying if not moralistic. It should deal with grand themes: historical, mythological, heroic, and so on. And it must be realistic, reproducing as minutely as possible exactly what the artist saw.

The first Impressionist painters—Monet, Cézanne, Pissarro, and others—were not interested in realism: The camera, they said, could now fulfill that function. Nor did they wish to paint traditional heroic, historical, or romantic images. They wanted instead to capture ordinary scenes of life as the eye encounters them for a moment in the changing day, to show the play of light on a surface. By orienting the artist's eye and the viewer's attention away from formal, artificial imagery and toward fleeting, ephemeral sensations, the Impressionist painters changed forever the Western world's conception of art. In this selection, an excerpt from American art historian Otto Friedrich's book *Olympia: Paris in the Age of Manet* shows how the close-knit Parisian Impressionists struggled for recognition in a world still dominated by a traditional, so-called academic style, and thereby laid the foundations for what we now call modern art.

Just as Beethoven didn't know that he had written the "Moonlight" Sonata until a minor critic named Rellstab bestowed its name upon it, just as Zola didn't know that he had written *"J'Accuse"* un-

til the editor of *L'Aurore* put that headline on the diatribe that Zola
had called "Letter to M. Felix Fauré, President of the Republic,"[1] so
the impressionists didn't know that they were the Impressionists.
They modestly announced that their show represented the Société
Anonyme des Artistes, Peintres, Sculpteurs, Graveurs, etc. [Corpo-
ration of Artists, Painters, Sculptors, Engravers, etc.].

The word had actually been in use for about ten years, notably by
Manet, who had said at the time of his solo exhibition in 1867 that
his goal was "to convey his impression." Critics occasionally applied the term to the landscapes of Corot, Jongkind and Daubigny,
and one of them specifically praised Manet for his skill in capturing
"the first impression of nature," but the full significance of the term
emerged only from the storms that surrounded the exhibition of
1874. The catalogue was late, as usual, and there were arguments
about the titles of various pictures. Renoir's brother Edmond, who
was trying to edit the catalogue, complained that Monet's landscapes
all seemed to have similar designations, *Morning in a Village,
Evening in a Village.* . . . Monet himself later recalled that the dispute centered on a misty view of the harbor of Le Havre. "I couldn't
very well call it a view of Le Havre. So I said: 'Put *Impression.*'"
The picture actually was listed as *Impression, Sunrise.* It was only
one of 165 pictures by thirty artists—among them Degas, Monet,
Renoir, Pissarro, Cézanne, Sisley, and Berthe Morisot, but not
Manet—but it inspired the malicious hostility of the critic Louis
Leroy in the satirical magazine *Charivari*, who entitled his review
"Exhibition of the Impressionists."

Leroy took with him to the exhibition an academic landscape
painter named Joseph Vincent, winner of various official medals and
prizes, and he wrote his review as a kind of mocking dialogue between the indignant voice of scholastic authority and himself as the
innocently inquiring interviewer. Vincent's first shock came on seeing the beautiful Degas *Dancer* that is now in Washington's National
Gallery of Art. "What a pity," said Vincent, "that the painter, who
has a certain understanding of color, doesn't draw better; his
dancer's legs are as cottony as the gauze of her skirts." Next came
Pissarro's *Ploughed Field:* "Those furrows? . . . But they are palette
scrapings placed uniformly on a dirty canvas. It has neither head nor
tail, top nor bottom, front nor back."

"Perhaps . . . but the impression is there," Leroy offered.

"Well, it's a funny impression!" snapped Vincent.

Then came Monet's marvelous scene of crowds strolling on the
snowy Boulevard des Capucines. "'Ah-hah!' he sneered. . . . 'Is that
brilliant enough, now! There's impression, or I don't know what it

---

1. an allusion to the famous appeal, entitled *"J'Accuse"* [I Accuse], that the French novelist Emile
Zola published in 1895, demanding justice for the wrongfully convicted Captain Dreyfus

means. Only be so good as to tell me what those innumerable black tongue-lickings in the lower part of the picture represent?'

"'Why, those are people walking along,' I replied.

"'Then do I look like that when I'm walking along the Boulevard des Capucines? Blood and thunder! So you're making fun of me at last!'"

And then, inevitably, the two nay-sayers arrived in front of Berthe Morisot's exquisite portrait of Edma admiring her new baby in *The Cradle*. Vincent was outraged by the delicate image of Edma's hand on the cradle. "Now take Mlle. Morisot," he protested. "That young lady is not interested in producing trifling details. When she has a hand to paint, she makes exactly as many brushstrokes lengthwise as there are fingers, and the business is done. Stupid people who are finicky about the drawing of a hand don't understand a thing about impressionism, and the great Manet would chase them out of his republic."

Leroy had been so unerringly accurate in singling out the most gifted of his contemporaries to be excoriated as "Impressionists" that the painters of the "Société Anonyme des Artistes" could hardly help accepting their new name. Like the "wild beasts" who later took pride in having been denounced as *"les fauves,"*[2] the impressionists remained the Impressionists.

They did not suddenly appear out of nowhere as a "school," of course. As often happens when the younger generation suddenly becomes famous, they were already approaching middle age at the time of their first exhibition in 1874. Monet, Cézanne, Renoir, and Berthe Morisot were all in their mid-thirties, Degas already forty, Pissarro forty-four (and Manet forty-two). But this emergence of the Impressionist group had been more than a decade in the coming. These young painters had been attracted from all over to the booming imperial Paris of the early 1860s. Claude Monet, for one, was the son of a prosperous grocer in Le Havre. He ignored his schoolwork, doodled in his notebooks, and soon became locally celebrated as a caricaturist. He inevitably encountered another local celebrity, Eugène Boudin, who devoted himself to the very unfashionable practice of painting seascapes, which the seventeen-year-old Monet regarded "with an intense aversion." Boudin was not to be discouraged, however. "Boudin, with untiring kindness, undertook my education," Monet later recalled. "My eyes were finally opened and I really understood nature; I learned at the same time to love it." Boudin urged the young apprentice onward to Paris, and so, with the reluctant approval of his parents, Monet headed for the capital. He refused to enroll in the stodgy École des Beaux Arts, however, preferring a simpler institution known as the Académie Suisse, where artists

2. an allusion to a group of painters called *Les Fauves* [the Wild Beasts]

could paint live models or work at whatever they liked, without any examinations. Monet's father promptly cut off his allowance.

Monet soon met a fellow student named Camille Pissarro, son of a storekeeper on the Caribbean island of St. Thomas, who had run away from home to become a painter. The two youths struck up a friendship and went out on painting expeditions together. That camaraderie was interrupted by Monet's being summoned to seven years' conscription in the army. His father offered to buy a substitute, as was common in those days; Monet refused. "The seven years of service that appalled so many were full of attraction to me . . ." he said. "In Algeria I spent two really charming years. I incessantly saw something new; in my moments of leisure I attempted to render what I saw. You cannot imagine to what extent I increased my knowledge, and how much my vision gained thereby. I did not quite realize it at first. The impressions of light and color that I received there were not to classify themselves until later; they contained the germ of my future researches."

Monet fell ill in Algeria, however, so he had to accede to his father's paying for his discharge. He returned to Paris early in 1862—by now bushy-haired and thickly bearded—and compromised with his father's desire for some professional discipline by enrolling in the studio of Charles Gleyre. An eminent conservative, Gleyre was nonetheless a relatively easygoing teacher whose other pupils included the young Renoir, Whistler, Sisley, and Bazille.

They were all, to some extent, Gleyre's black sheep. "The first week I worked there most conscientiously," Monet later recalled, "and made, with as much application as spirit, a study of the nude from the living model. . . . The following week, when he [Gleyre] came to me, he sat down and, solidly planted in my chair, looked attentively at my production. Then he turned round and, leaning his grave head to one side with a satisfied air, said to me: 'Not bad! not bad at all, that thing there, but it is too much in the character of the model—you have before you a short thick-set man, you paint him short and thick-set—he has enormous feet, you render them as they are. All that is very ugly. I want you to remember, young man, that when one draws a figure, one should always think of the antique. Nature, my friend, is all right as an element of study, but it offers no interest. Style, you see, is everything.' "

Renoir had similar problems. One of five children of a tailor in Limoges, he had started as an apprentice painter of the local porcelain, but he too, now twenty-one, had arrived in Paris in that same year of 1862 to fulfill a higher ambition. He too had copied the model as realistically as he could.

"No doubt it's to amuse yourself that you are dabbling in paint?" inquired the lordly teacher.

"Why, of course," said the ebullient young Renoir, "and if it didn't amuse me, I beg you to believe that I wouldn't do it!"

It is strange and striking how the great composers of the early nineteenth century—Chopin, Liszt, Schumann, Berlioz, Wagner— all recognized each other instantly when they were still in their early twenties. Much the same thing happened among the future Impressionists. Monet was still only twenty-two when he met the twenty-one-year-old Renoir at Gleyre's studio and they began going off to paint landscapes together. Cézanne, the schoolmate of Zola, had met Pissarro the previous year, and Pissarro already knew Monet. Manet and Degas met while copying in the Louvre, and Fantin-Latour introduced Berthe Morisot to Monet there. Most of these painters (not, of course, the ultrarespectable Berthe Morisot) met regularly at the Café de Guerbois, a small and relatively quiet establishment on the Grande Rue des Batignolles (now the Avenue de Clichy), and so the group came to be known as the Batignolles group. When Fantin-Latour painted his splendidly documentary *Studio in the Batignolles Quarter* (1870), he placed Manet before an easel in the center, then surrounded him with such younger admirers as Monet, Renoir, Bazille, and Zola.

The goal of the young painters' training was a showing at the official Salon, but as the students observed the Salon jurors' treatment of Manet, whose work they much admired, they began to think about alternative courses. The year after Monet and Renoir first encountered each other at Gleyre's studio was the year when they saw the Salon jurors reject *Le Déjeuner sur l'herbe* and *Mlle. V. . . in the Costume of an Espada,* and saw both these paintings of Mlle. Victorine Meurent appear before the mocking visitors to the Salon des Refusés. An even more important breaking point came four years later when both Manet and Courbet decided separately not to submit anything to the Salon but to build separate pavilions and exhibit their works to visitors to the World's Fair of 1867. After both these private exhibitions closed, both failures in any critical or commercial sense, Courbet hoped to rent out the pavilion he had built, and Monet and his friends hoped to move into it.

"I shan't send anything more to the jury," Bazille wrote to his family. "It is far too ridiculous . . . to be exposed to these administrative whims. . . . What I say here, a dozen young people of talent think along with me. We have therefore decided to rent each year a large studio where we'll exhibit as many of our works as we wish. We shall invite painters whom we like to send pictures. Courbet, Corot, Diaz, Daubigny, and many others whom you perhaps do not know, have promised to send us pictures and very much approve of our idea. With these people, and Monet, who is stronger than all of them, we are sure to succeed. . . ." But that time was not yet. Bazille soon wrote again to his family: "I spoke to you of the plan some young people had of making a separate exhibition. Bleeding ourselves as much as possible, we were able to collect the sum of 2,500 francs, which is not sufficient. We are therefore obliged to give up what we wanted to do."

Poverty affects the history of art as much as wealth. Just as Manet and Degas and Berthe Morisot could pursue their experiments without any worries about the next meal, some of the younger painters were severely handicapped by their penury. Renoir was so penniless during the unsuccessful 1867 fund-raising that he had to beg a friend to provide the canvas so that he could paint a portrait of the friend's sister-in-law. The following year, both Renoir and Pissarro were reduced to painting window blinds in order to survive. Perhaps the most afflicted of all was Monet, who had started in 1866 what he called "experimenting with effects of light and color." One of these experiments was to dig a trench in his garden near Saint-Cloud so that he could undertake a large painting entirely out of doors. The following year, he began his first cityscapes. But all through this period, his letters to various friends and acquaintances contain repeated appeals for money. Thus to Bazille, who had a modest allowance, in 1868: "I am writing you a few lines in haste to ask your speedy help. I was certainly born under an unlucky star. I have just been thrown out of the inn, and stark naked at that. My family have no intention of doing anything more for me. I don't even know where I'll have a place to sleep tomorrow. . . . I was so upset yesterday that I had the stupidity to throw myself into the water. Fortunately, no harm came of it."

Monet's finances were never much better than disastrous, but now they became worse than before because he had become involved with a nineteen-year-old girl named Camille Doncieux. She was not a great beauty but handsome, and a personality of considerable patience and character, as anyone would have to be to survive life with Monet. Just a few days after he met her, he quickly painted a full-length portrait for the Salon of 1866. It attracted considerable attention, for it is a remarkable portrait, the face barely visible, turned away to one side, the eyes closed, so that Monet the colorist could devote great attention to his beloved's flowing green-striped dress. He then had her pose—again with her dress, this time white-flowered, more important than her face—for a huge (eight-foot-high) painting called *Women in the Garden*. The practical problem was that Camille was now pregnant, and Monet could not even support himself, much less a family. Out of a mixture of admiration and charity, Bazille bought *Women in the Garden* on the installment plan, fifty francs a month. Monet then fled from the Paris suburb of Ville d'Avray to his native Le Havre to escape his creditors. In an effort to hide his unsold paintings from the creditors, he slit some 200 canvases from their frames and stored them away; the creditors found them and sold them off at the now-incredible price of thirty francs for each lot of fifty paintings.

Monet's only recourse was to beg his father for help, but be could not bring himself to that final humiliation. So it was Bazille who wrote the letter, describing not only Monet's poverty but explaining that his first child was soon to be born. The elder Monet's answer was chilling. He said that he had a sister living in the Le Havre suburb of Saint-Adresse, who would be kind enough to offer her scapegrace nephew his room and board, but no money. As for the pregnant Camille, the elder Monet disapproved of her and showed no interest in his prospective grandchild. He said that young Claude should abandon them both.

And Monet did. He went to live with his aunt, leaving Camille in Paris without a sou. The baby was born that July of 1867 and named Jean. Monet claimed that he could not raise the train fare to visit them. Later that summer, while working at his easel alongside Sisley at Honfleur, Monet mysteriously suffered a temporary blindness. Cézanne once said that Monet was "nothing but an eye, but what an eye," and we are too far away in space and time to do more than wonder at the frequency with which these Impressionist painters, so obsessed with their visions of light and color, suffered serious eye trouble. Degas spent much of his life struggling with a progressive blindness that finally forced him to shift from painting to sculpture. His highly gifted protégé Mary Cassatt endured the last ten years of her life blind. Renoir, Pissarro, Cézanne, they all saw their vision falter and fail. Monet, too, went blind near the end but was saved by a delicate eye operation.

He somehow recovered from this early crisis and got himself back to Paris, where he and Renoir shared Bazille's studio on the Rue Visconti. "Monet has fallen upon me from the skies with a collection of magnificent canvases," the ever-generous Bazille wrote to his sisters. And Camille took him back, so Monet painted a charming picture of her presiding over the young Jean's cradle. And the struggle went on. "My painting doesn't go, and I definitely do not count any more on fame," Monet wrote to Bazille in 1868. "I'm getting very sunk. . . . As soon as I make up my mind to work, I see everything black. In addition, money is always lacking. Disappointments, insults, hopes, new disappointments. . . ." At least Camille believed in him. They were finally married in June of 1870, less than two months before the war against Prussia suddenly broke out.

They were remarkably different people, these young Impressionists—Monet the passionate visionary, Renoir the carefree hedonist, Pissarro the idealistic socialist, Berthe Morisot the acerbic aristocrat—and yet they were bound together by their deep belief in a series of radical propositions. One was the conviction commonly held by ambitious young artists, that the gates of the establishment must be broken open. Let the new generation be heard. Another, more important, was that the tradition of historical painting must give way to scenes of contemporary life, *la vie moderne*. And that the tradition of studio composition must give way to a new process of painting out of doors, *en plein air*. And that a painting need not be "finished," in the sense that every detail must be fully shown by nearly invisible brushwork. . . .

"The coloring of shadows" . . . suggests what is perhaps the most important innovation among the Impressionists, a new sense of light and of how to convey light in pictures. In his authoritative *History of Impressionism,* [American art historian] John Rewald offers a succinct analysis: "Manet liked to maintain that for him 'light appeared with such unity that a single tone was sufficient to convey it and that it was preferable, even though apparently crude, to move abruptly from light to shadow than to accumulate things which the eye doesn't see and which not only weaken the strength of the light but enfeeble the color scheme of the shadows, which it is important to concentrate on.' But those among Manet's companions who had already worked out-of-doors, that is, all the landscapists in the group, must have objected to his manner of dividing a subject merely into lighted and shadowed areas. Their experience with nature had taught them otherwise. Little by little they were abandoning the usual method of suggesting the third dimension by letting the so-called local color of each object become more somber as the object itself seemed further away from the source of light and deeper in the shadow. Their own observations had taught them that the parts in the shadow were not devoid of color nor merely darker than the rest. Being to a lesser degree penetrated by the light, the shaded areas did not, of course, show the same color values as those exposed to the sun, but they were just as rich in color, among which complimentaries and especially blue seemed to dominate. By observing and reproducing these colors, it became possible to indicate depth without resorting to any of the bitumens customarily reserved for shadows. At the same time the general aspect of the work became automatically brighter. In order to study these questions further Monet, Sisley, and Pissarro began to devote themselves especially to winter landscapes. . . ."

"White does not exist in nature," Renoir explained long afterward in examining a young student's snow scene. "You admit that you have a sky above that snow. Your sky is blue. That blue must show up in the snow. In the morning there is green and yellow in the sky. These colors also must show up in the snow when you say that you painted your picture in the morning. Had you done it in the evening red and yellow would have to appear in the snow. And look at the shadows. They are much too dark. That tree, for example, has the *same* local color on the side where the sun shines as on the side where the shadow is. But you paint it as if it were two different objects, one light and one dark. Yet the color of the object is the same, only with a veil thrown over it. Sometimes that veil is thin, sometimes thick, but always it remains a veil. . . . Shadows are not black; no shadow is black. It always has a color. Nature knows only colors. . . . White and black are not colors.". . .

If the Impressionists' first effort to join forces in 1867 was thwarted by their poverty, their growing sense of community toward the end of the 1860s was shattered by the sudden outbreak of the Franco-Prussian War. While Manet and Degas joined the armed forces defending Paris, and Berthe Morisot remained in the besieged city, many painters were more interested in painting than in taking up arms for the dissolute emperor or his patchwork successors. Pissarro fled to London, leaving fifteen years' accumulated work behind him in Louveciennes. Monet, too, decided to go to London, once again leaving the indomitable Camille to fend for herself.

Monet and Pissarro soon found each other, through the good offices of the refugee art dealer Paul Durand-Ruel, the future sponsor of the whole Impressionist movement, who included new works by both of his new discoveries in a London exhibition of French artists. Monet and Pissarro then went off painting and museum-visiting together, just as though nothing were happening back in France. "The water colors and paintings of Turner and Constable . . . have certainly had influence upon us," Pissarro recalled. "We admired Gainsborough, Lawrence, Reynolds, etc., but we were struck chiefly by the landscape painters, who shared more in our aim with regard to *plein air,* light, and fugitive effects. . . . Turner and Constable, while they taught us something, showed us in their works that they had no understanding of the *analysis of shadow,* which in Turner's painting is simply used as an effect, a mere absence of light. . . ."

The young Impressionists liked to go out in pairs—Monet and Renoir, Pissarro and Cézanne—and to paint the same scenes from the same vantage point, all learning from each other's gifts and perceptions. Yet the doors of the official Salon still remained largely closed to them. Renoir submitted two canvases for the Salon of 1873, and both were rejected; Monet, Pissarro, and Sisley didn't even bother to try. So the scene was set for one of Zola's friends, Paul Alexis, apparently prodded by the painters of the Café Guerbois. He published an article in *L'Avenir National* in May of 1873 calling on the young painters to forget about the Salon and organize a showing of their own works. . . .

As happens every time that some young people start a new movement appealing to "all serious artists," the first question was, who would pay the bills? A rich participant? Someone's mistress? A social-climbing merchant? One person who could not pay was Durand-Ruel, the art dealer who had by now acquired the largest collection of the young painters' works. The postwar boom had ended abruptly in 1873, and Durand-Ruel had to cut back drastically on his investments. The most logical solution was for the painters to sponsor themselves, with each participant putting up an advance of sixty francs. Those who signed the founding charter on December 27, 1873, included Monet, Degas, Renoir, Pissarro, and Berthe Morisot. The main trouble with this system was that it gave everyone the right to argue about every detail. . . .

The new movement rejected the whole idea of a jury; the painters were to make their own selections, of their own works, and therefore the founders had to decide which painters to admit. To such natural leaders as Monet and Pissarro, it seemed obvious that the exhibition should concentrate on the new tendencies, the new concern with landscapes and light. But Degas felt very strongly that the exhibition should not appear radical, not a movement, simply independent of the official system. . . .

Somehow, the arguments did get settled. Pissarro, who had had experience in various Socialist enterprises, suggested a joint stock company, with each stockholder signing the official regulations. Each participant would give the group one-tenth of any sales. . . . Degas . . . proposed that the group adopt the neutral name of la Capucine (nasturtium); the others preferred the even more neutral name of Société Anonyme des Artistes, Peintres, Sculpteurs, Graveurs, etc. As for the touchy question of how the assembled works should be hung, Pissarro won approval for an elaborate system whereby pictures would first be classified according to size and then arranged by a drawing of lots.

The official opening took place on April 15, 1874—two weeks before the official Salon, to make it clear that this was no collection of castoffs, no new Salon des Refusés. Looking back, we can only marvel that such a magnificent collection of pictures could be assembled, all new, in one time and place. Degas's *Carriage at the Races,* for example, in which the serene expanse of a pale green meadow all comes into focus on a tiny baby being fed under a white parasol, watched by a man in a top hat and a large black dog. Or Renoir's *The Loge,* in which a handsome woman in a black-and-white-striped dress, with a pink flower in her red hair, gazes reflectively out at the theater audience while her escort surveys the balcony through his binoculars. And from Berthe Morisot not only the unforgettable *Cradle* but also the delicious *Hide and Seek,* a mother and her young daughter, both fully outfitted in beribboned hats, pretending to find and be found behind a transparent shrub.

The critics played their predictable roles as blind and ignorant buffoons, with Leroy leading the way in *Charivari*. The condemnation and derision caused Madame Morisot to worry that even though her difficult daughter was now at least engaged, her association with such controversial artists might bring disgrace upon the family. . . .

If the first Impressionist exhibition had relatively little effect on critics and other artists, it had even less on the public or the market. The number of visitors on opening day amounted to only 175—and many of them came only to jeer—as compared to a daily average of nearly 10,000 at the Salon. All in all, some 3,500 came to the Impressionists' month-long exhibit, 400,000 to the Salon. A few Impressionist paintings were sold, but the sales receipts no longer record which ones, and the sums involved were derisory. Total sales figures, derived from the 10 percent commission collected by the group, amounted to only 3,600 francs. Sisley earned 1,000 francs, Monet 200, Renoir 180, Degas and Berthe Morisot nothing, and this at a time when a popular hack like Ernest Meissonier, Manet's commander during the war, charged 100,000 francs for a commissioned painting.

The exhibition seemed for a time to have broken even on its entrance fees, catalogue sales, and commissions, but at the end of the year, Renoir summoned all available stockholders to his studio on the Rue Saint-Georges and told them that they still owed 3,435 francs, or 184.50 apiece. He therefore proposed liquidating the Société Anonyme des Artistes, Peintres, Sculpteurs, Graveurs, etc., and his proposal was approved unanimously. So the first exhibition of the group now known as Impressionists (though Degas still adamantly rejected the term) both was a historic event and was not a historic event. It was an almost total failure, and yet it established a landmark, created a new sense of common dedication and commitment. But the real history of the Impressionist movement, with its rending conflicts and controversies, was yet to come.

Gay Nineties Dance Hall Music

Ian Bradley

In the 1890s, writes British historian Ian Bradley, a new type of popular music emerged in the United States, Great Britain, and western Europe. The new music was explicitly designed to appeal to the mass audiences that were appearing in rapidly expanding cities. Performed in vaudeville theaters that often featured lavish staging and spectacular lighting effects (made possible by rapid advances in electrification), popular music endeared itself to people of all social classes who could afford the modest price of admission and who could reach places of entertainment using new urban transit systems, including electric-powered streetcars. Less pretentious than the self-consciously "highbrow" world of classical music, opera, and "serious" theater (all of which had earlier appealed across class lines), the new mass entertainment generally dropped the risqué tone of older popular theater, adhering to the strict limits of propriety that the era required of all entertainments intended for family viewing. Together with cheap—and usually sensationalistic—newspapers and professional sports, the new popular music shaped the taste and appealed to the common interests of almost all urban people at the end of the nineteenth century. It also laid the foundation for the style and content of the mass entertainment that new technologies of the twentieth century would create: movies, radio, television, theme parks, and the myriad outpourings of the recording industry.

In the Easter Vacation of 1898 [British writer] E.M. Forster, down from his second term at Cambridge, treated his mother and aunts to a trip to the music hall in London. He wrote an account of the ex-

Reprinted from "Changing the Tune: Popular Music in the 1890s," by Ian Bradley, *History Today*, July 1992. Reprinted with permission from *History Today*.

perience in schoolboy Latin for his old school magazine, *The Ton-bridgian,* recording his mother's anxious comment before the climax of the show—Albert Chevalier's rendering of 'Knocked 'em in the Old Kent Road'—'*Spero hoc non erit vulgare*'. In the event, there was nothing in the Cockney songs of the Coster Laureate to shock the sensibilities of his predominantly middle-class audience. The Forster party returned to their villas in the Home Counties with a sense of relief mingled with a tinge of excitement at having ventured into the still slightly *risqué* world of popular entertainment.

The 1890s was in many ways the golden age of the English music hall—the decade that saw Albert Chevalier, George Robey, Nellie Wallace, Florrie Ford and Vesta Tilley launched as stars and Marie Lloyd and Dan Leno at the height of their careers. As the Forsters' visit suggests, it was also the period when music hall became respectable. The seedy drinking dens with sawdust-covered floors and rough benches in the galleries, where proletarian audiences had gathered to swill beer and jeer at bad jokes, were being replaced by elaborately decorated palaces of varieties with plush seating and more refined acts calculated to appeal to a more genteel clientele.

To a large extent this transition was a result of increasing commercialisation in the world of entertainment. Music hall was ceasing to be essentially localised and amateurish and fast on the way to becoming a highly organised business, concentrated in the hands of a small group of entrepreneurs owning chains of theatres throughout the country. Song writing, too, was becoming an industry. The 1890s marks the start of Tin Pan Alley, the biggest and most successful popular music factory that the world has ever seen.

It is, indeed, tempting to see the decade as the one in which commercial forces began to take over as the main determinants of musical taste on both sides of the Atlantic, destroying the vitality and richness of genuine popular culture and paving the way for the bland mass-produced muzak and international pop industry that have so dominated the twentieth century. To some extent, purely commercial considerations lay behind many of the significant new arrivals on the popular music scene during the 1890s, which included pantomime and musical comedy as well as ragtime and recordings.

But this period also saw the flowering of the great tradition of amateur music-making in Britain. It has been estimated that there were some 40,000 brass bands in the United Kingdom in the 1890s. The vast majority were made up of amateur musicians, including the famous works bands which played against each other in competitions. There were also a growing number of municipal bands, especially in seaside and tourist resorts—one of the best-known was founded in Bournemouth in 1893. There were over 1,000 Salvation Army bands, kitted out from 1890 onwards in their distinctive uniform of blue tunic, faced with black braid and lined with narrow red trimmings. In December 1899 the first international Salvation Army bandsmen's council took place in London with representatives from bands from all over the world.

Like brass bands, choral societies were particularly a feature of the industrial communities of the Midlands and North, although there was also a strong amateur choir movement in London and the Home Counties. Their traditional repertoire of sacred oratorios, recently supplemented by Sir John Stainer's *Crucifixion* in 1887 was widened during the 1890s to include Elgar's new choral works, *The Black Night, The Light of Life, King Olaf* and *Caractacus*, and Coleridge Taylor's enormously popular *Hiawatha's Wedding Feast,* composed in 1898.

Singing, of course, was not just confined to organised choirs. It took place at home, in public houses, at smoking concerts, school reunions, weddings and wherever people got together. The music hall produced a constant flow of easily memorable choruses which were taken up with gusto and sung at work and at home. The 'hits' of the 1890s included 'My old man said follow the van', 'Oh, Mr Porter' and 'The man who broke the bank at Monte Carlo'. Student singing, which had long been a feature of university life in Germany and among college fraternities in the United States, was given a considerable boost in Britain with the publication of the *Scottish Students' Song Book* in 1891. Its compiler, Millar Patrick, who went on to become a leading Free Church minister and expert on metrical psalmody, began by collecting the songs which he heard students singing on the train journey to St Andrews University. He added a number of German drinking songs and American student favourites like 'Riding down from Bangor' and 'Abdul, the bulbul Ameer', together with English translations of Gaelic lyrics. The resulting book was to sell nearly half a million copies and was said to be found, along with the Bible, in nearly every Scottish home in the years before the First World War.

The decade also saw a significant folksong revival, spearheaded by Lucy Broadwood and J.A. Fuller-Maitland who produced an important collection of English county songs in 1893. Prominent among the new breed of collectors who roamed the countryside recording local ballads and songs were the Reverend Sabine Baring-Gould in the West Country and Frank Kidson in the North. In 1898 they helped to found the Folk Song Society. It had the backing of the musical establishment in the shape of Sir John Stainer and Sir Charles Stanford and was soon to be joined by the young Ralph Vaughan Williams. To a considerable extent the folk song revival, like the changing patronage of the music hall, represented a middle-class takeover of what had hitherto been a genuinely proletarian and popular musical culture. Traditional working songs which had been passed orally from generation to generation were now being written down and published, their words and tunes often cleaned up and prettified to turn them into parlour ballads. This was particularly true in Scotland where devotees of the Celtic twilight like Professor John Stuart Blackie and Marjory Kennedy Fraser were transforming the rough chants of the Highlands and Islands into flamboyant art songs suitable for suburban drawing rooms in Edinburgh and London.

But if the middle classes were showing an increasing enthusiasm for music hall and folk song, they were also getting more access to classical music. In 1895 Henry Wood established the Promenade Concerts at the Queen's Hall in London. Other cities followed suit and set up their own proms, featuring the music of popular classical composers like Beethoven, Schubert and Schumann. Among their patrons there was little enthusiasm or appetite for the more *avant garde* contemporary pieces which were giving classical music in other countries a distinctive frenetic and *fin de siècle* feeling. Such 'modern' pieces as Debussy's *Prelude à l'après-midi d'un faune* (1894) and Richard Strauss' *So Sprach Zarathustra* (1896) found few admirers or imitators among the British musical establishment. Composers stuck to oratorios, hymn tunes and part songs. Nostalgia and patriotism were much in vogue, particularly around the time of Queen Victoria's diamond jubilee. Sir Arthur Sullivan, who had begun the decade by writing his one and only grand opera, *Ivanhoe,* went on to produce an *Imperial March,* incidental music to *King Arthur,* and a ballet, *Queen Victoria and Merry England,* to celebrate the royal anniversary in 1897.

Most of the leading classical composers dabbled in what was undoubtedly the most popular and perhaps the most characteristic musical form of the decade, the parlour ballad. Stanford's 'Father O'Flynn' and Parry's 'When lovers meet again', not to mention Sullivan's 'The Lost Chord' were sung a great deal more often than their sacred oratorios and cantatas. Ballads formed the staple of the musical evenings which were such a prominent feature of late victorian middle-class life. There were few respectable homes that did not have a piano and a large stack of sheet music in the drawing room. Most of the ballads were strongly sentimental and many had an overtly religious flavour. One of the most popular. 'The Holy City', which dates from 1892, sold at the rate of 50,000 copies a year throughout the decade. The words were by Fred Weatherley, a lawyer who was also responsible for 'The Old Brigade', 'Danny Boy' and 'Roses of Picardy' and the music by Michael Maybrick, a distinguished singer who had been appointed organist of St Peter's Church, Liverpool, at the age of fourteen and wrote music under the pseudonym, Stephen Adams.

Ballads were sung not just at home but also at public concerts and recitals. If music hall still provided most of the household names in the world of entertainment, the recital circuit was creating its own stars. They included Adelina Patti and Jenny Lind who regularly brought the house down with their renditions of 'Home, Sweet Home'. Sometimes it was more than just the house that was brought down by the exertions of these powerful female soloists. The unfortunate Mme Patey-Whyttock, who secured her reputation on the basis of 'Kathleen Mavourneen' collapsed and died just after finishing 'The Banks of Allan Water' in 1894. Perhaps the greatest of all the recitalists, Clara Butt, made her debut as a contralto at the Lyceum Theatre in 1892 before the Prince of Wales. Her particular 'show-stoppers' were 'Abide with Me' and 'Softly Awakes my Heart' from Saint Saens' *Samson and Delilah*. Later she was to be one of the first singers of Elgar's 'Land of Hope and Glory'. Queen Victoria was one of her greatest fans, telling her: 'I have never liked the English language before, but in your mouth it is beautiful'.

In the jingoistic atmosphere induced by Kitchener's exploits in the Sudan and the build-up to the Boer War in the closing years of the decade the dominant theme in ballads switched from religiosity to patriotism. Yet things were not always what they seemed. One of the great British morale-boosters during the Boer War, 'Sons of the Sea', which sent audiences wild with its celebration of 'the boys of the bulldog breed who made old England's name', was actually written in 1896 by an Irish-born emigrant to the United States, Felix Mc-Glennon. From his Tin Pan Alley base he turned out a succession of highly successful vaudeville and music hall songs, including another great patriotic favourite, 'Comrades'. The song which, perhaps more than any other, was to be taken up during the Boer War and which came to epitomise the patriotic fervour of the last years of Queen Victoria's reign, 'The Soldiers of the Queen' started life as a send-up of jingoism. When war against the Boers was declared in 1899, its author, Leslie Stuart, a Manchester church organist who supplemented his income by writing popular ballads, did his patriotic bit and hastily re-wrote it as a recruiting song and morale booster for the British army.

The provenance of these two songs underlines one of the most important features of the 1890s—the emergence of the professional tunesmith, ready to turn out a song to order. The music business was becoming increasingly commercial and nowhere more so than in Tin Pan Alley, the area of railroad flats in New York City between 28th Street and Broadway where a group of music publishers set up shop to cash in on the booming demand for sentimental ballads on both sides of the Atlantic. The publishing houses were on top of each other and the cacophony of tunes which poured out of their open windows reminded journalist Monroe Rosenfield of the clashing of tin pans. In a piece for the *New York Herald* he coined the phrase 'Tin Pan Alley' for the new community of commercially-minded publishers, composers and lyricists who were to dominate popular music in America and Europe for the next fifty years.

Several of its early members were British emigrants like Harry Dacre, whose successes included 'Daisy Bell', written in 1892, and the Boer War song 'Two lively little lads in Navy Blue'. Perhaps the most successful of the native American songsmiths was Paul Dresser who wrote and composed 'On the Banks of the Wabash' in 1891. He specialised in tear-jerking ballads with titles like 'The pardon came too late' and 'Her tears drifted out with the tide'. Many of the most popular sentimental parlour ballads of the 1890s came from Tin Pan Alley, including 'The Volunteer Organist' and 'Silver threads among the gold'. So also did such great British music hall hits as 'After the Ball was over', 'A Bird in a Gilded Cage' and 'Where did you get that hat?'

Those music hall songs which were home grown were increasingly coming from the pens of British writers with the same new commercial outlook. Songs like 'Knocked 'em in the Old Kent Road', 'My Old Dutch', 'If it wasn't for the 'ouses in between' and 'It's a great big shame' sung by Albert Chevalier and Gus Elen did not, as they seemed, have their origins among the costermongers' barrows but were dreamed up by music publishers and writers who deliberately created a cult of Cockney songs among music hall goers in the 1890s. Nor was it just in the area of song writing that the rough and tumble was going out of music hall and a new calculated sophistication and commercialism coming in. The small independent provincial halls that had been the backbone of the business since it had begun in the 1840s and 1850s were closing down. They fell victim partly to stringent new licensing laws and fire regulations. It was true that many were serious fire hazards and some undoubtedly attracted disreputable customers. Prompted by moral pressure groups, several local authorities compulsorily closed down local halls. But commercial factors also played an important part in the demise of the old-style music hall. As popular entertainment became increasingly a business, bigger operators moved in. Like Mrs Forster, they felt that there was a certain vulgarity about the word 'music hall' which might put off more affluent patrons. They preferred the term 'variety theatre'.

The 1890s saw the emergence of national chains of variety theatres, dominated by three companies: Stoll, Moss and MacNaughton. They were designed to appeal to a richer and more respectable clientele than those who had paid a penny to crowd the gallery or stand in the pits of the old halls. Comfortable seating was installed throughout the auditorium and ceilings and walls were sumptuously decorated in a neo-Baroque style. To underline their magnificence these new theatres were often called 'The Empire' or 'The Palace'— the greatest of them all, the Hackney Empire, the ultimate in exotic plush, was to open in 1901.

The transition from music hall to variety theatre went hand in hand with a more organised and professional approach on the part of both managements and artistes and a change of style in the entertainment offered. The development of theatre chains enabled the new breed of entrepreneurs to tour acts around the country. Formal contracts came to replace ad-hoc engagements. The emerging entertainment industry developed its own trade unions—first in the field was the Music Hall Artistes Association which was formed in 1886 to negotiate contracts. Ten years later the Music Hall Artistes Railway Association was set up to secure travel concessions for those on tour. It is interesting to note that the artistes held to the term 'music hall' when the management was trying to abandon it in an effort to woo more middle-class customers. The same motivation lay behind changes which were made in the kinds of act on offer in the new variety theatres during the decade. A conscious effort was made to move away from the rougher elements of the old music hall turns. 'Nigger minstrels' were largely phased out although the black-faced crooner Eugene Stratton continued to have enormous success with the two songs Leslie Stuart had specially written for him, 'Little Dolly Daydream' and 'Lily of Laguna'. In their place there were more speciality musical acts and an increasing number of singers whose repertoire included songs from operetta and musical comedy as well as the more vulgar music hall and vaudeville numbers. Several music hall stars graduated to the status of recitalists. Albert Chevalier regularly gave recitals at the Queen's Hall to audiences who would never have entered a music hall. Another who was among the first to straddle the worlds of music hall, operetta and musical comedy was George Grossmith, creator of many of the comic roles in Gilbert and Sullivan's operas. He was particularly popular with Queen Victoria and was summoned to give a recital of ballads at Balmoral in 1890. It included, by special royal request, his own song 'See me dance the polka'.

As music hall diversified into variety two new forms of musical entertainment were born: the end of the pier show and the modern pantomime. The former was a direct result of the development of seaside holidays with the spread of the railways and the provision of paid summer holidays for most workers. The Follies, perhaps the best-known of the troupes of pierrots and minstrels who were to go on entertaining holiday makers until the advent of television produced a demand for a rather different type of seaside show, made their first professional appearance at Worthing in 1897.

The advent of Christmas pantomimes was a more direct result of the establishment of the new variety theatres. Managements soon saw the potential for filling their Empires and Palaces through the depths of winter by putting on humorous and tuneful shows that would appeal to whole families. So with the help of music hall star-turns like Dan Leno, the classic Italian *comedia dell'arte* was transformed into the romps with male dames, handsome princes played by glamorous girls, corny jokes and sing-along tunes which have continued to delight us ever since. It was, indeed, in one of the first of these new-style pantomimes, *Dick Whittington,* at the Grand Theatre, Islington, that one of the great hit songs of the decade was introduced to the British public on Boxing Night 1891.'Ta-ra-ra-boom-de-ay', based on a tune which a nigger minstrel had heard in a low-down dive in St Louis seven years earlier, had been a flop when it was performed in New York. But when Lottie Collins belted it out to the accompaniment of high kicks the London audience went wild and demanded encore after encore.

If music hall was moving up-market, operetta was also changing in a way that would bring it to a wider audience. The 1890s marked the end of the greatest partnership in the history of the British musical theatre with the last two collaborations between W.S. Gilbert and Arthur Sullivan. Neither *Utopia Limited* (1893) nor *The Grand Duke* (1896) were anything like as successful as their earlier works. In fact, they were not markedly inferior in quality to shows like *Patience* and *Ruddigore.* The duo who had dominated the world of operetta for nearly twenty years ended with comparative flops on their hands, not so much because they had lost their touch but rather because of a change in public taste and expectations. Perhaps partly as a consequence of increasing middle-class patronage of music hall, audiences were coming to demand more glamour and spectacle on the stage and were less attuned to a style which was closer to opera than to the lighter fare on offer in the palaces of varieties.

The future belonged to a new and rather different genre which had its origins in America in the 1860s. Musical comedy differed from Gilbert and Sullivan in having less complex plots and less 'difficult' music and more lavish decor and costumes. Dancing and pretty girls took the place of choruses and coloratura runs. Once again, the hand of commercialism was clearly at work. The managers of a number of West End theatres, notably the Gaiety, the Lyric and the Prince of Wales, saw the potential profitability of musical shows. The most enthusiastic was George Edwardes, who had learned the business of theatrical management under Richard D'Oyly Carte and ran the Savoy Theatre in its heyday as the home of Gilbert and Sullivan. As manager of the Gaiety during the 1890s Edwardes introduced a string of musical comedies to an increasingly appreciative public. The first, *In Town,* with music by Osmond Carr, opened in 1892. It was followed two years later by Owen Hall and Sidney Jones' *A Gaiety Girl* and in 1896 by the same duo's phenomenally successful *The Geisha* which produced the hit song 'Chin-chin Chinaman, muchee muchee sad' and introduced a whole line of Oriental musicals that had their climax in *Chu Chin Chow* in 1916. In 1899 Hall and Leslie Stuart collaborated on *Floradora*, famous for its song 'Tell me, pretty maiden'. With the transfer of these last three British shows to Broadway and the arrival in London in 1898 of Hugh Morton and Gustav Kerber's *The Belle of New York* that two-way traffic in musicals across the Atlantic had begun which has continued to boom throughout the twentieth century.

At this early stage, the British contribution was more substantial in both quality and quantity. Although America is credited with the invention of the musical, and certainly brought the genre to its peak of development in the work of Rodgers and Hammerstein and Lerner and Lowe in the 1950s and 1960s, in these pioneering days it was British composers and lyricists who were at the forefront of developing the new form. Perhaps it is more accurate to say that while Americans excelled in writing and staging musicals, the British excelled in the slightly different field of musical comedy. This was a gentler, more innocent world, epitomised by the work of Ivan Caryll and Lionel Monckton who gave a taste of things to come with their first joint work, *The Shop Girl* which ran for 546 performances in 1894. It was in later collaborative ventures between these two men, notably *The Quaker Girl, Our Miss Gibbs* and *The Arcadians* that musical comedy achieved its apogee in the Edwardian era.

But if much of the music emanating from both sides of the Atlantic in the 1890s was of a gentle, lyrical, sentimental kind far removed from any kind of *fin de siècle* angst or frenzy, there was one new sound which did have a distinctly frenetic quality. Ragtime gave the nineties their naughtiness, challenging the smooth modulations of the parlour ballad with wild rhythms and jerky syncopation. It came, of course, from America and specifically from black America where its origins are generally traced to a dance called the cake walk. The first piece of music to have ragtime in its title was 'Ma Ragtime Baby' written by Fred Stone and published in 1893. Four years later Scott Joplin published a medley of piano tunes called 'The Original Rags' and in 1899 he brought out what was to become one of the classics of ragtime, 'Maple Leaf Rag'.

The gradual spread of ragtime signalled several significant shifts in popular music style and taste. Instrumental playing, whether on piano, by jazz band or in orchestras, came to rival singing as an attraction and audience puller. At the same time singing began to give way to dancing as a communal activity. This was partly a result of the decline of the music hall which had been founded on the principle of lots of easy choruses which people would take up and sing. Along with the new palaces of varieties went the spread of *palais de dance*. Increasingly, popular music was being written primarily to dance to, rather than to sing to. Indeed, 'Knocked 'em in the Old Kent Road', the song whose potential vulgarity had concerned Mrs Forster, was one of the first to use the new tango rhythm. The jazz and dance band era was still some way off, to be heralded by the bugle call of *Alexander's Rag Time Band* in 1911. But already the seeds were beginning to be sown of that revolution in musical taste that would take thousands of people away from the parlour sing-song and on to the dance floor.

Some perceptive commentators detected a decline in amateur singing and music making towards the end of the decade. Various factors were blamed for this. In 1896 the *Musical Times* complained that 'there are literally thousands of young ladies whose leisure hours, formerly passed in large part on the music-stool, are now spent in the saddle of the 'iron bird' as a lady journalist has poetically described the bicycle'. It reported that pianos were being sold to pay for the new machine and that 'after bicycling for any length of time, many ladies find their wrists ache so much as to render pianoforte playing well-nigh impossible'. Other advances in transport were also held responsible for falling levels of musical appreciation and participation. The growth of trams and suburban trains made it possible for many people to get to professional concerts and musical shows and helped to kill off amateur choirs and brass bands.

Perhaps the most significant innovation of the decade, certainly in terms of its eventual impact on the whole development of popular music, was also the least noticed. In 1894 Emile Berliner, a German living in Washington, invented the gramophone. This was a distinct improvement on the earlier phonograph, which had gone into commercial production the same year, because it played discs rather than cylinders. The next few years saw the establishment of the Gramophone Company in London, Deutsche Grammophon in Berlin, the Compagnie Francais du Gramophone in Paris. A disc pressing facility was set up in Hamburg in 1899. At the end of the nineteenth century very few people had heard commercial music recordings, let alone possessed a gramophone. Most would have been astounded at the thought that within a generation or so, access to every kind of music would not involve a tram trip to the concert hall or the palace of varieties nor even a cluster round the piano in the drawing room but simply the winding of a handle and later the press of a button.

Perhaps it was as well that they did not guess the potential of the new machine with its cumbersome loudspeaker—for it was to introduce a vulgarity into popular musical culture of a kind infinitely more insidious and pervasive than Mrs Forster feared in her visit to the music hall.

Psychoanalysis and the Oedipus Complex

Sigmund Freud

Sigmund Freud, one of the giants of twentieth-century thought, was born in Austria in 1856 and studied medicine at the University of Vienna, from which he graduated in 1881. Moving into the new field of neurology, he became fascinated by the controversial work on hysteria of another Viennese physician, Joseph Breuer. Breuer maintained that patients could be cured of hysteria by subjecting them to hypnosis, during which they could be induced to recall painful, long-suppressed events. After studying with Breuer and a well-known Parisian specialist, J.M. Charcot, Freud gradually came to believe hypnosis insufficient for treating hysterical conditions. Instead, by the mid-1890s he pioneered the use of "free association," an analytical technique in which the patient reclines comfortably on a couch and describes his or her thoughts to an analyst who sits discreetly out of sight but takes careful notes. As his patients' thoughts wandered into the realm of dreams, childhood, and sexual experience, Freud became convinced that he could find the keys to human behavior there. Despite an internal conflict with his own puritanical sensibilities, a quarrel with his disapproving mentor Breuer, the opposition of Vienna's conservative medical establishment, and the loss of many of his patients, Freud persisted with his work. In 1900 he published *The Interpretation of Dreams*, from which this selection is excerpted. At the time it aroused mostly derision or hostility, and very few copies were sold. It is now regarded as one of Freud's most important works.

Excerpted from "The Interpretation of Dreams," by Sigmund Freud, translated and edited by A.A. Brill, in *The Basic Writings of Sigmund Freud* (New York: Modern Library, 1938). Copyright © 1938 by Random House, Inc.

According to Freud, it is the task of what he called psychoanalysis to delve beneath the repressions constructed by our conscious mind (the ego) and reveal the wellsprings of our actions and our personality that lie hidden in the unconscious. Dreams, he believed, operate as windows to the unconscious, allowing us a glimpse of the sexual feelings that our civilized nature forces us to repress. Among these basic sexual impulses is what Freud termed the Oedipus complex, the male child's secret desire to supplant his father and gain exclusive possession of his mother. (For girls, Freud posited a parallel Elektra complex, involving a desire to supplant the mother.) Freud held that maturation in modern society involves rejecting such impulses—a vain hope, he thought, because an unconscious residue of frustration will remain, producing adult neuroses.

Freud based his theories on thorough analysis of his patients' and his own dreams and fantasies, which he combined with his deep knowledge of European cultural history. His description of the Oedipus complex, for example, owes much to his understanding of the ancient Greek dramas of Sophocles (496–406 B.C.), which narrate the tragedy of Oedipus.

Modern research suggests that Freud was mistaken in his belief that patients who told him about their early sexual feelings were revealing fantasies born of unconscious desires. It is quite possible that real—albeit long-repressed—sexual abuses lay behind the stories that Freud was hearing in his consulting room. Freud's writings now seem more revealing of the tensions of upper-middle-class European life at the end of the nineteenth century than of universal aspects of the human condition. Today, as more becomes known about the genetic and biochemical basis for human behavior, the influence of Freudian psychology has declined significantly. Modern therapy is much more apt to involve medication rather than years of painstaking (and expensive) psychoanalysis. Yet Freud's theories became enormously influential throughout the Western world between the 1920s and the 1960s.

A ccording to my already extensive experience, parents play a leading part in the infantile psychology of all persons who subsequently become psychoneurotics. Falling in love with one parent and hating the other forms part of the permanent stock of the psychic impulses which arise in early childhood, and are of such importance as the material of the subsequent neurosis. But I do not believe that psychoneurotics are to be sharply distinguished in this respect from other persons who remain normal—that is, I do not believe that they are capable of creating something absolutely new and peculiar to themselves. It is far more probable—and this is confirmed by incidental observations of normal children—that in their amorous or hostile attitude toward their parents, psychoneurotics do no more than reveal to us, by magnification, something that occurs less markedly and intensively in the minds of the majority of children. Antiquity has furnished us with legendary matter which corroborates this belief, and the profound and universal validity of the old legends is explicable only by an equally universal validity of the above-mentioned hypothesis of infantile psychology.

I am referring to the legend of King Oedipus and the *Oedipus Rex* of Sophocles. Oedipus, the son of Laius, king of Thebes, and Jocasta, is exposed as a suckling, because an oracle had informed the father that his son, who was still unborn, would be his murderer. He is rescued, and grows up as a king's son at a foreign court, until, being uncertain of his origin, he, too, consults the oracle, and is warned to avoid his native place, for he is destined to become the murderer of his father and the husband of his mother. On the road leading away from his supposed home he meets King Laius, and in a sudden quarrel strikes him dead. He comes to Thebes, where he solves the riddle of the Sphinx, who is barring the way to the city, whereupon he is elected king by the grateful Thebans, and is rewarded with the hand of Jocasta. He reigns for many years in peace and honour, and begets two sons

Sigmund Freud

and two daughters upon his unknown mother, until at last a plague breaks out—which causes the Thebans to consult the oracle anew. Here Sophocles' tragedy begins. The messengers bring the reply that the plague will stop as soon as the murderer of Laius is driven from the country. But where is he?

> "Where shall be found,
> Faint, and hard to be known, the trace of the ancient guilt?"

The action of the play consists simply in the disclosure, approached step by step and artistically delayed (and comparable to the work of a psychoanalysis) that Oedipus himself is the murderer of Laius, and that he is the son of the murdered man and Jocasta. Shocked by the abominable crime which he has unwittingly committed, Oedipus blinds himself, and departs from his native city. The prophecy of the oracle has been fulfilled.

The *Oedipus Rex* is a tragedy of fate; its tragic effect depends on the conflict between the all-powerful will of the gods and the vain efforts of human beings threatened with disaster; resignation to the divine will, and the perception of one's own impotence is the lesson which the deeply moved spectator is supposed to learn from the tragedy. Modern authors have therefore sought to achieve a similar tragic effect by expressing the same conflict in stories of their own invention. But the playgoers have looked on unmoved at the unavailing efforts of guiltless men to avert the fulfilment of curse or oracle; the modern tragedies of destiny have failed of their effect.

If the *Oedipus Rex* is capable of moving a modern reader or playgoer no less powerfully than it moved the contemporary Greeks, the only possible explanation is that the effect of the Greek tragedy does not depend upon the conflict between fate and human will, but upon the peculiar nature of the material by which this conflict is revealed. There must be a voice within us which is prepared to acknowledge the compelling power of fate in the *Oedipus,* while we are able to condemn the situations occurring in . . . other tragedies of fate as arbitrary inventions. And there actually is a motive in the story of King Oedipus which explains the verdict of this inner voice. His fate moves us only because it might have been our own, because the oracle laid upon us before our birth the very curse which rested upon him. It may be that we were all destined to direct our first sexual impulses toward our mothers, and our first impulses of hatred and violence toward our fathers; our dreams convince us that we were. King Oedipus, who slew his father Laius and wedded his mother Jocasta, is nothing more or less than a wish-fulfilment—the fulfilment of the wish of our childhood. But we, more fortunate than he, in so far as we have not become psychoneurotics, have since our childhood succeeded in withdrawing our sexual impulses from our mothers, and in forgetting our jealousy of our fathers. We recoil from the person for whom this primitive wish of our childhood has been fulfilled with all the force of the repression which these wishes have undergone in our minds since childhood. As the poet brings the guilt of Oedipus to light by his investigation, he forces us to become aware of our own inner selves, in which the same impulses are still extant, even though they are suppressed. The antithesis with which the chorus departs:—

> ". . . Behold, this is Oedipus,
> Who unravelled the great riddle, and was first in power,
> Whose fortune all the townsmen praised and envied;
> See in what dread adversity he sank!"

—this admonition touches us and our own pride, us who since the years of our childhood have grown so wise and so powerful in our own estimation. Like Oedipus, we live in ignorance of the desires that offend morality, the desires that nature has forced upon us and after their unveiling we may well prefer to avert our gaze from the scenes of our childhood.

In the very text of Sophocles' tragedy there is an unmistakable reference to the fact that the Oedipus legend had its source in dream-material of immemorial antiquity, the content of which was the painful disturbance of the child's relations to its parents caused by the first impulses of sexuality. Jocasta comforts Oedipus—who is not yet enlightened, but is troubled by the recollection of the oracle—by an allusion to a dream which is often dreamed, though it cannot, in her opinion, mean anything:—

> "For many a man hath seen himself in dreams
> His mother's mate, but he who gives no heed
> To suchlike matters bears the easier life."

The dream of having sexual intercourse with one's mother was as common then as it is to-day with many people, who tell it with indignation and astonishment. As may well be imagined, it is the key to the tragedy and the complement to the dream of the death of the father. The Oedipus fable is the reaction of fantasy to these two typical dreams, and just as such a dream, when occurring to an adult, is experienced with feelings of aversion, so the content of the fable must include terror and self-chastisement. The form which it subsequently assumed was the result of an uncomprehending secondary elaboration of the material, which sought to make it serve a theological intention. The attempt to reconcile divine omnipotence with human responsibility must, of course, fail with this material as with any other.

A Century
of Invention

The 1800s "century of invention" can be interpreted as yet another consequence of the Dual Revolution. Without the Industrial Revolution, there would have been far less opportunity for technological innovation, far less accumulated wealth to provide the capital to invest in new discoveries and processes, and far less discretionary income that ordinary citizens increasingly could spend on the consumer goods that the inventors and industrialists provided. Without the impetus of political revolution, there could hardly have been the kind of democratic mass culture that arose over the span of the nineteenth century (and in particular its last quarter, 1875–1900), sparking the demand and the need for the consumer goods and services that flowed from the work of innovators like Louis Pasteur and Thomas A. Edison. Nor, without democratization, is it likely that so many inventors from humble social backgrounds—Edison is a particularly significant example—would have had the opportunity to put their natural genius to work at any task above those dull routines that traditional societies require for subsistence.

We must also credit that ultimate intellectual wellspring of discovery, the West's Scientific Revolution of the sixteenth through the eighteenth centuries. Out of the Scientific Revolution sprang the rational, quantifying, cause-and-effect state of mind that set and solved practical problems centering on the workings of the natural world. The accumulation of scientific knowledge, which accelerated every decade during the eighteenth and nineteenth centuries, increasingly found practical applications in ways that affected everyday life. Questions that "pure" scientists relentlessly pursued (for example, what is light, and what connection does it have to electricity and magnetism?) had profound implications for the development of electrical engineering and for the invention of electrical devices during the nineteenth century. Every advance stimulated dozens of others, often in unexpected directions.

The readings in this chapter capture some of the excitement of the nineteenth century's myriad new discoveries. The first makes clear how the great French biologist Louis Pasteur's dramatic discoveries about the world of microorganisms, which had profound implications for the control of disease, infection, and the processes of fermentation, were rooted in practices and agendas that were ultimately products of the Scientific Revolution. The second selection makes clear how enormously revolutionary was the discovery of how electricity could be harnessed for industrial production, and how far-reaching were the consequences of that discovery. The third selection returns to the personality and work of a great scientist, and of one of the most significant women in the history of science, Marie Curie. Her work in the 1890s on the hitherto mysterious problem of radioactivity was not only spellbinding to those many members of the general public who were becoming attracted to the progress of science, but was also an essential link in the rise of modern physics, which in the twentieth century would unlock many of the secrets of the atom and unleash natural forces of stupendous power. Ironically, Curie would give her own life to the cause of science by dying of leukemia contracted through excessive exposure to radiation—the medically curative capacities of which were only beginning to be recognized and exploited during Marie Curie's tragically shortened lifetime.

The final selection bridges the gap between nineteenth-century innovation and twenty-first-century global telecommunications. As a scientist, entrepreneur, and humanitarian, Canadian Alexander Graham Bell was another of the nineteenth century's great innovators. His invention of the telephone in 1876 was a spectacular success in his own time, but its true significance only began to be apparent a hundred years later, with the development of the computer, of digitalization, and of the means for instantaneous information transmittal. Bell's discoveries in telecommunications were among the most truly revolutionary innovations of a century of innovation.

Louis Pasteur: Scientist of the Wonderful Century

Lisa Yount

The nineteenth century saw a burst in science—in invention, in scientific principles, and in scientific research. Perhaps no other scientist epitomized the century like Louis Pasteur. Through testing and proving ideas by experiment, Pasteur made advances in chemistry, in microbiology, and in the diagnosis and treatment of disease that remain valuable today. In the following selection, Lisa Yount summarizes Pasteur's accomplishments and lasting significance. Yount is a graduate of Stanford University and the author of numerous books on science.

In 1899 biologist A.R. Wallace wrote a book called *The Wonderful Century*. He credited twenty-four basic advances in science and technology to the nineteenth century. He claimed that only fifteen such advances had taken place in the entire earlier history of humankind.

Wallace may have exaggerated, but not by much. Nineteenth-century inventions include photography, railroads, the telegraph, and the telephone. Nineteenth-century scientists found ways to control electricity and chemical reactions. Science improved many people's standard of living and made European nations wealthy and powerful. It is not surprising that the time period is called the "Age of Progress." By the end of the century, most Europeans were optimistic about the future. They believed that life would improve as long as science and technology continued to advance.

Pasteur in His Time

In many ways, Louis Pasteur was a typical scientist of the "Wonderful Century." Like other nineteenth-century scientists, he stressed the importance of testing and proving ideas by experiment. He also used science to solve practical problems. He devoted much of his research to the needs of farmers and factory owners. His discoveries saved millions of francs (French currency) for makers of wine, beer, and vinegar and for raisers of silkworms, chickens, sheep, and cattle. "There are not two kinds of science—practical and applied," he said. "There is only Science and the applications of Science, and one is dependent on the other, as the fruit is to the tree." Pasteur's studies, like the work of most other nineteenth-century scientists, were not aimed simply at understanding nature. They focused on controlling other living things in order to protect or help human beings. The usefulness of Pasteur's research helped to make him the ideal nineteenth-century representation of what a scientist should be.

Pasteur's strong nationalism was also typical of the nineteenth century. He felt great love for and pride in France. He devoted much of his science to advancing French interests. "If science knows no country, the scientist has one, and it is to his country that he must dedicate the influence that his works may exert in the world," he said. He also felt strongly, as did others in his time, that a country's strength was closely tied to its success in scientific research. He once claimed that "science is the highest personification of the nation."

Changing Scientific Thought

Though Pasteur was a typical nineteenth-century scientist in some ways, in other respects he was a revolutionary who changed nineteenth-century thinking. At a time when only a few biologists studied microorganisms, or living things too small to see without a microscope, his "germ theory" showed that these tiny creatures had immense power to either help or harm humans. (*Germ* means "seed," but the word also came to mean "microorganism." After 1878 the term *microbe* was also used for microorganisms.) At a time when doctors blamed disease mostly on changes in the body, Pasteur revealed that microbes could cause many contagious diseases. His research led to improved public health, safer surgery, fewer deaths in war, and new ways to protect people and animals against disease.

Physics and chemistry had made great strides during the early part of the nineteenth century. As a result, many scientists of the time came to believe that all changes in matter were strictly physical or chemical. Pasteur, however, showed that some chemical reactions required the presence of living microorganisms. He also proved that microbes could not arise from nonliving matter. They had to come from other microbes. This, too, showed that living things had qualities that nonliving substances did not.

Pasteur broke down barriers between sciences, sharing insights among biology, chemistry, and medicine. He also founded new sciences. His research on crystals marked the beginning of stereochemistry, which studies the way atoms are arranged inside molecules. His studies of microorganisms helped to found the science of microbiology. His work on vaccination was the basis of immunology, the study of the way the body defends itself against disease.

Because Pasteur presented new ideas, other scientists and thinkers constantly argued with him. Even after his greatest successes, challengers made him prove his points all over again. Yet by the end of Pasteur's century, people almost worshiped him. Dignitaries from around the world attended the jubilee honoring his seventieth birthday. After Pasteur's death, one writer called him "the most perfect man who has ever entered the kingdom of Science." Even today, if asked to name the person who symbolizes science at its finest, many people would choose Louis Pasteur.

Observation, Intuition, and Experiment

Pasteur was not the first person to come up with many of the ideas that made him famous, such as the belief that microorganisms could cause disease. Other scientists of the time also did important work that supported these ideas, yet none of these scientists became as well known. Why was Pasteur able to spread his ideas and change the thinking of his time so effectively?

One reason is Pasteur's devotion to work—he was one of the most productive scientists who ever lived. On the walls of the chapel where he is buried, carvings name nine areas of study to which he contributed. Each area could have occupied most scientists for a lifetime. Pasteur's productivity reflected his endless capacity for work. Even after years of study and experiment had weakened his health, he said, "It would seem to me that I was committing a theft if I were to let one day go by without doing some work." But work was not merely a duty. He once said, "Work . . . is the only thing which is entertaining."

Long hours were only part of the story, however. Pasteur was successful because of the way he used his time. He followed the same pattern in each of his investigations. He began with a scientific question that intrigued him. This might have been a puzzling finding by another scientist or a practical problem that someone asked him to solve. Pasteur then read everything he could find about the subject. He also visited farms or factories to see the problem for himself.

René Dubos, an important Pasteur biographer, writes:

> He had the ability, and the discipline, to focus all his physical and mental energies on a given target. . . . One gets the impression that the intense "field" of interest which he created attracted within his range all the facts—large and small—pertinent to the solution of the problem which was preoccupying him.

Pasteur's assistants described him staring at a sick sheep or a flask of microorganisms for hours. "Nothing escaped his nearsighted eye," said one co-worker, Emile Roux. Pasteur carefully wrote down everything he observed, or that his assistants reported to him, in little notebooks.

After observation, the second step in Pasteur's investigations was intuition. Pasteur was rightly famous for his devotion to experiments and factual proof, but imagination played an equally large part in his genius. He seemed to know what his experiments would show, even before he carried them out. Pasteur was probably speaking of intuition when he said:

Louis Pasteur at work in his laboratory. Pasteur was famous for his meticulous observation of tiny details.

The Greeks have given us one of the most beautiful words of our language, the word "enthusiasm"—[meaning] a God within. The grandeur of the acts of men is measured by the inspiration from which they spring. Happy is he who bears a God within!

Pasteur's power of concentration and attention to detail, combined with his intuition, help to explain what many have called his fantastic luck. When studying crystals, for example, he somehow chose one of the few groups of chemicals that shows a clear relationship between the structure of their crystals and the structure of their molecules. Pasteur himself explained his so-called luck by saying, "Chance favors only the mind which is prepared." Because he had prepared his mind, Pasteur noticed and used facts that other scientists missed. The result seemed like magic.

Pasteur tested all his ideas by painstaking experiment. As he told his co-workers and students, "Keep your . . . enthusiasm, . . . but let it ever be regulated by rigorous examinations and tests. Never advance anything which cannot be proved in a simple and decisive fashion." If the results of his experiments did not support Pasteur's intuitive guesses, he discarded his ideas without a second thought. He could be persistent, however, if he believed that a line of thought had promise. Emile Roux recalled Pasteur's approach:

> How many times, in the presence of unforeseen difficulties, when we could not imagine how to get out of them, have I heard Pasteur tell us, "Let us do the same experiment over again; the essential is not to leave the subject."

After experiments provided Pasteur with solid results, he used his imagination once more to make generalizations. These often went far beyond what his experiments had shown. For example, after doing studies on yeast, the microorganism involved in making wine and beer, he stated that some of the chemical processes that took place in yeast were probably found in all living things. His experiments had not given any evidence for this. Later research, however, showed the statement to be true. Basing a general theory on a small number of facts is a dangerous thing for a scientist to do, but the method almost always worked for Pasteur. Later research by other scientists supported most of his ideas.

Pasteur also had a strong effect during his era because he tried to make the public understand his work. Many educated people in the late nineteenth century were interested in science, and Pasteur took full advantage of this fact. He challenged scientists who disagreed with him to public demonstrations and contests. Some of these turned into social events that attracted the cream of Paris society.

In his public lectures, Pasteur proved his points with well-chosen words and simple, dramatic experiments. He often scolded and even made fun of his opponents. (He claimed, however, that his "lively and caustic manner" was used only "in the defense of truth.") These features guaranteed a good show for his audience. They also helped newspaper reporters write vivid stories about his performances.

Besides giving talks to the general public, Pasteur took his discoveries directly to the people who needed them. He personally showed farmers how to protect their sheep and cattle from disease. He showed wine and beer makers how to produce drinks that would not spoil. In the evenings he answered endless letters from people who requested his advice or help.

A Man of Contradictions

Finally, Pasteur became a hero to many because they sensed the warmth that lay behind his sometimes harsh or cold appearance. It was true that he rarely spoke much, even to those closest to him. Emile Duclaux, another of Pasteur's co-workers, described the "Olympian [godlike] silence with which he loved to surround himself." Pasteur's devoted wife, Marie, wrote to her children on her thirty-fifth anniversary, "Your father is absorbed in his thoughts, talks little, sleeps little, rises at dawn, and, in one word, continues the life I began with him this day thirty-five years ago." Yet Pasteur's speeches and letters are filled with deep affection for his parents, sisters, wife, and children. He suffered greatly when three of his five children died in childhood. He always spoke admiringly of his teachers, even after his fame outgrew theirs. In turn, his family, friends, teachers, and pupils were devoted to him.

Strangers also remembered Pasteur's kindness. Farmers, silkworm breeders, and factory owners recalled the patience with which he answered their questions. When he visited his rabies vaccination clinic, he knew each patient's name. He tried especially hard to comfort the children. He always kept candies and small coins in a drawer for them.

Pasteur, then, was a man of contradictions. He was intuitive yet methodical, interested in general theories yet expert at solving practical problems. He was completely focused on his work, yet he could demonstrate both public showmanship and deep private affection. He expressed both halves of each contradiction with all the "faith and fire" of his passionate nature. This many-sidedness, perhaps more than anything else, made Louis Pasteur both a great scientist and a great man. . . .

Pasteur's Ideas Today

Louis Pasteur contributed to many scientific fields. Scientists in all these fields are still exploring the lines of thinking that he began. Even more than practical tools such as pasteurization and the rabies vaccine, Pasteur's ideas are the heritage he left for the twentieth century. . . .

Chemistry

Pasteur founded the science of stereochemistry when he discovered, in his study of crystals, that the arrangement of atoms in a molecule could affect a substance's physical and chemical activity. Modern stereochemists have confirmed Pasteur's finding that living things often react differently to right-handed and left-handed molecules of the same chemical compound. Sometimes one form of a molecule is active as a drug, and the other is inactive. In other cases, one "mirror image" form of a drug is harmful. For example, a sleeping medicine called thalidomide caused tragedy in the early 1960s because it contained both right-handed and left-handed forms of a molecule. The right-handed form produced the drug's desired effect. The left-handed form, however, caused pregnant women who took thalidomide to give birth to deformed babies. Scientists are now learning how to make compounds with just one "handed" form. Thus, if a drug like thalidomide were invented today, scientists might be able to make a safe form of it.

Pasteur studied fermentation and other chemical processes by which microorganisms break down organic matter. He found ways to make fermentation more dependable and more useful to human beings. . . .

Microbes

While Pasteur was trying to find out whether spontaneous generation occurred, he performed experiments to learn where microbes lived. These studies, along with his research on the way microorganisms broke down organic matter, gave him an appreciation of microorganisms' part in nature. René Dubos has pointed out that, unlike most people of his time, Pasteur realized that microbes play a vital role in recycling living and nonliving matter.

Today scientists know that microorganisms play many parts in the complex web of natural life. Some microbes live in the roots of certain plants, such as peanuts and clover. These microbes change nitrogen from the air into a form that plants can use. Other microbes live in the stomachs of animals. They help the animals digest food. Discovery of these many roles bears out Pasteur's understanding that microbes play important and useful roles in our environment.

Pasteur once wrote, "A day will come, I am convinced, when microorganisms will be utilized in certain industrial operations on account of their ability to transform organic matter." Today his prediction has come true. Scientists have learned how to modify microorganisms to make substances they could not make in nature. These one-celled factories make drugs, vitamins, and industrial chemicals. They can even make substances normally found only in the human body. Because the microbes can make large amounts of these substances, they cut the cost of factory processes and medical treatments.

In his silkworm studies, Pasteur pointed out that the overall health of the worms helped determine whether they would become sick when exposed to the microbes that caused *flacherie*. He recommended preventing *flacherie* by providing plenty of air and space for the worms in the nurseries. These improvements in the worms' environment increased their resistance to disease. Keeping the worms healthy and strong, Pasteur said, was a better way of protecting them than trying to kill the disease microbes.

Doctors and other health care workers have learned that environment also affects human health. Poorly nourished children are more likely to catch germ-caused diseases than children who are well fed, for example. Breathing polluted air reduces resistance to lung diseases. A clean and healthful environment helps people as well as silkworms resist disease.

Tracing and Stopping the Spread of Disease

Pasteur, along with Robert Koch and other early microbiologists, worked out techniques for identifying the microbes that caused particular diseases. Pasteur used these techniques to identify the microbes that caused anthrax and childbirth fever. Other scientists later discovered the microbes that caused other contagious diseases.

Pasteur and the scientists who followed him showed that different disease-causing microbes spread in different ways. Anthrax microbes spread from dead animals to soil, then to plants that living animals ate. The germs that caused childbirth fever were carried on doctors' dirty hands.

Once scientists knew which microbe caused a contagious disease and how it was spread, they could often find ways to stop the disease. Bubonic plague, for example, is carried by fleas that live on rats. People therefore learned to kill rats to keep plague from spreading. Today, scientists are trying to control the spread of AIDS by teaching people to avoid actions that can transmit the disease.

After Pasteur created vaccines for anthrax and rabies, people hoped that vaccines soon could be made for all major diseases caused by microbes. This did not happen for many years, though vaccines for most of these diseases do exist today. Many contagious diseases have been partly or completely controlled by vaccination programs.

Pasteur did not know why his vaccines worked. Today scientists know that vaccines help the body's immune system prepare to fight disease. The immune system is like an army that defends a country. It goes into action whenever a microbe or harmful substance enters the body. Some parts of the system can "remember" foreign materials they have previously encountered. If these materials reenter the body, the reaction against them is quicker and more effective than it was the first time. Vaccines work by introducing weakened microbes or their products into the body. This lets the immune system have experience with the microbes. Then, if full-strength microorganisms enter the body later, the immune system is better able to destroy them.

The Pasteur Institute

When Pasteur could no longer do research, he comforted himself by watching the scientists at the Pasteur Institute continue his work. The Pasteur Institute is still one of the world's most respected medical research organizations. It celebrated its hundredth anniversary in 1988. It started with a staff of fifteen scientists; today it has over five hundred. Pasteur Institute scientists have won at least five Nobel Prizes.

The Pasteur Institute is a leader in the study of diseases caused by microbes, just as it was in Pasteur's time. For example, it is deeply involved in research on AIDS. In 1983, Luc Montagnier and other scientists at the Pasteur Institute discovered the virus that causes AIDS. Robert Gallo and other scientists at the National Institutes of Health in the United States also found the virus at the same time. Shortly afterward, these two laboratories codeveloped a test to identify blood that has been exposed to the virus. Several Pasteur Institute scientists are now seeking a vaccine or cure for AIDS.

The Pasteur Institute is a fitting symbol for Louis Pasteur's work. Like Pasteur, it contributed to the science of the nineteenth century. Like his legacy of discoveries and ideas, it still contributes to science today. The Pasteur Institute reminds us that, one hundred years after his death, science still has much to learn from Louis Pasteur.

Electrifying the Industrial Age

David S. Landes

The first stage of the Industrial Revolution enormously increased the harnessing of energy for human productivity. The source of that energy had been steam power generated primarily by burning coal or water power provided by rapidly flowing streams and falls. Machinery powered by these sources of energy produced the textiles, the metallurgical goods, and the means of mass transportation that transformed life in the industrializing societies of western and central Europe and North America between the mid-1700s and the mid-1800s.

But, as historian David S. Landes explains in the following excerpt from his classic book *The Unbound Prometheus: Technological Change and Industrial Development in Western Europe from 1750 to the Present* (1969), relying primarily on steam and water power limited what the Industrial Revolution could accomplish. Water power could only be put to use in places near suitable bodies of moving water; bulky steam engines—except of course for railroad locomotives and steamships—could not easily be moved. Ultimately, the answer was to develop ways of generating and transmitting electrical power. However, for this to happen scientists first had to gain a basic understanding of the fundamental force of nature called electromagnetism. One of the first steps in this direction had been Benjamin Franklin's dramatic (and dangerous) mid-eighteenth-century experiments with capturing the electrical energy that is inherent in lightning. Then, as Landes explains in this selection, came a series of breakthroughs from 1800 onward, leading up to the British scientist Michael Faraday's discovery of electromagnetic induction (1831) and a number of independent efforts to build self-generating electromagnetic generators in the late 1860s. By the 1880s, alternators and transformers were being developed that could produce and convert high-voltage alternating current. It was these technical and scientific breakthroughs that made it possible, in the last quarter of the nineteenth century, to develop a series of technologies and industries based on the exploitation of electricity—and out of these came a multitude of innovations: electrical lighting, transport systems, industrial machinery, the vast electrochemical industry, telephones, radio, the phonograph. . . . The social and cultural effects of these breakthroughs were no less startling and far-reaching: homes and workplaces that could be lighted at night, street railroads and subways that made possible enormous mass transport facilities, and a cornucopia of consumer goods that, once opened, has never ceased to pour out its wonders.

The electrification of life that began in the late 1800s has truly been one of the most significant of the multitude of changes that the nineteenth century wrought in human existence, and its impact continues to grow even now, as the twenty-first century begins.

From the standpoint of the economic historian, the significance of electricity lay in its unique combination of two characteristics: transmissibility and flexibility. By the first we mean its ability to move energy through space without serious loss. And by the second we mean its easy and efficient conversion into other forms of energy—heat, light, or motion. An electric current can be used to produce any or all of these, separately or together, and the user can switch from one to the other at will. He can so draw precisely the amount of power needed, large or small, and can change it when necessary without time-consuming adjustments or sacrifice of efficiency. And he pays for what he uses.

From these characteristics two major consequences emerge. On the one hand, electricity freed the machine and the tool from the bondage of place; on the other, it made power ubiquitous and placed it within reach of everyone. Both of these—and they are inextricably linked together—merit detailed consideration.

Up to the latter half of the nineteenth century, the machine had always been closely bound to its prime mover. It could not be placed too far off because of the inefficiency of belts and shafting as a method of distributing energy: each gear, joint, or wheel was a source of power loss, and the torsion on long shafts was such that rigidity and smooth rotation could be maintained only by the use of disproportionately heavy materials. Similarly, the machine was rooted to its emplacement or restricted to positions along the path of the shafts, for only there could it draw on the source of energy.

These were not serious disadvantages in such industries as the textile manufacture, where neatly aligned banks of equipment worked side by side at the same pace, although even there shafting longer than 200 feet posed costly problems. But they gave rise to all manner of difficulties in trades like iron or engineering, where the work was dispersed, the pace uneven, and much of the equipment was always being moved about. The answer in such cases was a multiplicity of steam-engines, large and small. It was an expensive solution, not only in capital outlays but in operating costs. These smaller engines, often working at less than full load, were extremely inefficient; by the same token, they had a voracious appetite for labour. Not least important, they were a nuisance, with their piles of coal scattered about, their noise and dirt, their exhaust gases, their need for separate maintenance.

Energy can be transmitted economically over longer distances than a few hundred feet only by fluids or gases, which can be delivered under pressure in rigid pipe or flexible hose, or by electric current. Each technique has its own merits and area of application; all are highly efficient. In the last half of the nineteenth century, all three of these methods began to be used, in the order given.

Fluid systems generally use water—there is no liquid cheaper—or oil, which lubricates as it works; gas systems almost always use air. They are especially suitable to short and medium-range transmission, at distances up to a few miles between prime mover and machine. Their forte is work where incompressibility is an advantage and the mechanical action is direct—in lifts, pumps, presses, punches, and brakes. Their effect in these operations has a certain inexorable quality, and their work is characterized more by force than by motion—as anyone who has ridden in a hydraulic lift will testify.

In principle, water and air pressure may also be used with turbines to produce rotary motion (cf. the windmill). Here, however, they are not so flexible as electricity nor so suitable to heavy work. But compressed air, especially, is excellent with light motors—it has found a new application today in dentistry, where it has proved the most convenient drive for high-speed drills—and is almost indispensable in fields like mining where the presence of inflammable dusts precludes the use of sparking motors.

Historically, pneumatic pressure systems have almost always been the work of the individual enterprise, whereas hydraulic pressure has usually been distributed from central power stations. The development of these installations dates from the invention in 1850 of the accumulator, which made it possible to store pressure and to economize on peak capacity. At first water was obtained simply by tapping public mains. But by the last two decades of the century, the technique had reached the point where private capital was ready to invest in independent pumping works and distribution systems. British enterprise was particularly active in this regard, and as late as the middle 1890's, there were engineers who were convinced that hydraulic pressure was superior to any other means of power transmission. In 1894 Antwerp actually tried to use it to distribute energy to electrical power stations scattered through the city, rather than send current directly from the central power plant. The operation was not profitable.

The fact was that hydraulic and pneumatic power owed much of their success to their priority. They came along first. But once electricity came on the scene, they were bound to lose ground. They were strongest where one or both of two conditions prevailed:

(*a*) Where the primary power source had been constructed for other purposes and existed independently, as in the case of public water works or of air pumps used in underwater excavation. In such circumstances, the water or air used for motor purposes is a by-product whose marginal cost is very low. The municipal hydraulic systems of Geneva and Lyons, both cities abundantly endowed with flowing water, fall in this category.

(*b*) Where the industrial operations of the area lent themselves to these techniques—in ports, for example, like Liverpool and London, where there is a great deal of lifting work to be done; or in a cotton town like Manchester, with its hundreds of packing presses.

Otherwise—beginning in the very last years of the nineteenth century—electricity had the field of power transmission to itself. The history of this development is worth following—as an example of scientific and technical co-operation, of multiple invention, of progress by an infinitude of small improvements, of creative entrepreneurship, of derived demand and unanticipated consequences. The symbiotic growth of electric power and electric motors is like that of textile machines and the steam-engine in the eighteenth century: a new technique and system of production were now available, with boundless possibilities. . . .

At the start of the nineteenth century, electricity was a scientific curiosity, a plaything of the laboratory. As the result of widespread investigation and experiment, however, it became a commercially useful form of energy, first in communication,* shortly thereafter in light-chemical and metallurgical processes, and finally in illumination. Of these, the last had the greatest economic impact because of its implications for power technology in general.

The invention of the incandescent filament lamp, especially Edi-

* A brief list of the key inventions and landmarks will be helpful: Electromagnetic telegraph, in Britain, by Cooke and Wheatstone, *c.* 1837; in the United States, by Morse and Vail, *c.* 1838; undersea cable, across the Channel, 1851; across the Atlantic, by C.W. Field, 1866. Telephone, by A.G. Bell, 1876. Wireless, by Marconi, 1895.

son's high-resistance variety, was crucial here. For the first time electricity offered something useful not only in industry, or in commerce, or on the theatre stage, but in every home. None of the earlier applications had been particularly voracious of energy; and each enterprise, given the scale of its requirements, could profitably generate its own. Now, however, a demand existed—incalculably large *in toto* yet atomized into a multitude of individual needs—that could be satisfied only by a centralized system of power generation and distribution. This too was Edison's conception, and it made all the difference between electric lighting for a wealthy few and for everyone.

The development of central power was the work of the last two decades of the nineteenth century. It was a tremendous technological achievement, made possible only by almost a century of large and small theoretical advances and practical innovations. The landmarks stand out: Volta's chemical battery in 1800; Oersted's discovery of electromagnetism in 1820; the statement of the law of the electric circuit by Ohm in 1827; the experiments of Arago, Faraday, and others, climaxed by Faraday's discovery of electromagnetic induction in 1831; the invention of the self-excited electromagnetic generator (Wilde, Varley, E.W. von Siemens, Wheatstone, *et al.*) in 1866–7; Z.T. Gramme's ring dynamo, the first commercially practical generator of direct current, in 1870; the development of alternators and transformers for the production and conversion of high-voltage alternating current in the 1880's. Less well known but equally vital, however, were advances in the manufacture of cable and insulation, in the details of generator construction, in the operation of prime movers, in the linkage of the component units of the system, in the choice of current characteristics, in the registration of flow and consumption.

The first public power station in Europe was established at Godalming in England by Siemens Brothers in 1881. Within the next decade and a half others sprang up throughout western Europe, a patchwork multitude of market-situated local units, each with its own equipment and method of transmission. . . .

Very early, however, entrepreneurs realized that important savings might be achieved if the generating plant were located at or close to the source of energy and the current were sent out from there. To be sure, the longer the lines the greater the loss of power, but this could be minimized by the use of high-voltage alternating current. The first large station of this kind was that which Ferranti built in 1887–9 at Deptford on the Thames to supply London at 10,000 volts. In the meantime, experiments on the Continent, where there was a great incentive to use hydro-electric power, were demonstrating the possibility of transmitting energy over even longer distances. . . . [I]n 1891 the decisive breakthrough came when Oscar Müller and the Swiss firm of Brown Boveri and Co. delivered 225 kW. over 179 km. at 30,000 volts, from Lauffen on the upper Neckar to Frankfurt-am-Main. Twenty years later current was being transmitted over lines operating at as high as 100,000 volts, and the principle of regional distribution grids was established. It was now possible to develop large, integrated power districts in which agricultural and industrial enterprises of all kinds, to say nothing of homes and shops, could draw on an efficient energy source in common. To the substantial economies of scale in the generation of power were thus added the advantages of diversification: the more heterogeneous the demand, the more favourable the load and capacity factors.

The Germans took the lead here. The most rapid development occurred in Westphalia [in northwestern Germany], where the waste heat of the blast furnaces and the gases of the coking ovens constituted an exceptionally cheap source of energy; even so, demand outstripped supply, and huge coal-fired steam generating plants were built to meet the needs of industrial and domestic consumers. . . . In the rest of Europe, however, the realization of these possibilities did not come until a decade or more later.

Yet electrical current was more than a convenient means of distributing established fuels. Thanks to long-distance transmission, falling water once again came into its own as a source of energy, which could now be delivered to the factory as coal to the steam-engine. The addition to the world's resources was enormous: in 1913 world output of water power, most of it used to generate electricity, was 510 million kWh., the equivalent of 800,000 long tons of coal (at a consumption of 3·5 lb. of coal per kWh.); sixteen years later, in spite of a world war, hydro-electric output was over 120 billion kWh., equivalent to slightly over 100 million tons of coal (at a more efficient rate of 1·0 lb. per kWh.) and representing 40 per cent of the total world production of electricity. By that time electric generating plants were taking up about two-thirds of the prime mover capacity of the principal industrial countries.

While the precipitating cause of large-scale generation of power was electrical illumination, this was soon surpassed as a demand factor by other and heavier applications of the new form of energy. The first of these was traction. It was in 1879, at about the same time as the incandescent filament lamp came on the market, that Siemens demonstrated the first electric railway at the Berlin Industrial Exposition. Within the next generation electrical drive had become standard in tramways and subways and had been successfully introduced into full-gauge rail systems. The second was heavy electrochemistry: both the Hall-Héroult method of aluminium manufacture (1886) and Castner's sodium, sodium cyanide, and caustic soda processes (1886 and 1894) required enormous quantities of energy. The third was electro-metallurgy: the key innovation was Sir William Siemens's electric furnace (1878). This technique, whose great virtues are its cleanness and high temperatures, received considerable impetus from the development of special alloy steels around the turn of the century.

The fourth and most important application was fixed motor power. Ironically enough, producers and engineers were long in appreciating its potential. As late as 1894, some six years after [Nicola] Tesla's invention of the a.c. induction motor and polyphase a.c. systems had 'made alternating current as suitable for power purposes as it had been for lighting', the President of the British Institute of Mechanical Engineers was saying that the chief purpose of public generating plants 'was, and probably always would be, to supply energy for lighting purposes'.

He could not have been more mistaken. By its flexibility and convenience, electricity transformed the factory. Now the motor could be fitted to the tool and the tool moved to the job—an especial advantage in engineering and other industries engaged in the manufacture of heavy objects. And now one could clear away the jungle of shafts and belts that had been the most prominent feature of machine rooms since the water mills of the 1770's—a threat to safety, an interference to movement, a source of breakdowns, and a devourer of energy.

But electricity did more than change the techniques and decor of the factory: by making cheap power available outside as well as inside the plant, it reversed the historical forces of a century, gave new life and scope to dispersed home and shop industry, and modified the mode of production. In particular, it made possible a new division of labour between large and small units. Where before the two had almost inevitably been opposed within a given industry—the one using new techniques and thriving, the other clinging to old ways and declining—now a complimentarity was possible. Both types could use modem equipment, with the factory concentrating on larger objects or standardized items that lent themselves to capital-intensive techniques, while the shop specialized in labour-intensive processes using light power tools. And often the complementarity became symbiosis: the modem structure of sub-contracting in the manufacture of consumers' durables rests on the technological effectiveness of the small machine shop.

New uses and cheaper power promoted capital formation. The increased efficiency of prime movers was more than compensated by the larger demand for energy and the multiplication of motors and machines, not only in industry but in agriculture and eventually the household. To be sure, the great expansion promised by electrification of the home still lay far ahead: in Europe, the refrigerator, electric heater, washing machine, and similar big power users (by contrast with electric lighting, the radio, and the gramophone, which consume little current) do not come in on a large scale until after the Second World War. As late as the 1950's the overwhelming majority of houses and flats made do with entry circuits of ten amperes or less; the hungriest piece of equipment was the electric iron. Yet this secular proliferation and diffusion of electrical equipment, which is far from exhausted, goes back to these decades before the First World War. There was now no activity that could not be mechanized and powered. This was the consummation of the Industrial Revolution.

Some of this investment represented simply a shift from working to fixed capital, as resources once set aside for fuel supplies and furnace labour were freed for other uses. But by far the greater part of it was new capital, created in response to the opportunities offered by new production functions. In this respect, one should not forget the electrical industry itself—tens of thousands of enterprises generating and distributing current and building and servicing electrical equipment.

Here, as in chemicals, the most striking achievements occurred in Germany. The parallels are numerous: the belated start, the rapid rise based on technological excellence and rational organization, the concentration of production, the strong position on the world market. Up to the very eve of the First World War, Britain was possibly still ahead in consumption of electrical power, though the statistics of the two countries were established on so different a basis that comparison is hazardous. Within less than a decade, however, Germany had overtaken her rival and left her far behind—in spite of heavy losses of territory due to the war. Thus by 1925, regular output of German prime movers totalled 21,186,825 h.p., as against 16,808,700 in Britain in 1924; the corresponding figures for electric generators were 13,288,800 and 8,510,000 h.p. respectively. What is more, as the higher German capacity factor implies, her stations and distribution nets were on the average larger: her current characteristics more uniform; and her performance more efficient.

Even more impressive was the progress of the German electrical manufacturing industry. It was the largest in Europe—more than twice as big as that of Britain—and second only by a small margin to that of the United States. The firms, as in the chemical industry, were large, well-financed enterprises, strongly supported by the capital market and the great investment banks. The largest, Emil Rathenau's Allgemeine Electricitäts-Gesellschaft (or AEG) and the Siemens-Schuckert combine, were holding companies of extraordinary versatility and complexity. Their products were ingenious, solidly made, competitively priced; financial support made possible generous credit to customers. As a result, German exports on the eve of the war were the largest in the world, more than two-and-one-half times the United Kingdom total, almost three times the American.

Yet one should not overemphasize the importance of capital. As in the chemical manufacture, scientific knowledge, technical skill, and high standards of performance weighed more heavily in the market place than price. Here too a small country like Switzerland was extraordinarily successful, and names like Brown-Boveri, Oerlikon, Eggi-Wyss, and C.I.E.M. (Cie de l'Industrie electrique et Mécanique) acquired international renown. And for the same reasons, even an agrarian economy like that of Hungary could produce an enterprise like Ganz of Budapest.

Marie Curie and the Discovery of Radium

Sean Grady

Marie Curie was a true pioneer, both as a woman and as a scientist. Curie chose a career in science in a time when women were actively discouraged from pursuing any career, let alone a male-dominated field such as science. She was also a pioneering and persistent researcher who made landmark contributions to the study of radioactivity. In this selection, journalist Sean Grady briefly profiles this remarkable woman.

M arie Curie was a true scientific pioneer. She was one of the first scientists to investigate radioactivity, and she was *the* first scientist to recognize that radioactivity is the result of changes in the atoms of an element. In addition, she discovered the radioactive elements radium and polonium, which exist only in microscopic quantities in nature.

Altogether, Marie's work helped open the field of atomic physics for study. And because of her research and achievements, she won two Nobel Prizes—one in physics in 1903 and one in chemistry in 1911. Today, only three people, including Marie Curie, have achieved this distinction.

But the effects of Marie Curie's work went beyond the laboratory. She began her scientific career in 1891 as a student at the University of Paris, when women scientists were virtually nonexistent. Women simply were not encouraged to study science, and they were often actively discouraged from studying it by universities and by society. Nevertheless, Marie Curie followed her dream of doing scientific research, and her achievements have inspired women scientists around the world.

Science in the 1890s

Marie Curie made her most famous discoveries in the late 1890s, during a period of worldwide scientific progress. Scientists were beginning to figure out the forces that hold the universe together. Every year, discoveries were made that showed flaws in the old ideas of how nature worked. This rapid progress and increase in knowledge happened in all scientific fields, from physics to chemistry to biology.

The discoveries made and the philosophies developed during this time still influence our lives today. British physicist Alex Keller, in his 1983 book, *The Infancy of Atomic Physics,* summed up the effect this period had on the world:

> For more than half a century we have been living on the intellectual muscle built up during the twenty years that ended with the . . . First World War. Our art and music, our politics—our physical science, and above all our scientific technologies are working out ideas born at the turn of the century. In a few short years old assumptions were challenged and overthrown in every field. . . . In science, at least, it was a time of renaissance, renewal, adventure, which it was hoped would make the twentieth century even more glorious than the nineteenth.

Marie Curie had a great deal to do with overthrowing one of these assumptions. Until the 1890s, scientists thought that atoms were the smallest particles of matter. Larger chunks of matter—houses, trees, people—were made up of atoms that somehow managed to stick together. Scientists did not know how these atoms were connected or how they stayed together. But they believed that there was no way to divide an atom into smaller parts.

Marie Curie's pioneering research provided the first major challenge to this theory. The elements she studied convinced her that atoms could break down into smaller parts. By studying radioactivity, Marie discovered that the atoms of radioactive substances were shooting out tiny pieces of themselves. This action could only mean that there were bits of matter smaller than atoms. Other scientists investigated Marie's theory. Before long, many scientists were using Marie's theory of radioactivity to redevelop models of how atoms were constructed.

Studying Science in a Man's World

Marie Curie was instrumental in challenging another idea: that women were not capable of original scientific thought. Male scientists and university directors in Marie's time believed that women's minds were arranged for "soft" tasks like caring for a home and children. Scientific thought, which involved unlocking the secrets of the universe, was thought to be a "hard" task. It was judged to be more suited for the supposedly superior and more flexible male mind.

Women scientists before Marie Curie had failed to overcome this assumption. The first female physics professor in a European university, Laura Bassi, began teaching in the 1730s. In the United States, amateur astronomer Maria Mitchell discovered a new comet in 1847 and became the first woman elected to the American Academy of Arts and Sciences in 1848. More women followed, or tried to follow, in the paths these two and a few other scientists set. But these women formed an extreme minority in the male-dominated world of science. And women who did receive their degrees were forced to take positions as assistants to male scientists.

Marie Curie, like other women in science, fought this mind-set throughout her career. She was accused of building her career on the work of her husband, Pierre, and other male colleagues. Some scientists said that she merely acted as a technician, percolating chemicals while Pierre made the truly great discoveries. And despite the fact that she was awarded two Nobel Prizes, Marie was never admitted to the French Academy of Sciences because she was a woman.

But her passion for her studies and her belief that being a woman was irrelevant to her pursuit of science allowed Marie Curie to press on with her research. In 1903, she became the first woman in France to earn a doctorate in science. Three years later, she was appointed a professor of physics by the University of Paris. She was the first woman in France to hold such a position.

Later in her life, Marie defined the basic unit of measurement for radioactivity—the curie—and prepared a standard sample of radium by which all other samples were measured. With the aid of her daughter Irène and a few assistants, she set up a network of X-ray examination stations throughout France during World War I. For many doctors, these stations were their first chance to use X rays to diagnose injuries. And Marie almost single-handedly created France's Radium Institute, which became a leading center for the study of radioactivity.

Marie Curie's life was not a series of successes, however. She suffered many personal hardships, including the accidental death of her husband when she was thirty-eight. Her reputation and her health were nearly destroyed by allegations that she had a relationship with a married colleague. And, worst of all, she suffered burns and other problems caused by her continual exposure to high levels of radioactivity. Yet her determination and her dedication allowed her to pursue her research, despite these setbacks.

Alexander Graham Bell Invents the Telephone

Robyn M. Weaver

Alexander Graham Bell revolutionized communications with his invention of the telephone. In the following selection, Robyn M. Weaver summarizes the impact of Bell's invention on the world. Weaver is a writer, editor, and continuing education instructor at Texas Christian University.

Calling a parent after soccer practice, logging onto the Internet, and sending a fax are all possible because of the accomplishments of Alexander Graham Bell. His original machine that reproduced speech—which he first called a talking telegraph—is what we now call the telephone. It used electricity to reproduce human speech and has become the basis for today's many forms of mass communication.

Bell's invention has evolved into a tool that allows businesses and financial institutions to transfer money electronically in their day-to-day operations. It allows family members who are separated by great distances to stay in touch through long distance telephone calls or e-mail communication. It allows doctors to fax medical records, which helps them provide better health care during emergencies.

As the editors of *Time for Biography* state, nearly the entire world is dependent on the telephone today:

Few Americans—indeed, few members of most of the world's nations can imagine life without the telephone. It is considered a daily essential like food, housing, clothing. But people haven't always had telephones, and the struggle of Alexander Graham Bell (1847–1922) is a tale of heartbreaking work and courageous dedication. The devotion of his wife and the loyalty of his friend and fellow inventor, Thomas Watson, kept Bell from total despair.

Although many inventors tried to reproduce speech over wires, Alexander Graham Bell was the first to successfully build a working telephone. The telephone of today does not look anything like Bell's first invention; however, it is a tangible reminder of the worldwide communication available because of Bell's original crude device. This fact was first reflected by Professor F.A.P. Barnard of Columbia University when he said: "The name of the inventor of the telephone would be handed down to posterity with a permanent claim on the gratitude and remembrance of mankind."

Bell's contributions to communication did not begin or end with the telephone, though. He was a student and teacher of speech, as were his father and grandfather. He devoted many more years to his career as a teacher than he did to the time he spent inventing the telephone.

A curiosity about sound and speech was only one of the many infatuations Bell had during his varied life of research and inventions. Later, he became a founder of the National Geographic Society as well as a contributor to its magazine. His interest in the organization stemmed from his desire to continue to research new inventions and fund other inventors who had inquisitive minds like his.

Bell and other inventors interested in the mechanics of flight began one of the first aviation groups in North America. This fascination with flight prompted Bell to help finance the group's many experiments with kites and other flying apparatuses. They accomplished many exciting firsts in aviation history.

Even as age caused him to cut back on his own inventions, Bell continued to encourage and fund his fellow inventors. He never forgot the struggles involved with building, adjusting, and experimenting on that first telephone. Many times during that process of creating, he often lacked the funds to purchase necessary materials for the project. Some biographers believe that Bell's support of other inventors was as important to modem technology as his first telephone.

In the past century, Alexander Graham Bell has been recognized as the premiere inventor of the telephone. Those who knew him well, however, remember Bell for his love of thinking and wondering as well as for his researching and teaching capabilities. Even after inventing the telephone, when Bell was asked to put his occupation on official forms and documents, he would write, "teacher of the deaf." One of his most famous pupils, Helen Keller, gave Bell credit for her successful career as a writer and a speaker.

But it is the telephone that Bell invented that he is remembered for most often. Historians agree that Bell's telephone has had an overwhelming influence on modern society, and it continues to impact daily life. This influence would not be possible without the first telephone, and for that accomplishment, Alexander Graham Bell remains a giant in the field of communication.

1801

U.S. Congress resolves political deadlock by electing Thomas Jefferson as president of the United States, initiating a peaceful transfer of political power.

1803

Louisiana Purchase, by which the United States acquires Louisiana from France and doubles its territory.

1804

Napoléon Bonaparte crowns himself Napoléon I, emperor of the French.

1804–1806

Lewis and Clark Expedition explores the trans-Mississippi West.

1806

Napoléon abolishes the Holy Roman Empire, which had existed in Germany since the Middle Ages, and establishes the Confederation of the Rhine, a French satellite; former Holy Roman emperor declares himself Emperor Francis I of Austria.

1807

American Robert Fulton builds first successful steamboat.

1808

Napoléon invades Spain; New Granada (later Colombia) affirms loyalty to legitimate Spanish king Ferdinand VII but overthrows rule of Spanish officials; Mexico declares independence.

1810

Río de la Plata (later known as Argentina) and Chile declare independence; independence movement in Mexico assumes a radical, popular character under Creole priest Miguel Hidalgo.

1811

Simón Bolívar, at the head of a Latin American army, defeats Spanish forces and liberates New Granada from Spanish rule; Hidalgo is captured and executed; Spanish rule is restored but significant opposition remains.

1812
Napoléon invades Russia and takes Moscow, but is forced to retreat and loses his Grand Army in winter storms; War of 1812 begins between United States and Great Britain.

1814–1815
Congress of Vienna meets and redraws map of Europe after Napoléon's defeat.

1815
Napoléon attempts to regain power but is defeated at Waterloo and exiled to St. Helena (where he dies in 1821); War of 1812 ends.

1817
David Ricardo publishes *On the Principles of Political Economy*, a fundamental work in the development of capitalist economic theory that also influences Karl Marx.

1819
British found city of Singapore at southern tip of Malay Peninsula.

1820
Crisis over Missouri's admission to the Union reveals dangerous sectional split in American politics.

1821
José de San Martín leads an army to Lima and declares the independence of Peru; Mexico reclaims independence under upper-class leadership; final separation of Brazil and Portugal takes place.

1821–1831
Greek war for independence from Ottoman Empire, ending with European support for a small independent Greek state.

1823
United States issues Monroe Doctrine, warning European nations not to recolonize the Western Hemisphere; British naval power effectively blocks European intervention and allows Latin American nations to retain their independence.

1825

Decembrist Revolt in Russia, an unsuccessful uprising of liberal-minded army officers, followed by intense political repression under Czar Nicholas I (reigns 1825–1855); world's first railroad line begins operation in Great Britain.

1828

Election of Andrew Jackson to the presidency marks the onset of the democratization of American politics at the national level.

1830

Wave of revolutions sweeps France, Belgium, and Poland; Louis Philippe becomes king of the French; French occupation of Algeria begins; Charles Lyell publishes *The Principles of Geology,* establishing the great age of the earth and the principle of geological evolution.

1831

Michael Faraday discovers electromagnetism.

1832

Enactment of Great Reform Act ends some abuses in British politics, widens the suffrage, and perhaps saves Great Britain from revolution.

1833

Parliament abolishes slavery in all British colonies; Alexis de Tocqueville publishes *Democracy in America.*

1835–1837

"Great Trek" of Dutch-speaking Boers from British-ruled Cape Colony into the interior of South Africa.

1835–1838

Forced removal of Indian nations from American Old Southwest over the Trail of Tears.

1837–1901

Reign of Queen Victoria in Great Britain.

1839

Belgium's independence and neutrality recognized by a treaty ratified by all major European states.

1839–1841

Opium War between Great Britain and China results in opening of the latter to greater European penetration and reveals the weakness of the Manchu dynasty.

1844

First telegraph message transmitted, by Samuel F.B. Morse in the United States.

1845–1846

Potato famine in Ireland causes death of more than 1 million persons and the emigration of several million others.

1846

Great Britain repeals the Corn Laws and adopts a policy of free trade.

1846–1848

Mexican-American War, resulting in the annexation of large western territories by the United States and in the worsening of north-south sectional tensions over the expansion of slavery.

1848

Karl Marx and Friedrich Engels write *The Communist Manifesto*, published by an obscure group of European revolutionaries; wave of revolutions sweeps through France, Germany, Italy, Austria, and Hungary; after overthrow of Louis Philippe and establishment of Second French Republic, Louis Napoléon Bonaparte (Napoléon's nephew) elected president; Seneca Falls Convention in the United States adopts first significant public statement on women's political rights.

1849

Discovery of gold in California and subsequent gold rush spark a global economic boom that lasts until 1857.

1850–1864

Taiping Rebellion in China, a massive popular uprising against the Manchu (Qing) dynasty, eventually defeated largely by Western support for the Manchu.

1851

Crystal Palace exhibition in London showcases industrial progress in the Western world.

1851–1852

Louis Napoléon Bonaparte carries out a coup d'état against the French Republic and proclaims himself Emperor Napoléon III.

1853–1854

Commodore Matthew Perry forces Japan to open itself to foreign commerce, setting in motion revolutionary changes in Japanese society and politics.

1853–1856

David Livingstone crosses the interior of central Africa.

1854–1856

Crimean War (Great Britain, France, Ottoman Empire, and Piedmont against Russia) blocks Russian expansion into the Balkan Peninsula and reveals Russia's need for modernization.

1855

Rifling introduced in the manufacture of small arms, making possible a great increase in the accuracy of military firepower.

1856

Henry Bessemer of Great Britain invents the blast furnace, making possible the development of the modern steel industry.

1857–1858

Sepoy Mutiny in India fails to overthrow British domination, but the rule of the East India Company ends and direct British control begins.

1857–1859

Serious economic depression, relieved by new discoveries of gold in the United States and Australia.

1859

France and Piedmont defeat Austria, initiating process of Italian unification (completed in 1870 with occupation of Rome by the kingdom of Italy); Charles Darwin publishes *On the Origin of Species by Means of Natural Selection.*

1860

Franco-British occupation of Beijing during Second Opium War; Anglo-French free trade agreement.

1861

Emancipation of the Russian serfs proclaimed by Czar Alexander II, the central event of the Great Reform Era in Russian history (1856–1863).

1861–1865

U.S. Civil War, resulting in the destruction of slavery and of the principle of secession.

1862

French occupation of Cochin China (southern Vietnam) begins.

1863

State-sponsored art show in Paris, the Salon, rejects the paintings of Edouard Manet and other innovative artists, who hold an exhibition (the "Salon of the Rejected") that is considered to mark the advent of modern painting.

1864

Marx helps found the First International Workingmen's Association to promote Marxian socialism.

1865

Gregor Mendel's experiments with genetics first published, but do not attract attention until the end of the century.

1865–1866

First transatlantic cable laid, enormously increasing speed of global communications.

1866

Prussia defeats Austria in a short war, resulting in Austria's exclusion from Germany and Prussian leadership of the process of German unification.

1867

Second Reform Act in Great Britain further widens the suffrage, opening the way for the democratization of British politics and the emergence of modern political parties; political compromise in Habsburg empire creates the "dual monarchy" of Austria-Hungary; Canada achieves internal self-government; Marx publishes first volume of *Das Kapital,* purportedly revealing the scientific laws of economics and history.

1868

Meiji Restoration in Japan ends the shogunate and brings to power advocates of Western models to modernize the Japanese economy, society, and political system.

1869

Declaration of papal infallibility by Pope Pius IX, according to which Catholics must believe that when the pope speaks authoritatively on matters of faith and morals he cannot err; Suez Canal completed and opened to international shipping.

1870–1871

Franco-Prussian War, resulting in the overthrow of Napoléon III and proclamation of the Third Republic, the unification of Germany under Prussian leadership, and the defeat of the radical Paris Commune by conservative and rural forces in French society; papacy loses control of Rome to the kingdom of Italy.

1871

Henry M. Stanley finds the "lost" David Livingstone at Lake Tanganyika in the interior of East Africa; Darwin publishes *The Descent of Man*, applying evolution by natural selection to human beings.

1873

Panic of 1873 ushers in a global economic depression that lasts most of the 1870s.

1875

Establishment of the German Social Democratic Party, first mass socialist party in Europe.

1875–1878

Series of revolts and wars in the Balkans sets in motion the rise of national states in the region, as well as the European powers' determination to prevent Russian domination there.

1876

Establishment of the International Association for the Exploration and Civilization of Africa under the sponsorship of Belgian king Leopold II; Alexander Graham Bell invents the telephone.

1877

End of Reconstruction era in the American South; federal support for black civil liberties withdrawn, leading to the establishment of white racist governments throughout the former Confederacy; Queen Victoria proclaimed empress of India, symbolizing triumph of British rule over the subcontinent; Thomas A. Edison invents the phonograph.

1879
Great Britain and France assume direct control of the Suez Canal and of Egypt's finances; Edison invents the incandescent electric lamp; electric streetcars introduced in Germany.

1880–1881
Revolt of Boers against British rule and establishment of Republic of the Transvaal.

1881
Assassination of Czar Alexander II of Russia by the People's Will, a small terrorist organization.

1881–1885
Louis Pasteur of France applies the principle of immunization to rabies and shows that fermentation is caused by microorganisms— among the most fundamental breakthroughs in biology and public health achieved by scientists internationally in the 1880s.

1882
Creation of the Triple Alliance (Germany, Austria-Hungary, and Italy), supplemented by Germany's informal alliance with Russia, ensures the isolation of France in international affairs; Great Britain becomes dominant power in Egypt; compound steam turbine invented in Great Britain.

1885
Berlin Conference partitions Africa among colonial powers—notably Great Britain, France, Germany, and Portugal—and establishes the Congo Free State under the administration of Belgium's King Leopold II; French rule consolidated over most of Indochina (Vietnam and Cambodia, later Laos).

1886
Defeat of the Liberal Party in British general election ensures failure of Home Rule Bill, which would have given Ireland self-government; discovery of gold in the Transvaal Republic raises Anglo-Boer tensions; Gottlieb Daimler invents the internal combustion engine in Germany.

1888

Slavery abolished in Brazil, last country in the Western world to maintain the institution.

1889

Japan adopts an authoritarian but Western-style constitution; formation of the Second International, the worldwide (but mainly European) federation of socialist parties; Edison perfects the motion picture; Friedrich Nietzsche goes insane but his writings and ideas (often in badly distorted form) become highly influential in the 1890s.

1890

Forced resignation of German chancellor Otto von Bismarck.

1892

Franco-Russian alliance begins the polarization of European international politics into hostile alliance systems.

1893–1897

Devastating global economic depression.

1894–1895

Japan defeats China in Sino-Japanese War, forcing China to pay a large indemnity, to cede Taiwan, and to recognize the "independence" of Japanese-influenced Korea.

1894–1906

Dreyfus Affair in France, involving the conviction of Jewish colonel Alfred Dreyfus on charges on spying for Germany, revelations of his innocence and of the guilt of others, coverups in the military, the polarization of pro- and antirepublican forces in France, powerful anti-Semitic agitation, and Dreyfus's ultimate vindication.

1895

Guglielmo Marconi invents wireless telegraphy, the basis for radio; Wilhelm Roentgen discovers X rays.

1896

Italian attempt to conquer Ethiopia ends in defeat at Battle of Adowa.

1897–1898

European powers and Japan vie for concessions in China, threatening its virtual partition into spheres of influence.

1898

Foundation of the Russian Social Democratic Party, a Marxist party (of which one important member is Vladimir Ilich Ulyanov, known as Lenin) that in 1903 will split to form the Bolshevik faction, out of which eventually grows the Communist Party; Spanish-American War, in which United States defeats Spain, establishes effective control over nominally independent Cuba, and annexes Puerto Rico and the Philippines; Pierre and Marie Curie discover radiation and isolate radium.

1899–1902

Boer War in South Africa, ending with British annexation of the Boer republics and establishment of the Union of South Africa (later South Africa).

1900

Boxer Rebellion in China, an antiforeign uprising defeated by European, Japanese, and American intervention; Sigmund Freud publishes *The Interpretation of Dreams;* Max Planck publishes the quantum theory, part of a revolution in physics that also includes Albert Einstein's theory of relativity, introduced in 1905.

FOR FURTHER READING

Stephen F. Ambrose, *Undaunted Courage: Meriwether Lewis, Thomas Jefferson, and the Opening of the American West.* New York: Simon & Schuster, 1996.

Benedict Anderson, *Imagined Communities: Reflections on the Origin and Spread of Nationalism.* 2nd ed. London: Verso, 1991.

Gunther Barth, *Bitter Strength: A History of Chinese in the United States, 1850–1870.* Cambridge, MA: Harvard University Press, 1964.

Winfried Baumgart, *Imperialism: The Idea and Reality of British and French Colonial Expansion, 1880–1914.* Rev. ed. New York: Oxford University Press, 1982.

C.A. Bayly, *Indian Society and the Making of the British Empire.* New York: Cambridge University Press, 1988.

Isaiah Berlin, *Karl Marx: His Life and Environment.* 4th ed. New York: Oxford University Press, 1978.

Robert Blake, *Disraeli.* London: Methuen, 1969.

Jerome Blum, *The End of the Old Order in Rural Europe.* Princeton, NJ: Princeton University Press, 1978.

E. Bradford Burns, *The Poverty of Progress: Latin America in the Nineteenth Century.* Berkeley and Los Angeles: University of California Press, 1980.

David Bushnell and Neill Macauley, *The Emergence of Latin America in the Nineteenth Century.* 2nd ed. New York: Oxford University Press, 1994.

P.J. Cain and A.G. Hopkins, *British Imperialism: Innovation and Expansion, 1688–1914.* London: Longman, 1993.

Hsin-pao Chang, *Commissioner Lin and the Opium War.* New York: W.W. Norton, 1964.

Owen Connelly, *Blundering to Glory: Napoleon's Military Cam-*

paigns. Wilmington, DE: Scholarly Resources, 1987.

Robert Conrad, *The Destruction of Brazilian Slavery, 1850–1888.* Berkeley and Los Angeles: University of California Press, 1973.

William J. Cooper, *The South and the Politics of Slavery, 1828–1856.* New York: Knopf, 1978.

Albert M. Craig, *Choshu in the Meiji Restoration.* Cambridge, MA: Harvard University Press, 1961.

Gordon Craig, *Germany, 1866–1945.* Oxford: Clarendon, 1978.

Pamela Kyle Crossley, *Orphan Warriors: Three Manchu Generations and the End of the Qing World.* Princeton, NJ: Princeton University Press, 1990.

Bernard De Voto, *The Year of Decision: 1846.* Boston: Houghton Mifflin, 1943.

Frank Dobbin, *Forging Industrial Policy: The United States, Britain, and France in the Railway Age.* New York: Cambridge University Press, 1994.

David Herbert Donald, *Lincoln.* New York: Simon & Schuster, 1995.

Ann Douglas, *The Feminization of American Culture.* Garden City, NY: Doubleday, 1978.

Ellen C. Du Bois, *Feminism and Suffrage: The Emergence of an Independent Woman's Movement in the Nineteenth Century.* Ithaca, NY: Cornell University Press, 1984.

Stewart Edwards, *The Paris Commune 1871.* London: Eyre and Spottiswoode, 1971.

Richard J. Evans, ed., *The German Working Class, 1888–1933: The Politics of Everyday Life.* London: Croon Helm, 1982.

Peter Ward Fay, *The Opium War, 1840–1842: Barbarians in the Celestial Empire in the Early Part of the Nineteenth Century and the War by Which They Forced Her Gates Ajar.* Chapel Hill: University of North Carolina Press, 1976.

D.K. Fieldhouse, *Colonialism, 1870–1945: An Introduction.* London: Weidenfield and Nicholson, 1981.

Carter V. Findley, *Bureaucratic Reform in the Ottoman Empire: The Sublime Porte, 1789–1922*. Princeton, NJ: Princeton University Press, 1980.

Eric Foner, *Reconstruction, 1863–1877*. New York: Harper & Row, 1988.

Eugene D. Genovese, *Roll, Jordan, Roll: The World the Slaves Made*. New York: Vintage, 1974.

Alexander Gerschenkron, *Economic Backwardness in Historical Perspective*. New York: Praeger, 1965.

Peter Geyl, *Napoleon, For and Against*. New Haven, CT: Yale University Press, 1949.

Siegfried Giedion, *Mechanization Takes Command*. New York: W.W. Norton, 1948.

David Gillard, *The Struggle for Asia, 1828–1914: A Study in British and Russian Imperialism*. London: Methuen, 1977.

Michael D. Green, *The Politics of Indian Removal: Creek Government and Society in Crisis*. Lincoln: University of Nebraska Press, 1982.

Liah Greenfeld, *Nationalism: Five Roads to Modernity*. Cambridge, MA: Harvard University Press, 1992.

H.J. Habakkuk, *American and British Technology in the Nineteenth Century*. Cambridge, England: Cambridge University Press, 1962.

Tulio Halperín-Donghi, *The Contemporary History of Latin America*. Durham, NC: Duke University Press, 1993.

Theodore S. Hamerow, *Restoration, Revolution, Reaction: Economics and Politics in Germany, 1815–1871*. Princeton, NJ: Princeton University Press, 1958.

Daniel Headrick, *The Tentacles of Progress: Technology Transfer in the Age of Imperialism, 1850–1940*. New York: Oxford University Press, 1988.

———, *The Tools of Empire: Technology and European Imperialism in the Nineteenth Century*. New York: Oxford University Press, 1981.

Christopher Hibbert, *The Dragon Wakes: China and the West,*

1793–1911. New York: Harper & Row, 1970.

Eric Hobsbawm, *The Age of Revolution, 1789–1848.* New York: New American Library, 1962.

————, *Industry and Empire: The Making of Modern English Society, 1750 to the Present Day.* New York: Pantheon, 1968.

Robert Huttenback, *Racism and Empire: White Settlers and Colored Immigrants in the British Self-Governing Colonies, 1830–1910.* Ithaca, NY: Cornell University Press, 1976.

Huri Islamoglu–Inan, ed., *The Ottoman Empire and the World-Economy.* New York: Cambridge University Press, 1987.

Barbara Jelavich, *History of the Balkans.* 2 vols. New York: Cambridge University Press, 1983.

Roy Jenkins, *Gladstone: A Biography.* New York: Random House, 1997.

Douglas W.J. Johnson, *France and the Dreyfus Affair.* New York: Walker, 1966.

Paul Johnson, *The Birth of the Modern: World Society, 1815–1830.* New York: HarperCollins, 1991.

Ira Katznelson and Aristide R. Zolberg, eds., *Working-Class Formation: Nineteenth-Century Patterns in Western Europe and the United States.* Princeton, NJ: Princeton University Press, 1986.

Walter Kaufmann, *Nietzsche: Philosopher, Psychologist, Antichrist.* 4th ed. Princeton, NJ: Princeton University Press, 1974.

Paul M. Kennedy, *The Rise of the Anglo-German Antagonism, 1860–1914.* Boston: Allyn & Unwin, 1980.

Jay Kinsbruner, *Independence in Spanish America: Civil Wars, Revolutions, and Underdevelopment.* Albuquerque: University of New Mexico Press, 1994.

Henry Kissinger, *Diplomacy.* New York: Simon & Schuster, 1994.

Leszek Kolakowski, *Main Currents of Marxism.* 3 vols. New York: Oxford University Press, 1978.

Walter LaFeber, ed., *John Quincy Adams and the American Continental Empire.* Chicago: Quadrangle, 1965.

David Landes, *The Unbound Prometheus: Technological Change and Industrial Development in Western Europe from 1750 to the Present.* New York: Cambridge University Press, 1972.

Patricia Nelson Limerick, *Legacy of Conquest: The Unbroken Past of the American West.* New York: W.W. Norton, 1987.

Patricia Mainardi, *The End of the Salon: Art and the State in the Early Third Republic.* New York: Cambridge University Press, 1993.

Arno J. Mayer, *The Persistence of the Old Regime, Europe to the Great War.* London: Croom Helm, 1981.

William S. McFeely, *Frederick Douglass.* New York: W.W. Norton, 1991.

James M. McPherson, *Battle Cry of Freedom: The Civil War Era.* New York: Oxford University Press, 1988.

Alan S. Milward and S.B. Saul, *The Development of the Economies of Continental Europe, 1850–1914.* Cambridge, MA: Harvard University Press, 1977.

Joel Mokyr, *The Lever of Riches: Technological Creativity and Economic Progress.* New York: Oxford University Press, 1990.

George L. Mosse, *Toward the Final Solution: A History of European Racism.* Madison: University of Wisconsin Press, 1978.

Noël Mostert, *Frontiers: The Epic of South Africa's Creation and the Tragedy of the Xhosa People.* New York: Knopf, 1992.

Lewis Namier, *1848: The Revolution of the Intellectuals.* New Introduction by James Joll. Oxford: Published for the British Academy by Oxford University Press, 1992.

David Northrup, *Indentured Labor in the Age of Imperialism, 1834–1992.* New York: Cambridge University Press, 1995.

Walter T.K. Nugent, *Crossing: The Great Transatlantic Migrations, 1870–1914.* Bloomington: Indiana University Press, 1992.

Roland Oliver and Anthony Atmore, *Africa Since 1800.* 4th ed. New York: Cambridge University Press, 1994.

Roger Owen and Bob Sutcliffe, eds., *Studies in the Theory of Imperialism*. London: Longman, 1972.

Thomas Pakenham, *The Scramble for Africa, 1876–1912*. New York: Random House, 1991.

Merrill Peterson, *Thomas Jefferson and the New Nation: A Biography*. New York: Oxford University Press, 1970.

Otto Pflanze, *Bismarck and the Development of Germany*. 2nd ed. 3 vols. Princeton, NJ: Princeton University Press, 1991.

D.C.M. Platt, *Latin America and British Trade, 1806–1914*. New York: Barnes & Noble, 1973.

James M. Polachek, *The Inner Opium War*. Cambridge, MA: Harvard University Press, 1992.

Bernard Porter, *The Lion's Share: A Short History of British Imperialism, 1850–1970*. 3rd ed. New York: Longman, 1996.

David M. Potter, *The Impending Crisis, 1848–1861*. New York: Harper & Row, 1976.

Roger Price, *A Social History of Nineteenth-Century France*. London: Hutchinson, 1987.

Nicholas V. Riasanovsky, *A History of Russia*. 5th ed. New York: Oxford University Press, 1993.

Philip Rieff, *Freud, the Mind of the Moralist*. 3rd ed. Chicago: University of Chicago Press, 1987.

Ronald E. Robinson and John Gallagher, *Africa and the Victorians: The Climax of Imperialism*. Garden City, NY: Doubleday, 1968.

A.J.R. Russell-Wood, ed., *From Colony to Nation: Essays on the Independence of Brazil*. Baltimore: Johns Hopkins University Press, 1976.

D.R. SarDesai, *Southeast Asia: Past and Present*. 4th ed. Boulder, CO: Westview, 1997.

Carl E. Schorske, *Fin-de-Siècle Vienna: Politics and Culture*. New York: Vintage, 1981.

Roger Shattuck, *The Banquet Years: The Origins of the Avant-Garde in France, 1885 to World War I*. Rev. ed. New York: Vintage, 1968.

James J. Sheehan, *German History, 1770–1866*. New York: Oxford University Press, 1989.

————, *German Liberalism in the Nineteenth Century*. Chicago: University of Chicago Press, 1978.

Bonnie G. Smith, *Changing Lives: Women in European History Since 1700*. Lexington, MA: D.C. Heath, 1989.

Jonathan D. Spence, *God's Chinese Son: The Taiping Heavenly Kingdom of Hong Xiuquan*. New York: W.W. Norton, 1996.

Jonathan Sperber, *The European Revolutions, 1848–1851*. New York: Cambridge University Press, 1994.

Peter N. Stearns, *1848: The Revolutionary Tide in Europe*. New York: W.W. Norton, 1974.

————, *The Industrial Revolution in World History*. 2nd ed. Boulder, CO: Westview, 1998.

Fritz Stern, *Gold and Iron: Bismarck, Bleichröder, and the Building of the German Empire*. New York: Knopf, 1977.

Philip A.M. Taylor, *The Distant Magnet: European Emigration to the U.S.A.* London: Eyre and Spottiswoode, 1971.

S.Y. Teng, *The Taiping Rebellion and the Western Powers: A Comprehenisve Survey*. Oxford: Clarendon, 1971.

F.M.L. Thompson, *The Rise of Respectable Society: A Social History of Victorian Britain, 1830–1900*. Cambridge, MA: Harvard University Press, 1988.

Louise A. Tilly and Joan W. Scott, *Women, Work, and Family*. New York: Holt, Rinehart and Winston, 1978.

Conrad D. Totman, *The Collapse of the Tokugawa Bakufu, 1862–1868*. Honolulu: University Press of Hawaii, 1980.

Robert C. Tucker, *Philosophy and Myth in Karl Marx*. Cambridge, England: Cambridge University Press, 1960.

Robert M. Utley, *The Indian Frontier of the American West, 1846–1890*. Albuquerque: University of New Mexico Press, 1984.

Franco Venturi, *Roots of Revolution: A History of the Populist and*

Socialist Movements in Nineteenth-Century Russia. New York: Grossett & Dunlap, 1960.

Ronald G. Walters, *American Reformers, 1815–1860.* Rev. ed. New York: Hill and Wang, 1997.

Eugen Weber, *France, Fin de Siècle.* Cambridge, MA: Belknap Press, 1986.

————, *Peasants into Frenchmen: The Modernization of Rural France, 1870–1914.* Stanford, CA: Stanford University Press, 1976.

Hans-Ulrich Wehler, *The German Empire, 1871–1918.* Dover, NH: Berg, 1985.

Stanley Weintraub, *Victoria: An Intimate Biography.* New York: Dutton, 1987.

Martin J. Wiener, *English Culture and the Decline of the Industrial Spirit, 1850–1980.* New York: Cambridge University Press, 1981.

Sean Wilentz, *Chants Democratic: New York City and the Rise of the American Working Class, 1788–1850.* New York: Oxford University Press, 1983.

Peter Booth Wiley and Korogi Ichiro, *Yankees in the Land of the Gods: Commodore Perry and the Opening of Japan.* New York: Viking, 1990.

Roger L. Williams, *Gaslight and Shadow: The World of Napoleon III, 1851–1870.* New York: Macmillan, 1957.

George M. Wilson, *Patriots and Redeemers in Japan: Motives in the Meiji Restoration.* Chicago: University of Chicago Press, 1992.

Eric Wolf, *Europe and the People Without History.* Berkeley and Los Angeles: University of California Press, 1982.

INDEX

abolitionist movement
  American, 121, 122
  British, 121–22, 125–27
    and class tensions, 131
    denunciations of, 130–31
    and factory reform, 128–29, 130
    political motives, 129–30
    politico-economic cycles of, 127–28
    survival of, 131–32
  see also emancipation
Adams, Henry, 75
Africa
  colonialism in, 24
  in 19th vs. 20th century, 15–16
  Western imperialism in, 229
  see also Congo Free State
African Americans
  on Emancipation Proclamation, 156
  and Spanish-American War, 293–94
  see also slavery/slaves
Alaska, 25
Albert (prince of England)
  death of, 215
  and Lord Melbourne, 211–12
  marriage of, to Victoria, 211
  and Sir Robert Peel, 212–13
  unpopularity of, 212, 213–14
Alexander II, czar of Russia, 119, 133, 174
American Revolution
  vs. Spanish-American revolt, 50–51
  turmoil following, 32, 33
Ampudia, Pedro de, 280
Anthony, Susan B., 224
anthrax vaccine, 339–40
apprentice system, 82–83
Arista, Mariano, 281
aristocracy, vs. democracy, 64
Articles of Confederation, 33
artisan industry
  apprentice system in, 82–83
  and emergence of working class, 99–100
  and suffrage movement, 98
arts, the, 297–98
  see also Impressionists
Ashton, T.S., 84
Astor, John Jacob, 76
Australia, 25, 120

Austrian Empire, 20–21
automobile, 13–14

Bachrach, Deborah, 289
Baldwin, Stanley, 208
Barbados, 24
Baring-Gould, Reverend Sabine, 316
Bascom, Ansel, 221
Bassi, Laura, 352
Bazille, 307–308
Belgium, 46, 119
Bell, Alexander Graham, 28, 331, 353–55
Bell (Herzen), 186
Bengal Army. *See* sepoys
Benton, Thomas Hart, 284
Berliner, Emile, 323
Bessemer, Henry, 28
bicycles, 323
Birdzell, L.E., Jr., 81
Birmingham Chartist rally (1838), 131–32
Blackie, John Stuart, 317
blast furnace, 28
Bolívar, Simón, 51, 58
Bolsheviks, 23, 79–80
Bolton Political Union, 92
Bonaparte, Napoléon. *See* Napoléon Bonaparte
Boudin, Eugéne, 305
Boxer Rebellion, 26
Bradley, Ian, 314
Brazil, 124
Breuer, Joseph, 324
Brewster, Sir David, 180
Bricusse, Georges, 266
Briggs, Asa, 209
Bristol Political Union
  and riots, 93–95
Broadwood, Lucy, 316
Brock, Michael, 86
Broers, Michael, 41
Büchner, George, 187
Butt, Clara, 318
Butt, Isaac, 197

Canada, 15, 25
  during the Civil War, 120
  and Irish emigrants, 200